JEROME FRANK: JURIST AND PHILOSOPHER

# JEROME FRANK:
## JURIST AND PHILOSOPHER

By

J. MITCHELL ROSENBERG

Philosophical Library
New York

For Helen

A judge should always think of himself as if he had a sword hanging over his head and Gehenna gaping under him.

—Babylonian Talmud,
Tractate Sandhedrin, p. 7a

# Contents

# PREFACE

This book will record the contributions made by Judge Jerome Frank to the literature of jurisprudence and of judicial opinions. Few, if any, will challenge the statement that this distinguished jurist in his intellectual equipment stood head and shoulders above most judges of his time. Frank's equally lofty moral endowment—his passion for justice—made his a truly great judge in the liberal tradition.

Recognition is accorded to the late, lamented Professor Otto Kirschheimer of the New School for Social Research, later of Columbia University, who suggested the topic of this undertaking. The author's gratitude to Professor Jacob W. Landynski of the New School for his help in the preparation of the doctoral dissertation, which has been slightly expanded into this book, is indeed immense and is acknowledged with a deep sense of appreciation. Without his guiding hand and warm devotion, this book would not have been possible. He devoted many hours uncomplainingly to the improvement of the thesis and made erudite suggestions. The author's debt is further cheerfully acknowledged to Professors Saul K. Padover and Adamantia Pollis of the New School for helpful advice and for the cordiality they displayed. Gratefulness is also expressed to Professor Felicia J. Deyrup of the New School who was gracious enough to read the galley proofs of the text as an act of supererogation, which is warmly prized, and to advise a number of improvements in style. To Mrs. Lucie Jurow, librarian of the Brooklyn Law School, who placed the facilities of the school's library at the author's service, due appreciation is recorded. Last but not least, an understanding wife allowed for uninterrupted time for work. None of the professors listed above can, of course, be held responsible for any possible errors or for any of the opinions expressed in this volume.

# INTRODUCTION

No systematic analysis of Judge Jerome Frank's judicial opinions has heretofore been undertaken. This study is the first such attempt.

Many of Judge Frank's opinions show an abiding concern for the underprivileged. He was solicitous about each individual—the humble, the poor, the unknown—caught in the meshes of the law. He was moved by the question: Does the law, in its operation, favor the wealthy to the detriment of the poor, thus running afoul of the ideal of equal protection of the laws? Yet there has been no systematic analysis of his judicial opinions.

Frank's judicial opinions in three major areas of the law—*stare decisis*, civil liberties in general and freedom of speech and press in particular—have been selected for analysis in these pages. *Stare decisis*, the doctrine of following previous court decisions, is essential for the purpose of attaining stability in the law. The legal realists, including Frank, have been attacked as "nihilists,"[1] seeking to abrogate *stare decisis* and substitute in its place a regime of judicial whim. This study will seek to demonstrate that this accusation was an exaggeration, and that in truth Frank's quest was for a greater stability which can only be attained by due recognition of the conflicting claims of stability and progress in the law. Civil liberties are the basic personal rights of the individual in a democratic state. From Frank's opinions in this area it will become apparent that he had a deeply etched empathy for those suffering injustice at the hands of the law. for the final area of discussion, a vital civil liberty—freedom of speech and press—has been singled out, since it is critical to the lifeblood of a democracy. We shall hear Frank's voice raised in powerful defense of this freedom against those who wish to curtail it.

Frank was the author of a number of books, mainly on jurisprudence. Two features strikingly emerge from a reading of his judicial opinions and one of his books on the philosophy of free will and determinism. Firstly, it is rare for a judicial opinion to transcend the metes and bounds of its genre: a narrative of a factual summary and an analysis of the relevant law. In consequence, the bulk of judicial opinions is in its nature prosaic, humdrum. It is only the rare judge who will seize the appropriate occasion to embellish his opinion with ideas in which he is steeped. Judges of this quality have been Holmes and Cardozo. In this constellation of judges one must place the name of Jerome Frank. Many of his opinions, in diverse areas of concern, transcend the shackles of technical, legalistic terminology and incorporate ideas transported from the realms of philosophy, economics, literature, history, psychology, sociology and anthropology, and they make for enjoyable reading. In the view of Justice Douglas, Frank's opinions were "literary treasures" and "inspiring exceptions to the dull literature which the courts turn out."[2] Secondly, it is uncommon for a judge to set forth, as did Frank, his purely philosophical *Anschauungen* as distinguished from his legal philosophy. He engaged in a polemic against determinism and built up a case for free will as a philosophy consonant with the American faith.[3]

In the 1930's and 1940's, legal realism was the dominant school in American jurisprudence and Jerome Frank was one of its main spokesmen. This movement and Frank's relationship and contributions to it have been of profound interest to this writer. Frank was a "supreme provocateur"[4] in the currents of American legal thought, more obviously in his jurisprudential writings than in his judicial opinions. He fought against dogmatic authoritarianism not only in jurisprudence but in all spheres of though. Thus his contributions, both as legal philosopher and as judge, to the American liberal tradition will be studied on these pages.

Jerome Frank was born on September 10, 1889 in New York City into the German-Jewish family of Clara New Frank and Herman Frank, a lawyer. In his childhood, the family, which included two daughters, moved to Chicago. After attending Chicago's public schools, Frank entered the University of Chicago and took his Ph.B. degree in 1909.[5] He became secretary to Professor Charles E. Merriam, the political scientist who had taught him at the university, when Merriam was elected a Chicago reform alderman (1909-11).[6] Years later Merriam was to refer to the young Frank as "passionate in his hatred of wrong and injustice, keen and subtle in his intellectual processes."[7] In 1912 Frank was graduated from the University of Chicago Law School, where he was considered "one of the two brightest students of the pre-War generation."[8] In July, 1914 he married Florence Kipper, a poetess and playwright.

From 1912 until 1929, Frank engaged in the practice of the law with the Chicago firm of Levinson, Becker, Cleveland and Schwartz, which specialized in corporation law. He became a full partner of the firm in 1919. His particular specialty was corporate reorganization work. Between 1921 and 1925, he helped negotiate a settlement for the tangled trolly car affairs of Chicago, but it was defeated in a referendum due to the opposition of the magnate, Samuel Insull.[9]

In 1929 Frank joined the prominent New York law firm of Chadbourne, Stanchfield and Levy. The members of this firm "often said, 'It's worth $50,000. a year to us to have Jerry around just to hear him talk.' "[10] In New York he renewed a previous acquaintance with Felix Frankfurter. Among his other friends Frank counted Professor Morris Raphael Cohen, as well as Carl Sandburg, Rebecca West, Sherwood Anderson, Max Eastman and Harry Hansen.

In 1929 Frank decided to undergo psychoanalysis; this lasted a half year. He cut the duration of the analysis in half by arranging for two daily sessions: one in the morning and a second in the late afternoon. He was disturbed by feelings that the law might not be the right profession for him. However, the analysis seems to have allayed the doubts about his choice of profession. He thought that it did him "a great deal of good"[11] and enabled him to stop wasting his energies in inner friction. "I'd say it was a turning point in my life. I think I would have been a very distracted, unhappy kind of fellow ... I would have been constantly rebelling against being a lawyer—doing it competently but still interiorly objecting to it."[12]

Thus, when Frank in his subsequent writings specified the need for prospective or incumbent judges to undergo psychoanalysis or a "self-exploration,"[13] he was speaking not only from an intellectual interest in psychoanalysis and its anticipated utility in the administration of justice, but also as a result of a personal involvement which had led to his own catharsis.

Attaining fame as a legal philosopher and protagonist of the school of "legal realism"[14] through the publication in 1930 of his first major work, *Law and The Modern Mind*,[15] he was appointed a research assistant at Yale Law School in 1932.[16] Earlier, in 1931, he had given some lectures in law and anthropology at the New School for Social Research in New York City.[17] After Roosevelt's elevation to the Presidency, he wrote Professor Frankfurter of his wish to get out of the "Wall Street racket"[18] and "join up for the duration"[19] of the crisis then confronting the country. Thereupon Frankfurter recommended that Frank, "a lawyer who watches the bread-lines more closely than the price-quotations,"[20] be named to head the legal division of the Department of Agriculture. James Farley blocked this appointment,[21] but in May, 1933, Secretary of Agriculture Henry Wallace designated Frank as general counsel to the Agriculture Adjustment Administration. In addition, Frank became general counsel to the newly created Federal Surplus Relief Corporation.[22]

Arthur M. Schlesinger, Jr., in *The Coming of the New Deal*,[23] has painted a glowing profile of Jerome Frank of New Deal days, as a brilliant personality, possessed of "omnivorous . . . curiosity," boundless energy and exciting leadership. Frank surrounded himself in the AAA with a remarkable group of men, consisting of Thurman Arnold, Abe Fortas, Adlai Stevenson, Alger Hiss, Lee Pressman, John Abt and Nathan Witt, among others. Schlesinger quoted Frank's wife as having remarked: " 'Being married to Jerome is like being hitched to the tail of a comet.' "[24]

During Frank's tenure at the AAA, there occurred clashes between the "consumer-minded New Dealers,"[25] including Frank, and the industry-minded administrator of the AAA, George N. Peek. [26] Peek's main concern was for the "large-scale commercial farmer."[27] "[S]o long as Frank was there, every marketing agreement promised a struggle."[28] This conflict eventually led to Peek's resignation. Roosevelt summoned Rexford G. Tugwell, Acting Secretary of the Department of Agriculture, to the White House, and Peek was reassigned to a new position in the foreign trade field.[29] Chester Davis was appointed Peek's successor.

But Davis's appointment did not resolve the conflict. Clashes broke out between Davis and Frank's group. During Davis's absence on a field trip in 1935, Frank and others in his department, without consulting Davis or other top AAA officials, prevailed upon the Acting Administrator to send out a new AAA directive which reinterpreted the tenant provisions of the AAA contracts with farmers, to include the interests of the hard-pressed southern sharecroppers. It was Frank's legal opinion that under the cotton-benefit contracts, the sharecroppers too were entitled to some protection.[30] On his return, an infuriated Davis cancelled the directive as an act of insubordination and because it put the AAA "into the reform business."[31] As a consequence, Frank and his staff were fired by Wallace.

President Roosevelt's reaction was that he had "the highest regard for all parties concerned,"[32] but that if in a government department the officials are at loggerheads and a reconciliation is impossible, one or the other side must go. Roosevelt, who had a "high regard for Jerome Frank,"[33] immediately appointed him as special counsel to the Reconstruction Finance Corporation, where he remained a short time. Frank was then asked by Secretary of the Interior Harold L. Ickes to help prepare the government's case in behalf of the Public Works Administration against the Alabama Power Company.[34] The Federal Emergency Administration of Public Works had entered into loan and grant agreements with four Alabama municipalities for the construction of electricity-distribution systems, pursuant to the provisions of the National Industrial Recovery Act.[35] The power company contended that governmental competition was unconstitutional. In a unanimous decision, the Supreme Court upheld the government.[36]

Because of financial pressure, Frank resumed the private practice of law in 1936, though he had loved the trial work with PWA.[37] Helping to reorganize the Union Pacific Railroad Co. earned him a fee of $38,000.[38] But money was never a primary goal in Frank's career,[39] and soon his "nostalgia for the public service . . . overrode his instinct for financial security."[40] At the request of William O. Douglas, then Chairman of the Securities Exchange Commission, he returned to government service in 1937 "at a great monetary loss."[41] Frank served first as a member of that commission and later as its chairman for two years, having been recommended for the post by Douglas, who resigned in 1939 for a seat on the United States Supreme Court. While serving with Frank on the S.E.C., Douglas had observed Frank's "brilliance make dull problems sparkle."[42] During his tenure, Frank had occasional bouts with Wall Street and with the Investment Bankers' Association.

In the early days of the New Deal, while serving as general counsel to the AAA, Frank had delivered a talk at a meeting of the Association of American Law Schools in Chicago,[43] in which he aptly portrayed his philosophy as a dedicated servant of a forward-looking government concerned with the welfare of all the people. He discussed his brand of legal orientation which has been dubbed "realistic jurisprudence,"[44] as being akin to and congenial with "experimental economics." Because the word "realism" had too many historic connotations and conflicting meanings, he preferred to call his brand of thinking "experimental jurisprudence."[45] The exponents of his school were not "rigid determinists, but 'possibilists.' "[46] They were "humble servants to that master experimentalist, Franklin Roosevelt."[47] Positing a premise which was to be his refrain throughout his life, in his books and in his judicial opinions, namely, that "principles are what principles do,"[48] he advocated that principles be jettisoned when they produce an economic depression, such as America had just experienced. He said that judges like Marshall, Story and Holmes were effective because for conclusions they deemed desirable, they were able to find or create the appropriate legal premises to justify their conclusions. Frank visualized an important function for experimental jurisprudence in making the profit system workable by means of a conscious direction to promote the general welfare.[49]

In 1938, Frank published a book, *Save America First*,[50] which he had started to write in 1932. It was a topical economic tract and does not represent one of his major efforts. It embodied a defense of isolationism for the Unittd States, which Frank later recanted.[51] It was also a challenge to Marxian economics.[52] Throughout his career Frank was an opponent of all totalitarian creeds. In this volume, however, Frank presented some interesting views on the wise statesmanship needed to save and ameliorate American democracy and capitalism in order "to make in America a unique civilization—an economic-political democracy every citizen of which will have a full life."[53] He conceived of statesmanship as a "handling of the folkways,"[54] the traditions and institutions of a people. A great leader will realize when the folkways breed trouble and will gauge the pace at which they can be changed. He expressed his views on wages, depressions and monopolies. Frank looked at wages not only as an item in the cost of production, but as the preponderant element in the purchasing power of consumers. To avoid depressions, as the national income rises, "an increased share of the aggregate income must go to the citizens with low incomes, and a smaller share to those with large incomes."[55] But Frank was no revolutionary. Asserting that we never have had a "nonmonopolistic economy,"[56] he concluded that the giant corporations have advanced our standard of living. He opposed an indiscriminate destruction of monopoly, favoring its suppression or control only when the public interest demanded it.[57]

On May 1, 1941, Jerome Frank was appointed to the United States Court of Appeals for the Second Circuit—comprising New York, Vermont and Connecticut. This was widely regarded as the "'strongest English-speaking court,'"[58] including among its judges luminaries like Learned Hand, Augustus N. Hand and Charles E. Clark. The ten circuit courts of appeals and the District of Columbia Circuit Court of Appeals are intermediate courts between the federal district courts in their respective circuits and the United States Supreme Court. They hear appeals from decisions of the district courts and the federal regulatory agencies and on federal constitutional issues from the highest state courts via the district courts. If an appeal from a decision of a circuit court of appeals is entertained by the Supreme Court, an opinion in the lower court may influence its decision. Unless appealed from and overruled by the Supreme Court, opinions by the circuit courts of appeals are binding on lower federal district courts in their circuit and on federal regulatory agencies on all questions, but on the state courts only on federal constitutional questions as between or among the specific parties in litigation.[58a] We can thus gauge the importance of the circuit courts of appeals in the judicial constellation.[59] On this eminent bench Frank served with distinction until his death in 1957.

In 1942 Frank completed his important volume, *If Men Were Angels*,[60] which was largely a ringing defense of, and a brief for, administrative agencies, a subject which he could discuss from first-hand knowledge. In this volume he also replied at length to some of the criticism which had been levelled at his volume, *Law and The Modern Mind*.[61] In 1945, he published his philosophical volume, *Fate and Freedom*,[62] and in 1949, his most important legal treatise, *Courts on Trial*.[63] His final volume, *Not Guilty*,[64] was published posthumously in 1957. It represented the collaborative efforts of Frank and his only child, Barbara, and it detailed the lurid histories of thirty-six cases in which innocent men had been wrongly convicted by a jury and subsequently set free.

The pages that follow will seek to demonstrate through the legal writings of Jerome Frank—his judicial opinions, books and articles—that he was a legal scholar imbued with a passion for justice as the paramount goal of the law.

# Chapter I

## LEGAL REALISM AND JEROME FRANK

In the Preface to his volume, *Fate and Freedom—A Philosophy for Free Americans*,[65] Jerome Frank modestly characterized himself as "not a philosopher but an ordinary person humbly reflecting on some of man's major problems."[66] Although this humble person—very far from ordinary—was not cloaked in the mantle of a philosopher in its technical denotation, he came to be regarded in the 1930's and 1940's as one of the leading exponents of the school of "legal realism." He restricted his jurisprudence principally to a study of the area of "what courts do and should do in fact and more directly to the effects of specific court decisions on citizens."[67] An iconoclast, he was a "supreme provocateur"[68] in the currents of American legal thought, an "enfant terrible"[69] who rocked the complacency of staid legal minds.

### Four Schools of Jurisprudence

In the history of jurisprudence there have been, broadly speaking, four major schools of thought: (1) the philosophical,[70] exemplified mainly by natural law but including German transcendental idealism, (2) the historical, (3) the analytical, imperative or positivist, and (4) the sociological, of which legal realism was an offshoot.

The most venerable of these schools, dating back 2,500 years to ancient Greece, has been the school of natural law. Its influence has alternately waxed and waned.[71] But its history has been continuous from Aristotle, the Stoics, Cicero, the Roman jurists and the medieval scholastic philosophers down to our day,[72] Natural law specifically represents man's search for absolute justice, his quest for an ideal higher than the law of the state, the positive law of his time. The positive law is to be judged by the degree of its conformance with natural law. Natural law posits a body of fundamental, rational principles

1

which should govern mankind and which man can ignore only at his peril. It is a view of law as "dictated by eternal reason."[73] "'Reason' and 'the nature of man' are the starting points of all natural law thinking."[74] But the forms it has assumed have varied in accordance with the social and political setting. At times it was harnessed in the service of reform or revolution. At other times it has served as a justification for the perpetuation of the status quo.

The historical school of jurisprudence originated in the early nineteenth century in Germany and spread to England and the United States.[75] The proponents of this school believe that each nation has its distinctive *Volksgeist* (national spirit) and particular characteristics, which aid its jurists in directing the nation's development, legal and otherwise, in a specific course. This school studies both the contemporary and primitive legal institutions of a people.[76] It is opposed to the glorification of Reason[77] and the speculations of those who have sought to establish a law of nature. It advocates scientific research into legal traditions and seeks to "replace the rationalistic inquiries into the ideal nature, purposes and social objectives of the law."[78] Although it had a profound influence in England and the United States in the nineteenth century, contemporary Anglo-American scholars have neglected it.[79] Since it related law to the life of the community, it was a foundation stone for the subsequent rise of the sociological school.[80]

The analytical, imperative or positivist school of jurisprudence emerged in modern times with the rise of the modern state.[81] It seeks to analyze the law as is rather than the law as it ought to be. It states that the law as it ought to be is the concern of the ethical philosopher. The Anglo-American contribution to legal theory—particularly the English—has been mainly in the analytical field.[82]

The father of modern analytical jurisprudence or analytical positivism was John Austin (1790-1859).[83] He stressed a sharp cleavage between law and morals.[84] His analysis was concerned solely with positive laws after they have come into existence and with their analysis without regard to an ethical study of their goodness or badness.[85] Jurisprudence, according to this theory, was concerned exclusively with the study of positive law

2

—the law "set by a sovereign person or a sovereign body of persons."[86] Analytical jurisprudence has been called, with justification, a "command theory" of law.[87] Moral, ethical and political speculation were referrable to entirely different studies, which he denominated "positive morality" and the "science of legislation"[88] as distinguished from the "science of jurisprudence" or "philosophy of positive law."[89] Austin was influenced by the Pandectists of the nineteenth century, the German exponents of Roman law, who worked on Justinian's massive code, the Corpus Juris.[90] This code represented an achievement in logical consistency. Austin favored the adoption of a code of laws for England to supplant the common law. He wrote on the Roman and English systems of law, seeking a logically structured scheme into which the various propositions of law of those countries could fit.[91] He sought principles and distinctions common to developed systems of law.[92] His quest was for certainty, for consistency, for security in the law. Austin's view of a closed, self-consistent, strictly logical, conceptual system of law leaves very little room for the exercise of judicial discretion, and the little discretion allowed must follow syllogistically from the major premises of the established law.[93] A rigid application of this theory would prevent law from developing organically of its own vitality within the social fabric. For half a century after Austin, positivism monopolized English jurisprudence and exercised a great influence in America.[94]

At the turn of the century, the leading Austinians in America were Dean Christopher Columbus Langdell and Professor Joseph H. Beale of the Harvard Law School.[95] They were of the belief that at the basis of all law were a few principles. The correctness of a judicial decision was to be judged by its conformance to "fixed legal concepts."[96]

## Forerunners of Sociological Jurisprudence

It was against this petrification of the vital and creative forces of a living law, responsive to the social changes of each new generation, that Oliver Wendell Holmes, Jr., later United States Supreme Court justice and a forerunner of sociological

3

jurisprudence, expressed himself on the opening page of his legal-historical classic, *The Common Law*.[97]

> . . . The life of the law has not been logic; it has been experience. The felt necessities of the time, the prevalent moral and political theories, intuitions of public policy, avowed or unconscious, even the prejudices which judges share with their fellow-men, have had a good deal more to do than the syllogism in determining the rules by which men should be governed. The law embodies the story of a nation's development through many centuries, and it cannot be dealt with as if it contained only the axioms and corollaries of a book of mathematics . . .[98]

In a famous article, *The Path of The Law*,[99] Holmes amplified his views. They can be placed side by side with the views later expressed by Frank in his volume, *Law and The Modern Mind*, and the acknowledged inspiration will be clearly discerned. Holmes disputed the notion implicit in judicial opinions that logic is the sole force in the development of law.[100] The "logical method and form flatter that longing for certainty and for repose which is in every human mind."[101] We add his famous utterance: "But certainty generally is illusion, and repose is not the destiny of man."[102]

> Behind the logical form lies a judgment as to the relative worth and importance of competing legislative grounds, often an inarticulate and unconscious judgment, it is true, and yet the very root and nerve of the whole proceeding. You can give any conclusion a logical form . . .[103]

Holmes's nominalistic definition of law in this article was later to be adopted by Frank.[104] Holmes disputed the textwriters who defined law as a system of reason or a deduction from principles of ethics.[105] He defined law in terms of the courts' decisions, which may or may not coincide with the alleged logic or ethical maxims of the court.[106] "The prophecies of what the courts will do in fact, and nothing more pretentious, are what I mean by the law."[107] The crucial difference between Holmes and the analytical positivists was that they stressed rules and logic; he stressed decisions and experience.[108]

4

Holmes's inspiration had not been a "private revelation,"[109] but came from the European writers on history, sociology and philology who had flourished during the course of the previous century.[110] The development of science, the evolutionary ideas of Darwin and Huxley, and the teachings of the great reformers, the Utilitarians, notedly Jeremy Bentham, who believed in such legislative measures as would realize the greatest happiness of the greatest number exerted their influence upon Holmes.[111] And above all, the influence upon Holmes, of his friends, William James and Charles Peirce, was marked. James and Peirce, the founders of the philosophic school of Pragmatism, were two towering figures in American philosophy. In 1870, they and other young Bostonians, including Holmes, had founded the Metaphysical Club in order to discuss "none but the tallest and broadest questions."[112]

Pragmatism was a positivistic philosophy[113] since it was opposed to a priori reasoning. Its emphasis, however, was not on logic, but rather on "last things, fruits, consequences."[114] As such it was a social philosophy. James denied that it was a brand new doctrine and called it a "new name for some old ways of thinking."[115]

James postulated that theories have significance only in relation to their consequences in the lives of men.[116] He opposed a perspective which looked at "first things, principles, 'categories,' supposed necessities."[117] He criticized closed rationalistic systems, pretended absolutes, "the magic played by w o r d s ('God,' 'Matter,' 'Reason,' 'the Absolute,' 'energy' . . .)"[118] He opposed the use of these terms as "solving names" and as the end of one's metaphysical quest.

William James had never analyzed jurisprudence as such. It was left to his great colleague, John Dewey,[119] to write several articles on the issue of the place of logic in law. James had referred to the influence on him of the work of F.C.S. Schiller and Dewey in connection with their pragmatic analysis of truth,[120] an "instrumental" view of truth—"the view that truth in our ideas means their power to 'work.'"[121] To attain such power to "work," ideas have to harmonize with the other parts of our life experience. Dewey formulated as his view the relativity of logic; this has become known as "instrumental logic."

5

This has been his chief importance for legal philosophy.[122] He viewed logic not as the closed system postulated by the analytical positivists, but as an "empirical and concrete discipline."[123] He deprecated the view that logic represented a pure, deductive process from fixed, eternal concepts. Rather, it was a process of "inquiry into probable consequences."[124] Logic should be *relative to consequences rather than to antecedents,* a logic of prediction of probabilities rather than of deduction of certainties."[125] Legal rules and principles are hypotheses; as such they must be constantly tested in the crucible of concrete situations. General principles thus are not immutable but are only tools requiring justification by the way they work. Since law to Dewey was "through and through a social phenomenon,"[126] the functioning of legal rules, decisions and legislation must be investigated in a concrete social setting rather than in a vacuum of their logical interrelationships.[127] Dewey felt that the concept of "antecedent universal principles" interfered with intelligent social reforms in general and social advance in law in particular. There was both an intellectual and a social need for an "experimental and flexible logic."[128] This approach has been succinctly summarized as follows: "How the rules of law work, not what they are on paper, is the core of the pragmatic approach to legal problems."[129]

## Sociological Jurisprudence

The sociological school, originating around the turn of the century, considered law in relation to all other social problems. The adherents of this school looked upon Holmes as their patron saint. They found philosophic support in Pragmatism. The basic tenet of this school is that for a proper understanding of law, we must not only know what it says but must study what it does.[130] It is "both the youngest and, juristically, the most active field of jurisprudence."[131] Whereas analytical positivism had insulated and divorced "legal propositions from the world of psychological, social, political and economic facts,"[132] these factors are at the very heart of sociological jurisprudence.[133] The approach of the sociological jurist is therefore functional.[134]

6

His outlook upon law is a melioristic one directed to a dynamic social institution.

The outstanding proponent of sociological jurisprudence in America was Dean Roscoe Pound of the Harvard Law School. He first outlined the need for a sociological jurisprudence in an article published in 1905.[135] He followed in the footsteps of several important sociological jurisprudents on the Continent,[136] as well as a number of American sociologists.[137] Pound proclaimed that in law truth is relative; there is no dogmatic, metaphysical truth. With Rudolf von Ihering[138] he believed that "'interests are the chief subject matter of law, and that the task of law in society is the 'satisfaction of human wants and desires.' "[139] Pound was concerned with the manner in which law operated in the lives of men.[140]

The task of "social engineering," which Pound assigned to law, was to formulate the social interests governing a particular age. The function of law, in this view, is to balance these interests, which are modified by the flux of circumstance.[141] In the course of time the catalogue of social interests underwent change in Pound's own writings.[142] He classified these interests in three main categories: public, social and private.[143]

We shall briefly enumerate several of the "practical objectives of the study of law in society"[144] as visualized by Pound. A number of his objectives became those of the legal realist school. (1) He distinguished between law in the books—the inert decisions of the appellate courts—and law in action—the law as meted out in the trial courts. Was there a discernible difference between "paper formulae and social reality?"[145] (2) He proposed a study of the social effects of legal precepts and doctrines in the whole area of the law.[146] (3) He aimed at the individualization of justice, as opposed to a mechanical jurisprudence, through a consideration of the relevant particular factors.[147] (4) He urged scientific study as an essential preliminary to the introduction of any legislation. Legislative reform should not be the result of legislators' guesswork or of armchair speculation.[148] (5) He called for an analysis of legal history in its social context.[149] (6) Finally, he urged the establishment of ministries of justice in common law countries to help implement his program.[150]

7

## John Chipman Gray, A Mental Father of the
### Realist Movement

Professor Gray of the Harvard Law School started to write at about the same time as Pound.[151] Holmes and Gray have been singled out as the two great representatives of the field of law who, above all others, were the "mental fathers" of American legal realism.[152] Frank called Gray's contribution "invaluable."[153] Agreeing with Austin on the need for a dichotomy between law and ethics in analyzing the law as it is, Gray nevertheless diverged from Austin in a sharp modification of analytical positivism.[154] He relegated statutory legislation from the center of the law, where Austin had enshrined it, to the status of one source among several for the formation of law. He mentioned custom and morality, for example, as other sources of law. But the crucial divergence from analytical positivism in Gray's formulation is that the law has shifted from Austin's center of gravity in the sovereign to the judges who declare what the law is.[155] In Gray's view the law is what the judges declare it to be; statutes, precedents, opinions of learned experts, customs and morality are but the sources of law.[156] And although Gray considered law-making essentially a logical process[157]—and Frank criticized him for defining law in terms of the "rules" which courts lay down rather than in terms of the "decisions" in particular cases[158]——nevertheless

> his own definition as well as his comments admit and emphasize the great influence of personality, prejudice and other non-legal factors upon the making of the law. The illustrations which Gray gives from English and American legal history show how political sympathy, economic theories and other personal qualities of particular judges have settled matters of the gravest importance for millions of people and hundreds of years.[159]

Gray repudiated the fiction that judges merely state the law, never make it. He saw law as law in action, an approach which was rich in potentialities and served as an inspiration to the American realists.[160]

8

## Joseph W. Bingham, The Initiator of the Realist Exegesis

Professor Bingham of the Stanford Law School was the first to write articles devoted exclusively to formulating a nominalistic theory of law.[161] His views on that issue are identical with those later formulated by Frank.[162] Frank suggested Bingham's "forbidding style" as the possible reason for the scant notice he had received.[163] Although Bingham had published his first article in 1912, Frank did not hear of him until *Law and The Modern Mind* was substantially completed.[164] Frank and Llewellyn first brought Bingham to public notice.[165]

Bingham appeared to be a thoroughgoing "legal realist." He was the first to formulate at length the notion, so much emphasized by Frank, that the law consists of discrete, atomic decisions.[166] This had been Holmes's position, too, but his was a brief analysis. In addition, Holmes was a great architect and historian of the law and he incorporated in his studies, alongside his nominalistic approach to law, a penetrating logical analysis of legal doctrine.[167] To Bingham, rules, principles and generalizations are but "mental implements"[168] and guides to the judge. They are not necessarily binding and are not "the law." They can be criticized for inaccuracy or for other defects.[169] Precedents, which have a limited weight, should not be used to perpetuate bad law.[170] Legislative enactments have more force than judicial rules, but they too are subject to judicial interpretation.[171] Judges create law in certain areas, and instinct no less than logic is important as a source of judicial creativity.[172] Judicial opinions cannot record the instinctive processes by which judges arrive at decisions; their written opinions may be rationalizations.[173] Frank was later to urge this idea in his discussion of the "hunch" in the judicial process.[174]

## Legal Realism

Legal realism[175] was an offshoot of the sociological school. The legal realists represented the yeast in the ferment of the sociological school. They were its most dynamic representatives. Despite Pound's vast erudition and his social philosophy, he had few direct disciples.[176] The legal realists, who flourished in the nineteen thirties and forties, assumed a leadership which Pound

9

did not exert.[177] They were more fertile than he in studying concrete legal problems and suggesting reforms in the judicial system.[178] They emphasized more than Pound the social forces in the shaping of the law. They added a new dimension to the law by an emphasis on the subjective factors which contribute to the shaping of the law.

Pound's sociological jurisprudence has been labeled the "right wing" of themovement and legal realism its "left wing."[179] In similar fashion, the realist movement in American jurisprudence has been labeled as "a radical wing" of the sociological school of law.[180] Frank himself characterized Pound as representing "the right-wing of the Holmes' movement."[181] The main difference between these two wings of the sociological school consisted in this: Pound emphasized equally both facets of Holmes's thinking—the normative or prescriptive element in the law—its rules based on logic—as well as the social and psychological forces which animate it as a going institution. The legal realists, on the other hand, in de-emphasizing the pre-eminence of logic, emphasized greatly the social and particularly the psychological forces which produce an element of uncertainty in the law. The realists placed great stress in their studies on the personal characteristics of the judges. An impressionistic interpretation of some of the writings of the legal realists would lead to the belief that they assigned a minor role to logic as a force in the law's development. In criticizing legal realism, Pound characterized it as the "cult of the single decision."[182]

Frank acknowledged the tremendous debt of American jurisprudence to Pound for "quickening our legal institutions and making the law effective for the task of wise 'social engineering.' "[183] He nevertheless felt that Pound had obstructed the full growth and diluted the potency of Holmes's views.[184] For side by side with Pound's elaborate formulation of the doctrine of a sociological judicial empiricism, he demonstrated a lack of consistency by holding the doctrine that "the *fundamental* idea of law is that of a rule or principle underlying a series of decisions."[185]

The gospel of both Pound and Frank was that an imperative duty rests upon the jurist to study empirically how law functions in society.[186] In the pursuit of this objective a different emphasis arose between Pound and the realists.[187] Because of Pound's belief that the normative element was the *fundamental idea of law*,"[188] he was unable to exert the influence which the more iconoclastic and dynamic legal realists, including Frank, were able to. Yet, as Professor Paton concluded, it would seem that after the settling of the dust of the early conflict between these two wings, there is less difference between them than had been supposed.[189] This is discernible, for example, in the case of Frank, in whose later writings the approach to the place of logic in the law became more moderate than in his early writings as he extended greater recognition to its role in the judicial process.[190]

Both Pound and Frank were lawyers. But whereas legal theory from Aristotle through the Stoics, scholastic philosophers, Spinoza, Kant, Fichte, Hegel, Hobbes, Locke and Rousseau was part of their general philosophy,[191] in modern times most legal theorists have not been philosophers as such but lawyers—usually professors of law or judges—who have been confronted in their professional work with problems of social justice[192] and whose acquaintance with the actual problems of law has been thorough.[193] Most of the systematizers of the analytical, historical, sociological and realist schools of jurisprudence have been distinguished lawyers.

Sociological jurisprudence, and particularly its most dynamic variant, legal realism, represented a protest principally against analytical positivism.[194] Their healthy skepticism took sharp issue with the complacency of the closed system of analytical positivism which still held considerable sway.[195] They opposed its mechanistic approach to the law—an approach which Professor Cohen (a critic of legal realism in other respects)[196] dubbed "the phonograph theory" of law.[197] According to this theory, all the judge need do is turn on the record of the code or treatise and the law will issue tailored for use. Frank called this process the "Columbus theory"[198]—the judge never makes or invents new law but only discovers it, just as Columbus discovered America.

Henry Steele Commager stated the issues involved in the revolt against a mechanistic jurisprudence:

11

The revolt against mechanistic doctrines in law, like that against mechanistic doctrines in the other social sciences, was a revolt from forms to functions, from concepts to activities, from statics to dynamics, from individual ends to social ends, from the satisfaction of intellectual ideals to the satisfaction of human wants . . .[199]

And in the words of Dean Rostow, the exponents of a mechanical jurisprudence did not treat law as a body of "tentative hypotheses advanced to explain shifting bodies of social behavior, but as fixed propositions, laws of nature and of 'reason' in some magical sense, sustained by autonomous authority and capable of surviving unchanged for indefinite periods of time."[200] Legal propositions, however, cannot be arranged with logical consistency, as analytical jurisprudence sought to do. The application of justice to the kaleidoscopic and constantly changing facts of life calls for the frequent revisions of legal propositions.[201]

Positivism was not a concept original with the nineteenth century. It was simply a new word for an old idea.[202] Philosophy has been an eternal battleground between empiricists or positivists and metaphysicians.[203] The former placed their trust in observation; the latter in a priori or first principles.[204] With the growth of modern science, positivism spread its wings.[205] Thus, Auguste Comte (1798-1857) preached the gospel of "scientific positivism" for the study of society. His method was empirical and excluded any first principles or preconceived ideas.[206]

The adherents of the positivistic school of law excluded any a priori principles from their studies and were chiefly concerned with ascertaining the principles and corpus of the law as *is* (positus) rather than the law as it ought to be.[207] We shall see that legal realism too was a positivistic movement, concerned with knowing the law as *is*, but with this very profound difference: The motivation of its concern with knowing the law as *is*, in addition to any scientific interest, was that thereby it should be able intelligently to construct the law as it *ought* to be. The positivism of legal realism was positivism in a social matrix, imbued with a goal of law reform, which analytical positivism was not. "[P]ositivism in jurisprudence comprises legal move-

12

ments, poles apart in every respect, except for their common aversion of metaphysical theories."[208]

## Legal Realism Not a Homogeneous School

The legal realists were not a homogeneous school. In fact, the usage of the term "school" would be a misnomer in designating the exponents of "realistic" jurisprudence.[209] On many points they sharply disagreed with one another.[210] The realists were related only, as Frank stated it, "in their negations, in their skepticisms and in their curiosity."[211] They were a "formidable lot,"[212] including in their ranks, besides Frank, Professors Walter Wheeler Cook, Karl Llewellyn, Leon Green, Hessel Yntema, Herman Oliphant, Max Radin,[213] and Thurman Arnold, among others.[214] Professor Llewellyn, one of the most brilliant minds in the legal realist movement,[215] characterized it as a "ferment."[216]

Whatever the approach of the particular realist scholar— whether, e.g., he approached the study of law by way of the economic order, as in the instance of Thurman Arnold,[217] or by way of a psychological analysis, as in the instance of Frank, or by way of several empirical investigations conducted by realist scholars in various branches of the law—[218], all the approaches had a common point of departure, namely, a desire to study the law *in action*.[219] A knowledge of the law as *is* is a prerequisite to any formulation of the law as it *ought* to be. And instead of utilizing the single avenue of logic in analyzing the law as *is*, as did the analytical posivitists, the realists sought "to utilize the multiple avenues, which modern science has opened or is opening up, for a more exact and detailed knowledge of the many factors that compose modern life . . ."[220]

Several main currents and trends united the otherwise individualistic legal realists. They all attacked a formal conceptualism.[221] Rules may be plausible in the abstract but will often be found to have little correspondence with the concrete.[222] They called in question the possibility—not the desirability—of certainty in the law, though in the best of circumstances a modicum of uncertainty would be desirable in an open, progressive world.[223] Skepticism was the keynote of their approach to all traditional doctrines.[224] They put stress upon the human factor in the judicial process.[225] After positing the lack of a cohesive point of view among legal realists, Llewellyn enumerated detailed characteristics which he had found common to the movement.[226]

Frank divided the legal realists into two groups, "roughly speaking": the "rule skeptics" and the "fact skeptics." [227] He thought that Llewellyn was perhaps the leading representative of the first group, in which he included Professors Walter Wheeler Cook and Edward Levi, as well as Felix Cohen.[228] Their objective was the attainment of greater legal certainty. It was their belief that behind the courts' "paper rules" could be discovered some "real rules" which would describe uniformities in judicial behavior. [229] Such a discovery would be serviceable to lawyers in enabling them to predict decisions for their clients. [230] In this endeavor, the "rule skeptics" concentrated on upper court decisions. Consequently, their analysis neglected a consideration of the trial courts and the procedures of the latter in arriving at decisions. Like the rule skeptics, the fact skeptics too engaged in "rule skepticism" and looked beyond the "paper rules".[231] "Together with the rule skeptics, they have stimulated interest in factors influencing upper-court decisions, of which, often, the opinions of those courts give no hint. But the fact skeptics go much further." [232] Unlike the rule skeptics, their primary concern was the trial courts. Their tenet was that regardless of the definiteness and precision of formal legal rules, or any discoverable uniformities behind them, it would always be impossible to predict most future decisions because of the elusiveness of the facts. [233] As representatives of the latter group Frank listed, besides himself, Dean Leon Green, Professor Max Radin, Thurman Arnold, Justice William O. Douglas, and "perhaps" Professor E. M. Morgan. [234]. Within each group there have been diversities of opinion. In Frank's view, the rule skeptics as well as anti-skeptics exaggerated the extent of legal certainty in their exclusive concern with upper-court decisions and in their neglect of the morass of factual uncertainty at the trial-court level. "The rule skeptics are, indeed, but the left-wing adherents of a tradition. It is from the tradition itself that the fact skeptics have revolted." [235] And so he characterized the rule skeptics as dwelling in a "two-dimensional legal world,"

14

whereas the fact skeptics live in a "three-dimensional legal world."[236]

## Frank's Psychological Interpretation of the Law

In 1930 Jerome Frank made his debut in the arena of legal philosophy with his "literary bombshell,"[237] *Law and The Modern Mind.*[238] He set out to explode the myth, denominated by him "the basic legal myth," that law "is or can be made approximately stationary and certain."[239] He sought to analyze the psychology of illusive yearning for certainty in the human breast. To accomplish this he relied chiefly on the psychological writings of Jean Piaget, an eclectic psychologist who had had considerable experience in the study and treatment of children. [240] Although Frank's main thesis that certainty in the law is unattainable was well-reasoned, its psychological underpinning was widely disputed. In effect, in fighting one myth, Frank was creating another myth, ingenious though it was.

Frank raised the question as to the source of the "basic legal myth." In substance, his reply was as follows: In the womb all the child's limited needs are met and he feels omnipotent. After severing the umbilical cord, the child confronts a "chancy, crushing, unpredictable world." The certainty and the serenity he experienced in the womb have vanished beyond retrieve. But the need for a feeling of certainty and omnipotence gnaws at him. That need seeks realization anew through a transference. In the eyes of the child, the father is all-powerful, and the child finds satisfaction vicariously through him for his womb-engendered feeling of omnipotence. In contrast to the mother who in the child's psyche is the tender parent, the father is the omnipotent and omniscient parent, a strict judge who "lays down infallible and precise rules of conduct"[241] and who "sits in judgment and punishes misdeeds." [242] He is able to solve all difficulties and extricate him from all predicaments. However, as the child matures out of infancy, the infallibility attributed to the father collapses in the face of stern reality. The childish notion deeply imbedded in the child's psyche requires a replacement. The yearning for certainty, though submerged, seeks a new outlet. It is the Law which serves to satisfy that emotional need. [243] The Law serves as the replacement for the forfeited

15

omnipotence of the father. Thus the law comes to be regarded as omnipotent, fixed, certain, predictable, capable of solving all difficulties. [244]

Even though the demand for "exactly predictable law" arises in part from practical considerations rooted in reality, Frank nevertheless contended that the practical need was usually exaggerated. [245] He offered the subconscious "father-substitute" notion as a "partial explanation" [246] of the so-called "basic legal myth." But since the father-substitute causation is largely unconscious and has been neglected, he felt that it should be emphasized. He utilized it in the form of a useful fiction as if it were the sole explanation, in order to focus attention on it as a potent factor preventing the development of a realistic movement in law. [247] Conceding that psychology was still in its infancy, he nevertheless felt that it was the best instrument at present available to study human nature.[248] He described at length "childish thought-ways" [249] he adapted from Piaget. [250] Frank, however, failed to show any scientific evidence for the synapse he assumed between the "childish thought-ways" described and his father-substitute theory. This theory is relegated today to the limbo of forgotten theories. But in the day of its creation it aroused a furor, which few theories in the field of law have produced.[251]

Frank's friend and fellow legal realist, Professor Llewellyn, found the book exciting, but could not swallow Frank's venture into a psychoanalysis of the law by way of an "unproved and unapprovable" [252] womb-yearning concept. His friend, Professor Cohen, could not see why the craving for certainty, if it is a general human trait, should be fastened only on the law and not in all areas of human endeavor. [253] Is there any evidence, asked Cohen, that children reared without paternal authority crave less certainty in the law than do others? When youth ceases to respect paternal authority, it does not transfer its awe to the law, but defies the law as well as paternal authority. And if adults become more conservative and steeped in routine as they grow older, why drag in the father-substitute notion to explain it? And Allen could not understand the need for a Freudian explanation of the simple fact that in the precarious circumstances of life, men seek more certainty than they can actually obtain. [254]

What did Frank seek to accomplish by his attack on the myth of legal certainty? In one word: Emancipation. His aim was to make the law "avowedly pragmatic" through the realization that "man is not made for the law, but that the law is made by and for man."[255] His aim was the emancipation of the law from the mortmain and incubus of legal abstractions. This can result only from a pragmatic observation of the working results of the generalizations. [256] But in espousing such advocacy he disclaimed any intention of indiscriminate rebellion. "It means questioning—not hastily, angrily, rebelliously, but calmly and dispassionately—our bequests from the past, our social heritage." [257] Divorced of its theoretical and mythical psychological underpinning, *Law and The Modern Mind* still represents a landmark volume in the annals of jurisprudence.[258]

## Frank's Attack on Conceptualism

The jurisprudential views of Frank are presented mainly in his two volumes, *Law and The Modern Mind* and *Courts on Trial,* and in numerous legal articles. Frank chose as the target of his attack upon analytical positivism a leading American proponent of that school, Professor Joseph H. Beale.[259] He assailed Beale's espousal of Legal Fundamentalism—"Bealism"[260] to use Frank's coinage. Beale looked upon law in the abstract—the law of statutes, rules and principles. "Law must be, Beale asserts, UNIFORM, GENERAL, CONTINUOUS, EQUAL, CERTAIN, PURE." [261] Law must be predictable. The application of law must be an exercise in pure conceptualism. Frank, on the other hand, looked upon law in the concrete—the law of specific decisions. The approach is nominalistic. To Frank "law" meant "for any particular lay person ... with respect to any particular set of facts, a decision of a court with respect to those facts so far as that decision affects that particular person." [262] "The law of any case is what the judge decides." [263] To Frank the rules were "incidental, the decisions are the thing." [264] His constant refrain was that "[T]he law consists of decisions, not of rules." [265] Past decisions are "actual law;" a guess as to a future decision is "probable law." [266] He spoke of the reality of the contingent, the accidental, the chancy, the iffy in the day-to-day decisions of judge and jury. He waged a relentless war against universals, against the extra- or trans-experiential, against the "brooding omnipresence in the sky."[267] Law is not static and certainty is a will-o'-the-wisp. "Such denaturalized but sonorous terms as Uniformity, Continuity, Universality, when applied to law by the legal Absolutist, have the same capacity for emotional satisfaction that terms like Oneness, Eternity, or the True have when applied by the metaphysicians to the Absolute."[268]

Frank sought to de-emphasize the overlordship of rules in law since he considered them as purely functional in character. Rules can be useful only if recognized as "psychological pulleys, psychical levers, mental bridges, or ladders, means of orientation, modes of reflection, 'As-Ifs,' convenient hypostatizations, provisional formulations, sign-posts, guides."[269] He admitted that rules have some prognosticative function in the law, but they are not the sum total of what constitutes law.[270] And since the purpose of rules is the realization of "justice," it is intolerable when they are used by judges automatically and blindly for the promotion of injustice in a particular case.[271]

Since rules are only words, they can be translated into action only through the concrete decisions of judges.[272] Rules are only one source among many to which judges resort in making the law.[273] Holmes had stated that the law was to be looked at from the standpoint of a "bad man" who was not interested in legal axioms or the vaguer sanctions of conscience, but in what the courts are likely to do in fact if he acted in a certain manner.[274] Concurring, Frank stated that the hypothetical "bad man" does not care what the rules are so long as the decisions go in his favor.[275]

Before ascending the bench, Frank had assigned a "subordinate role"[276] to rules. He later modified their role to a "significant" one.[277] But regardless of the extent of their role, they are but one of the factors in judicial decision-making.[278] Thus, in Frank's view law cannot be defined in terms of rules, but in terms of individual decisions. One cannot predict whether a judge will follow an old rule, consider the case an exception to the old rule, or formulate a new rule. "His decision is primary, the rules he may happen to refer to are incidental...If so, *whenever a judge decides a case he is making law.*"[279]

Legal fundamentalism to Frank was "word-worship"[280] or "word-magic"[281] —the kind of worship or magic which Plato in his metaphysics had indulged in when constructing his world of abstract realities, "immortal entities or Universals."[282] Plato had treated individual things as imperfect copies of eternal universals.[283] Plato posited universalistic Ideas—the ideas of *man, goodness, unity, beauty* and all other conceivable manifold categories of thought—as real entities, eternal, fixed, changeless, and possessed of a higher order than their concrete, sensible manifestations in individual men who, and in objects which, pass away into doom and oblivion. Frank was of the opinion that lawyers have inherited an ancient attitude which considers concepts as more real than concrete occurrences.[284] He equated the legal fundamentalism—the conceptualism—of his bête noire,[285] Beale, with a belief in a perfectionist kind of law and in the resultant possibility of certainty in the law.[286] Belief in such a magical process was a misdescription of the facts of life.

In a historical glimpse, Frank referred to the magic spell cast by words on primitive peoples who concretized words, making of them independent entities with power over things and the forces of nature, rather than the labels and symbols they really are.[287] He cited the studies of Ogden and Richards which conclude that words have become the masters of people in their belief that the mere existence of words proves their independent reality.[288] Frank would rid us of the "narcotizing and paralyzing"[289] effect of mere verbal contrivances, including emotive words like victory, liberty, democracy and freedom, which are used in total disregard of the circumstances which brought them forth or nurtured them.[290]

Logically included in Frank's attack on the conceptualism of Beale was an onslaught on "formal logic" which avoids a consideration of substance in thought in general and in law in particular.[291] He referred to F.C.S. Schiller's book which contained a catalogue of the vices of "formal logic" in the general area of thought.[292] Formal logic, according to Schiller, posits as an ideal of perfection the notions of fixity and immutable truth and a belief in verbalistic Universals as real entities.[293] It has an

19

abiding faith in the absoluteness of authoritative rules divorced from a consideration of concrete cases and the novelties they may present. [294] This was not Frank's conception of a realistic functional logic. [295] He would consider concrete individual situations which tend to make truth with respect to them relative. [296]

Frank's opposition was to a syllogistic reasoning based upon given, fixed, unalterable major premises. The most important task of a thinker is the choice of premises. [297] That choice is not an exercise in formal logic. It is a judgment rendered on the social values of conflicting options. He conceded a role to formal logic when the judge checks his conclusion with rules theretofore acceptable. [298] If the checking proves negative, he must then consider the wisdom of his tentative conclusion both with repect to the case before him and its possible implications for future cases. [299] One almost glimpses William James incarnate in Frank when he asks lawyers to

> catch *the spirit of the creative scientist,* which yearns not for safety but risk, not for certainty but adventure, which thrives on experimentation, invention and novelty and not on nostalgia for the absolute, which devotes itself to new ways of manipulating protean particulars and not to the quest of undeviating universals ... The constant effort to achieve a stable equilibrium, resembling sleep, is regressive, infantile, and immature. [300]

In contrast to the spirit of incessant adventure in science since the eighteenth century, the outlook in law has been to find self-evident, unchanging principles. [301] The practical work of lawyers in the adjustment of human relations has been at variance with this illusory ideal. [302]

Frequently the accusation has been leveled at Frank that he was an "extreme" nominalist who refused to believe in any rules and who sought to demolish any certainty in the law by allowing each judge to act on his own uncontrolled hunches. This view is incorrect. His adulation of Holmes as "the completely adult jurist" [303] mirrors Frank's own outlook on the law. Referring to Holmes's "judicial opinions and other writings," Frank wrote:

... There you will find a vast knowledge of legal history divorced from a slavish veneration for the past, a keen sensitiveness to the needs of today with no irrational revolt against the conceptions of yesterday, *a profound respect for the utility of syllogistic reasoning* linked with an insistence upon recurrent revisions of premises based on patient studies of new facts and new desires ... [304]

Frank correctly rejected a pejorative reference to himself as an "extreme nominalist," an unbeliever in rules, as a "distorted account" of his work. [305] He insisted that legal rules have existence and must be studied, but that a definition of law in terms of rules obfuscates clear thinking about law. In his view, the difference between the realists and many respectable non-realists regarding the need for flexibility in many legal rules was mainly one of emphasis. [306] He claimed that Professor Morris Raphael Cohen had misread Holmes by failing to place the proper emphasis on the word "life" in Holmes's aphorism: "The life of the law has not been logic; it has been experience."[307] Legal realism was selecting and emphasizing one facet of Holmes's thinking—experience—which had been greatly neglected, and debunking not logic itself but the preeminence which had been attached to it in the evolution of the law. Logic without life was as inconceivable to this new school, as life without logic. Holmes was "the completely adult jurist" because he had helped undermine the conception that law can be worked out, like pure geometry, from axioms and corollaries.[308] Frank acknowledged Holmes's inspiration to the legal realists in their attempt to revise the conventional descriptions of how the courts work. [309]

In his attack on conceptualism, Frank was on common ground with all the legal realists. While he performed a salutary service in helping dethrone logic from its supremacy in the legal process, he realized in his later writings that he had exaggerated in his earlier writings the extent of uncertainty in the legal rules.[310] With the passage of the years, his emphasis shifted from rule-skepticism to fact-skepticism, to which we now turn. Many realists were not concerned with fact-skepticism, of which Frank was the chief exponent. He had advanced it from the start, but without the stress and the commanding thrust of his later writings.[311]

## The "Judging Process" and the Role of Fact-Skepticism

The conflict between theory and practice engaged much of Frank's attention. Thus, in a discussion on the judging process, he distinguished between its theory and its practice. In theory the judge starts with a rule of law as his major premise, applies it to the minor premise of the facts in the case, and then arrives at his decision. The "heretical" conception that a judge works backwards from conclusion to rule of law has seldom found expression. [312] According to this conception, the judge begins with the decision he deems desirable, and working backwards, will select such facts and apply such rules as will make his decision appear logical. [313] This "judging" of the facts, Frank commented, is usually an unconscious process and is not dishonesty. [314]

Support for this "heretical" view was found by Frank in Judge Hutcheson's concept of the judgment intuitive, the function of the "hunch" in judicial decisions.[315] According to this view, the judging process is the result of a hunch, "an intuitive flash of understanding that makes the jump-spark between question and decision." [316] The judge's reaction to the trial is a total, undivided one—not an analytical one. The judge may thereafter experience some difficulty in reporting his experience analytically.[317] On this analysis, ratiocination follows after "hunching." Opinion-writing, precedent-citing are part of the process of ratiocination utilized to justify the hunch. The published justification is in reality "ex post facto."[318] The judge must appear reasonable and make an effort to find a category which will at least appear to support his view.[319]

The main thesis of Gestalt psychology, in Frank's view, substantiated Hutcheson's notion of the hunch in the judging process. He outlined this thesis as follows: "All thinking is done in forms, patterns, configurations. A human response to situations is 'whole'. It is not made up of little bricks of sight, sound, taste, and touch. It is an organized entity which is greater than, and different from, the sum of what, on analysis, appear to be its parts ... " [320] In a play on words, Frank remarked that "we need not swallow whole this notion of the 'whole.' " [321] But it illuminates some of the reactions of men to experience, including a

22

trial judge's reaction to a trial. The trial judge experiences a "gestalt."

The decisional process in Frank's analysis is more an artistic than a logical one. Language is not the sole means of articulation. There are the fine arts and music which utilize a "wordless symbolism."[322] They are to be understood and truly appreciated only through a Gestalt—the meaning of the whole. It was to the artistic process that Frank analogized the decisional process of the judge who has heard conflicting testimony, has formed his hunches, and is then called upon to articulate the foundations of his "hunch." Emotion, intuition and feelings "that words cannot ensnare" [323] are involved. The judge "lets down as it were a bucket into his subconscious." [324] The articulation of his decision will not reflect these subconscious forces.[325]

From the premise that the law consists of the decisions of judges, Frank deduced that if their decisions are based upon hunches and intuition, the key to the judicial process is the way in which judges come by their hunches. "Whatever produces the judge's hunches makes the law." [326] In enumerating the hunch-producers, he listed rules and principles as only one element or class of stimuli, often exaggerated in importance. There are many concealed elements, not often discussed in analyses of the nature of law. [327] In addition to the political, economic and moral prejudices of the judge, Frank added the innumerable unique traits of each judge. [328] Deeply buried biases of a personal nature, which may be immune from scrutiny, may influence the judge's reactions to witnesses. [329] "His own past may have created plus or minus reactions to women, or blonde women, or men with beards, or Southerners, or Italians, or Englishmen, or plumbers, or ministers, or college graduates, or Democrats." [330] To Frank these individual traits of judges often loom larger in arriving at decisions than the socio-economic biases of judges. Further, these characteristics have a dual intertwining function: they help determine not only the decision which the judge thinks fair on the given set of facts, but unconsciously the very selection of the facts he chooses to believe. [331] This subjective element in the decisional process leads to a greater unpredictability of decisions. The sociological school of Pound sought wisely to demonstrate the influence of social,

23

economic and political views on judges sitting in the upper courts, where rules are formulated, but it neglected to consider the idiosyncratic influences and unconscious biases of judges in their reactions to witnesses when finding the facts on a trial court level. [332] Legal rules usually represent the more or less objective moral norms of a community, but the trial judge's evaluation of the oral testimony at a trial is subjective in character. [333]

In the concrete framework of the judicial process, fallibility is compounded: that of witnesses and that of the judge or jury. [334] Witnesses may be mistaken on any one of three scores: (1) faulty observation; (2) Correct observation but faulty or imaginative memory; and (3) an inaccurate or inadvertent reporting by an honest witness for any number of causes. [335] "For the ordinary witness, then, it is not true that a fact is a fact is a fact ..." [336] Aside from mistaken witnesses, witnesses may be outright liars or they may be biased. [337] An honest witness may appear untruthful because of fear, irascibility, overscrupulousness or exaggeration. [338] Aggravating this picture of subjectivity and chanciness may be the fact of a dead or missing witness or of a destroyed important document.

In addition, the judge and the jury too are witnesses; they are the silent witnesses of the witnesses in the courtroom. [339] Their reactions to the testimony are subjective. They are subject to defects in comprehension and they suffer from the same human frailties as the testifying witnesses. Thus, there arises a dual refraction from the facts as they actually occurred: first by the witnesses who testify and second by the witnesses who must find the "facts". And since the trial judge or jury observed the witnesses and their demeanor—"this language without words" [340] —, an upper court, which has before it only a cold printed record of the lower court proceedings, seldom will disturb the lower court's fact-finding, provided there is some support for it in the record. If the fact-finding can be supported by reasonable inferences drawn from the testimony of some witnesses, though it is flatly contradicted by other witnesses, the upper court will rule only on questions of law. In this entire process, the pivotal factor in Frank's assessment is the judge, and the decision handed down may vary with his personality. [341]

In Frank's later writings, the major cause of legal uncertainty was not that of rule but of fact.[342] If the court for any reason misapprehends the real facts, it decides an unreal, a hypothetical case. [343] Even if all the rules were certain, no one can predict what facts the court will "find" so as to be able to guess which rule will consequently be followed as a precedent. "For no rule can be hermetically sealed against the intrusion of false or inaccurate oral testimony which the trial judge may believe." [344]

Frank sought to rebut the commonly held notion that the most difficult function in the administration of justice is the determination of which rules to apply to the facts of a case. [345] He was haunted by the specter of fact-uncertainty. He considered fact-finding by the trial court the "toughest" part of the judicial function. He schematized the conventional theory of court operation with the mathematical formula: $R \times F = D$, [346] in which R stands for Rule (the major premise), F for Fact (the minor premise) and D for Decision. He argued that no matter how certain legal rules may be—and some are—, the decisions are at the mercy of correct fact-finding by the court. [347] The facts to be decided are not objective data which "walk into court". [348] On the contrary, they must be ferreted out by judge or jury in a subjective process. As a result, they may be "hopelessly incorrect." [349] In view of the subjective factor in the decisional process, Frank would modify its conventional description and reformulate it to read: $R \times SF = D$, in which S stands for Subjective, since the "facts" in litigation are subjectively arrived at.[350]

Injustice results from the application of the correct rule to mistaken facts as much as from the application of an incorrect rule to the actual facts.[351] As a matter of fact, greater injustice usually results in the former instance, since an appellate court will ordinarily not reverse on a factual basis but will do so on a rule basis. The policy behind a rule is "wrecked" when it is misapplied because applied to erroneously found facts. [352] Sitting on an appellate court, Frank stated that he considered rules to be of "great importance",[353] and he felt sorely troubled when they are foiled by application to the wrong facts due to unnecessarily faulty fact-finding. His distress was keen because "probably" ninety five per cent of all cases tried are not appealed, and in those cases which are appealed, the appellate courts in most instances accept the facts as found by the trial court. [354]

Although acknowledging the salutary effect of John Dewey's pragmatic approach to the law, Frank nevertheless felt that Dewey had omitted one dimension from his discussion on judicial logic.[355] Dewey had not discussed the "weakest spots" in the administration of justice —the faultiness of witnesses' observations and the methods of determination by trial judges of the reliability of witnesses.[356] Dewey's analysis, according to Frank, was mostly relevant on an appellate court level, where the courts are concerned only with the correct application of the rules to facts already "found" in the trial court and consequently where the question of the "logical method" is more germane. Dewey's analysis, however, was not relevant on the trial court level, where the gravest problem is the selection of the "correct" facts. But Frank's critique of Dewey was unfair, since Dewey was not directing his study to the concrete problems of the trial courts. This was a matter for other students more familiar with the details of the trial courts, for reformers like Frank, to come to grips with.

In Frank's view Aristotle was a better pragmatist than Dewey because of Aristotle's first-hand observations of the functioning of the courts. [357] Aristotle reported in his *Rhetoric* on the nonrational and irrational ingredients which often mightily affect judicial decisions—such as the all-too-human emotions of judges. [358] Frank was profoundly disturbed by the fact that no matter how noble the ideals of a legal system, "that system works shocking evils when, because of its avoidable 'unruly' features, its courts sentence men to death for murders they did not commit or mulct men in money damages for acts they did not do."[359]

Despite Frank's analysis of legal decisions as rooted in non-logical hunches, he felt it very desirable that trial judges be required to write special findings of fact since that would compel them to scrutinize their decisions carefully.[360] For while most of the conclusions arrived at by men in their daily lives are hunch-products, frequently their correctness can be tested by means of a logical analysis. [361] "Logic," said Frank, "need not be the enemy of hunching." [362] But after all is said, Frank still had one basic reservation gnawing at his inner peace: it can never be known that the facts as found by the judge are, in the well-known Kantian phrase, das *Ding-an-sich*—adapted and pluralized by Frank as "the facts in themselves."[363]

Frank's stress on fact-uncertainty rendered a beneficent service to court-house government, since it had been largely a neglected area in jurisprudential studies, but he engaged in hyperbole in raising the specter of an almost boundless fact-uncertainty in the law courts. He furnished no scientific support for his extreme skepticism. It was considerably based on assumptions.[364] His onslaught on the jury system, as we shall later see, was similarly based on abstract thinking and was not the result of empiric studies, such as would be in consonance with a basic tenet of legal realism.[365] But as has been pointed out, "he alerted juristic minds to the always present possibility that the facts as found by judge or jury do not correspond to the actual facts. In the process he pointed the way to reforms in an area of crucial human significance."[366]


## Fact-Skepticism and Capital Punishment

Frank's deeply ingrained fact-skepticism was clearly discernible in his attitude towards capital punishment. After citing in his volume, *Not Guilty*,[367] thirty-six instances of defendants convicted of all manner of crimes, including homicide, who were later proved incontrovertibly innocent, Frank concluded with a call for the abolition of capital punishment in the vein of fact-skepticism. "Such instances demonstrate the intolerably monstrous nature of any death sentence: It cannot be undone. It may mean the judicially sanctioned governmental murder of the guiltless."[368] Frank's concern for the innocents wrongly convicted represented a lifelong passion. His words bear the stamp of a deeply etched empathy for those suffering injustice at the hands of the law. "A man in prison when he should not be there is brother to us all."[369] Or as he well expressed it in an address before the Chicago Bar Association: *"To have convicted the innocent is horrible.* For the innocent to have been irresponsibly charged with a serious violation of law, is but little less so: The power to prosecute can be power to destroy."[370]

In a brief sociological analysis of crime, Frank stated that "roughly speaking, crimes of violence are committed by the poor."[371] The rich, on the other hand, *"do not beat, they cheat their victims; they do not rob banks, they wreck them."* [372] Such men as Richard Whitney and Coster may well be more destructive to our civilization than gangsters. It is true, he said, that "pathological criminality" is responsible for some crime, but often the roots of crime are to be found in "debased economic and social living conditions." [373] Consequently, prosecutors should have a very high regard for civil liberties since "[T]o brow-beat poor men, to coerce or trick them into confessing or pleading guilty to crimes they did not commit is thus relatively easy ... Repeated and unredressed attacks on the constitutional liberties of the humble tend to destroy the foundations supporting the constitutional liberties of everyone." [374]

The *cause célèbre* of *U.S.* v. *Rosenberg*[374a] involved a charge of espionage brought by the United States government against the alleged conspirators, Julius and Ethel Rosenberg, husband and wife, Morton Sobell, David Greenglass and Anatoli Yakolev, charging that they had communicated to the Soviet Union, both towards the end of World War II when the United States was an ally of Russia and during the ensuing Cold War—from 1944 to 1950—documents, sketches and information relating to the national defense of the United States. In writing the Court's opinion confirming the death sentence imposed by a federal district court judge on the Rosenbergs after a trial by jury, Judge Frank did not express his abhorrence of the death sentence, as might have been expected. In our subsequent discussion of Frank and the jury system, it will be seen that though he was a pronounced advocate of abolition of the jury system in civil cases, he upheld the obligation of every judge, so long as the jury system prevailed and was guaranteed either by the constitution or by statute, to enforce punctiliously all the rules governing juries. Yet, he never ceased in his opinions, as well as in his jurisprudential writings, to advocate the abolition of the jury system in civil cases.[374b] Why did Frank not follow a similar path in discussing the death sentence in the Rosenberg case? We are not concerned with the many substantive issues of law raised in this case, since they are not germane to any of our areas of discussion. Our analysis is confined to the sole issue raised by the imposition of the death penalty.

28

The issue raised lends itself to several conjectures. One is the gravity and enormity of the crime, which, according to the opinion of the trial judge, quoted by Frank, did incalculable damage to the security and vital interests of the United States. As a parallel, one may feel an inherent revulsion against capital punishment in general and yet approve its use in the instance of the crime of genocide, where a multitude of lives are involved. But the enormity of the crime still does not dispose of the question whether a particular defendant may possibly have been guiltless. Of course, since Frank wrote the Court's opinion, he expressed the views of his colleagues as well as his own. Yet a brief explanation of his own personal position—if such be the case—clearly indicated as such, would have been possible, but we find no such brief expression of Frank's personal view. A candid statement of his general views on capital punishment, as well as his views on the special facts of the case before him, would certainly not have been amiss, if he had definite views against capital punishment when he wrote his opinion. Another conjecture is that Frank's opposition to capital punishment, despite his fact-skepticism, did not crystallize until shortly before his death; it was in his last book, *Not Guilty*, that he expressed his abhorrence of capital punishment.

The Circuit Court of Appeals was asked by the defense to modify the death sentence. In a strict adherence to the doctrine of *stare decisis*, Frank replied:

Unless we are to overrule 60 years of undeviating federal precedents, we must hold that a (federal) appellate court has no power to modify a sentence . . .

In England, Canada and in several of our states, upper courts have held that they may reverse sentences while affirming convictions. But these rulings were based on statutory authority . . .

Because, however, for six decades federal decisions, including that of the Supreme Court in Blockburger v. United States, *supra*, have denied the existence of such authority, it is clear that the Supreme Court alone is in a position to hold that sec. 2016 (of 28 U.S.C.A.) confers authority to reduce a sentence which is not outside the bounds set by a valid statute. As matters now stand, this court properly regards itself as powerless to exercise its own judgment concerning the alleged severity of the defendants' sentences.[374c]

Without expressing his own views, though perhaps they may obliquely be gleaned by reading between the lines, Frank referred to the long-standing suggestion of some commentators that upper courts have or should have power to reduce harsh sentences. See, e.g., Hall, Reduction of Criminal Sentences on Appeal, 33 Col. L. Rev. 521, 764 (1937). The existence of such power may seem the more desirable in these days when, in the recent words of the Supreme Court "retribution is no longer the dominant objective of criminal law. Reformation and rehabilitation of offenders have become important goals of criminal jurisprudence." (citing *William* v. *New York*, 337 U.S. 241, 248. . .)[374d]

Frank was also confronted with the issue of "cruel and unusual punishment" prohibited by the Eighth Amendment of the Constitution. Is the death penalty the infliction of "cruel and unusual punishment"? Frank ruled that under the federal decisions the death penalty is not a violation of the Eighth Amendment.[374e]

The test of a "cruel and unusual punishment" urged by the defendants—i.e., that it shocks the conscience and sense of justice of the people of the United States—is not met here. . . . And in any context, such a standard—the community's attitude—is usually an unknowable. It resembles a slithery shadow, since we can seldom learn, at all accurately, what the community, or a majority, actually feels. Even a carefully-taken 'public opinion poll' would be inconclusive in a case like this. Cases are conceivable where there would be little doubt of a general public antipathy to a death sentence. But (for reasons noted below) this is not such a case . . .[374f]

. . . Assuming the applicability of the community-attitude test proposed by these defendants, it is impossible to say that the community is shocked and outraged by such sentences resting on such facts . . .[374g]

## Frank and Natural Law

Natural law,[375] that eternally puzzling and ever-recurring problem, must engage the attention of any writer on jurisprudence, even if he restricts himself to a study of the courts and judicial reform, as did Frank.[376] Frank believed that the fundamental principles of natural law set forth by Thomas Aquinas must be accepted today by every "decent" man as the basis of modern civilization.[377] But the application of the general principles has varied according to time, place and circumstance. In a survey from the Greeks to his day, Frank furnished a kaleidoscopic view of how natural law has been used over the centuries and espoused alike by revolutionary and reactionary, each to suit his own purpose and as justification for his views. Frank would therefore substitute the nomenclature Justice for natural law. Of course, this represents the mere substitution of one symbol or label for another and Frank conceded that the substituted word he proposed lack precision.[378] But he felt that it would have the advantage of not being impregnated with "the misleading connotations and embarrassing historical associations of the words natural law, which today must be translated to be understood by most non-Catholics." [379] If the objective of natural law is the quest for justice, he believed in speaking of justice directly.

Frank linked his analysis of natural law with his dominant leitmotif of the crucial importance in the judicial process of correct fact-finding, and he concluded that natural law principles cannot solve that problem. Natural law does not assure uniformity in that area. And it is in that area that abstract justice is concretized. Frank asked the question with which all his writings are instinct: Of what utility are justice in the abstract and the universals of natural law, if justice is lacking in concrete instances?[380] And contrary to the pronouncement of some of Frank's critics that legal realists, including Frank, favored a dichotomy of law and ethics in the judicial process, Frank wrote that it would be a perversion of the judicial process to separate ethics from it. But ethicizing the work of the courts would have little utility if it were not done on the trial-court level.[381] Frank

31

sounded what has been held to be the distinct contribution of legal realism to modern jurisprudence: reverence for the individual man. [382]

> ... Here is the practice, the devotion, which comes from the very heart of democratic justice: reverence for the man—not the abstraction in capital letters but the man, the individual, seeking a good life...
>
> We may be thankful that justice is not a word of precise, fixed meaning. Its meaning changes as civilization grows... Only so can the quest for justice be pursued by men of good will through the ages.[383]

## Frank's Views on Free Will and Democracy

A "polemic against fatalism" was the leitmotif of one of Frank's volumes.[384] He posited that free will—"possibilism" as it is called by him at one point[385]—is in consonance with the American faith and is supported by a solid scientific corpus of proof—particularly modern—, and that conversely, determinism, fatalism or inevitabilism—he used all three as synonyms—runs counter to the American faith. He felt that, viewing the consequences of determinism—regardless of the support it has received from many quarters throughout history—its rejection is required for the free world.

Both inevitability and freedom, in Frank's view, could be seen in the universe. He debunked the inevitabilism of the so-called "scientific historians" who read their subjectivities into their historical analyses.[386] He refused to see men as mere puppets of fate.[387] "We must assert our faith in the power of free men to preserve a civilization in which freedom will seem to have been inevitable—because free men have effectively willed that it would persist..." [388] He roamed over the history of philosophic ideas from the perspective of determinism and free will, including Pythagoras, Democritus, Plato, Aristotle, Zeno, Locke, Hegel, Marx, Freud, the Greek skeptics Aenesidemus and Sextus Empiricus and the modern skeptic David Hume, Charles Peirce and William James, as well as outstanding modern scientific thinkers. He attacked "anyone who does not fit into his synthesis, but this is the beauty of a crusader who believes in his cause."[389]

Since neither causality nor acausality can be scientifically proved, Frank's criterion for the selection of one rather than the other was the pragmatic result of an assaying of their consequences.[390] Conceding that in either case the choice would be a "faith axiom," he opted for free will and acausality because they aid in promoting the ideals cherished by free Americans and are more compatible with them. He dreamt of a leisure society and a richer civilization, in which man would enjoy adequate material comforts, civil liberties and an abundance of economic and non-economic activities, individual initiative, social fellowship and co-operativeness.[391] With Jefferson and Lincoln he felt that democracy offered the best road to this goal. Democracy offers the best opportunity for man to express himself as a social individual. Frank looked forward to an ever-increasing role for the individual in democratic government on all levels.[392] And as part of his democratic faith, he believed in a vast measure of free self-expression by and lack of restraint upon the creators of thought and culture. "Abandonment, inventiveness, creation, individual initiative should there be at a premium." [393]

The defeat of Nazism in Europe did not assure its rejection in America.[394] Democracy required a constant vigilance in behalf of "the American tradition of individual and group freewill." [395] Frank sounded a ringing affirmation of his faith in democracy, providing it is administered by the right kind of men—in line with his emphasis that a "government of laws" is not self-executing and is insufficient to guarantee good government.[396]

Frank was pleased that many law schools now emphasize the role of lawyers in policy making and stress the need for incorporating democratic ideals in the legal rules.[397] He was in accord with the view that emphasis should be placed in the law school curriculum upon democratic values and ideals.[398] Among the democratic values Frank listed in which a law school should interest itself "mightily"[399] are the overhauling and improving of our trial methods. He advocated law school studies on the effect of corruption and political pull on trial judges.[400] Although interested in the creation and improvement of all institutions which have community value, of foremost concern to him was the "vaunted" democratic community value of the right to a fair trial.[401] A sound legal education, in his opinion, should stimulate the interests of budding lawyers in that direction. Encouragement should be given to law students to feel that the pressing for improvements in the judicial process and for amelioration in the social and economic spheres through legislation and wise administration is an important part of their future task.[402]

## A Program of Reform

> I am—I make no secret of it—a reformer, one of those persons who (to quote Shaw) 'will not take evil good-naturedly.'[403]

If the judge is the "pivotal factor" in the administration of law, Frank asked whether it is possible that a more discriminating technique of judging can be developed. He warned against over-optimism[404] and was not ready to jump overboard with Schroeder into the assumption that a blending of psychology with law would promptly bring about remarkable results.[405] But he stressed the importance of "ventures of self-discovery" by the judges themselves and the "tentative" idea of prospective judges undergoing psychoanalysis.[406]

As a preliminary to ventures of self-discovery, Frank thought it valuable to undertake studies of judges from the outside, such as the psychological study by Haines of judges' motives and biases in their judicial decisions.[407] Haines had outlined a blueprint for such a study of the justices of the Supreme Court. He listed as the factors which were likely to be influential in molding judicial decisions, the "judges' education, general and legal; their family and personal associations; their political affiliations and opinions; their intellectual and temperamental traits."[408] Such studies could prove of great value if they led to a "searching self-analysis" on the part of the judges themselves. No one but the judge himself or a psychologist can ferret out his intimate experiences and comprehend their emotional significance.[409] And since many of the influences in one's life are subconscious and subliminal, Frank advocated that each prospective judge undergo "something like a psychoanalysis." [410] Frank well understood the psychological phenomenon of projection and the hazards it presents when sadism is operative in the subconscious of a judge. The judge will "self-deceptively" project onto others his own aggressiveness and imagine it is in others. By this process he seeks to whitewash his own aggressiveness of which he is unaware. "... [T]hat tendency," said Frank, "operative in a judge, may produce hideous consequences in sadistic decisions which he will self-deceptively rationalize."[411] In addition, Frank urged that trial judges first function as trial lawyers, serve as apprentices to trial judges, and pass a "stiff examination." [412]

Whether or not a more discriminating technique of judging can be developed, Frank concluded that the personality of the judge is the pivotal factor in the judicial process.[413] Consequently, there is no hope for "complete uniformity, certainty, continuity in the law."[414] An undesirable uniformity of decisions and "stability" could result only if all judges were narrow-minded or bigoted. But the elevation of enlightened and intelligent judges to the bench must bring about divergent reactions in response to unique facts in legal controversies.[415] However, a deeper uniformity will ensue from the greater readiness of such judges to detect and check their prejudices and from their keen realization that rules and precedents are not their masters but rather their servants for the attainment of justice.[416] The outward semblance of uniformity will be diminished, but the conviction will be greater that justice is being done when decisions are rendered by judges who have attained self-knowledge and self-scrutiny as had, in his view, such judges as Holmes, Cardozo, Hutcheson, Lehman and Cuthbert Pound. To Frank, creativeness was the very life of the law, as he claimed it was to Aristotle in his classical description of judicial discretion or "equity" in his volume, *The Nicomachean Ethics*.[417] To Aristotle, the generality of legal rules prevented their application to the divergent facts of particular cases, which frequently required modified treatment through supplementation by equity in order to avert an injustice.

Frank set out to effectuate court reform in a broad spectrum. He anticipated no "millennium." [418] He knew that the trial process can never become a thoroughly scientific inquiry for ferreting out the true facts. But he was anxious for palliative measures to ameliorate the defects which he saw in the judicial process. In addition to the fact that witnesses, judges and jurors are fallible, Frank posited that the present method of trial procedure—the "contentious" or "adversary" system as distinguished from the "investigatory" or "truth" system—frequently precludes the presentation of all available important evidence. [419] Our trial methods still bear the traces of their genesis as substitutes for private brawls out-of-court. Frank recognized the merits of the "fight theory" of the adversary system, such as the marshalling before the court by partisan contestants of the facts and the law, some of which might be overlooked in a dispassionate investigation. But since a lawyer is interested in victory and not in aiding the court in the discovery of the facts, he concluded that the adversary system had become "dangerously excessive." [420] A lawyer may not call a witness he knows of who may be helpful to his opponent. "Our present trial method is thus the equivalent of throwing pepper in the eyes of a surgeon when he is performing an operation." [421]

Frank's critique was directed not at the lawyer, but at the system tolerating a "battle of wits and wiles." [422] The stratagems of lawyers are considered a legitimate corollary of the "fight theory." Frank pointed to Dickens and Trollope who had ridiculed the expectation that an ordinary witness could give accurate testimony when attempts are made by undignified bellowing and other antics to browbeat him on cross-examination. [423] These novelists felt that more use should be made in witnesses' testimony of narrative recitals rather than the usual question-and-answer method. The folly of this method, Frank thought, should be exposed by psychologists and psychiatrists, leading to its drastic modification.

A deviation in part from the "fight theory" has occurred in both federal and state jurisdictions through the medium of the "discovery" procedure in non-criminal cases. This compels one's adversary before trial to disclose evidence in his possession and prevents belated surprise at a trial. [424] Frank proposed the adoption of the English practice—not followed in most American jurisdictions and "narrowly limited" in some—which compels the prosecutor before trial to divulge to the accused all the evidence he intends to offer at the trial. [425]

Another advance seen by Frank towards implementing the

"truth theory" of trials has been the greater insistence that judges exercise more latitude in examining witnesses at trials and in summoning witnesses they have become aware of but whom neither side has subpoenaed. He regretted that as yet few judges avail themselves of this power. [426] He urged the extension into all jurisdictions of the reform instituted in some states by which indigent persons charged with crime are represented by a publicly paid official, a Public Defender. [427] But when an error in the channels of justice is discovered, Frank stated it was only right that the government assume the responsibility, as it has in some jurisdictions, of compensating an innocent convicted person.

A number of situations not conducive to the discovery of truth agitated Frank. A party, because of lack of funds, may be unable to procure evidence, not in the possession of his adversary. Neither his lawyer, nor any legal aid institution, if it represents him, will supply such funds.[428] This creates a mockery of our vaunted "equality before the law."[429] Or detectives may be needed to scour vast territories to unearth papers or locate witnesses. Or the services of an expert—an engineer, a chemist, an accountant—may be required, involving substantial outlays of funds. It was shocking that justice often becomes an "upper-bracket privilege." Frank was of the opinion that the government should take an active part in civil, as well as in criminal, cases.[430] To remedy such situations, in civil cases, Frank proposed a "public prosecutor of civil actions."[431]

In civil actions there is no official analogous to the public prosecutor in criminal cases. Because of the incompetence or lack of diligence of a lawyer or the lack of funds, available crucial evidence may not be produced in court. [432] A man may as a consequence lose his job or his savings. Frank urged that the government even in the area of so-called private rights should assume some of the burden of enforcing such rights through the creation of the office of "public prosecutor of civil actions." This office was first proposed in 1927 by Samuel Willoughby.[433] This "impartial government official" would dig up evidence which may have been overlooked or which could not be procured by one of the parties. His employment would be optional, and if he were retained, private counsel could still assist him. His first efforts would be directed towards settling the dispute himself or through arbitration. Public funds would be at his disposal to produce essential evidence. The innovation would at first be tested experimentally in some cases. Frank granted that these officials would make their share of mistakes and at times might become partisan. [434] But he was analogizing from his own experience as chairman of the Securities Exchange Commission and the fact that many of the administrative agencies have expert staffs to conduct their investigations. [435]

An excellent suggestion was made by Frank regarding the selection of criminal prosecutors. To be rid of unfair prosecutors he would require special education for that office, rather than the usual present political method of selection. He would require the prospective prosecutor to pass a stiff written and oral examination demonstrating his moral and intellectual aptness for the position.[436] On the Continent a prospective prosecutor must first serve an apprenticeship with an experienced prosecutor.[437] The present belief that a trial is essentially a battle or a sporting contest between prosecution and defense places innocent accused persons in jeopardy. Only high-minded prosecutors can transcend such a belief.

Reference was made by Frank to the suggestion that trained psychologists be allowed to testify as court experts regarding the capacities of witnesses.[438] These experts would interview a witness prior to trial, and at the trial they would testify concerning the capacity of the witness in the area of the five senses, his capacity for sustained memory, and any abnormal tendencies he may display, such as pathological lying. Like any other witness, they would be subject to cross-examination, and their testimony would not be binding on court or jury.[439] It will be recalled that during the *cause célèbre* of Alger Hiss, the defense called as a witness a psychiatrist who had observed Whittaker Chambers, the star prosecution witness, during the course of his testimony in the courtroom, to give evidence as to his testimonial capacity. But the psychiatrist had not been accorded an opportunity for a clinical examination of or an interview with the witness. Frank was doubtful that the expert testimony can be of help where such an opportunity is not extended to the psychiatrist.[440] He believed further that the judge should have the power to call neutral experts.

Frank realized that this proposal—which had been espoused by Wigmore, the great expert on evidence—if applied to all witnesses in all trials, would result in much longer trials.[441] But as a realist, he felt it merited experimentation. Are not scientific experts of all varieties called upon to give testimony with regard to their specialties for the court's guidance? Since, in Frank's opinion, juries and most judges are amateurs in sizing up witnesses, the use of expert aid might help minimize the hazards of fact-finding.

Concern was expressed by Frank with the state of legal education and he proposed reforms in that area as well. He launched a grass-roots attack on a system of legal education which he deemed responsible for the perpetuation of "legal rule magic."[442] He was highly critical of the exclusively law-library method of American legal education introduced by Professor Christopher Columbus Langdell of the Harvard Law School—the "Harvard system."[443] To Langdell law was restricted in meaning to library-law—examining published authorities and writing briefs. The atmosphere of a law office and a law court and the non-rational factors permeating a trial, according to Frank, were virtually unknown to him.[444] In distinction to "library law-schools, book-law schools,"[445] Frank urged the establishment of "lawyer-schools." Students at such law schools should be "doing" and not merely "learning."[446] Frank briefly traced the history of American legal education from its origin as an apprentice system, under which the law student "read law" in the office of a practicing attorney.[447] In this atmosphere the student constantly observed what the courts and lawyers were doing. Before his eyes legal theories became intertwined with legal practices.[448] Judge Reeves, who founded the first American law school in 1780, applied the apprentice system on a group basis. But it was under the impact of Langdellism that legal apprenticeship practically disappeared in the universities and the students became quarantined in law libraries.

In addition to the current study of cases in the law schools, Frank advocated a close re-alliance with the actualities of court practice and law office work.[449] In his view a considerable proportion of law instructors—contrary to the prevailing situation—should have had actual and varied law practice before the courts and administrative agencies and in law office work.[450] Although there is need for a "library-law" teacher in the law school since part of the lawyer's function is brief-writing for appellate courts, his dominance of the law schools should end.

Law students, Frank argued, should read and analyze not merely the judges' opinions under the Langdell case system, but also elaborate complete records of cases, from the filing of the first papers through the proceeding in the trial and appellate courts.[451] Students should observe at first hand courthouse procedures and operations. Law teachers frequently should accompany the students to trial and appellate courts.[452]

What would our opinion be, Frank wondered, of a medical school which gave its students no clinical experience? He proposed the establishment of a legal clinic or dispensary in each law school to be run by experienced professors with the assistance of students for a nominal charge or none at all.[453] The staffing of these "clinics" by professors and some top-notch members of the local bar would render more skilled advice than is presently provided by the Legal Aid Societies, in addition to the fact that far more varied cases would be handled. This system would provide for the interlacing of theory and practice.[454] The learning of legal rules would thus be transferred to the "exciting context of live cases."[455] The difference between that method and the present method, said Frank, is "like the difference between kissing a girl and reading a treatise on osculation."[456] The current relevance of Frank's "interne plan" for law schools is apparent from a recent item appearing in the New York Times.[457]

In addition, Frank was an enthusiastic advocate of the inclusion of the social studies—history, ethics, economics, politics, psychology and anthropology—in the law school curriculum.[458] Legal studies should be considered in the light furnished by the other social studies.[459] In these studies Frank urged severe criticism of the "errors" of determinism—economic or otherwise—and of behaviorism.[460] These courses should teach the students the need for openmindedness and the folly of dogmatism.[461]

40

Legal theory was not ignored in this reorientation of the law school curriculum. Frank would lay "much stress" on legal theory.[462] "For practices unavoidably blossom into theories, and most theories produce practices, good or bad."[463] Even one who has no express philosophy has an inarticulate and unexamined philosophy.

The claim has been made that

The most important immediate consequences of legal realism were in the field of legal education. While outside of academic halls the realists seemed to many to be merely cynics or iconoclasts, within those halls legal realism was a vital constructive influence . . .

"Cases and Materials" became the standard heading for the classbook, revised to include, besides the traditional collection of reported judicial decisions, "materials" showing economic or social theory or fact, relevant business practices, excerpts from works on psychiatry, forms of contracts, and frequently just straight legal text from law reviews or treatises. The realist drive for 'factual" or "extra-legal material" to be studied in connection with reported cases, as a means of "integrating" law and the social sciences, or as a means of showing the place of law in society . . . concurred with a movement toward the use of textual material in casebooks, heterodoxy to Langdell's earlier followers . . .[464]

## Pound's Controversy With Legal Realism—The Battle of the "Is" and the "Ought"

A continuous battle was waged for many years over the IS and the OUGHT in the law—the law as it is and the law as it ought to be. Some critics have contended that legal realism was concerned only with the IS to the neglect of the OUGHT and thus to the neglect of any value-system.

Writing in 1931, Dean Pound lauded legal realism as an important jurisprudential movement which sought to found a "science of law"[465] on the basis of actualities, as well as for its recognition of the "alogical and non-rational" element in the judicial process which had been ignored by nineteenth century jurisprudence.[466] He then criticized legal realism on two scores. First, for its refusal "to recognize the function of the quest for

41

certainty as contributing to the general security ... There is as much actuality in the old picture as in the new. Each selects a set of aspects for emphasis. Neither portrays the whole as it is."[467] Second, Pound argued that a science of law cannot be exhausted by a descriptive catalogue of actualities. The crucial question is: What then? "The question of OUGHT, turning ultimately on a theory of values, is the hardest one in jurisprudence."[468] It was Pound's contention that legal realism furnished no criteria for a valuation of the materials selected in its studies—no axiology with which to create a science of law, such as other schools of jurisprudence, each in its way, havs attempted. The significance of a fact selected for study can only be determined by a preconceived notion of the ideal sought. The fact that many legal realists use the psychological method in their studies is a question of methodology. But what is the OUGHT sought? Pound would not be taken in by the prevalent psychological "dogma," aside from the fact that there were clashing psychological dogmas. He was of the opinion that psychological neo-realism was not wholly free of the a priori dogmatism with which it charged the older jurisprudential schools.[469]

A reading of Frank's books and articles indicates that he at least recognized the need for a consideration of the OUGHT in jurisprudence. He argued that his negation of certainty in the law was not to be construed as a renunciation of ideals. On the contrary, he said that the question of what the law oughtto be represents "no small part of the thinking of the judges and lawyers. Such thinking should not be diminished, but augmented." The OUGHT, however, should consist not of illusions and day-dreams but only of ideals which are possible of realization.[470]

In subsequent writings, in reply to his critics, including Pound, Frank stated that he had included in his writings "men's 'ideals' as part of the 'description of men's ways,' asserting that 'men's hopes and desires' are part of the phenomena to be described . . . , that some present 'oughts' will become future 'is-es.' "[471] He repudiated the charge that he and the other legal realists had distinguished between the IS and the OUGHT in order to purge the law of the latter.[472]

In accord with William James, Frank expressed a belief that

42

we are suffering today from the consequences of the dogmatic nineteenth century faith in science as offering man's sole means of salvation.[473] He asserted that neither legal thinkers, nor economists, can legitimately profess a disinterest in ethical ideals and values.[474] Social ideals must direct their thinking and their selection of data. While rejecting the "scientific method" for law and the social sciences, Frank championed the "scientific spirit" —"the discipline of suspended judgment..; the questioning.. of the respectably accepted and seemingly self-evident;.. what I would call 'constructive skepticism.' "[475] The subject-matter of law is more complex and "baffling" than that of science, and their methods must accordingly be different.[476] Like medicine, law and government are not sciences, but arts which they must always remain.[477] A social ideal, whether in the law or elsewhere, represents an aspiration and should be approached in a scientific spirit to see if it can be realized and one should chart the road it must travel in order to be actualized.

Professor Llewellyn also replied to Dean Pound's article.[478] He asserted that legal realists posited only a temporary divorce of the IS and the OUGHT for purposes of study. "To men who begin with a suspicion that change is needed, a permanent divorce would be impossible." Although value judgments will set objectives for inquiry, nevertheless during an inquiry into the IS of a judicial system, the inquirer's values are to be set aside so as not to interfere with the accuracy of his description.

Writing two decades after Pound's article, Professor Stone concluded that further debate on this issue would be "unreal."[479] He stated that a court's view of what is correct policy or justice— the OUGHT—may affect its decision. From the court's standpoint, the decision was arrived at by means of an OUGHT. But from the perspective of an historian, that OUGHT became converted into an IS in the very process of arriving at a decision. In the description of any legal system, the ideals of the actors, since they frequently affect decisions and become the law, are an indispensable part of the observable facts.[480] It is clear from Llewellyn's remarks that he was asking *not for the observer to ignore the actor's ideals, but for the observer to put aside his own* so that the accuracy of his observation and description shall not be interfered with."[480a] Furthermore, the realists began to turn to a consideration of the question of justice, of the problem of the OUGHT, which originally they had postponed.[481] Stone pointed out that in various articles by Llewellyn and "others"[482] the problem is discussed. He felt that the realists could make further contributions to such an evaluation.

Whatever the merits of the above criticism with respect to any particular realist, it certainly was not applicable to Frank. Frank's proposed reforms in judicial administration were his OUGHT for the realization of a greater degree of justice. It was not enough for him that courts function to halt brawls and bring peace to society. He envisioned a far greater and nobler function for our courts—that they be courts of justice. His goal was an improvement in fact-finding, and for its realization he deemed it essential that the martial spirit in litigation be diminished.[483] He saw as the main function of the courts the rendering of just decisions in individual lawsuits. "Courthouse justice is . . . done at retail, not at wholesale."[484]

A more trenchant accusation has been levelled at legal realism, particularly by natural law exponents—that it sanctions no permanent objective values and that consequently anything which the state seeks to enforce capriciously is law.[485] Holmes is specifically included in this charge. A host of charges have been brought against legal realism, such as: Godlessness, negation of divine reason in man, and the elevation of a "blind unfolding dominant social pattern of force to the throne of omnipotence."[486] In Father Lucey's view, for example, the logical result of legal realism, though soft-pedaled by the realists, is that physical force is the ultimate justification of law. In his view, those realists who delimited their functional IS by ideals and ends and "ultimate abstract norms" were in effect contradicting legal realism.[487] A skepticism as to God and moral values, he charged, must end with a justification of physical force.[488] But Lucey's comparative delineation of legal realism and natural law is not that of a Zoroastrian dualism: the contentiousness of the forces of Ormazd against those of Ahriman. He acknowledged that the realists must be credited as one of the most dynamic groups clamoring for procedural reforms and for reformation of a rigid process of judicial interpretation.[489] However, the fly in the ointment as viewed by Lucey was his appraisal of legal realism as a jurisprudence of the IS. As such, he accused legal realism of contradicting the "fundamental principles of Democracy,"[490] and because of its relativism and skepticism, it is as applicable to a totalitarian or absolute government as to a democracy. And in a somewhat similar vein, though not from a natural law premise, barbs have been levelled at Frank for swinging the pendulum too far from a reliance upon rules to a reliance upon men, taking into consideration our recent experiences with European totalitarian regimes.[491]

The above criticism has been termed "a distortion of the theories of most positivists and realists."[492] This rejoinder concedes that judges would not be constrained by an imaginary law of nature, but "they would be held in check just as effectively by their allegiance to the scientific attitude, by their training in objectivity and the understanding of human nature, and by their devotion to the principle that law is an instrument of the general good."[493] To this defense can be added the consideration that there is available in the United States a reservoir of constitutional and political power to check the Supreme Court in the exercise of its judicial authority, and in recognition of which the court has imposed rules of self-restraint upon itself.[494]

A cogent argument has been presented that a realist jurisprudence could not arise in a totalitarian system, since such a regime does not permit the free play of social and economic forces in society.[495] "The realist movement has arisen and can operate only where there is sufficient freedom in the play of social forces to make this scientific weighing possible in the administration of law; it therefore demands a society which admits objectivity, that is a fundamentally tolerant society."[496]

Since law operates in the lives of men only through the interpretation placed upon it, it would seem that important as a theory of law may be, the manner of functioning of the law is of greater importance. As Justice Jackson put the matter: "Indeed, if put to the choice, one might well prefer to live under Soviet substantive law applied in good faith by our common law procedures than under our substantive law enforced by Soviet procedural practices."[497] And it was to the proper functioning and the prevention of the malfunctioning of law in a democratic society that Frank devoted his major efforts.

It is difficult to catch any distinction at all between Frank's moral ardor and passion for justice and that manifested by exponents of natural law. Of interest is his reply to such charges in his article on Judge Learned Hand.[498] He stated that "moral relativism neither implies nor induces cynicism or moral indifference."[499] The problem is not what "a man's formal philosophy is," but what his "actual working creed is."[500] Frank asked whether any of Hand's decisions would have been different if he had spoken in terms of natural law and adopted its philosophy. He could think of none. And he concluded: "For pragmatism, wrote C. S. Peirce, 'is only an application of the sole principle of logic which was recommended by Jesus: "Ye shall know them by their fruits." ' "[501] The identical question may be asked by us regarding Frank: Would any of Frank's decisions have been any different had he espoused natural law rather than legal realism? We can think of none.

Abuses can occur in practice regardless of whether or not the philosophical formulation of a system of government is grounded in natural law. But Frank's reliance was not upon human leadership as such in the American democracy which he loved,[502] but, as he continuously stressed, upon democratic leadership. And does not democratic leadership pre-suppose rules and the adherence to rules by an enlightened leadership? The basic theory of a constitutional democracy is rule by the majority but constitutional guarantee for the rights of dissenting minorities. In addition to an enlightened democratic leadership, Frank preached the gospel of "self-guardianship" on the part of the people, if they are to assume their rightful role as responsible members of a democratically functioning society.[503] An alert citizenry has no need of a bevy of Platonic guardians. The latter concept is inimical to the basic concept of democracy.[504]

A critic of legal realism in 1940 has in later years modified his acerbity.[505] In his view the conflict and interaction in the 1950's between the psychological school of legal realism and the school of revived natural law hold great promise for the future of jurisprudence: a synthesis of the psychological insights from the school of legal realism with the "problems of norm-

46

ative valuation and moral conflict" provided by a revival of natural law ideas will lead to a collaboration and a rapprochement between the two.[506] He conceded that the realists were not oblivious to the problem of "justice," but claimed that they have a functional approach to the law and are more interested in results. They have an apprehension that a philosophical formulation of justice would be too elusive and subjective to permit of a scientific analysis.[507] It will be recalled, however, that Frank specifically restricted his jurisprudence principally to a study of what courts do and should do, and had no intention of presenting a history of the concept of justice as it had been conceived by different thinkers or his own abstract notions on justice. Yet prodded by critiques of his volume, *Law and The Modern Mind,* he finally did present in subsequent writings his views on natural law and justice.[508] So it cannot accurately be said that Frank neglected and completely omitted an analysis of this crucial problem in jurisprudence. Besides his fundamental commitment to democratic justice, Frank was guided by a profound "sense of injustice."[509]

## Chapter II
## STARE DECISIS

An analysis of *stare decisis,* the doctrine of following previous court decisions, will be found both in Frank's jurisprudential writings and in a number of his judicial opinions. He has been portrayed by critics as compounded of two Franks: the Frank of his early jurisprudential writings, and the Frank of his later period, especially after ascending the bench.[1] The early Frank is depicted as one in revolt against the doctrine of *stare decisis,* and the later Frank is limned as a traditional judge imbued with a respect for precedent. It is, to be sure, far easier to be revolutionary and radical in theoretical discussions than in the decision of concrete cases, and such was the case with Frank. But we shall seek to demonstrate that though there is a fair measure of truth in this accusation against the early Frank, it is an exaggeration.

### A. *The Doctrine of Stare Decisis*

The Latin phrase, *stare decisis,* lending itself to a literal translation: to stand by decisions, is the doctrine of respect for precedent. The source of this legal phrase is the maxim: *stare decisis et non quieta movere,* which means "adhere to the decisions and do not unsettle things which are established."[2] The rationale for the doctrine of following previous court decisions has been succinctly summarized by Dicey: "If the courts were to apply to the decision of substantially the same case one principle today and another tomorrow, men would lose rights they already possessed."[3] *Stare decisis* thus has been a force for the attainment of stability in the law.

Yet, as was pointed out by Justice Cardozo, there is an antinomy of stability and progress in the law, which presents "the need of a philosophy that will mediate between the conflicting claims of stability and progress and supply a principle of growth."[4] Certainty is essential if law is to be any guide to conduct. But undue emphasis on certainty as conducive to stability leads to "the worship of an intolerable rigidity,"[5] which in turn breeds stagnancy. The strains inherent in law by reason of the opposing pulls of stability and progress have been recognized by all modern writers on the subject.

It would be misleading, however, to infer that the dilemma posed by Cardozo was meant to be applicable to the whole realm of the law. Of such a notion he was quick to disabuse us. "Stare decisis is at least the everyday working rule of our law."[6] In the bulk of litigation, the law is clear and an exercise of discretion by the judge is uncalled for. "We shall have a false view of the landscape if we look at the waste spaces only, and refuse to see the acres already sown and fruitful . . ."[7]

Dean Roscoe Pound, too, in the early decades of this century, viewed the paradox of stability and motion in the law. "Law must be stable and yet it cannot stand still."[8] He distinguished between cases relating to property and commercial transactions on the one hand and cases concerned with human conduct and human relations on the other. In the latter area, he declared, a large degree of free judicial play should be exercised and progress and motion are desirable. But, he contended, it was in the former area, involving the commerce and property interests of the nation, that the principle of *stare decisis* was primarily useful, and a mechanical application of established rules can with justice be enforced in order to produce stability.[9]

In a later discussion, Pound classified the American cases which have dealt with the *stare decisis* doctrine into three categories.[10] In the first type, the courts refuse to abrogate a rule or doctrine established by judicial decision, claiming that after its entrenchment in the law, any change should be made by the legislature.[11] In the second type, the court, after deciding that an old doctrine no longer accords with reason, or with accepted principles of law, concludes that there is no need to await legislative change and abrogates the rule. In the third type, of recent vintage, the court accords recognition to an encompassing doctrine that *stare decisis* is a principle of guiding social policy, rather than an inflexible rule of law. Compelling reasons of social policy may thus dictate to a court that it change even well-established rules of property—an area where the doctrine of *stare decisis* has long been recognized as pri-

49

marily useful. The last type accords with Pound's view that what we need on the bench and in the law schools are social engineers, and that a judge's work is to be judged "by its adherence to the purposes for which it is done, not by its conformity to some ideal form of traditional plan."[12]

C. K. Allen in his treatise, *Law in the Making*,[13] traces the development of the doctrine of *stare decisis* from its soupçon in the Roman law. In the English law, by the thirteenth century judges showed "a distinct desire to tread the beaten path"[14], but there was no doctrine of binding precedents, and judges rejected decisions deemed by them ill-founded.[15] The great faith in precedent evinced by Sir Edward Coke, Chief Justice under James I in the seventeenth century, was conditioned upon its intelligent use.[16] It was in the eighteenth century that *stare decisis* became an integral part of judicial machinery[17] and a potent force in Anglo-American law. However, at the same time that Lord Mansfield, the great legal personality of this period, insisted on the importance of precedent for certainty and consistency in the law, like Coke he disdained a mechanical use of precedent, without searching to see if the underlying situations may not require different solutions and different principles.[18]

Allen refers to the "time-lag of the law;" law limps behind changing social circumstances, due to the fact that under a system of *stare decisis* judges frequently have to say: "Whatever the anachronism of inconvenience, we must abide by the established rule.'"[19] Yet he points to many indications in his own country, England, of progress during the forties and fifties in the direction of a working compromise between precedent slavishness and precedent iconoclasm and consequently a greater flexibility and less rigidity in some areas of the administration of English law. Courts have overruled previous decisions or sterilized them by means of a "distinguishing" process. The two highest courts in England, the House of Lords and the Court of Appeal, do not overrule their own prior decisions (with certain exceptions in the case of the Court of Appeal).[20] Yet today the prevailing disposition in the House of Lords is to apply the "distinguishing" process, when the occasion so demands, to its own prior decisions, in order to purge the law of anomalies.[21] This distinguishing process may not always be in consonance with perfect logic, but at times it has the effect of overruling a previous decision without saying so in so many words.

In our own country, the Supreme Court has overruled itself about one hundred times expressly, in addition to overruling itself by indirection on many other occasions.[22] The statistics furnished by Justice Douglas show that between 1860 and 1890 the Supreme Court on eighteen occasions overruled precedents expressly or in effect, and that in the short span between 1937 and 1949, the Court accelerated its pace and overruled thirty of its earlier cases—twenty-one on constitutional grounds.[23] In the Jehovah's Witnesses flag-salute cases, the Supreme Court overruled itself after a lapse of but three years.[24] In *Reid* v. *Covert*,[25] the Supreme Court overruled itself within a period of one year. Justice Roberts in 1944 acidly compared Supreme Court decisions, because of the frequency with which they are overruled, to restricted railway tickets "good for this day and train only."[26]

Justice Douglas and Judge Frank shared views in various areas of legal thinking—*stare decisis* among them. Douglas, whom Frank characterized as an adherent of the "fact-skeptics" among the legal realists,[27] cited Frank in support of their concordant views on *stare decisis*. He referred approvingly to Frank's treatment of this subject in *Law and The Modern Mind*,[28] which posited the need for a blunt candor on the part of the judiciary when effecting changes in the law. Douglas is an outspoken protagonist of the need for flux in the law so that one age should not be fettered "by the fears or limited vision of another."[29] In his advocacy of this need so to render any body of law, but particularly constitutional law, immune to the mortmain of a prior generation, Douglas felt that it was more in accord with democratic traditions that the changes induced by the flux be undisguised by any verbal legerdemain.[30]

## B. *Stare Decisis in Frank's Jurisprudential Writings*

What were Frank's expressed views on the subject of *stare decisis*? The first clue to his views is discernible from the title

51

of his chapter, "Illusory Precedents," in *Law and The Modern Mind*.[31] He adopted the thesis of Professor Hessl Yntema, a legal realist, that in arriving at a decision "'principle and logic play a secondary part' "[32] in the judge's mind—the "emotive experience" plays the primary role. He asserted that excepting the most simple cases, every case has unique circumstances, making it an "'unprovided case' where no well-established rule 'authoritatively' compels a given result."[33] Judges are not trained to observe all their mental processes; in addition to this there are unconscious motivations. As a result, many operative factors are concealed in the formulation of a decision, which is frequently arrived at in a logical form after the prior determination by the judge of his decision in a psychological matrix.

The average judge, in Frank's view, believes that in opinion writing, his intellect is functioning as "'a cold logic engine.'"[34] This is a product of "rule-fetishism"[35] and precedent veneration. A judge should not sacrifice the unique facts of a case before him in order to mould the case into a generalized rule. He should seek to do "equity" in the particular case. Law cannot be mathematically certain, since the judicial process involves constant individualization.[36]

To Frank the aspect of "rule-fetichism" that was particularly objectionable is that which impels judges in writing opinions to feel that they are "addressing posterity."[37] They pay excessive heed not only to past judicial formulations but also to the imagined future effects of their own generalizations. They seek to formulate their opinions in such word-patterns as will cover a large variety of cases, even though they may not be doing justice to the unique facts of the case before them, which require individualization of treatment. Although ends have a future bearing, they "obtain their significance in present consequences."[38] The present should not be sacrificed to a hypothetical future which will produce problems different from those envisaged for it. Frank referred to the wisdom of Valery's reference to the "'anachronism of the future.'"[39]

Frank criticized Pound's dichotomy between cases relating to property and commercial transactions on the one hand and human conduct cases—such as "fraud, good faith, negligence, or fiduciary duties"[40]—on the other.[40a] Frank conceded that in cases involving primarily economic activities, there is greater reason for a close adherence to precedents.[41] But he felt that the two types of cases were too much intertwined. Legal controversies relating to commercial transactions often involve questions of human conduct, raising questions of fact which pertain to "fraud, negligence, mistake, alteration or estoppel,"[42] and, Frank contended, there cannot be a mechanical application of rules to them. But, granting the difficulty of drawing a sharp line between the two types of cases, Pound's dichotomy is a valid one and Frank's polemic with Pound was overdrawn and too acerbic in tone.[43]

This represented Frank's early treatment of *stare decisis*. It was psychologically oriented and at times abstruse. Frank exaggerated the extent of unique circumstances in cases. He underestimated the extent of uniformities. He saw unprecedented problems constantly arising in the law. He visualized the social and industrial conditions as constantly changing. Although he did not favor making changes lightly, he emphasized the experimental nature of law. "Much of the uncertainty of law is not an unfortunate accident; its is of immense social value."[44] But was not Frank's kaleidoscopic picture of the social and industrial landscape a hyperbole and not in conformance with reality? An element of truth, worth emphasis, was exaggerated by Frank out of all proportion.

A more comprehensive and more balanced discussion of *stare decisis* is to be found in Frank's later volume, *Courts on Trial*, published after eight years on the bench. Here he divided law-making into legislative and judicial components. Most of the rules governing the law of torts, contracts, assault, libel and slander have been the result of judicial law-making. They have been fashioned over the centuries in the crucible of court litigation and have evolved as expressions of the social policy of the period. If that is so, Frank asked, what should be the desirable course if a subsequent court believes the previously expressed social policy to be harmful and that a new or previously submerged policy should replace it?[45] Is the attainment of the goals of so-called certainty, uniformity, continuity and stability more desirable than the attainment of the goal of justice? Does continuity outweigh justice? Frank's reply was an emphatic NO.

In reply to the argument advanced in support of *stare decisis* that to upset precedents would open the floodgates of instability, Frank stated that a court might well declare to an individual relying on an unwise precedent: "Prove to us that, in actual fact, you did thus rely. If you did not, we will not hesitate to overrule this undesirable precedent. If you did rely on it, then we'll follow it in your case; but we hereby serve notice that we will not follow it in any other subsequent case unless actual reliance is also proved in those cases."[46] Only a few courts had adopted such a position. He then criticized the distinction made by most courts which overrule precedents in cases involving rules of evidence, procedure or negligence, but not in cases involving rules of property. Since a change in a rule involving evidence, procedure or negligence may lead to a litigant losing a case he might otherwise have won, is it not in effect a parting with "property"? Thus he attacked the dichotomy as unrealistic. The only test Frank would apply was that of reliance or lack of reliance by the litigant on the old rule, regardless of the nature of the rule.[47]

Frank poked holes in the argument sometimes advanced that only a legislature should undo a harsh or unjust court-enacted rule. But what if the legislature does not act, or is tardy in its efforts? Why is more instability caused by the court's annulment of its prior act than by the legislature's action? Frank would require that a court never change its rule retroactively in its application to a person who has relied on it to his harm, but it "would be free to change an unjust rule as to all other persons, both retroactively and prospectively."[48] Let the legislatures repeal their acts, and the courts theirs with the reservation expressed.

After assaulting the argument of stability posited for adhering even to unjust precedents and other arguments tendered in justification of *stare decisis*,[49] Frank attempted to explain *stare decisis* and the adherence to precedent in general as founded first and foremost on habit—the maintenance of habit patterns so familiar in all walks of life.[50] Inertia is a regnant force in men's lives. Resistance and hostility to change are encouraged by apparently deep-rooted physiological and psychological bases of comfortable reliance upon the accepted, the known, the customary.[51] Lawyers and judges have no monopoly on inertia and "stick-in-the-muddism."[52] Physicians and even natural scientists are "precedent-ridden."[53]

Frank conceded that the precedent system does not "bite" when a judge follows a just, a sagacious or a neutral kind of precedent.[54] Precedents, he said, often aid thinking and "allay inner doubts" about a solution and "help, as rationalizations, to persuade others."[55] He then proceeded to demonstrate how courts have taken the "bite" out of obnoxious precedents by indirectly sterlizing them by means of three methods, and they have thus found a way out of a strict adherence to a rigid rule.

(1) The most common method: The "Distinguishing" or "Precise Question" Device: Courts have often said their decision in a previous case must be limited to the "precise question" in that case and since somewhat different facts are involved in most cases, a "distinguishing" way out, when desired, has been effectuated by the application of a different or competing rule or analogy.[56] Frank stated that this "distinguishing" process, in truth, often involved an "extinguishing" process.[57]

On the other hand, a court will often want to treat a case only partly alike "as if" it were identical with a decision involving a somewhat different fact situation. It will then indulge, merely for convenience, in an "as if" or "let's pretend" formulation of a complete identity between the two cases. Frank warned of the pitfalls which maye at times be involved by refusing to distinguish between fact situations sufficiently discrepant to warrant a disregard of the likenesses and an emphasis of the differences.[58]

(2) Verbal Stability: The old rule is maintained, but new meaning is poured into the old words. The old rule, in effect, becomes a new rule. This is but a "stability of words."[59] Yet, as Frank stated, it is a blessing that many concepts—such as "democracy"—and the words in our Constitution have not been frozen into "inflexible definitions."[60]

(3) *Ratio Decidendi* Device: According to this postulation, the authoritative part of a case is neither the decision nor the rule enunciated in the case, but rather the *ratio decidendi*, the

55

"right principle upon which the case was decided."[61] Frank called it "something" lying back of decision and rule. It is ordinarily taken to mean the reason or spirit of a case, rather than the letter, considered in conjunction with the facts treated by the judge as material in arriving at his decision as distinguished from the immaterial facts.[62] And should a subsequent judge feel that the right principle was not laid down, he may declare the "true principle." This can lead to considerable subjectivism, as is evidenced in judges' varying interpretations of precedents.[63]

In view of the multiplicity of devices for deviations from precedent, Frank concluded that it cannot be asserted *stare decisis* breeds, or has ever bred, certainty. He posited "pliancy and fluidity" and uncertainty as essential to the health of any legal system.[64] He underpinned the inevitability of uncertainty with the eternal clash of policies and principles and the need by the courts to work out compromises,[65] and pointed to the fact that "highly respectable" lawyers of the non-realist persuasion had also written on the desirability of flexibility in many legal rules.[66] He wrote elsewhere: "The difference between the 'realists' and those other writers has been, in this respect, chiefly one of emphasis and shading."[67]

The proper role of *stare decisis*, according to Frank, is mainly in "indifferent" situations where no change or deviation is called for—"like the rule about driving on the right side of the road"[68] —or where rules have become strongly entrenched or the judges have a "strong hunch" that they have so become in the community mores despite the judge's belief that they may be unjust or unwise, or, most importantly, in situations where actual reliance to one's detriment has been placed upon a precedent.[69] But Frank failed to mention, as he should have, the most important role of *stare decisis*—the assurance of stability in the daily enterprises and lives of men by means of rules not deemed unwise, but desirable or even beneficent. Men rely on uniformity and continuity in the law for their daily undertakings. They draw up contracts, write wills, draft conveyances on the assurance and confidence that the laws applicable to them will not be impaired.[70] The issue of men's reliance upon the law's stability is also closely linked up with that of the law's integrity and equal justice—the fact that the courts will not apply one rule in the morning to one individual and a different rule in the afternoon to another.

Frank did not believe in change as an "inherent virtue."[71] Sometimes the longing for change may be neurotically motivated and has to be resisted. But when a change is to be made in a rule, a straightforward overruling of a precedent is more candid and is preferable to an oblique and evasive deviation in the various manners he had indicated that the courts sterilize precedents.[72] In a democracy, the judge should practice "judicial candor."[73] "For that reason I admire the way in which our present Supreme Court Justices often straightforwardly overrule precedents instead of chloroforming them by indirect methods, as their predecessors were more inclined to do."[74]

In a chapter of *Courts on Trial*, "Legal Classicism and Romanticism,"[75] Frank spoke of the polarities of "classicism" and "romanticism." He traced classicism to formal Roman legal and artistic canons, and romanticism to medieval popular "romances" which deviated from the classical norms of Rome.[76] Classicism, he said, dwelt on the typical, recurrent, non-unique types in art as well as in law. Conversely, romanticism referred to the spontaneous, diverse, non-rational and unique types. Concretely translating this to trial court administration, he stated that one of the chief functions of the trial courts is to do justice to the "unruly" and the unique situations and not subsume them under general rubrics. This calls for an intelligent and discriminating application of *stare decisis*. Conjoined with the recognition that "the legal rules and principles will ever be indispensable as guides,"[77] Frank insisted equally that "such 'classicism' should be tempered by a recognized 'romantic' respect in our courts for the unique individual"[78]—the unique case. Critical of "excessive classicism" and of "excessive romanticism", he posited a pragmatic synthesis of classicism and romanticism.

In a further analysis of the concept and role of "judicial legislation," Frank queried whether it is the function of the judge merely to find and declare the law, as most judges and lawyers in the nineteenth century had conceived the judicial role.[79] This would deny the existence of any judicial legislation. Is reason the sole guide for the judge in finding the law, hovering over him like a brooding omnipresence in the sky,[80] so that if a court should later reverse itself, one must say that the old rule was an error since it was not in consonance with reason? Can it be said that once a judge has found and declared the "correct" law, the law should then be stabilized and it should be the duty of judges to adhere to it under the doctrine of *stare decisis?* Or is the function of the judge rather to exercise some discretion and creative capacity in stating the law? Does not much of the law represent social policy hammered out by the judiciary as a result of compromises between "conflicting social interests"?[81] According to this conception, judge-made rules akin to statutes which are passed by a legislature represent a balancing of rival interests. And since social policy changes from time to time, there can be no rigid doctrine of *stare decisis* in this area of the law. The latter is Frank's view. And today the existence of some judicial legislation is a fact of life acknowledged by all writers on jurisprudence.

Frank questioned whether the judge in interpreting statutes has any creative function or is merely a passive tool of interpretation of the legislative "will." The latter thesis would deny the existence of any judicial legislation in connection with statutes. The bulk of legislation today emanates from legislatures. But not always is the legislative will ascertainable. Sometimes a question is raised which never occurred to the legislature. The function of the court then is to guess what the legislature would have done on this point had it been raised. The legislature cannot anticipate the multitude of particular situations which are bound to arise within the general scope of legislation.[82] The court is thus called upon to exercise a creative role of interpretation. Still another complication arises when there is ambiguity arising from a careless wording of a statute—careless draftsmanship—and the court must then interpret as best it can. Not infrequently the legislature will be purposely vague because it cannot foresee the full contours of the situation, and it will leave it to the court to fill them in as specific situations arise. The legislature may purposely not define the word "employees," for example, in a statute in order not to tie the hands of a court as multiple types of situations confront it. Words are, after all, "condensed symbols,"[83] and judges frequently differ as to the proper degree of expansion to extend to them. In addition, many statutes abound with words such as "reasonable, fair, equitable, proper."[84] These generalized concepts must be concretized by the courts. It is thus apparent that "judicial legislation" is a necessary complement of "legislative legislation."

An interesting thesis was presented by Frank, for which he claimed "priority."[85] He cited as his inspiration the criticism by Krenek, a musical composer, of musical "purists" who insist that there is a "work-fidelity," one authentic interpretation of a musical composition. Krenek observed that some great composers know that interpretation is not a mechanical process. There are variant readings of musical compositions and variant performances. At times a literal interpretation is called for; at other times an imaginative one, produced by an insight transcending the literal interpretation. And thus it is with statutes. Sometimes a literal interpretation is the correct one; at other times so to construe a statute would nullify the legislative purpose.[86]

Frank roundly criticized those judges, like Justices McReynolds[87] and Butler,[88] who, under the guise of a theory that judges never legislate, eviscerated social legislation and sabotaged legislative purposes through a literal interpretation of statutes. The imaginative, creative approach which Krenek attributed to intelligent musical performers, Frank said, had been that of the great Supreme Court justices in interpreting the Constitution. There is no "paradise" where all words have a fixed meaning. "The serpent in the imagined garden of Eden is the irrepressible semantic problem."[89] Frank would apply to judges Krenek's attitude to musical performers. The judge is the imaginative interpreter of the legislative composition. The judge's creativeness is a limited one, but "within proper limits, it is a boon, not an evil."[90]

There is hardly any topic discussed by Frank where the specter of the subjectivity of fact-finding is not introduced. It seems like the commingling of two separate issues. So we must not overlook what is of cardinal importance to Frank in his analysis: his relating of the subjectivity of fact-finding to the precedent system. Thus, if a judge or jury arrived at the wrong facts in a trial, and as a result applied the wrong rule because the correct facts had not been found, the aggrieved person is not receiving true equality of treatment with a person in whose case the correct facts had been found. The aggrieved person will have a rule applied to his facts contrary to that which he had substantial reason to rely upon. The correct rule is not applied to the actual facts in his case and this serves to frustrate the precedent system. "No rule can be proof against the subjectivity inherent in fact-finding."[91]

Legal realists did not have a uniform view of the *stare decisis* doctrine. Thus, Professor Karl N. Llewellyn, dubbed by Frank "the most brilliant of the rule-skeptics" among the legal realists, was somewhat critical of Frank's analysis of *stare decisis*. Llewellyn denominated our legal system a "regime of precedents,"[92] and stated that neither virtual nor outspoken overruling of precedents is a daily diet, but on the contrary, is found in a very low percentage of the cases. He likened the "flat overruling and the newly minted principle" to a freeze or a hurricane in Florida. He viewed the following of precedent as the leitmotif in the bulk of cases.

## *"Two Franks" On Stare Decisis?*

Llewellyn claimed that Frank in his jurisprudential writings evinced a "deliberate obtuseness" to the fact that precedent is the rule and overruling precedent is the exception, whereas as a governmental official—as counsel to the AAA, as chairman of the SEC, and finally as a Circuit Court of Appeals judge—"he is working, day by day, in the most careful and responsible response to the things which, via intangibles, make a man's own conscience seek the *regular*."[93] Llewellyn thus attributed to Frank an inconsistency between his jurisprudential writings on the one hand and his official opinions on the other.

Professor Edward McWhinney likewise offered a view of others, which he did not share, of two Franks: the Jerome Frank as he appeared in his early writings and the Jerome Frank of the later period, especially after his ascension to the bench.[94] He wrote that many of the American realist group in their early gropings favored free-law finding, akin to the European free-law schools.[95] Some contended that although Frank in his early writings, when he was a champion of revolt against the rigidities of the legal system, was a free-law finder, this was no longer true in his later period, especially after his ascension to the bench. In writing opinions, he saw the need for continuity and certainty in the law.[96] But McWhinney was of another opinion. He preferred to believe that in view of Frank's philosophy of "eclectic humanism," the latter could never adopt an absolutist position in matters of technique, and that if Frank advocated the abandonment of *stare decisis* in his early writings, it was meant "largely as a tactical device to correct rigidities of the then current orthodoxies of juristic thinking."[97]

Are Frank's critics correct in their depiction of a two-gestalt Frank? The answer is: Partly. The truth of the matter is that even in his early period Frank never advocated the abandonment of *stare decisis*. There are, it is true, a number of passages in *Law and The Modern Mind* which lend credence to the belief that Frank was in open revolt against the *stare decisis* doctrine. Thus he wrote: "On the continent there is a movement in favor of 'free legal decision'[98] which emphasizes the 'subjective sense of justice inherent in the judge' . . . The question is not whether we shall adopt 'free legal decision' but whether we shall admit that we already have it."[99] Frank could not possibly have been arguing, contrary to fact, that the *stare decisis* doctrine has already been abandoned. That this passage did not signify, furthermore, advocacy of a total abandonment of *stare decisis* is seen from Frank's detailed analysis. He referred to the three wings of the continental Freirechtslehre[100] movement: its right wing, left wing, and moderates. This movement arose on the Continent where the law had been largely codified. Frank then portrayed the viewpoint of this school as garnered from an English translation of one of the moderates of the movement, Gmelin, justice of the Court of Appeals of Stuttgart. It basic notion was that the sense of justice of the judge should always prevail excepting in those exceptional instances where the explicit language of the code compels the judge to reach an unjust decision. Where the code could not be rationalized to accord with the judge's sense of justice, it was the code in such unusual instances which prevailed and not the sense of justice. So that although this doctrine considerably limits the potency of *stare decisis* and allows free range to the possibly manifold subjectivities of judges, it nevertheless goes beyond merely recognizing the code as a point

61

of departure in decision making; it conceded its compelling force in a limited number of instances. Frank added that regardless whether we are considering the rules in codes, statutes or decisions, it is a vain effort to turn them into dogmas. Rules, while entering into a decision of a case, are neither the whole of law nor "the most important part of it,"[101] but are of "relatively subordinate importance."[102] It would indeed be fatuous for anyone to deny the existence of rules. All that Frank was saying was that rules are of limited importance and that *stare decisis* consequently is a doctrine of limited significance.

Elsewhere in *Law and The Modern Mind* Frank wrote: "The number of cases which should be disposed of by routine application of rules is limited. To apply rules mechanically signifies laziness, or callousness to the peculiar factors, presented by the controversy."[103] The latter statement is explicable by the need, as conceived by Frank, of weighing the unique facts in many cases, so that they cannot be said to fall mechanically and automatically into a definite groove. In making this statement, it is true, Frank overlooked the large extent of uniformities in cases. Nevertheless, in this quotation Frank recognized the binding force of rules in some situations. He was opposed to their routine application, but not to the application of the proper rule.

Although Frank contended that "the rules and principles did not constitute law,"[104] he nevertheless admitted that rules are part of law. After arriving at a conclusion, the judge should check to see if it is in accord with the rules accepted previously. If it is not, he should consider whether his conclusion is a wise one. The rules thus aid the judge in a tentative testing of his conclusions, and he may decide to adopt them in the solution of the case before him. But in the final analysis, the personality of the judge was to Frank the "pivotal" factor in the judicial process. In this process, we have seen,[105] Frank took cognizance of the factors of "hunching," including the various "hunch-producers," and ratiocination. This represented a recognition of the psychological ingredient in the judicial process which had theretofore been either overlooked or unstressed.

One year after the publication of *Law and The Modern Mind*, Frank wrote: ". . . (1) Many of the legal rules are unsettled and vague. (2) Some legal rules are clear and precise . . ."[106] But regardless of the quantum of vague rules, there are some clear and precise rules which, when applicable, have to be followed. And in a later volume, *If Men Were Angels*, Frank referred to his difference with the critics of realism in the area of *stare decisis* as one of emphasis and degree rather than of kind.[107]

Frank characterized rules, in his Preface to the Sixth edition of *Law and The Modern Mind*,[108] as embodiments of social values, and as such they stand in need of periodic re-examination. He then made a significant remark, which seems to indicate an evolution in his views about rules after ascending the bench. He wrote that since for the preceding seven years he had been sitting as a judge on an appellate bench, the main concern of which is rules and not fact-finding, it should be obvious that he regarded "the rules as significant."[109] Naturally, we would expect him to add, as he did, that the rules are not "self-operative," and are frustrated whenever there is faulty fact-finding.[110] But this was the first time that Frank had ever referred to rules as "significant."

A half year later, in his mature legal treatise, *Courts on Trial*, Frank wrote: ". . . For all these reasons, although many persons (myself included) believe that the theory of precedent ought to be restated so as to conform more nearly with the precedent practice, no sensible person suggests that *stare decisis* be abandoned."[111] He stated that his opposition to *stare decisis* was only in its formulation whereby the attainment of certainty was deemed to outweigh in importance the attainment of justice. His fight was against the slogan: "Let certainty be achieved though injustice be done and the heavens fall."[112] This was a valiant fight and Frank deserves recognition for his contribution towards a proper delimitation of the scope of *stare decisis*. But even in this late volume of his, in delineating the proper roles of *stare decisis*,[113] Frank omitted mention of its significant role in bringing certainty into the daily transactions and enterprises of people. People conduct an infinite variety of daily transactions, business and otherwise, on the basis of the certainty of legal rules. Any impairment of this certainty will wreak havoc with the daily drawing up of contracts, writing of wills, drafting of conveyances on the assurance and confidence that the laws applicable to them will not be impaired.[114]

Nevertheless, it is certain that after ascending the bench an evolution occurred in Frank's expressed views on *stare decisis*, regardless of whether his original formulation was a "tactical device" as claimed by Professor McWhinney.[115] Frank significantly changed his view with respect to the volume of cases which can be disposed of by routine application of rules—from his original estimate of a "limited" number[116] to his later estimate of a far greater number. Thus, in an article in 1951 he wrote: ". . . For, in the great majority of cases, the lawyers have not the slightest difficulty in foreseeing what legal rules the courts will apply, since most of those rules are well settled and precise . . . the sole issues are the fact issues."[117] Frank had shifted his emphasis from rule uncertainty to fact uncertainty. This represents an evolution in his views on legal rules as a result of his tenure of judicial office. If it is known in advance what legal rule will be applied in the great majority of cases, it can only be as a result of the doctrine of *stare decisis*.

Justice Cardozo, although acknowledging that the realists were not a unified school of thought, stated that their teachings had been of great value to jurisprudence in helping rid *stare decisis* of its "petrifying rigidity."[118] It was his feeling that any excess of accent by the realists in expressing contempt for symmetry and order in the legal system was mere "hyperbole of phrase" and "missionary ecstasy" indulged in by enthusiasts, rather than constituting the "essence of the movement" and the "leit-motif of the symphony."[119] On the other hand, he would brand realism as a "false and misleading cult"[120] if its avowed intention was to "degrade" order in the legal system and deem it "an illusion, a mirage."[121] But he was persuaded that extravagant utterances to be found in the writings of the realists were "not of the essence of the faith."[122]

In a specific reference to Frank as "the most thoroughgoing of the realists,"[123] Cardozo stated that even Frank did not doubt the efficacy of rules, but predicated a smaller volume of cases than commonly supposed in which the only ingredient in the "judicial cauldron" for arriving at a decision was a precedent. Cardozo felt that there was a sufficient basis for an entente between the realists and others to engage in a common task of enlightenment.

Frank's reply to Cardozo constitutes the crux of his legal realism.[124] He no longer subordinated the importance of the rules, but he elevated the importance of the facts. He wrote that the facts-skeptics' criticism of the *stare decisis* doctrine was not based upon any instability of the rules. Even if all the rules were indubitably clear, and the courts always adhered faithfully to precedent, the facts as determined by the trial courts are often unforeseeable. For that reason the certainty that *stare decisis* is claimed to yield is often only an illusion. Fact-uncertainty in Frank's view militates against the exaggerated extent of legal certainty described by Cardozo and other writers on jurisprudence as resultants from the *stare decisis* doctrine.

There is no better summary of the respective positions of Cardozo and Frank on this issue than in a reference by Cardozo to the function of the litigated facts in jurisprudence and Frank's reply to it. Cardozo admitted that he may have thrown too much into the shadow the cases involving disputed facts, and not disputed rules of law, since most cases turn upon a determination of disputed facts. The issue is undoubtedly important to the litigants and it calls for discernment on the part of the judge. But it leaves "jurisprudence where it stood before . . . Jurisprudence remains untouched, regardless of the outcome."[125] Frank's reply was brief: "These choices of the 'facts,' resulting from the exercise of the trial courts' guessy discretion, may 'leave jurisdiction untouched,' but if so, they leave it looking pretty lifeless, indeed inhuman."[126]

It seems that Frank was adding to the concept of *stare decisis* a consideration essentially extraneous to it. *Stare decisis* refers to the legal rules. There can be no gainsaying that the facts are a very important aspect in litigation, but they are not a part of the *stare decisis* doctrine, to which Frank sought to attach them. He sought by showing the conjectural nature of fact-determinations, to prove the illusiveness of certainty which the *stare decisis* doctrine is supposed to bring into the law. But *stare decisis* makes no claim of producing certainty in the facts. Its only claim is that of producing certainty in the rules of law, to a lesser or greater degree. Frank's confusion was the result

65

of his obsession with fact-uncertainty and his attempt to attach it synthetically to a doctrine where it does not belong.

## Stare Decisis in Frank's Judicial Opinions

The cases in the Circuit Court of Appeals in which Frank discussed the issue of *stare decisis*—usually in connection with his desire to overrule a prior decision of his circuit—were relatively few in number. These cases represent a small fraction of the many cases he decided or participated in. In most of the cases he followed precedent. The view he had expressed in *Law and The Modern Mind* that, excepting the most simple cases, every case has unique circumstances[127] was obsolete by the time he ascended the bench. It is far easier to be revolutionary or radical in theoretical discussions than in the decision of actual cases. It is true that he dissented more often than the other members of his court, but his agreement with them was more frequent than his disagreement.[127a] In most of the cases in which he dissented—usually cases involving personal rights as distinguished from property or commercial rights—he interpreted precedent differently from the majority of the court. This was no attempt at an evasion of *stare decisis* under the guise of precedent interpretation. The fact that he dissented more frequently than his colleagues in cases of significance had nothing to do with his views on *stare decisis*. It had to do with his perspective on life and his views on social policy. He used a social lens a little more often than his colleagues. So-called liberal and conservative judges alike cite precedents in an attempt to bolster their respective positions. Frequently, the representatives of each viewpoint are convinced that precedent supports their position. The most that can be said with respect to Frank's position on *stare decisis* as culled from his judicial opinions is that he was a little more ready than his brothers to overrule precedents of his court. It represented a difference of degree, but of a relatively minor degree.

One fact emerges from Frank's opinions in which he called for an overruling of precedent, to which he had made no reference in his jurisprudential writings. In his opinions he stressed the greater importance of criminal cases, which involve the individual's liberty, than civil cases. The only way he could demonstrate this emphasis was in the procedure he adopted: In civil cases he concurred in an established precedent of his court but urged his colleagues to overrule it, whereas in criminal cases he dissented.

Frank also decided cases involving the question whether judge-made rules of very long standing, when found undesirable, should be overruled by the courts or be left to the legislature for its action. *In Courts on Trial* he had called for the abolition or modification of some exclusionary rules of evidence, such as the hearsay rule.[128] The implication from his general statement was that it should be left to the courts to overrule all judge-made rules. "Legislatures repeal rules legislatures have made. Why should not courts do the same with rules they have made?"[129] In his opinions, however, he circumscribed the call in connection with the hearsay rule. He stated that despite the fact the hearsay rule is judge-made in origin, it has become so embedded in our traditions that its abolition should be left to the legislature. This was a clear recognition of the overriding importance that *stare decisis* at times assumes.

A number of cases were also decided by Frank involving the interpretation of statutes, which inevitably raises the issue of judicial legislation. The question is to what extent a judge may exercise creativeness in interpreting statutes or conversely, to what extent he is bound by the terms of the statutes. Frank adhered to the thesis he had presented in *Courts on Trial*.[130] The role of the judge in legislating is a limited or interstitial one —one merely of filling in the legislative gaps. Sometimes a liberal interpretation is the correct one; at other times so to construe a statute would nullify the legislative purpose. And so in his cases Frank decided that a court may not ignore the language and purpose of a statute in order to achieve a "more just result."[131] A court should not annul legislation out of disagreement with legislative policy. The court is not a policy-making branch of the government, since, unlike the legislature, it is not the representative of the people's will. At times a literal interpretation—the "plain language" construction—was adopted by Frank. At other times so to construe a statute would nullify the legislative purpose, as Frank saw it, and he adopted an "equitable" construction. Thus, he adopted the "plain language" construction in a commercial case, where he interpreted a statute as calling for a stringent accountability by the chairman of the board of directors of a bank to its stockholders.[132] But when the issue involved a suit for personal injuries, he so interpreted a statute in an "equitable" manner that an injured member of the public should not be denied recovery for the injuries sustained.[133] In none of these cases, however, did Frank apply the principle of "free judicial decision." He was no starry-eyed iconoclast bent on demolishing rules in accordance with his subjective whims, but rather a staid interpreter of the laws of his government.

## Stare Decisis and Civil Cases

A brief sampling of Judge Frank's judicial opinions will demonstrate how he reacted concretely on the bench to the issue of *stare decisis.*

Should the doctrine of *stare decisis* prevail if the court, in arriving at its decision in an earlier case, had overlooked certain important considerations? Judge Frank's answer in a dissenting opinion in *In Re Marine Harbor Properties*[134] was that if the prior circuit court erred, a subsequent court should not perpetuate its errors. In his opinion Frank expressed his full accord with the *stare decisis* doctrine in order to effectuate equality before the law and legal certainty.[135] Thus, if a prior decision had assigned to specific words in a document specific legal consequences, a retroactive deviation by a subsequent court would harm any person who had acted in reliance thereon. Any overruling of a decision, even if the latter was conceived in error, must be applied only prospectively. But where, as in this case, there was no issue of a party acting in reliance upon a prior decision, if the previous court was in error Frank would disregard its decision as a binding precedent.[136]

In another opinion, Frank expressed his accord with John Chipman Gray that most of the laity do not act in reliance upon court decisions.[137] It should therefore not be automatically assumed that men have changed their position because of a prior decision, without the opportunity to prove the contrary, and on the ground of such an unwarranted assumption "to refuse to wipe it out, no matter how erroneous, does not seem to me to be an intelligent method of administering justice."[138]

Judge Frank employed a unique technique of adhering to a precedent, when it involved a Supreme Court decision or trend, but simultaneously advocating its change. Thus, in *Hammon-Knowlton* v. *United States*[139] Frank felt he was bound by a trend in Supreme Court decisions which had narrowly construed statutes involving suits against the government. He supplicated the Supreme Court to relax the asperity of its interpretation. He favored a liberal construction in favor of a plaintiff who was suing the government for a refund of an overpayment of federal estate taxes.[140]

Thurman Arnold expressed approval of Frank's technique in this case. He characterized it as "a unique and useful technique whereby a lower court judge could pay allegiance to precedent and at the same time encourage the processes of change."[141] He said further: "When forced by stare decisis to reach what he considered an undesirable result, he would write a concurring opinion analyzing the problem and plainly suggesting that either the Supreme Court or Congress do something about it."[142]

An extended analysis of "rule fetichism", which Frank had touched upon in *Law and The Modern Mind*,[143] was made by him in *Aero Spark Plug Co.* v. *B. G. Corp.*[144] He discussed the "rule" aspect of opinions and the effect of rules on future litigation—the heart of the issue of *stare decisis*. "*Stare decisis*," he said, "within limits, has undeniable worth."[144a] But he urged that judges should not base their rulings upon an undue interest in their anticipated future consequences. It is true that in our daily lives we all attempt to anticipate the consequences of our actions, but what Frank was stressing was an undue interest in such consequences to the neglect of the equitable interests of the parties in a pending lawsuit. No representative of the future can appear as protagonist or antagonist in the formulation of a rule to govern the future. The judges' expanded ego as guardians of the future should play no role in determining the present interests of the parties before the Court.

The formulation of legal rules by courts implies that there is some judicial legislation. "But courts should be modest in their legislative efforts to control the future, since they cannot function democratically, as legislative committees and administrative agencies can, by inviting the views of all who may be affected by their prospective rules."[145] It is true that since the present "is only a moving line between yesterdays and tomorrows,"[146] inevitably the court, in formulating rules, must give some reflection to their future consequences. But despite the need for some continuity linking the present to the past and the future, there should not be too much tinkering with the veiled future to the neglect of a proper solution of the immediate problems before the court, of their present aspect. Frank deprecated posterity-worship as much as ancestor-worship.

Translating this somewhat abstract discussion into concrete terms, Frank cited instances from Dean Leon Green's analysis of factors which, insofar as they direct upper court thinking to future horizons, at times sacrifice the impact of cases before them.[147] Thus, under the rubric of the "administrative factor," the court considers the workability of a rule. The upper court may determine that by allowing compensation in a particular species of lawsuit—such as mental anguish in tort suits—the floodgates of litigation would be opened in situations where it may be easy to feign an injury without detection. And so a workable rule has been arrived at by some courts on an alleged pragmatic basis barring recovery in all suits of that nature.[148] In its effort to obtain an impossible uniformity resulting from anticipated future consequences, the court has adopted a generalized rule, fitting perhaps a variety of cases, but nevertheless sacrificing an equitable solution of a particular case before the court. And under the rubric of the "prophylactic or preventive factor," the court considers fashioning legal rules for a "healthy future." Thus, penalties and damages to be imposed by judges will be scaled so as to serve not only as a lesson to the offender but equally to others in the hope of preventing future harm. Frank did not deny the importance of some future assessments in rule making, but he deprecated it when the future factors were weighed to the exclusion of the primary importance of the parties and the concrete case before the court, which should be decided equitably and not abstractly. This discussion by Frank undoubtedly has merit and it serves to highlight his conclusion that courts should not hesitate to change their previous formulations when a change is highly desirable.

After he had been on the bench for a few years, Frank altered his tactic when in disagreement with established precedent in civil cases. In *U.S.* v. *Bennett et al.*,[149] a criminal case, he enunciated a distinction in his procedure dependent upon whether the disagreement with his colleagues was in a civil or a criminal case. He stated that his policy in civil cases would be to concur with the established precedents of his court, though he deemed them erroneous, but in criminal cases he was to continue dissenting until the Supreme Court told him he was wrong.[150] Instead of dissenting in civil cases,[151] he would concur with reluctance, while urging his colleagues to overrule the precedent. It was a formalistic change, yet one calculated to demonstrate his respect for the doctrine of *stare decisis*, despite his disagreement with the particular precedent. Thus, in *Zamore* v. *Goldblatt*,[152] Frank stated in a concurring opinion that he felt constrained to follow the recent precedents of his court. However, he expressed his regret at this "new manifestation of procedural rigidity in appellate practice."[153]

At times Judge Frank sought to extend the range of a legal doctrine in order to effectuate a more advanced social policy. This represented a refusal to worship precedent when he felt a change desirable. Thus, in *Ricketts* v. *Pennsylvania Railway*,[154] he sought to extend the doctrine of his earlier decision in *Hume* v. *Moore-McCormack Lines Inc., et al.*[155] The latter case involved a general release of all claims executed by a seaman for burns when neither he nor his employer knew of the tubercular condition he had contracted. Upon learning of his malady, Hume instituted an action for damages against the line, claiming negligence in failing to supply proper sleeping quarters. Reversing the district court which had entered summary judgment in favor of Moore-McCormack on the theory that the general release was binding, and remitting the case for trial, Frank launched upon an excursion into maritime legal history and economics to explain why seamen, as distinguished from other types of employees, have been considered historically as "wards of admiralty" and entitled to a special solicitude.[156] In similar situations, however, involving employees who were not seamen, some courts have disallowed relief and other courts in a desire to extend relief have found on very slight evidence fraud, innocent misrepresentation or material mistake. In the *Ricketts* case, in a concurring opinion,[157] Frank sought as a matter of social policy to extend the admiralty rule governing seamen to a waiter on a railway dining car and to all manner of employees when, for an incommensurate consideration at a time neither party is aware of the true nature of the injuries, they sign general releases. "The usual non-maritime employees, because they are under similar economic pressures, are no less helpless in their trafficking with their employers . . . I believe that the court should now say forthrightly that the judiciary regards the ordinary employee as one who needs and will receive the special protection of the courts when, for a small consideration, he has given a release for an injury. Justice Holmes often urged when an important issue of social policy arises, it should be candidly, not evasively, articulated. In other contexts, the courts have openly acknowledged that the economic inequality between the ordinary employer and the ordinary individual employee means the absence of 'free bargaining.' I think the courts should do so in these employee release cases."[158] In addition to his apostleship of procedural reforms in the law, Frank thus was an advocate of substantive changes in line with his vision of a more advanced social policy.[159]

Legal principles and precedents may be differently interpreted in the light of the social policy adopted by a judge. Judge Frank used a social lens somewhat more often than did his colleagues. Thus, in *Hentschel* v. *Baby Bathinette Corp.* et al.,[160] an action in tort and breach of warranty was instituted when a fire broke out in an apartment causing a baby bathinette to catch on fire and emit sparks which burned Hentschel in an adjoining room. Magnesium alloy supports on the bathinette were burning fiercely.

Writing for the majority of the court, Judge Chase held the defendants not liable on the ground that in normal use the bathinette was not dangerous and it was not the proximate cause of the injuries by reason of the intervening fire. He felt the injuries were too remote and could not be anticipated.[161] In his dissent, Judge Frank argued that a fire is not an improbable occurrence, the inflammatory material in the bathinette was the foreseeable cause of the injuries sustained and defendants should respond in damages.[162] To Frank, "no foggier phrase than 'proximate cause' could be contrived for use in negligence cases."[163] He engaged in a philosophical-legal discussion of proximate and remote causation.[164] Both judges cited precedent in support of their respective positions, and thus the issue was one of interpretation of legal principles in the light of the social policy advanced by the respective protagonists. Frank refused to accept a hidebound concept of proximate cause. He could see no "social value" in freeing a defendant of liability in a case of this sort.[165]

Judge Frank's interpretation of legal principles and precedents differed from that of his colleagues in several trade name infringement cases.[166] In these cases, Frank analyzed the concepts of competition and monopoly and their impact on the social welfare. Trade name protection is an instance of a lawful monopoly. Frank embarked upon an analysis of the democratic co-existence in a world of compromise of conflicting public policy considerations.[167] He posited as a basic "common law"[168] public policy "deep-rooted in our economy and respected by the courts . . . the assumption that the social welfare is best advanced by free competition."[169] A conflicting public policy consideration is the protection of trade names, despite its curtailment of competition and possible financial loss to the public.[170] The law recognizes the protection of monopolies in trade names as "a secondary and limiting policy"[171] upon competition. But, at the same time, in a keen social-economic analysis, Frank interpreted precedent in such a way as to limit as much as possible the granting of trade name monopolies. Thus, in *La Touraine Coffee Co.* v. *Lorraine Coffee Co.*,[172] Judge Clark, speaking for the Court, held that the defendant by its name had infringed plaintiff's trade name monopoly of a registered-trade mark. In his dissenting opinion, Frank subjected the facts to a pragmatic analysis. He felt that even if plaintiff had established a trade name monopoly in Manhattan and New England, where it sold the bulk of its products, it had not by user established it in the other areas—Staten Island and northern New Jersey—where defendant chiefly traded.[173] Disputing the majority's reference to plaintiff's "property right," Frank called it "circular (boot-strap lifting) reasoning."[174] The court must determine if public policy warrants granting such a property right to a plaintiff.[175] Whereas the court majority adhered to precedent rigidly by granting a trade name monopoly, Frank analyzed the facts pragmatically and dissented. He advocated a liberal interpretation of the social policy favoring the freest possible competition, when warranted by the facts.

## Stare Decisis and Criminal Cases

The issue of *stare decisis* confronted Judge Frank in a number of criminal cases. In this area he never changed his procedure, as he had done in civil cases,[176] of dissenting when in disagreement with an established precedent—until the Supreme Court told him he was "wrong." Apparently Frank thought that a dissent in a criminal case is a more dramatic approach. But whether he concurred in an established precedent but urged his colleagues to overrule it, as became his wont in civil cases, or he dissented, as he invariably did in criminal cases, the purport is the same. However, a dissent does represent a greater candor, and candor was Frank's leitmotif. Yet, by making his distinction in procedure between civil and criminal cases, his aim was to stress the greater importance of cases involving the individual's liberty.

In the course of his remarks in *U.S.* v. *Bennett et al.*,[177] Frank enunciated the distinction in procedure he was henceforth to follow, dependent upon whether the disagreement with his colleagues was in a civil or a criminal case. Since this was a criminal case, he dissented. Frank disagreed with the cases in his circuit cited by the majority of the court and he would have overruled them.[178]

To Frank a quest for certitude must never be substituted for a quest for justice, whether in a civil or a criminal case, but in a criminal case the court should "particularly" be guided by a quest for justice. *In United States* v. *On Lee*,[179] after On Lee had been convicted of the sale of opium, he moved for a new trial upon the ground of newly discovered evidence. The burden of the newly discovered evidence was that subsequent to the trial an undercover agent, Laurance Lee, a witness at the trial, had been compelled to resign from the Bureau of Narcotics by reason of "improper acts" in other matters, and the government then dismissed several indictments requiring Lee's testimony.

Writing for the majority of the court, Judge Swan was of the opinion that the other evidence adduced at the trial was sufficient to sustain a conviction and further, the newly discovered evidence would "probably" not result in an acquittal. He ruled that the new material must tend to establish defendant's innocence in order to entitle him to a new trial.[180]

In his dissenting opinion, Judge Frank wrote that the fact there was other evidence in the record of sufficient quality to convict On Lee was immaterial since agent Lee's testimony may have been the factor which induced the jury's verdict.[181] The majority had relied on another decision in the same circuit—*U.S. v. Forzano*[182]—to the effect that newly discovered evidence "merely impeaching" a major government witness, as distinguished from evidence of a defendant's innocence, is insufficient ground for granting a motion for a new trial. Frank, on the other hand, claimed that this part of that decision was *obiter dictum*. In addition, he sought to distinguish the two cases: the newly discovered evidence in the *Forzano* case was nowhere as damaging as in this case where agent Lee, the sole government witness to a confession, is so untrustworthy that the government is no longer willing to vouch for his credibility and has dismissed indictments in other cases requiring his testimony. This represented no attempt at an evasion of *stare decisis* under the guise of precedent interpretation. On the contrary, it represented a genuine distinguishing process.

If the *Forzano* pronouncement relative to newly discovered evidence was necessary to the decision in that case and the case as a result became a precedent, said Frank, he would feel constrained to follow it as the accepted doctrine of his court, but he would urge his colleagues to overrule it. But in view of the fact that the *Forzano* rule refers to criminal cases, why did not Frank say, in accordance with his policy, that he would feel constrained to dissent from it? This seems to have been an oversight.

Frank cited with approval a recent case by the English Court of Criminal Appeals overruling a prior decision of that court.[183] It enunciated the doctrine that in a civil case that court is bound by its earlier decisions, but in dealing with cases involving the liberty of the subject, it would feel free to overrule a bad precedent favoring the prosecution. The latter procedure had been adopted by Frank several years before its formulation by the English court.[184] In a criminal case, Frank stated, a court should "particularly" be guided by a quest for justice. But he would go further than the English court. He asserted that even in civil cases, the quest for certitude should not be substituted for a quest for justice. In this case, the government cannot contend that it will be harmed by a rejection of the *Forzano* precedent, if such it be. "Its only harm will be, at most, the expense of another trial, a price certainly worth paying to prevent the conviction of a man who may be innocent."[185]

In a criminal case Frank used the technique previously employed by him in a civil case[186] of suggesting to the Supreme Court the formulation of a new rule. *United States* v. *Scully*[187] was an appeal from a conviction for defrauding the government. Scully had originally been subpoenaed to testify before an investigative grand jury as a witness. Subsequently, formal proceedings were instituted against him as a defendant. He raised the claim that he had not been apprised at the grand jury of the constitutional privilege against self-incrimination. Judge Medina, citing precedents from his circuit, ruled that the mere possibility that a witness may subsequently be indicted does not entitle him to be advised of any rights under the Fifth Amendment. In his opinion, Judge Frank stated that he would not be constrained by his court's precedents on this subject. He was very emphatic in the formulation of his differentiation between civil and criminal cases in the area of *stare decisis*. In criminal prosecutions, where a man's liberty is at stake, *stare decisis*, when invoked by the government, should have "far less significance than in civil suits . . ."[188] However, he felt bound by "virtual" old rulings of the Supreme Court that a witness, "if not at the time the target of a prospective criminal action," need not be advised of any constitutional rights. Frank felt that that position could be justified when a prosecutor has no reason to believe that an answer to his question will incriminate a witness before a grand jury. But when, as in this case, the prosecutor cannot help knowing that a question is of such a nature that an answer will incriminate the witness, there should be a warning requirement. The formulation of a new rule which he suggested to the Supreme Court would be based both upon constitutional doctrine and "as part of the wise and just administration of the federal courts."[189]

The government, Frank argued, cannot be said to act in reliance upon a precedent as does a businessman in buying property or incurring a business risk. The government cannot object to a change in the interpretation of the law governing its procedure any more than an individual can to a change in the procedural rules of evidence or even in the substantive rules of negligence. People do not act in reliance upon the continuance of such rules. *Stare decisis* has little vigor in these areas. And, Frank added, this is particularly so in the area of constitutional interpretation, where precedents "have even less vitality."[190] Precedent cannot stand in the way of the pronouncement of a correct constitutional principle.[191]

Frank was on solid ground in his assertion that precedents have less vitality in the area of constitutional interpretation than in other areas. Although, in general, *stare decisis* helps insure a measure of certainty and stability in the law for the proper guidance of the community's affairs, it is otherwise when it comes to a question of constitutional construction. An error by the Supreme Court in construing a statute or the failure of the Court to align the law with reality may easily be corrected by legislative action. But an error by the Court in constitutional interpretation cannot be corrected simply by legislative action. Such errors are final excepting for correction by the cumbersome machinery of constitutional amendment provided by the Constitution. Hence, in the area of constitutional construction, as indicated by Justice Brandeis, the Supreme Court has frequently overruled prior decisions, based on "the lessons of experience and the force of better reasoning."[192]

Where the Supreme Court had specifically ruled on an issue, though by a closely divided court, and the Circuit Court of Appeals was asked to reconsider the ruling, Judge Frank claimed that an inferior court, such as his, may not modify a Supreme

Court doctrine "in the absence of any indication of new doctrinal trends in that Court's opinion . . . Accordingly, the argument must be addressed not to our ears but to 18 others in Washington, D.C."[193] Frank's short opinion in *U.S. v. Ullmann*[194] was a clear indication of a respect for precedent.

Frank developed the thesis that there has been a different degree of adherence to *stare decisis* dependent upon whether a general clause of the Constitution—such as "due process"—or a specific clause—such as the right against self-incrimination—was involved. Thus, in *U.S. v. Pierre*,[195] involving a question of the interpretation of the Fifth Amendment against self-incrimination, Pierre had admitted before a grand jury the commission of a crime, but the evidence he furnished was insufficient to establish a prima facie case of a crime in court. The issue raised was whether by his answer he had waived the privilege against self-incrimination so as to be held in contempt of court for his failure to supply the lacuna in his testimony. During the course of his remarks Frank differentiated between the general and the specific clauses of the Constitution. Commencing with Chief Justice Marshall, he said, greater pliancy has been the rule with respect to the interpretation of the general clauses in the Constitution—such as "due process'—to prevent them from becoming a "strait--jacket." Consequently, in this area *stare decisis* has not been rigidly adhered to by the Supreme Court. These elastic clauses of the Constitution were purposely left so in order to be "adaptive" to changing circumstances and needs. But specific clauses—such as the Fifth Amendment—were not intended by the framers of the Constitution to be flexible. They had a defined meaning when adopted. They should, therefore, be given their "historical" meaning, since this can be ascertained. In this area, *stare decisis* should be the governing principle.

What was the historical meaning which Frank claimed was intended for the Fifth Amendment? He stated that it had its origin in the history of the seventeenth century Puritans, who had to submit to the oath ex officio,[196] which they insisted was unlawful. They would not have been *ashamed* to confess to the crime of "heresy" of being Puritans—in fact, they would have been elated to do so—, but they feared the punishment which would follow. The Fifth Amendment, resulting from the experience and efforts of these Puritans, was intended to shield persons from punishment for any crimes through their compelled testimony. It was not intended to shield them from disgrace. It follows from Frank's analysis that if a person confesses to a disgraceful act—even to the bare fact of the commission of a crime—but not to facts sufficient to constitute a crime in a trial, he does not come within the purview of the Fifth Amendment, and it cannot be argued that he has waived its provisions by confessing only to a disgraceful act.[197]

In a case where an alien's life might be at stake—though technically not a criminal case—Judge Frank refused to be bound by a prior decision deemed by him unjust, even though he had been a member of the bench in that case. In *U.S. ex rel. Fong Foo* v. *Shaughnessy*,[198] Fong Foo moved for a stay of deportation before Frank sitting alone during the vacation period. Although an alien deportation proceeding, its consequences can be as drastic as those following a criminal conviction. The government contended that *U.S. ex rel. Moon* v. *Shaughnessy*[199] was on all fours with this case. Frank, however, retorted that since life and liberty were at stake, he would reconsider the previous decision and see if any significant factor had been overlooked. Frank concluded that the administrative determination by the Attorney General placed before the Court in the prior case was arbitrary and capricious. Accordingly, the *Moon* case should not be used as a binding precedent. "Illegal entry into this country should not be punished by death . . . For *stare decisis* should not govern in a case like this where a man's life is involved."[200]

## Opinions in Judical Legislation[201]

Judicial legislation arises in two situations: (1) a consideration of a change in judge-made law. The issue then is one of judicial policy-making; (2) an interpretation of a statute. The first situation was presented in *Slifka* v. *Johnson*,[201a] in which the main issue was the admission of hearsay evidence[202] during the trial. The exclusionary rule of hearsay evidence is a judge-made rule of very long standing. It is part of the common law. Frank had no doubt that the rule prevents a court from coming as close as is humanly possible to ascertainment of the actual facts in a case. Theoretically, this should dictate an abandonment or a modification of the rule by the courts themselves. Frank felt, however, that in this area there was an overriding doctrine of *stare decisis*. Despite the fact that the rule is judge-made in origin, nevertheless it is so deeply "embedded in our traditions that I think courts should not thus virtually abolish it without legislative authorization."[203] Frank thought the following legislative change desirable: An abandonment of the rule in juryless trials, and a grant of discretion to trial judges in jury trials to retain the rule and continue excluding hearsay only when they are of the opinion that the jury could not intelligently handle the hearsay on the facts of any particular case. The change proposed, however, had one reservation. It would not apply to criminal trials, since the abandonment of the hearsay rule in such cases may sometimes constitute a violation of the Sixth Amendment which grants a defendant in a criminal prosecution the right of confrontation with all witnesses against him.[204]

The second situation giving rise to judicial legislation or at least the issue of judicial legislation, namely, an interpretation of a statute, was presented in *Commissioner of Internal Revenue v. Beck's Estate*.[205] The litigant in effect urged the court to ignore the language and purpose of the statute in order to achieve "a more just result." In rejecting this request, Frank retorted that legislatures hold committee hearings at which interested parties may appear before they agree upon policy and enact legislation. Courts are not equipped to do that and such is not their function. Courts cannot remake legislation.[206] He referred to "judicial legislation" as "one of the facts of life, an inescapable and necessary one."[207] But in dealing with "legislative legislation," the sole function of the court is to fill in "small gaps left by the legislature . . . in accord with what appears to have been the legislative purpose."[208] The function of the court when dealing with legislative legislation, clear on its face, is, in the phraseology of Holmes, merely an "interstitial" one, that of closing gaps.

Judge Frank examined the process indulged in by courts of interpreting statutes in the light of their own notions—perhaps "largely unconscious"—of public policy. Thus, in *M. Witmark & Sons v. Fred Fisher Music Co. et al.*[209] he stated that unless the aims of Congress are carried out divorced from judicial notions of what public policy should be, there would result a "demolition" of the congressional purpose.[210] Frank was of the opinion that the majority of the court was reading its own notion of laissez-faire, of complete freedom of contract, into a congressional act and was frustrating a congressional policy.[211]

The problem frequently arises of an equitable interpretation of the words of a statute versus a "plain language" construction. Judge Frank was not always latitudinarian in approach. Thus, he adopted the "plain language" construction in a commercial case, *Michelsen* v. *Penny*,[212] when he interpreted a statute as calling for a stringent accountability by the chairman of the board of directors of a bank to its stockholders.[213] The majority of the court limited recovery to the chairman's negligent acts. In his dissenting opinion, Frank would have allowed recovery for non-negligent acts as well. In this case we have an instance of a very strict interpretation by Frank of a statute to attach liabiliy to all its violations, regardless of any connection between them and the loss. This appears as a variation from the latitudinarian brush which he usually wielded in painting his legal canvases. But in a number of other instances Frank refused to espouse the "plain language" construction of a statute adopted by the court's majority and he favored an equitable interpretation. Thus, in *Dincher* v. *Marlin Firearms Co.*,[214] Dincher brought a negligence action for personal injuries suffered when a rifle of defendant's manufacture back-fired and he lost an eye. The rifle had been manufactured in 1946 and changed hands among firms several times before it reached the hands of a purchaser, Dincher's cousin, in 1949. In 1950 it was loaned to Dincher, and the injury was sustained on the very day of its borrowing. Under the Connecticut law held applicable,[215] there was a one year statute of limitations for negligence actions, which had to be instituted "within one year from the date of the act or omission complained of." The omission complained of was inherent in the gun upon manufacture, but had never been detected.

Writing for the majority of the court, Judge Chase dismissed the action as barred by the statute of limitations. He gave the statute a very narrow, strict construction. In his dissenting opinion, Judge Frank felt that his colleagues were ascribing "an unreasonable purpose to the legislature."[216] He asked how a statute of limitations can begin to run before a cause of action arises, "before a judicial remedy is available to the plaintiff."[217] "But no student of such legal somnolence has ever explained how a man can sleep on a right he does not have . . ."[218] There can be no gainsaying that this was an equitable interpretation of the statute in contradistinction to a "plain language" construction.[219]

Frank was guided by the discoverable legislative purpose even though the "plain language" construction might lead to another result. In *Schwartz* v. *Mills*,[220] Frank repudiated in a dissenting opinion the "plain language" construction of a statute "when the legislative purpose is discoverable, although ambiguously expressed."[221] He traced back to Aristotle the view of the inadequacy of the "plain language" as the sole key to a correct interpretation of a statute. He was in accord with the view of Learned Hand who had criticized both the school of thought which sanctioned a judge's decision based on his own notions of justice as well as the school of literalism which Hand dubbed the "dictionary school."[222]

Judicial legislation is engaged in by administrative agencies as well as by courts. Administrative agencies have been a potent force in American economic life, particularly since the establishment of the Interstate Commerce Commission in 1887.[223] In *Guiseppi* v. *Walling*[224] Judge Frank stated that the "transfer of 'subsidiary legislation' to administrative officers" by Congress[225] is akin to judicial legislation. In this case the Administrator of the Fair Labor Standards Act was granted statutory power to fix minimum wages in the embroidery industry. An attack was made on his action upon the ground that the statute in question represented an unconstitutional delegation of legislative power to the Administrator.

Writing the Court's opinion, Judge Frank traced the delegation of legislative power back to Aristotle's *Politics*. In a learned discussion he demonstrated that there never has been a rigid separation of powers in either our or the British governmental structure, and that, as has frequently been observed, Montesquieu was in error when he spoke of the clear-cut separation of powers in the England of his day. The administrative agencies, like the courts, are possessed not only of judicial powers, but of legislative powers as well. The legislative rule enacted by the Administrator was accordingly upheld.[226] It follows that all law does not emanate solely from the legislature. Frank could have pointed out, however, this distinction between administrative and judicial legislation: Whereas delegation of authority to administrative agencies by the legislature is express, judicial legislation is not an express legislative grant, but an acknowledged and unavoidable fact of life.

From his judicial opinions in the area of *stare decisis* there emerges an image of Frank as a traditional judge with a liberal bent of mind. Any revolutionary or radical notions which appear in his early jurisprudential writings were obsolete by the time he ascended the bench. It is far easier to be revolutionary in theoretical writings than in the decision of concrete cases. On the bench he abided by *stare decisis* as a fundamental tenet of our legal system, conducive to stability and certainty in the daily affairs and enterprises of men. But he was no worshiper of tradition and precedent for the sake of certainty in transactions when, in his opinion, they interfered with a just disposition of a case or were out of line with changed circumstances.

# Chapter III
## CIVIL LIBERTIES

Judge Frank's decisions in the area of civil liberties will be analyzed in this chapter. We reserve for a separate chapter an analysis of his decisions in a vital civil liberty, namely, freedom of speech and press, since it is critical to the lifeblood of a democracy.

Civil liberties are the basic personal rights of the individual in a democratic state. The individual is guaranteed by the Constitution due process of law, a right against self-incrimination, a right to be free of "unreasonable" searches and seizures, a right to trial by jury in criminal prosecutions, a right to the assistance of counsel in the defense of criminal prosecutions, as well as other rights.[1] These are protected against federal interference by the Bill of Rights and against state interference when incorporated by the Supreme Court into the "liberty" provision of the "due process" clause of the Fourteenth Amendment.

The preamble to the Constitution refers not only to the "blessings of liberty", but to the "general welfare" as well. Often the courts are confronted with an issue posing the antinomy of personal rights and societal interests. The problem of balancing the two, of resolving these antagonistic poles is fraught with difficulties and is not easy of solution. This chapter will discuss how Judge Frank resolved these constitutional problems. Further, it will discuss those decisions which, while not constitutionally based, resulted from standards promulgated by the Supreme Court in order to establish civilized standards of justice.

It should be noted at the outset that an analysis of many of the civil liberties to be discussed will be found only in Judge Frank's judicial opinions and not in any of his jurisprudential writings, with four exceptions: (1) Frank's critique of the jury system which is articulated both in his books and in his judicial opinions;[2] (2) an analysis of a case based on his view of fact-skepticism, to be found in *In re Fried;*[3] (3) an analysis of *U.S. v. Roth,* in which Frank fused the law with social science, a fusion often advanced by him in his jurisprudential writings;[4] and (4) the area of poverty and equal justice, discussed both in his writings and in judicial opinions.[5] Many of the civil liberties to be analyzed raised issues not directly related to any of his jurisprudential doctrines, and though one would anticipate a legal realist—who is essentially a reformer—to be liberal in his interpretation of principles of law, a liberal need not be a legal realist to subscribe to Frank's views in his civil liberties opinions. The following pages will prove that Frank was a pronounced liberal on the bench. But a liberal judge need not assent to Frank's *emphasis* on the subjective factors which contribute to the shaping of the law, and yet as a liberal interpret the law as did Frank. He may not be as concerned, as was Frank, with studying empirically how law functions in society. Although Frank's opinions demonstrate a judge of deep humanity and evince a strict adherence to the Bill of Rights in accordance with his interpretation of its provisions, it cannot be said that they are exclusively the product of a legal realist philosophy. Many of them, however, transcend the shackles of technical, legalistic terminology and incorporate ideas transported from the realm of philosophy, economics, literature, history, psychology, sociology and anthropology. None of his opinions, it may finally be noted, can be explained as a resultant of a deviation from the doctrine of *stare decisis*.

This and the following chapter are thus, with the exceptions enumerated, not studies in Frank's jurisprudence, but studies in legal analysis which help mold for us the Frank *gestalt*. Of pertinence is Pound's cogent observation on the training common to judges brought up in the common law tradition, which forges among them a basic universality in the techniques of applying the law.

It is true that the personality of a judge will affect his interpretation and application of a legal precept to some degree. But he has been trained in the tradition of the law, as have his fellow judges also. From judges steeped in that tradition we may expect to get, and experience shows that we do get, substantially the same technique of reading and interpreting a precept and applying it. It is chiefly in application of the standard of reasonableness, where the tradition

85

is not clear and settled, and in interpretation of legislation to be applied in the light of new and not clearly defined ideals, that the so-called realist finds the material for his doctrine. To judges well brought up in the common-law tradition the main body of its precepts speak alike no matter what their individual social or economic backgrounds or temperament.[6]

Even in the many areas—involving commerce and property interests—where common techniques of applying the law do or may be expected to lead to uniform results in the interest of a stable economy,[7] cases frequently arise which evoke divergences of opinion among judges. A fortiori is divergence to be expected in those areas of the law where new ideals keep on breaking through. It is in the latter area that civil liberties are embraced.

One note of caution: The line of demarcation between liberal and conservative judges is not strictly delimited. One simply senses the liberal and conservative tendencies of judges except in clear instances of a pronounced liberalism or a pronounced conservatism. And liberals—as well as conservatives—may differ among themselves in the interpretation of some legal doctrines. A difference of opinion will be seen between the writer and Frank in the analysis of some of his cases—not, it is hoped, from a liberal-conservative perspective, but as a family quarrel between liberals. The notion must be dispelled that there can be any uniformity or certainty in an important area of the law where reasonable men differ.

## Coerced Confessions

In his eulogy of Frank, Justice Douglas referred to Frank's concern that even-handed justice be done not only to those who are influential, but to the lowly, the indigent, and the despised. This appears in his repeated denunciations of the use of third degree by the policy. He wrote in *U.S. ex rel. Caminito* v. *Murphy*: "The test of the moral quality of a civilization is its treatment of the weak and powerless."[8]

The issue of a psychologically coerced confession in a case emanating from a state court was presented in *U.S. ex rel. Caminito* v. *Murphy*.[9] As we shall see, the law at that time regarding confessions arising from decisions rendered in state jurisdictions differed radically from that evolved in cases stemming from decisions rendered in federal jurisdictions.

Coerced confessions are of two types: (1) those resulting from physical violence inflicted by the police, colloquially denominated the "third degree"; (2) those resulting from the more subtle, more sophisticated forms of mental or psychological pressures.

In England, during the course of five centuries—from the thirteenth to the middle of the seventeenth—a person refusing to answer a criminal charge and persisting in his silence was "pressed" under heavy weights "until he either grew less stubborn or was crushed to death."[10] Not until the mid-seventeenth century did recognition dawn in England that silence in the face of a criminal charge should not be regarded as an admission of guilt.[11] Professor Gellhorn has written that the revolt in American law against police brutality, like many other good things in our law, is of relatively recent origin, "stimulated by reformers who were not afraid to challenge imperfections no matter how well entrenched they had become."[12]

The Wickersham Commission's "Report on Lawlessness in Law Enforcement," issued in 1931, was an official study confirming the widespread use of third degree methods by American police against defendants suspected of crime.[13] Until as recently as 1936, the weight to be attached to a confession in a state court, despite undisputed evidence of violence by the police on a defendant, was "one of the questions that was left to the fact finders in each case."[14] In 1936, in *Brown* v. *Mississippi*,[15] the first confession case to reach the Supreme Court from a state court, there was proof of a coerced confession resulting from police violence. In a unanimous opinion the Supreme Court categorically excluded the defendants' confessions as evidence. Reversing the conviction of three Negroes for murder based solely on confessions which followed callous beatings admitted by the police, the court held the submission of these confessions to a jury was in violation of due process guaranteed by the Fourteenth Amendment. "The rack and torture may not be substituted for the witness stand . . ."[16]

In 1940, the Supreme Court in another unanimous opinion

in *Chambers* v. *Florida*[17] extended the doctrine of the *Brown* case to a situation where the confession was a result not of physical violence but of mental coercion and psychological pressure. The confession, which followed a relentless questioning of defendant during a period of five days, was ruled to have been psychologically coerced and inadmissible as evidence.[18] Reversing the conviction, the Supreme Court refused to be bound by the state jury's finding of the confession's voluntariness, but made an independent search of the record to determine the constitutional issue of procedural due process under the Fourteenth Amendment.[19]

Commencing with *Lisenba* v. *California*,[20] a division set in in the resolution of psychological coercion cases by the Supreme Court. The problem has been a difficult one for the Court, and its opinions have not always been consistent with one another concerning the criterion for a determination of psychological coercion. This case involved somewhat prolonged questioning,[21] not of an ignorant boy as in the *Chambers* case, but of an intelligent business man. A majority of the court found the confession voluntary. It found that the defendent had exhibited self-possession and acumen both during his police interrogation and at the trial. It ruled that protracted questioning per se does not constitute a denial of due process. The Court set up as a criterion on the issue of psychological coercion a determination from all the facts whether there had been a deprivation of free choice by the particular defendant to admit, deny or refuse to answer.

A majority of the court in *Ashcraft* v. *Tennessee*[22] held a confession obtained following twenty-eight hours of continuous questioning of a substantial business man to have been psychologically coerced. It did not apply the criterion advanced in the *Lisenba* case on the issue of psychological coercion—namely, whether there had been a deprivation of free choice by the particular individual. Rather, it held that the unremitting interrogation of defendant was "inherently coercive" and raised a conclusive presumption of coercion regardless of who the defendant was and what his powers of resistance were. Even five hours of questioning in the dead of night was held by the majority of the court in *Haley* v. *Ohio*[23] to be psychologically coercive when a fifteen-year-old Negro boy was involved. In *Watts* v.

*Indiana*,[24] a majority of the court held a confession following relentless questioning during a period of five days psychologically coerced and the "product of the suction process of interrogation."[25] "There is torture of the mind as well as the body; the will is as much affected by fear as by force . . ."[26] Of relevance to our later discussion is Justice Douglas' concurring opinion, representing a minority view, in which he expressed the view that *any* confession obtained by the state during a period of unlawful detention should be held invalid, since "the procedure breeds coerced confessions."[27]

Several other leading cases from state courts resulted in reversals by the Supreme Court on the issue of psychologically coerced confessions.[28] Then, in *Stein* v. *New York*,[29] a majority of the court held that a confession obtained following twelve hours of intermittent questioning had not been psychologically coerced. Justice Jackson[30] refused to find any abstract inherent coercion divorced from an appraisal of all the circumstances, including the personality and power of resistance of the particular defendant. Although the facts of this case and those of the *Ashcraft* case may be distinguished in explanation of the opposite results arrived at, this Court nevertheless appears to have abandoned the inherent coercion test of *Ashcraft* and was reverting to the *Lisenba* test.[31] It announced as the criterion on the issue of psychological coercion a determination whether or not the circumstances testified to had a coercive effect on the particular defendant making the confession.[32] The Court stated that what might be coercive to a weak-willed person might be ineffective insofar as an experienced, hardened criminal was concerned.

The discussion thus far has dealt with confessions in state courts. Confessions are admissible in state court proceedings if the fundamental concepts of justice and liberty embodied in due process of law have not been violated.[33] Nearly all states have statutes providing for the prompt arraignment of a defendant before a magistrate after arrest..[34] Nevertheless, if the confession is found voluntary, the fact that it was obtained during a period of illegal detention—in violation of the requirement of prompt arraignment—does not constitute a violation of due process so as to vitiate the confession.[35]

89

The Supreme Court has applied a different standard of scrutiny to confessions in federal courts. In *McNabb* v. *United States*,[36] involving the murder of revenue officers, defendants had not been taken upon arrest before a United States Commissioner or judge as required by federal law, but were subjected to lengthy questioning.[37] The Supreme Court held that a confession is inadmissible in a federal court if obtained during a period of illegal detention, regardless of its voluntariness. This rule is not based upon the due process clause of the Fifth Amendment,[38] but was promulgated by the Court "in the exercise of its supervisory power over the administration of criminal justice in the federal courts" in order to maintain "civilized standards of procedure and evidence."[39] The motivation for the rule was a desire to check a resort to the reprehensible practice of the third degree.[40] The Court also felt it would prevent a stultification of congressional policy which requires arresting officers to make an immediate arraignment before a United States Commissioner or judicial officer. The Supreme Court, however, lacks the general power of supervision over state criminal trials which it possesses over federal trials, and its supervision over state criminal trials arises only when there is a claim of a denial of due process of law under the Fourteenth Amendment.[41] The due process test for state trials exacted by the Supreme Court has therefore been that of the voluntariness of the confessions. The fact of illegal detention is no criterion for exclusion of confessions in state trials, but is only a factor which may be weighed by the jury or court together with all the circumstances in the case in determining the question of voluntariness.[42]

A clarification of the *McNabb* rule holding that the sole fact of illegal detention vitiates a confession in a federal court, regardless of the existence of aggravating circumstances, such as the lengthy detention present in *McNabb,* was made by the Supreme Court in *Upshaw* v. *United States.*[43] The exclusion of the confession is intended as a prophylaxis against the possibility of any coercion, psychological as well as physical.[44]

An issue of a confession arising from a decision in a state court confronted Judge Frank in *U.S. ex rel. Caminito* v. *Murphy.*[45] Caminito, a twenty-six-year-old dress cutter never previously arrested, was apprehended with two others for a felony murder. Following conviction in a state court, he was sentenced to a life term. After the lapse of several years, Caminito sought a writ of habeas corpus in a federal district court, claiming that his signed confession—the sole evidence against him—had been coerced.

Judge Frank wrote the Court's opinion, reversing the District Court and granting the writ. He furnished an array of facts which, he stated, were "not disputed." A perusal by the writer of the trial record casts some doubt on the full accuracy of Frank's "not disputed" statement of facts.[46] Whether the accurate undisputed facts would have altered his position is speculative. But in view of his strong insistence and relentless emphasis in his various writings—books and articles,[47] and in his important decision in *In Re Fried*[48]—on the primary importance of correct fact finding in the judicial process, one may question whether his zeal carried him away in this instance to the extent of unconsciously considering the facts as of secondary importance to a passionate indignation at police methods. An abstract passion for justice should not blind one to facts which conceivably might not warrant its exercise in a particular instance.

Among Frank's listed "undisputed" facts was one that Caminito had been interogated "almost continuously for 27 hours," with only a brief interval for rest during the night, in a cell badly equipped for sleeping purposes.[49] The unlawful detention was not an unconstitutional act, but Frank claimed that the continuous questioning was. He also contended that keeping Caminito incommunicado from his lawyer, friends and family who came to the station house to consult with him was in effect a kidnapping and was an unconstitutional act.[50]

But is Frank's statistic of "almost 27 hours" interrogation in accord with the facts? Even if it was continuous from 9 P.M. until 2 A.M. and from 10 A.M. until 9 P.M.[51]—which is not conceded in the People's testimony—on Frank's own figures Caminito had been interrogated at most sixteen hours. But these were sixteen hours broken up by seven to eight nighttime hours spent alone in his cell. One would have to throw in seven or eight allegedly sleepless hours[52] to constitute twenty-three or twenty-four hours. On the People's testimony, although no

91

accurate figure can be deduced, a fair estimate would be a total questioning of nine to twelve hours, and not continuous questioning at that.

The belief was expressed by Frank that psychological torture may be more sadistic and may break one's will more readily than physical torture. It is also more reprehensible in that it leaves no discernible mark on the victim. It is bad enough when there are convictions of innocent men in fairly conducted trials. This should not be compounded by countenancing confessions by torture.[53] Frank shuddered at contemplating what happens to an innocent men sent to jail. He expressed his concern with the plight of humble, inconspicuous men like Caminito when unconstitutionally convicted.

> For repeated and unredressed attacks on the constitutional liberties of the humble will tend to destroy the foundations supporting the constitutional liberties of everybody. The test of the moral quality of a civilization is its treatment of the weak and powerless.[54]

Frank stated without explanation that the "undisputed" facts of this case distinguished it from the recent *Stein* case.[55] This implied, for one thing, that in this case the psychological pressure was greater than in the *Stein* case.[56] But in asserting that the continuous questioning was an unconstitutional act, without further elucidation, Frank was in effect deciding contrary to the principle of the *Stein case*.[57] Whether his opinion was well-founded or not, as a judge in an inferior court, Frank could not enunciate the doctrine that *all* confessions, obtained during a period of unlawful detention in cases emanating from state courts, are invalid, as that would have been contrary to the Supreme Court decisions we have discussed. But it certainly would have been more consonant with his general views on fact-skepticism,[58] which we have come to recognize as a dominant feature of his legal philosophy, to be able to reverse the *Caminito* case on the basis of what may go on in police stations during *any* unlawful detention, and in line with what Justice Douglas has stated in concurring opinions in several state coerced confession cases.[59] Such an opinion in the Caminito case by Frank could have been superimposed as an *orbiter dictum*[60] on the reasons he assigned for his decision. It would have served as an expression of a deeply felt conviction. The most he said in this case was that defendant's testimony resembled the reports of those who, behind the Iron Curtain after similar treatment, had confessed to crimes they had not committed.[61]

An issue of a confession arising from a decision rendered in a federal court was presented in *U.S.* v. *Leviton.*[62] Leviton was found guilty in a federal court of wilfully filing false export declarations and of wilfully exporting wheat flour and lard to Italy in violation of a presidential proclamation. Customs officers asked him to accompany them to the Custom Agents' office to discuss some office export files, and he readily complied. Shortly after his arrival and while waiting for the arrival of the Customs Agent, a questioning officer, Leviton admitted to a customs officer that he had tried "to make a dishonest dollar." Later, Leviton referred the Customs Agent to a specific office file. Upon the Agent's return, several hours elapsed in a search for a stenographer. In the ensuing confession, Leviton furnished details of his involvement. The next day he was arraigned before a United States Commissioner.

Did a seven- and-a half-hour intervention between the detention and the detailed confession automatically taint it under the federal rule? Affirming Leviton's conviction, Judge Clark, writing the Court's opinion, held that the delay was not in violation of the *McNabb* rule. He had found no definitive interpretation in the cases of the term "unnecessary" in Rule 5 (a) of the Rules of Criminal Procedure, which required the arraignment of a defendant before a judicial officer "without unnecessary delay."[63] Although delay may not be used by the authorities to induce a confession, it may nevertheless be demonstrated to have been "reasonable when it is induced by the voluntary act of the accused in freeing himself of the burden of guilt."[64] When the officers first approached Leviton, he almost immediately demonstrated a sense of guilt and a spirit of cooperation with them in the search for documents. Had the officers been more "sophisticated" in their approach, Leviton would have provided them with a full confession at the time of his arrest. The questioning, Clark concluded, was that of a "willing accused."[65]

In an eloquent dissent, Judge Frank felt that the admission of Leviton's confession was in flagrant violation of the *McNabb* rule. Between his arrest at 1:45 P.M.[66] and 5:30 P.M.—when court was open—, Leviton could have been arraigned and advised of his rights. No judicial officer passed upon the "probable cause" for his detention. He was being held in order to establish a good case against him before the agents could justify his arrest to a judicial officer. Frank emphasized that detention frustrates the purpose of the *McNabb* case to procure for an arrestee the protection of Rule 5(b) of the Rules of Criminal Procedure,[67] promulgated by the Supreme Court to effectuate the *McNabb* doctrine, and which requires a judicial officer to advise a defendant of his rights. Otherwise, an opportunity is afforded for improper pressures upon a defendant before he has the benefit of a judicial officer's statement. The only exception in favor of the admission of a confession is in the instance of a spontaneously voluntary confession, as in the case of *U.S.* v. *Mitchell*.[68] Frank refused to equate Leviton's "meager remark about 'making a dishonest dollar' "[69] with a confession, since, standing alone, it was insufficient to secure a conviction.

A reading of the facts in this case does not disclose a scintilla of denial by Leviton of the charge against him. From his first brief statement that he had tried "to make a dishonest dollar," his referral of an agent to a specific file, until the securing of a stenographer to record his confession, there appears to have been a chain of willingness on his part to confess. Leviton was apparently a businessman, a man of the world. It is true, as Frank said, that similar to *Upshaw* v. *United States*,[70] Leviton was being detained so the agents could obtain a good case against him in order to justify his arrest before an arraigning officer.[71] But contrary to Frank's opinion that the *Upshaw* case was duplicated here "in every essential respect," this case is distinguishable from the *Upshaw* case where the defendant had denied the charge for many hours. Nowhere in the *Leviton* case is there an intimation of a denial. Perhaps the officers should have obtained some degree of specific confession from Leviton before proceeding to secure his files, as Judge Clark intimated. But despite Frank's eloquent language, it does not seem entirely relevant to the facts. This does not appear to be a situation

94

where one can say with conviction that fact-skepticism should be called into play on the basis of what may go on in police stations or Custom offices during *any* unlawful detention.

The *McNabb* rule is a clear example in an important area of the criminal law of fact-skepticism. To the leading exponent among legal philosophers of fact-skepticism—which has been deemed Frank's "outstanding contribution to contemporary American legal philosophy . . . as an incisive tool of legal analysis"[72]—the *McNabb* rule is a logical instance of an ethicizing influence which fact-skepticism, whether labeled as such or not, has brought about in the law. But laws and rules, as Frank frequently wrote, are not self-operative. Their operation may furnish greater difficulties than their formulation.[73]

## Advance Suppression of a Coerced Confession

An issue of coerced confessions in a federal jurisdiction, but where the dispositive question before the Court was different from that presented in the previous section, was presented in *In Re Fried*.[74] It was one without a precedent from the Supreme Court.

Involved was a charge of grand larceny of rubber from foreign commerce. Fried and others applied to a federal district court for an order directing the United States Attorney to suppress their confessions in advance of their submission to a grand jury. Customarily, this issue is raised at trial, which follows a grand jury indictment. The facts set forth by Fried and the others with respect to continuous questioning of them for approximately eleven hours through the night and their physical ailments constitute a pathetic picture. The District Court refused to consider the evidence surrounding the confessions on the ground of lack of power to do so before the return of an indictment by a grand jury.

The Court's opinion reversing the lower court was written by Judge Frank, and he remanded the case to the district court to pass upon the issue raised. He could see no logical distinction between the illegal seizure of tangible articles by federal officials, in which situation the district court is possessed of power to restrain their use even though no indictment is pending, and the taking of illegal confessions, albeit intangible. He denounced

95

the government's contention that no harm would ensue from an indictment founded upon such illegal evidence, since at the trial such evidence must be suppressed.[75] A wrongful indictment which may work irreparable harm was no "laughing matter" to Frank. The stigma of an indictment may not be erased even after a subsequent acquittal; the public may remember the accusation and suspect guilt despite the acquittal. Accordingly, Frank asserted, a prosecutor should not be permitted to offer to a grand jury illegal evidence.[76]

In a concurring opinion Judge Learned Hand would have suppressed any confession, provided it resulted from a constitutional violation of the Fifth Amendment,[77] but not if it was the result of a statutory violation.[78] He could see no rational distinction between the suppression in advance of trial, which the courts have sanctioned, of the use of property illegally seized under the Fourth Amendment,[79] and that of a confession coerced in violation of the Fifth Amendment. Hand would not have suppressed a confession where there was no proof of coercion but only proof of the violation of a statute commanding immediate arraignment. Judge Frank, a more daring spirit, would have gone further. He would have suppressed in advance of indictment any confessions which resulted not only from constitutional violations but from federal statutory violations as well —such as a statute commanding immediate arraignment.[80] He felt that since Congress is the law-making agency under the Constitution, the restrictions it imposes upon official behavior are entitled to as much respect by the courts as those imposed by the Constitution itself.[81]

Frank spoke of the polarity of interests involved in many of the confession cases. The Constitution itself by reason of the Fourth and the Fifth Amendments impeded at times the apprehension and conviction of criminals. So did Supreme Court decisions, not constitutionally required, which have extended procedural safeguards to defendants.[82] He expressed puzzlement at the opposition engendered by the decisions of the Supreme Court in this area. Frank asked us to remember that a democratic society in its criminal procedure necessarily pursues conflicting aims—that of convicting the guilty without at the same time endangering the innocent. A democratic society must

96

pursue both aims and not sacrifice the latter aim in its effort to attain the former. A culprit may escape, but an innocent person will not suffer.

Frequently Frank wrote that the function of the law is to enforce the social values, the "social value judgments" embodied in substantive rules, civil and criminal. But their enforcement is not on a wholesale scale. It is on a retail scale—case by case.[82a] In each case the rules have to be applied by the court to the particular facts it has "found." If a court by reason of the subjectivity of fact-finding misapprehends the facts, it will apply a wrong rule and thus thwart the social policy embodied in the rule applicable to the true facts. Frank was worried that a coerced confession may bring about mistaken fact-finding. He expressed deep concern lest substantial harm result from a failure to suppress in advance an illegal confession.[83] Preventive justice is usually the best sort of justice.[84] Any other view, Frank thought, would be cynical.

## Entrapment

Police entrapment usually inveigles into its net drug addicts, homosexuals, and generally weak-willed individuals. It may, however, ensnare into the commission of an offense an individual otherwise innocent and not intending the preparation of a crime. A violation of the law would not occur but for the persuasion and luring by the police official. In Justice Brandeis' terminology, this is provoking, creating crime.[85] This area of the law is not constitutionally based. It is the result of the Supreme Court's exercise of its supervisory power over the federal courts.

The leading case on the subject is *Sorrells* v. *United States*.[86] Sorrells, regularly employed and never convicted of a crime, was introduced to Martin, a prohibition agent posing as a tourist, by one who had been a member with both of them in the same division of the American Expeditionary Force during World War I. During the exchange of reminiscences and after three importunings by Martin, Sorrells left his home for a half gallon of liquor which he sold to Martin for five dollars, allegedly for his partner in the furniture line back home. There was no evidence that Sorrells had ever possessed or sold liquor previously, but three government witnesses testified that he had a general reputation as a rum-runner. The trial judge ruled as a matter of law that there was no entrapment on these facts. A jury then convicted Sorrells for violation of the National Prohibition Act.

Writing for the Supreme Court, Chief Justice Hughes severely condemned Martin's act as one of entrapment. The government was not out to detect and punish crime, but to create a synthetic criminal. He read into the statute a legislative intention not to prosecute for the entrapment of innocent people through the "creative activity"[87] of governmental officials. He reversed and remanded the issue of entrapment for determination by a jury. Upon a trial of this issue, proof of defendant's reputation or past record, where it exists, is permitted as indicative of a predisposition on his part and as a possible rebuttal of entrapment.

In a concurring opinion, Justice Roberts (joined by Justices Brandeis and Stone) based the Court's policy against entrapment not on an alleged legislative intention but on a judicial policy to preserve the "purity" of a court of justice and prevent a "prostitution of the criminal law."[88] The government may not instigate the commission of a new crime even by a defendant previously convicted or who enjoys a bad reputation. Justice Roberts voted to quash the indictment and discharge Sorrells.

The issue of entrapment confronted Judge Frank in *U.S.* v. *Masciale*.[89] Masciale had interposed a plea of entrapment to an indictment charging a sale of narcotics. Marshall, a government agent, had been introduced as a big narcotics purchaser to Masciale by Kovel, a government informer—a stool pigeon. Masciale had known Kovel for some time, but was unaware of his undercover activities. Marshall testified at the trial that although Masciale had boasted he was primarily a gambler, he knew however someone high up in the narcotics traffic to whom he would introduce him. Masciale's version at the trial was he had told Marshall at their first meeting that through his gambling activities he knew about the narcotics traffic, but he denied advising Marshall that he then had any available source of narcotics. In the following six weeks, Masciale and Marshall met or spoke to each other telephonically many times. Masciale testified that in the beginning he strung Marshall along in order to increase Kovel's prestige in Marshall's eyes. He told Marshall he was experiencing trouble in establishing a contact. His first source did not show up. Finally, Masciale effected an introduction between Marshall and one other, who, on the following day, sold heroin to Marshall.

In the Court's opinion affirming the conviction, Judge Hincks wrote that although the sale had been induced by Marshall, nevertheless the Government had proven a sufficient excuse for the inducement, namely, the fact that Masciale needed no persuasion but was "ready and willing to commit the offense whenever the opportunity offered."[90] He ruled that despite the fact Masciale had not been involved in the past commission of any act in the area of the present offense, the defense of entrapment would not lie if he needed no persuasion. From the record he deduced that Masciale was an easy mark.

In his dissenting opinion, Judge Frank was primarily persuaded by the fact that before meeting Marshall, Masciale had never been guilty of the crime of selling narcotics or anything like it.[91] As he interpreted the *Sorrells* case, entrapment occurs whenever a government agent induces a person "previously innocent of a substantially similar crime"[92] to commit it. It is only when a defendant's past conduct justifies the belief he would commit the crime or a substantially similar one, without an officer's persuasion, that the government may use stratagem and set a trap.

The reasoning of Judge Frank predicated upon the presence or absence of past conduct in the specific or "substantially similar" area of criminality appears reasonable on the surface. But as a realist, Frank should have known that if any individual is engaged in one area of criminality—such as illicit gambling—, he is in a better position and more prone than the law-abiding individual to move into another criminal area, although new to him. Is a suggestion to such an individual, which he readily seizes upon and which involves him in a new area of criminality, to be considered an act of entrapment? Is he to be judged on the basis of a strict, formalistic dichotomy? Is he really on a par with one who has theretofore been fully a law-abiding individual? To Frank, however, gambling was a

crime so "wholly different" from narcotics dealing that he
would have refused to consider it a factor in rebuttal of the
defense of entrapment.[93] He felt that without any prior conduct
on Masciale's part in the area of narcotics to indicate he was
ready to engage in such an operation, there could in the nature
of things be no proof that he was "ready without persuasion
and was awaiting any propitious opportunity to commit the
offense."[94]

Frank could see no rational basis for the distinction drawn
by his colleagues between a situation where the officer's persuasion of a defendant is difficult and one where it is easy. In
this case the majority felt the proof had established an easy
persuasion—in fact, suggestion without the need for any persuasion. Frank queried as to what the measure of an "easy
seduction" is. He felt the government should not spend its time
and money on converting potential into actual criminals. "In
such circumstances, the police have not caught a criminal; they
have taught a man how to become a criminal."[95]

Although in the *Sorrells* case the government had introduced
reputation evidence to establish that Sorrells was a rum-runner,
and this, in the majority opinion, presented a question for a jury
as to whether it was sufficient to rebut Sorrells' proof of entrapment, nevertheless in all other respects the *Sorrells* case represents a much stronger case in entrapment than this case—
if this case represents any entrapment at all. Sorrells had no
criminal record; there was no proof of the past commission of
any offense by him, and he needed persuasion. There had
been several refusals by him before compliance. The government agent took "advantage of the sentiment aroused by reminiscences of their experiences as companions in arms in the
World War."[96] But though Masciale had no criminal record in
the area of the offense charged, he did have a criminal record,
and on the facts narrated, it is hard to see that he needed
persuasion. A "ready complaisance"[97] by him to commit the
crime was abundantly established.

In a genuine case of entrapment, and not one of "ready
complaisance," like the *Masciale* case, it would be just to disregard a defendant's past criminal record, not only in a different

area of crime but even in the identical area of the committed crime. This would be because society should not tolerate an ensnaring by the police of anyone into further crime, regardless of his past record or reputation. The government should not stimulate the weaknesses of human nature.[98] This is the enlightened view of the concurring minority opinion by Justice Roberts in the *Sorrells* case and of a concurring opinion by Justice Frankfurter in *Sherman* v. *United States*.[99]

Justice Frankfurter was of the opinion that the evidence for sustaining the defense of entrapment in the *Masciale* case was "rather thin."[100] Judge Frank, zealot though he was in protection of the rights of the inconspicuous man—the weak and powerless—, at times evinced too much zeal in a situation not calling for its exercise. This case is perhaps an instance of misguided zeal in behalf of one who on the facts did not seem to merit it.

## Eavesdropping

In the course of Judge Frank's dissenting opinion in *U.S.* v. *On Lee*[101] on the issue of eavesdropping, he gave fresh utterance with such fervor to the ancient concept that a man's home is his castle, that Alan Barth was moved to state: "The need for such sanctuary, expressed eloquently two centuries ago by William Pitt and James Otis, was restated for twentieth-century Americans by the late Judge Jerome Frank."[102]

"The concept that a man's home is his castle developed very early in English law,"[103] and was applicable to all alike—to the law-breaker as well as to the law-abiding member of the community. In 1776, in a famous parliamentary address on the subject of "general warrants," William Pitt declared that "the poorest man may, in his cottage, bid defiance to all the forces of the Crown. It may be frail; its roof may shake; the wind may blow through it; but the King of England may not enter; all his force dares not cross the threshold of the ruined tenement."[104]

Prior to the dawn of the modern electronic age, eavesdropping was usually accomplished by means of a trespass on private property, a violation of law. The illegality of a trespass constituted the consequent search and seizure illegal. With the advent of the Prohibition era, wiretapping became the main device used by the authorities in ferreting out mammoth syndicates engaged in conspiracies to violate the Volstead Act, such as was divulged in the famous case of *Olmstead* v. *United States*.[105] Involved were annual sales in excess of $2,000,000. and the employment of fifty persons, a small fleet, a central office, and storage facilities. With the use of wiretaps the federal officers listened into conversations among the executives, payoff promises to Seattle policemen, and arrangements for the release of arrested employees. Although wiretapping required no physical trespass upon defendants' property,[106] it was claimed that the Government had violated the Fourth Amendment against unreasonable searches and seizures and the Fifth Amendment against self-incrimination. Chief Justice Taft, writing the Court's opinion, held that the use of wiretaps violated neither amendment. He stated that an unlawful search and seizure requires a physical entry into a home or office and the seizure of "material things." The wires for the tapping were beyond defendants' homes and offices, and consequently did not constitute a trespass upon which an illegal search could be predicated.[107] Nor were the messages which were overheard "material things" necessary to constitute an illegal seizure.[108]

In his famous dissent, Justice Holmes referred to any illegal activity by Government officials—in this case the violation of a state statute which had made wiretapping a misdemeanor—as "dirty business."[109] In an equally famous dissent, Justice Brandeis emphasized the "right to be let alone" as "the right most valued by civilized men."[110] Regardless of the means employed, he deemed any "unjustifiable intrusion" upon privacy a violation of the Fourth Amendment.

In 1934, Congress enacted the Federal Communications Act. Its best-known provision—Section 605—forbids the divulgence of any information obtained by the interception of a communication without the consent of the "sender." The Supreme Court later construed this act as intended to outlaw wiretapping. But despite this prohibition, wiretapping—of an official as well as of a private nature—has remained widespread throughout the United States.[111]

A case which involved an interpretation of Section 605 of the Federal Communications Act as well as of the Fourth Amendment was *Goldman* v. *United States*,[112] in which the electronic device used for eavesdropping was a detectaphone. Federal agents, with the assistance of the building superintendent, gained access to a room adjacent to an office where a bankruptcy swindle was being concocted. They placed a detectaphone against the partition wall, and in this way overheard the conspirators' conversations as well as a telephonic conversation of one conspirator. Speaking for the Court, Justice Roberts held that there was no violation of either Section 605 or of the Fourth Amendment. Since there had been no mechanical interception of the telephone wires by wiretapping or other mechanical means, the Court held that Section 605 had not been violated. The means of communication is protected in the course of the transmission of a message, but not the words spoken into a telephone and overheard by someone without any mechanical interception of the wires.[113] Nor did the use of a detectaphone violate the Fourth Amendment since there had been no physical trespass on defendant's office, and the conversations among the conspirators were thus properly admitted into evidence.[114] The case was held indistinguishable in principle from the *Olmstead* case.

It was a somewhat similar issue of electronic eavesdropping with which Judge Frank was confronted in *U.S. v. On Lee*.[115] The facts were these: Chin Poy, an undercover agent for the Federal Narcotics Bureau, paid two "friendly" visits to the laundry of his former employer, On Lee. Concealed in Chin Poy's pocket was a microphone with a small antenna running along his arm, which transmitted their conversation to a receiving set atached to an agent, Chin Lee, stationed down the block. These visits occurred while On Lee was out on bail awaiting trial on narcotics charges.

Chin Poy was not called by the government to testify but Chin Lee was. He testified that by means of his receiving set he had heard On Lee admit to Chin Poy the sale of opium to Ying, his co-defendant, on behalf of a narcotics syndicate. On Lee's conviction followed.

On appeal, On Lee contended that the introduction at the trial of the microphone-heard conversation violated Section 605 of the Federal Communications Act. On the basis of the *Goldman* decision,[116] Judge Swan, for the Court, held that this contention could not be sustained. The microphone device was similar in use to the detectaphone in the *Goldman* case—"merely a mechanical means of eavesdropping" and not an "interception of a communication by wire or radio . . ."[117] The secrecy of a conversation as such is not protected by the Federal Communications Act. On Lee's further contention that the Fourth Amendment had been violated was not sustained because there had been no physical trespass by the agent. Swan also concluded from a reading of the Fourth Amendment and the *Olmstead* case that for a search to be unconstitutional, it must be a seizure of tangible things, not of words as in this case.[118]

In his dissenting opinion, though not pleased with the *Goldman* doctrine, which he thought restrictive of Fourth Amendment privacy,[119] Judge Frank sought to distinguish the two cases. He reasoned that though Chin Poy was in the store by permission of Lee, his concealed microphone had been brought into the store without his permission. The fact that it was concealed on Chin Poy's person rather than secreted inside the store was immaterial. The concealment permitted an "unlawful invasion" by the government agent though physically he was on the outside, tantamount to his sneaking into the premises when On Lee's back was turned and listening while concealed in a closet. To Frank this "illegality" distinguished this case from the *Goldman* case, in which the officer had listened through a detectaphone installed in an adjoining room, which constituted "no part of one's constitutionally protective precincts."[120] A man's place of business, though customers may enter at will, is as immune from illegal search and seizure as are his kitchen and bedroom.[121]

Judge Frank disagreed with the majority contention that illegal search and seizure are restricted to tangible, material objects; that words overheard during a search are outside the orbit of the Fourth Amendment, and are admissible in evidence despite a trespass. If a federal officer unlawfully breaks into a house, it should be immaterial whether he seizes something tangible or overhears a self-incriminating statement.[122] In either case, the original trespass taints it under the Fourth Amendment. The majority decision had relied on the *Olmstead* case to bolster its contention.[123] But Frank retorted that since no physical entry had been effected in the *Olmstead* case, any remarks by that court as to what constitutes an illegal seizure—whether it must be something tangible, as that court held—were dicta and as such "superfluous" to the decision. He felt the majority doctrine on this point contravened 180 years of constitutional history. Frank's position on this issue has been ultimately upheld by the Supreme Court.[124]

It was Frank's conviction that On Lee's right to a sanctuary —regardless of whether it was his home or his place of business— had been violated by the government agent, and he gave utterance to these memorable words:

> A man can still control a small part of his environment, his house; he can retreat thence from outsiders, secure in the knowledge that they cannot get at him without disobeying the Constitution. That is still a sizable chunk of liberty—worth protecting from encroachment. A sane, decent, civilized society must provide some such oasis, some shelter from public scrutiny, some insulated enclosure, some enclave, some inviolate place which is a man's castle.[125]

Frank brushed a few strokes of an Orwellian horror picture of what could be expected if the use of electronic devices— "knockless, sneaky, unknown"[126]—were to be allowed. He feared that the majority opinion invited the installation of frightening instruments like Orwell's "telescreen," on which private affairs in every household would be recorded.

The analysis by Frank that Lee, though physically outside the store, was nevertheless a "trespasser," strikes one as casuistry. Justice Jackson, writing the majority opinion of the Supreme Court affirming the conviction in a 5-4 decision, called this argument "frivolous."[127] Chin Poy made no affirmative misrepresentations of any sort and he was an implied, if not an express, invitee in the laundry. Anyone in an exposed position talking to another—be the other civilian or police officer—must take his chances that the other person may be "bugged." And the person armed with a microphone is under no obligation to inform his interlocutor of that fact, nor ask his permission to use it. There was no physical contact between the microphone inside the store and the receiving set on the outside, upon which one

105

might predicate a trespass. Technically, the case is no different from the line of Supreme Court cases which have held that so long as the observation is conducted on the exterior of the premises, information gleaned of activities on the inside of a house by means of eavesdropping, flashlight beams, spyglasses, etc. is not objectionable and is admissible in evidence.[128]

The issues presented by the *On Lee* case, however, run deeper than a technical analysis of what constitutes trespass. If invasion of privacy is involved, one might ask what difference it makes whether the instrument or detection is outside the premises or inside.[129] Why should the result be dependent upon fine-spun legalistic doctrines of whether or not a trespass had occurred? The answer seeems to be that once again we are confronted with the antinomy of private rights versus societal interests,[130] a most difficult issue defying easy resolution. And so the courts have, consciously or subconsciously, evolved a compromise based upon a geographical dividing line, whereby certain cases will be held to favor private rights and others societal interests. In this decision Frank sought unsuccessfully by an ingenious inter-pretation to extend the orbit of those cases which favor private rights. He sought to relax the geographical barriers by a legal transplantation into the inside of the premises of what was physically on the outside. One cannot quarrel with Frank's denominating the right of privacy "one of the most cherished constitutional rights, one which contributes substantially to the distinctive flavor of democracy."[131] As a judge in an inferior court Frank could not go all the way in enunciating a doctrine that any invasion of privacy, even in the absence of a trespass, is invalid, as that would have been contrary to Supreme Court pronouncements. But his effort to establish a trespass on the facts of the *On Lee* case was a daring exercise in casuistry.[132]

## Self-Incrimination

The self-incrimination clause of the Fifth Amendment to the Constitution is household currency. No other provision in the Constitution has aroused so much controversy in contemporary America as has this one. Dean Griswold has called the privilege against self-incrimination "one of the great landmarks in man's struggle to make himself civilized."[133] He links its genesis with the abolition of torture, "once used by honest and conscientious public servants as a means of obtaining information about crimes which could not otherwise be disclosed."[134]

This privilege is not mentioned in the great historical English documents—Magna Carta, the Petition of Right and the Bill of Rights.[135] In the early part of the seventeenth century, during the period of persecution of the Puritans under Charles I, there were in England two "special prerogative courts"[136]—the Court of High Commission for so-called religious heterodoxy,[137] and the Court of Star Chamber for so-called political heterodoxy. Those were dark days when the privilege against self-incrimination was unknown and one committed to the exercise of freedom of thought ran a grave risk. In the 1630's and 1640's, the trials of "Freeborn John" Lilburne resulted in the first vindication of a privilege against self-incrimination.[138] This privilege found a place in American laws from the 1640's on, and before 1789 we find it enumerated in the constitutions of seven American states.[139]

Frank wrote several opinions in this area. An issue of whether a disclosure before a grand jury of involvement in a crime without the furnishing of any details constituted a waiver of the privilege against self-incrimination so as to compel a full disclosure, was raised in *U.S. v. St. Pierre*.[140] St. Pierre was sentenced to a term of five months for criminal contempt because of his refusal to answer a question before a grand jury. After admitting to the grand jury his embezzlement of money and its transfer beyond New York State—a federal crime under the National Stolen Property Act—, he refused any further disclosure as to whose money it was he had embezzled. The money represented the winnings of a bet given to him by a bookmaker for transmission. No prosecution against him was possible without the undisclosed information, since his confession standing alone without the corroborative testimony of the embezzlee would be insufficient.

In the majority opinion by Judge Learned Hand, affirming the sentence, he wrote that St. Pierre need not have spoken at all, but having chosen to make some disclosure, it was not for him to decide when to stop speaking. He felt that St. Pierre had confessed to a crime and had omitted only a "detail."

Judge Frank wrote a vigorous dissent. He made a distinction

between evidence involving an admission to the commission of a crime, where the evidence furnished is, however, insufficient to effect the arrest and punishment of the individual, and evidence involving an admission to the commission of a crime, with sufficient facts furnished to make possible an arrest and punishment. Under the first situation there are lacunae in the evidence, so that the full contours of a punishable crime are not in view. It is an established principle of law that a person may wish not to avail himself of the privilege against self-incrimination, in which case he may waive it. In Frank's view, his colleagues had adopted as their conception of an effective waiver of the privilege the mere furnishing of evidence involving the disgrace of an admission to the commission of a crime, even though the disclosure does not furnish facts sufficient to effect the arrest and punishment of the party. And once waived, the party cannot stop talking at his discretion. It was Frank's belief, however, that a situation involving an admission to the commission of a crime wtih sufficient facts furnished to make possible an arrest and punishment would be required in order to constitute an effective waiver of the privilege. He claimed that the decisions and the history of the privilege demonstrated the validity of his position.[141]

This problem bears analysis as just one more instance of the conflict confronting the courts in manifold situations—that of private rights versus societal interests. So long as an individual exercises his right of silence, there can be no cause for conflict. But once he chooses to speak and he admits the commission of a crime, albeit without its details, it would seem that he has so far waived his right of silence that the societal interest becomes paramount. His waiver thus starts a process which will make possible an arrest and punishment. Should he balk, he can be held in contempt. But it was he who in the first instance brought this about by electing to talk. If the analysis is correct that St. Pierre effected a waiver, then the compulsion upon him to disclose the details of his crime or be punished for contempt, is no violation of the Fifth Amendment.

Frank's emphasis on the prime importance of correct fact-finding to a proper administration of justice has been previously discussed.[142] He consequently believed in the essentiality of the "fullest practicable disclosure to the courts of all important evidence bearing on the facts of cases."[143] And so he directed his attention in this case to the problem whether the various privileges granted to witnesses interfere with the desideratum of the fullest disclosure of evidence. Specifically, he asked whether his decision in this case could have the undesirable effect of barring the court from learning all the evidence. He agreed with the critics of the privileges that each privilege needed periodic examination to determine whether the original policy underlying its formation still outweighs in importance its interference with the presentation of certain evidence. He did not, however, feel that the Fifth Amendment was one of the privileges needing periodic examination with a view towards its repeal.[144] His decision in this case was not based upon any sentimental desire to "protect criminals" or prevent a "full judicial scrutiny"[145] of all the facts. He was motivated by respect for specific, unrepealed constitutional provisions. But in the final analysis, he was convinced that even if all the privileges and all the exclusionary rules (such as the hearsay rule) were abolished and the floodgates were opened to allow in more evidence, it would not make a particle of difference insofar as jury trials were concerned. For outspoken critic of the jury system that he was,[146] he was convinced that the juries would "hear more evidence which they will disregard."[147]

May a prosecutor at a trial make reference to the prior silence of a defendant, who had exercised his privilege against self-incrimination when he was a witness before an investigative grand jury, but who later testified at his trial? That was the issue in U.S. v. Grunewald et al.,[148] a prosecution for conspiracy of a tax-fixing ring. One of the defendants, Halperin, had originally been summoned before an investigative grand jury, whose questions he refused to answer. Subsequently, a regular grand jury indicted him.[149] On trial, during the cross-examination, the prosecutor was permitted to ask Halperin "whether he had invoked his constitutional privilege against self-incrimination before the Grand Jury in response to the same or similar questions in response to which he had testified fully on the trial."[150]

Writing the majority opinion affirming the conviction, Judge Medina relied on the Supreme Court case of *Raffel* v. *United*

*States*.[151] The trial judge had charged the jury that Halperin's prior silence was not to be deemed an implied admission of guilt, since it was an exercise of his privilege not to testify. He further charged that the jury could consider his prior silence only on the issue of the credibility of his present testimony. This meant that it could be used in a negative fashion only, to ascertain if the reason Halperin assigned for his prior silence discredited his present testimony. This was held a proper charge.

In his dissenting opinion, Judge Frank thought the case relied on by the majority was "wrong,"[152] and had in effect been overruled by the subsequent Supreme Court case of *Johnson* v. *United States*.[153] He felt it would require a feat in mental gymnastics for a jury to understand the trial judge's finespun distinction regarding the proper use of Halperin's prior silence. In his view it was unfair to submit to a jury in any fashion the question of the propriety of a defendant's prior exercise of his constitutional privilege against self-incrimination. The error of the prosecutor's question of Halperin could not be considered harmless for two reasons: first, the evidence against Halperin was not overwhelming, and he could reasonably have been acquitted by a jury, and second, an error involving a constitutional right never can be classified as "harmless."[154]

In a historical exposition of a criminal defendant's right of silence, Frank referred to the fact that at the time of the adoption of the Fifth Amendment, a defendant charged with a felony[155] was disqualified from testifying.[156] Accordingly, no inference of guilt could be drawn from his failure to testify. In 1878, Congress enacted a law conferring upon such a defendant the choice whether or not to testify.[157] Seemingly this was a beneficient measure according to an innocent man an opportunity to defend himself. But, noted Frank, this statute often coerces a defendant into abandoning his privilege not to testify and forces an innocent man, who does not make a good witness, to give testimony which, on cross-examination, may turn out to be damaging to his defense. He testifies out of fear that if he does not, a jury may infer guilt from his silence, despite admonitions by the court.[158] Applying this logic to this case, Frank commented: "For, if my colleagues' ruling stands, the accused, virtually coerced by the statutory option into testifying at his trial, will discover that, as an added result of so choosing, he must tell the jury that he had previously exercised the privilege as a witness before the Grand Jury."[159] And the rationale for silence by a witness before a grand jury is stronger than in open court. A grand jury proceeding, unlike a trial, is *ex parte*: a witness is not confronted with adverse witnesses, who thus cannot be cross-examined;[159a] he cannot object to the introduction of evidence; he cannot summon witnesses on his behalf; he cannot have counsel present in the grand jury room, nor is a judge present to make any rulings. In open court, cross-examination and judicially supervised proceedings "provide safeguards for the establishing of the whole, as against merely partial, truth."[160]

## On Trial by Jury

Judge Frank was an iconoclast of an institution which to many Americans has an aura of venerability. His critique of the jury system for civil cases, articulated both in his books and in his judicial opinions, was trenchant. He deemed it an anachronism.

The origin of the trial or petit jury is somewhat shrouded in mystery. It has been "variously attributed to a Scandinavian institution, to Alfred the Great and to a primitive mode of Anglo-Saxon trial known as compurgation."[161] Magna Carta makes no reference to trial by jury. The germ of the modern trial jury[162] would seem to lie in an institution introduced into England by the Normans under William the Conqueror after 1066, whereby at the King's pleasure "groups of distinterested neighbors were required to disclose under oath information that was used to establish royal rights"[163]—such as, information for the assessment of royal taxes and revenue, the conduct of suspected royal officers, or conspiracies against the king or the public peace. The utilization of the jury for the determination of private rights had to wait until the reign of Henry II (1154-1189). Until Henry II, the traditional modes of trial were: (1) compurgation —an oath by defendant's friends that he was an honorable man and thereby exonerating him; (2) various ordeals of torture which, if successfully endured by the defendant, were thought to have proved his nnocence; and (3) "trial by battle" introduced by the Normans, in which the contestant believed guilty

111

was either killed or he surrendered.[164] Henry II innovated a limited use for trial by jury: the determination of disputes involving land. Ultimately, by extension we arrive at the modern full-scale trials by jury. After Pope Innocent III (1198-1216) proscribed the participation of priests in trials by ordeal, they were shortly thereafter no longer used as a mode of trial. In 1219 King Henry III ordered that judgment by neighbors be substituted for trial by ordeal. By the end of the thirteenth century, the older modes of trial had been largely superseded.[165] Originally jurors had to come from the neighborhood of the litigated incident, and they arrived at verdicts, in both civil and criminal cases, on the basis of what they themselves knew or had heard. The use of eyewitnesses to give testimony before a jury which itself had no knowledge directly or indirectly of the facts was a gradual development. The principle that a verdict was to be reached solely on the evidence presented in court was not established until the end of the seventeenth century.[166]

The first statute providing for the right to trial by jury in criminal cases seems to have been the Bill of Rights of 1688.[167] In the colonial period of America, jury trials in both civil and criminal cases were in wide use. Many colonial constitutions guaranteed trial by jury. Colonial juries flouted many unpopular British laws.[168] The Constitution of the United States in Article III guaranteed federal jury trials in criminal cases only. Many of the state ratification conventions objected to the absence of a similar guarantee for civil cases. The result was the enactment of the Seventh Amendment in the Bill of Rights, preserving jury trials in federal courts for all suits at common law, where the "value in controversy" exceeded twenty dollars.[169] The Sixth Amendment requires jury trials in criminal cases with some safeguards in the conduct of the trial.

Frank wrote extensively in *Law and The Modern Mind* and in *Courts on Trial* in sharp criticism and severe indictment of the jury system in civil trials.[170] His reflections on juries were mordant. Thus: "A better system could scarcely be imagined for achieving uncertainty, capriciousness, lack of uniformity, disregard of former decisions—utter unpredictability."[171] Although the judge in his charge to the jury pontificates on the law governing the case—akin to a ritualistic incantation, reminiscent in part of primitive ritualism and "cabalistic formulas"[172]—, it is the jury which in actual fact decides the legal controversy and thus, for all practical purposes, the law. The rules in their recitation by the judge to the jury are certain, "pure and unsullied,"[173] but in practice they are honored in the breach by the jury.

Reference was made by Frank to the fact that some rules are excessively inflexible.[174] In addition, law, in order to cover a wide variety of situations, is ordinarily written in general terms and may not take account of a situation not "broadly typical." Frank noted the contention advanced by some writers in defense of the jury system that juries wisely nullify these general rules which often work injustice.[175] However, he deemed this defense a curious one. It elevates each jury to the rank of an "ephemeral legislature."[176] But he did not believe that juries acted in that sophisticated manner. Rather it was his belief that juries often do not understand the legal rules in the judge's charge and react emotionally to the case. "They do like an artful lawyer for the plaintiff, the poor widow, the brunette with the soulful eyes, and they do dislike the big corporation, the Italian with a thick foreign accent."[177] Juries capriciously nullify excellent as well as bad rules. He felt they were hopelessly incompetent as fact-finders. Although a great believer in the need for individualization of cases, it should be accomplished with candor —not in the arbitrary fashion of juries. Legal rules which work injustice should be made more flexible, but not through reliance upon juries.[178]

The view has often been expressed that juries represent the average conscience, the contemporary social sense of what is right.[179] A diversity of opinion by different juries on any issue, Frank pointed out, quickly dispels the validity of this argument. The capriciousness of juries makes them the worst enemies of our ideal of the "supremacy of law."[180] Juries wipe out the principle of "equality before the law" sought to be established by that ideal. "If anywhere we have a 'government of men,' in the worst sense of that phrase, it is in the operations of the jury system."[181]

Jury trials to Frank were a waste of time and money. Not only do juries not understand many points of law heard by them for the first time, but lawyers at times do not grasp all the "niceties" of the principles of law elaborately pronounced by the judge. Many cases tried for weeks are reversed by appellate courts because a judge included in his charge or omitted from it a phrase or a sentence meaningless to the jury.[182] Such a reversal results in a new trial "at which the judge will intone a more meticulously worded rule to another uncomprehending jury"[183] or in an unfair settlement by a litigant wearied by the experience and the expenses. The unintelligible words intoned by the judge "resemble the talismanic words of Word-Magic."[184]

Conceding that there was force to the argument that a jury is often sought as a refuge from a corrupt or political judge, Frank countered that this argument simply points to the pressing need for honest, competent trial judges.[185] The resort to juries was a feeble refuge in his opinion. Moreover, the law in many types of cases does not provide for a jury trial.[186]

Frank's opposition to the jury system was that of a crusader. But hit attitude was not unique and he cited a distinguished galaxy of men who had expressed opinions critical of the jury system.[187] Most of the trial judges whose abilities he respected, he claimed agreed with him that juries' verdicts were usually incorrect.[188] The presence of a jury in the courtroom, he contended, creates an atmosphere of melodrama and tension and prevents a calm, orderly and dispassionate progression in a trial, whose sole aim should be the realization of justice. The jury thus aids in keeping alive the "fight" theory of justice, of which he was critical. Since, as is well known, deep-rooted customs and habits become man's second nature, he posited the survival of the jury system as resting on the force of tradition which men come to regard as inherently right.[189]

Frank granted that the historic popularity of the jury system was deserved; it had served well in seventeenth century England as a check on royal judges of the Stuart kings and in eighteenth century America on judges controlled by a hostile British government.[190] Little wonder that both the federal constitution and the state constitutions embodied guarantees of trial by jury. The jury system had been "acclaimed as essential to individual liberty and democracy."[191] But, claimed Frank, it had outlived its usefulness. He limited his barbs to civil juries and advocated

114

the abolition of the jury system in civil lawsuits only. This would require a constitutional amendment. Despite Frank's limitation of his goal to civil juries, he nevertheless asked us to recall the innocent defendants listed in Borchard's book, *Convicting the Innocent,* who had been wrongly convicted by juries of various crimes. He felt that honest, competent judges would probably have done better.[192] If so, why did not Frank advocate the abolition of jury trials in criminal lawsuits as well—through constitutional amendment? The only answer he gave is to be found in a footnote to his dissenting opinion in *United States* v. *Antonelli.*[193] He said that it was an "awful responsibility" for a conscientious judge, rather than for a jury, to decide in a criminal case which witnesses told the truth and arrive at a judgment whether another human being is to be imprisoned or executed.[194]

The exclusion by Frank of criminal trials from his devastating critique of juries is indeed puzzling. Are juries in criminal trials endowed with any more wisdom than their brethren in civil trials? If they are as utterly incompetent as depicted by Frank, why entrust them with the fate of what is most sacred to man—his life and his liberty? His exclusion of criminal juries appears strange in light of his reference to Borchard's book.[195] Granted it is an "awful responsibility" for a judge to pass upon the innocence or guilt of a defendant and upon the nature of his sentence, can he for that reason abdicate his duty and render a defendant unsafe in the hands of incompetent jurors? Frank's inclusion and exclusion smacks of inconsistency.

The trenchant critique by Frank of the jury system was coupled with several suggested reforms, if the jury system is to be retained. One was the extended use of "fact" or "special" verdicts in lieu of "general" verdicts. A general verdict is the end product of a jury's deliberations. It announces: We find for the plaintiff or for the defendant. It does not disclose, however, whether the jury correctly applied the law, discarded it or failed to understand the law. The general verdict, coupled with the refusal by courts to inquire into the jury's method of arriving at its verdict, permits jurors' biases free play.[196] "For prejudice has been called the thirteenth juror."[197] Frank referred to instances where jurors have been known to flip coins or to average out arithmetically the amount of an award.[198] The general verdict, which Frank would replace, indiscriminately merges the law and the facts into a final decision. In the special verdict, which he favored, the jury answers specific question of fact submitted to it by the judge who then applies the appropriate law to the facts as found by the jury.[199] The jury is thus shorn of its power to ignore or to make the rules.[200] Frank also dealt with the "related device" of retaining the general verdict but in company with written answers to special interrogarories concerning specific facts, so as to furnish the judge with an analysis of the jury's reasoning in arriving at its verdict and to test the consistency of the general verdict in light of the written answers.

The special verdict is not a recent innovation. It was used centuries ago in England and at an early date was imported into this country.[201] It fell into disrepute by reason of the complicated manner of its use in many states, which included in its scope all evidentiary data introduced at the trial, regardless of their materiality. A few states seem to have avoided this complication. Since 1938 the use in civil cases of a streamlined form of special verdict or special interrogatories has been optional with federal courts, and it is optional in the courts of some states. However, the judges seldom use it. Frank felt that one of the other of these devices should be compulsory in "most" civil suits.[202]

Frank was aware that in a relatively simple case a jury, if it wishes, will be able to circumvent the law.[203] While a greater use of the special verdict would, in his opinion "slightly" reduce the inherent evils of the jury system, it could not eliminate them.[204] He was convinced that twelve inexperienced men, selected at random, never can be as competent as a judge "with a trained intuition."[205].

In a further analysis of the jury system, Frank distinguished between two types of rules which exclude evidence at a trial. There are exclusionary rules—such as those directed against evidence secured as a result of the rights against self-incrimination and unreasonable search and seizure—which are based upon "important reasons of public policy."[206] These have a constitutional basis. But there are exclusionary rules of another stripe, without constitutional provision—such as that against hearsay evidence—which, regardless of their genesis, have been perpetuated, in Frank's opinion, primarily because of the incompetence of jurors.[207] Conceding that hearsay should often be received with caution, he nevertheless believed that ninety percent of the evidence upon which business people and industrialists rely in their daily dealings is based upon "the equivalent of hearsay."[208] In addition, hearsay evidence is accepted by administrative agencies, juvenile courts and legislative committees. Yet because of a distrust of jurors that they will not be able to make due allowance for the character of hearsay as second-hand evidence, they usually do not learn of matters which would be helpful in establishing a more accurate picture of the facts. Consequently, if the jury system has to be retained, Frank advocated that at least exclusionary rules like the hearsay rule be abolished or modified so as to let more light in at a trial.[209] His exasperation with the jury system, however, was such that in *U.S. v. St. Pierre*,[210] previously discussed, Frank remarked that even if juries were allowed to hear more evidence, it would make no difference since the juries disregard the evidence.

Comments were made by Frank on a number of other suggested reforms to improve the jury system. Thus, he thought deserving of consideration Judge Galston's recommendation that a stenographic record be made of jury deliberations in order to ascertain if any impropriety entered into the verdict.[211] Endorsed as having some merit was a practice adopted in one California court of requiring prospective jurors to pass both a written and an oral test of jury aptitude. But even that scheme fell "short of the bull's eye." Disapproved as ineffective were suggestions for greater care in the selection of jurors who—after all, have no "special training"—, the distribution of brief handbooks to jurors detailing their duties, or short talks by judges to juries. He approved as more helpful a plan urged by Judges Galston and Clark whereby courses of instruction would be made compulsory in the public schools or in adult education classes on the "function of the jury and the nature of trial court fact-finding."[212] These courses would constitute "schools for jurors." How a course would remedy the basic difficulties he outlined was not elaborated upon.

117

As the upshot of the matter, after a consideration of the proposals which he felt would make a jury trial "less dangerous"[213] than at present, Frank maintained his verict that juryless trials were more desirable than jury trials, with the exception "perhaps" of criminal trials.[214] His conviction was firm that the administration of justice was better served by a trained and honest judge than by twelve inexperienced laymen, selected helter-skelter.[215]

In a bird's-eye view of the present status of the jury system, Frank demonstrated that excepting the United States, it had fallen into disfavor in this century. Several Swiss cantons abolished it; pre-Hitler Germany and France considerably limited its use. "Liberty-loving" Scotland has had a seesaw history with it: it virtually eliminated it in non-criminal cases in the sixteenth century, re-adopted in in 1815, and subsequently has almost dispensed with it. Even before World War II it was seldom used in civil suits in England and was abondoned in criminal prosecutions except for major crimes—and increasingly even there. "Surely that attitude in England, the birthplace of the modern jury, should give us pause."[216]

Though and advocate of jury abolition, Frank stated his obligation, as that of every judge, while the jury system prevailed and was guaranteed either by constitution or statute, to enforce punctiliously all the rules governing juries. A judge's private views become irrelevant on the bench. Thus, in *U.S.* v. *Farina*,[217] Frank dissented because he felt the trial judge's charge to the jury might have been misleading.[218] He dissented again in *U.S.* v. *Antonelli*[219] because he deemed some of the prosecutor's remarks to the jury in the course of his summation had been inflammatory.[220]

The battle surrounding trial by jury in civil actions still rages, and particularly in New York.[221] The current issue of heavily congested court calendars caused by jury trials, particularly in negligence cases, and the proposal consequently to abolish jury trials in negligence or in all civil actions, is often interlarded with a critique or a defense of juries. A recent article by a Lord Justice of Appeal of England, Sir William Diplock, has expressed the view that jury trials were inefficient, not even-handed, and that judges were better qualified than juries to pass on evidence.[222] A diametrically opposite view was expressed in another recent article to the effect that juries are closer to the mores of the people and can render fairer decisions than judges.[223] Of interest is also Justice Douglas' view set forth during his eulogy of Frank that imperfect as the jury system is, it is nevertheless the best system man has evolved for fact-finding.[224]

A number of empiric studies have been conducted on the utility of juries. Such studies are in consonance with the tenets of legal realism, which is opposed to lifeless abstractions in the law.[225] A rudimentary and unsuccessful beginning was made in 1952 through questionnaires forwarded to judges. They had been prepared by third year law students at Yale Law School at the suggestion of Lecturer Jerome Frank.[226] In Frank's introduction to an article written by two of these students, he made a telling confession regarding the weakness of his critique of the jury system. He conceded the difficulty in proving that "more than anything else in the judicial system the jury, I believe, blocks the road to bettering the ways of finding the facts and applying to those facts the correct legal rules."[227]

More recently, Professor Harry Kalven, Jr., Director of the University of Chicago Jury Project, reported the results of an empiric study it had undertaken.[228] Six hundred judges, canvassed throughout the United States, supplied information about eight thousand jury trials over which they had presided. They had been asked to keep a tally sheet signaling their agreement or disagreement with the jury verdicts in the cases on which they were to submit their reports. Agreement was reported in 80% of the criminal cases tried. In the 20% of the cases in which disagreement was reported, the jury generally was more lenient to the defendants. "Massive agreement" was also found between jury and judge in the personal injury case statistics which were compiled separately. This led Professor Kalven to conclude that "the armchair indictment of the jury must go awry somewhere . . . its intellectual incompetence has been vastly exaggerated . . ."[229] And he asked the same pointed question we have posed: "If the jury operates in a civil case, as its critics say, can we justify retaining such an archaic and incompetent institution in criminal cases?"[230] It would seem that Frank's indictment of the jury system went awry in its severity.[231]

## Poverty and Equal Justice

One opinion by Judge Frank in the area of growing judicial concern for the legal rights of indigent defendants places him in the tradition of America's liberal judges. In *U.S.* v. *Johnson*[232] a convicted defendant moved for leave to appeal *in forma pauperis*[233] and for the assignment of appeal counsel. On his trial in a federal court he had had a court-appointed lawyer.

One year before this decision, the Supreme Court by a closely divided court had ruled in *Griffin* v. *Illinois*[234] that a state must in consonance with the due process and equal protection clauses of the Fourteenth Amendment provide a method in all felony cases whereby some sort of transcript of the trial proceedings will be supplied to a destitute defendant in order to have adequate appellate review. Only an indigent defendant sentenced to death was provided by Illinois with a free transcript, while indigent defendants on all other charges had to purchase their transcripts. The Supreme Court equated discrimination on account of poverty with that on account of religion, race or color. The dispositive question in *U.S.* v. *Johnson*[232] was whether this doctrine was applicable to the federal government as well under the due process clause of the Fifth Amendment.

Judge Hincks, writing the opinion of the court, interpreted the *Griffin* case restrictively, positing certain distinguishing features which he claimed made it inapplicable to the facts of this case. One feature was the existence of a federal statute providing for certification by the trial judge that the appeal was not taken in good faith, in an effort to obviate the clogging of appellate court calendars with "frivolous appeals."[235] This statute, he asserted, did not constitute a violation of the due process clause of the Fifth Amendment.[236]

Judge Hincks denied appellant's application on the ground that under federal law if the trial judge certifies that the appeal is not taken in good faith—as was certified in this case—, a defendant cannot appeal *in forma pauperis*. In the absence of a showing that the trial judge had not acted in good faith, he ruled that the trial judge's determination was final. The avowed purpose of the federal code was to obviate the clogging of appellate court calendars with "frivolous appeals."

In a vigorous dissent, Judge Frank stated that there was "no unqualified finality" to a trial judge's bad faith certificate, as is obvious from a showing that he had acted in bad faith. Manifestly, it would be very difficult for many defendants, without some expert assistance, to present a basis for their claim that the trial judge had erred. A rich man can afford to hire counsel to prosecute an appeal, whether or not it is frivolous. Is a poor man to be discriminated against because of his poverty? Frank asserted that a literal interpretation of the code would prevent the appellate courts from ascertaining whether or not the appeal is frivolous. Such discrimination against the poor, Frank contended, is a violation of due process of law and possibly of the Sixth Amendment guarantee of assistance by counsel. Since convictions are sometimes reversed on appeal, how can one place blanket faith in a trial judge's certificate of "bad faith"? If the government were to deny justice to the poor in these circumstances by failing to supply them the funds needed, it would represent "an upper-court bracket privilege."[237] The poor man would be punished for the "crime" of poverty.

> Surely, even if but one out of a hundred attempted appeals by indigents has merit, justice compels the conclusion that that appeal should be heard . . . But I, for one, cannot sleep well if I think that, due to any judicial decisions in which I join, innocent destitute men may be behind bars solely because it will cost the government something to have their appeals considered . . .[238]

A lawyer should accordingly be appointed by the court to help him procure a statement of the trial proceedings.[239] The court-appointed counsel would procure a statement of the trial proceedings based on the judge's notes, or a transcript of the trial record of which a judge may avail himself free of charge, or trial counsel's recollection to serve as the equivalent of a stenographic transcript of the record for the purposes of this preliminary motion. Then the court would be in a position to decide whether to grant Johnson's motion, entailing his right to a transcript of the trial record gratis.[240]

Judge Frank's concern for the plight of indigent defendants

121

had been made manifest by him on several occasions prior to this case—in articles and in his volume, *Courts on Trial.*[241] With justice he could write in this case: "For thirteen years I have been calling attention to the problem and urging a solution."[242] His plea in this case did not go unheeded by the Supreme Court.[240]

## Aliens

In the course of his judicial career, the rights of aliens engaged Judge Frank's attention in a score of cases. Many were of a routine nature. Three of his decisions merit study as links in the formation of a composite Frank gestalt.

Until 1882 our government pursued an open-door policy, admitting to its hospitable shores immigrants of a world-wide complexion. This policy reflected the need in the first century of the republic's existence to help poulate an underdeveloped country.[243] In 1882 Congress enacted its first racial exclusion statute—the Chinese Exclusion Act—barring Chinese laborers from our shores for a period of ten years.[244] Other Chinese Exclusion Acts followed.[245] As an incident of sovereignty Congress may exclude any type of aliens it wishes to. The ground for non-racial exclusion of aliens was steadily expanded since 1875 to include "health, morality, economic conditions, criminality, illiteracy, political views and the like ..."[246]

A number of basic concepts have crystallized in the constitutional law applicable to the alien. The plenary power of Congress, in the exercise of the rights of a sovereign nation, summarily to *exclude* aliens knocking on our doors has never been questioned by the Supreme Court.[247] The alien at our gates claiming exemption under an exclusionary act has no constitutional claim to a court review of an administrative decision—that of the Immigration Authority—barring him pursuant to Congressional authority.[248] "Whatever the procedure authorized by Congress is, it is due process as far as an alien denied entry is concerned."[249] Congress may even exclude an alien by granting the Attorney General authority to bar him without a hearing, solely on his determination that it would be prejudicial to the interests of the United States to admit him.[250]

Similarly, the plenary power of Congress to *deport* aliens

resident in our country was sustained by a majority of the Supreme Court in *Fong Yue Ting* v. *United States*,[251] but not without eloquent voices of dissent. Although not derogating from the plenary power of Congress to deport resident aliens, a number of cases decided subsequent to the *Fong Yue Ting* case have held that the resident alien has some constitutional claim for a court review of administrative action on his contention that he is not within the purview of the congressional act.[252] Whittling down somewhat the rigor of the *Fong Yue* opinion, these cases have held that while constitutionally the resident alien is not entitled to a judicial trial (unless provided by Congress as a favor), he is nevertheless entitled to a fair administrative hearing. When fairly conducted, such administrative hearingh are conclusive. The gauge of fairness is the furnishing of reasonable notice to the resident alien to provide for the hearing and a final order supported by "some" evidence.[253] If there is some evidence sustaining the administrative conclusion, it is not reviewable, though the court passing upon it feels it would have reached a different determination. This provides for a modicum of constitutional protection, but it is a far cry from the constitutional protection accorded citizens— such as proof of guilt beyond a reasonable doubt in criminal trials, trial by jury and illegality of ex post facto laws.[254] The alien in a deportaion proceeding, as in an exclusion proceeding, is not entitled to all the constitutional rights with which the Bill of Rights cloaks a defendant in a criminal proceeding. However, the resident alien is entitled to procedural due process, to which the alien knocking on our doors is not entitled, for the obvious reason that as to him the proceedings are far more drastic.[255]

There is a third situation: A person halted at our gates and sought to be excluded or a resident sought to be deported as an alien, but each of whom claims to be an American citizen— in the former instance, either a native American returning from a visit to a foreign country (often, but not necessarily, China) or one born on foreign soil to American citizens. Is he entitled to a judicial trial or will an administrative hearing suffice? The Supreme Court has made a distinction depending on whether the person is knocking at our gates seeking admission or is a resident who faces deportation. In the former case, an administrative hearing suffices; in the latter, a judicial trial is required.

The issue of a claimed citizenship was first squarely met in *U.S. v. Ju Toy*.[256] Detained upon arrival in the United States, Ju Toy claimed he was a native American returning from a temporary visit to China. The Immigration authorities sought to deport him to China under the Act of 1902 excluding all Chinese laborers. Upon appeal to the Supreme Court, Justice Holmes, speaking for a majority of the court, held that regardless of the claim of citizenship, due process does not require a judicial trial. He ruled that, under the act, the administrative decision was final.

Some modification of this harsh doctrine was effected in *Quon Quon Poy v. Johnson*.[257] Arriving in the United States, a fifteen-year-old Chinese boy claimed to be the foreign-born son of a native American—whose citizenship was conceded—and thus an American citizen. Upon appeal to the Supreme Court, the administrative finding was held to be final, provided there had been a fair hearing, such as disclosed in the record of this case. This case modified the *Ju Toy* case[258] to this extent only: Although it denies a petitioner in an exclusionary proceeding the right to a judicial trial on the issue of American citizenship, it does require the administrative hearing to be a fair hearing, and it is subject to judicial review for an abuse of discretion.

A different rule for a resident claiming citizenship during a deportation proceeding had been enunciated by the Supreme Court in *Ng Fung Ho v. White*,[259] decided before the *Quon Quon Poy* case.[260] Such a petitioner was held entitled to a judicial trial. Upon arrival in the United States, the petitioners in this case claimed that they were foreign-born sons of native citizens. After extensive hearings, they were ordered admitted as citizens. They had resided here fifteen and six months respectively before the Secretary of Labor arrested them on a warrant. Justice Brandeis held that a claim of citizenship by a legal resident in a deportation proceeding creates a jurisdictional issue—i.e. a challenge to the jurisdiction of an administrative agency. The guarantee of due process in the Fifth Amendment against the deprivation of life, liberty or property requires a judicial trial in this situation.

A situation involving a claim of citizenship and conceded past residence in the United States by one sought to be excluded as an alien was presented to Judge Frank in *U.S. ex rel. Madeiros v. Watkins*.[261] Madeiros arrived in the United States in 1945. Until 1940 for a period in excess of twenty years he had continuously resided in the United States. During that period he was convicted of crimes, of unlawful entry and robbery. Following his release from jail in 1939, and after the authorities became convinced that he had been born in Bermuda, a warrant for his deportation to Bermuda was issued on the ground that an alien convicted of a felony was deportable. In 1940 he voluntarily left the United States. After capture by the Germans as a crew member on a British ship, he was repatriated in 1945 to the United States. Contesting the immigration authorities' effort to exclude him, he claimed that he could establish American citizenship through birth in San Francisco on March 16, 1902.

Speaking for the majority of the court, Judge Clark held that since this was an exclusion case, albeit by one claiming citizenship, Madeiros was entitled only to a fair administrative hearing.[262] The fact of past residence in the United States was held immaterial, and the Court found on the record that Madeiros had been given a fair hearing.

In a vigorous dissent, Judge Frank felt that Madeiros was entitled to a judicial trial on the issue of citizenship. Although Madeiros may not have possessed a savory character, Frank was concerned that whenever a citizen leaves the country, upon his return the immigration authorities may challenge his claim to citizenship. Frank claimed shock by the majority contention that on these facts an administrative order would be final, provided only the evidence before the administrative body on the issue of his citizenship was conflicting and the hearing was fair.[263] There should be no jurisdictional distinction when there is a claim of citizenship, in Frank's view, between deportation cases and those exclusion cases in which the petitioner had in the past resided in the United States. He derided a distinction based on soulless categories of "exclusion" or "deportation."[264]

But what was Frank to do with the Supreme Court cases cited by the majority as binding? This case was identical in type with *U.S.* v. *Ju Troy*,[265] in which the administrative officer's determination was held final. However, Frank regarded the *Ju Toy* case as considerably weakened by *Ng Fung Ho* v. *White*.[266] Although in that case which held a judicial trial mandatory, the petitioners were residents of the United States at the inception of the action, the court had placed emphasis not only on the fact of residence but also on the "substantial evidentiary support of the claimed citizenship as requiring judicial determination."[296] Frank would apply the *ratio decidendi* of that case to one of past residence in the United States when the petitioner offers to submit substantial proof of citizenship, though disputed (and though, of course, he may ultimately not succeed in his quest). In effect Frank was asking a logical question: What difference does it make when petitioner's residence occurred—whether at the inception of the proceedings or sometime in the past, if he offers to submit substantial proof of citizenship? But since the *Ng Fung Ho* case did revolve about resident petitioners, Frank placed his greatest support on *Quon Quon Poy* v. *Johnson*.[268] Although in that case the petitioner had claimed citizenship through birth to an American citizen abroad, the court ruled that a judicial trial was not mandatory when petitioner "had *never* resided in the United States."[269] From the wording of this statement Frank deduced that the "critical factor" was not residence at the inception of the administrative proceedings, but residence at any time in the past.[270] From the usage of the word "never", Frank concluded that the moment of undisputed residence—whether present or past—was immaterial. On this interpretation, the court was not simply stating as a fact in the case without any judicial overtones that petitioner "had never resided in the United States," but it was a fact laden with judicial significance, constituting part of the *ratio decidendi* of the case.

Judge Frank's dialectical skill demonstrated in his analysis of the Supreme Court decisions may profitably be read in conjunction with our discussion of the judicial process.[271] Undoubtedly, he had first arrived at a conclusion regarding a just decision on the facts. Then started the process of fitting the Supreme Court decisions into the mould of his thought, if this could be done. In deportation cases the Supreme Court had ruled that a claim of citizenship coupled with a showing that the claim is not frivolous entitles the petitioner to a judicial trial. Frank could not believe that in an exclusion proceeding a similar claim coupled with a similar showing that the claim is not frivolous should lead to a different result based on the fortuitous circumstance that petitioner's residence in the United States happened to have been in the past rather than in the present.[272]

A principle of an entirely different complexion, one regarding the propriety of the discretion exercised by an administrative agency in applying an act to suspend deportation, confronted Judge Frank in *U.S. ex rel. Accardi* v. *Shaughnessy.*[273] Accardi's action was brought pursuant to the Immigration Act of 1917, which authorized the Attorney General to suspend the deportation of an alien who had proven good moral character for the preceding five years, if he finds that the deportation would work a severe economic hardship upon the alien's spouse, parent or child who is a citizen or a legally resident alien.

Accardi, an alien of Italian citizenship, illegally entered the United States in 1932 at the age of 21. In 1940 he married a legally resident alien. At the time of this appeal they were the parents of a two-year old American-born child. At a deportation hearing commenced in 1947, Accardi was found deportable because of his illegal entry into the United States. His application for suspension was denied after an administrative hearing. The Board of Immigration Appeals, which was appointed by the Attorney General under his regulations and served at his pleasure, affirmed the denial.

The charge of illegal entry was not disputed by Accardi. His contention was that his name had been included in a secret list of undesirable aliens prepared by the Attorney General, who had decided on their expulsion from the United States.[274] He charged that the list had been circulated among all the Attorney General's subordinates in the Department of Justice, including the Board of Immigration Appeals. He challenged the proceedings on the ground that the Board had failed to exercise its discretion in a legal manner because of its consideration of confidential information outside the record—the list of undesirable aliens—and on the further ground that the Attorney General had prejudged he case.[275] The Board denied this charge in an opposing affidavit.

Writing for the majority of the Court, Judge Swan held that the record of the Board of Immigration Appeals hearing amply supported its discretionary denial of deportation suspension. The Board's opinion had also included Accardi's criminal record and "his tenuously explained affluence."[276]

In his dissenting opinion, Judge Frank wrote that the district court judge was in error when he refused to hear testimony intended to show that the hearing at the Board of Immigration Appeals was a "farce". What if facts could be offered that the Board knew of the promulgated list of its superior, the Attorney General, was influenced by it and consequently could not exercise its independent judgment as required by the regulation?[277] Courts cannot review administrative discretion if it has been exercised, but they can compel its exercise by one vested with discretion but who fails to exercise it. It would be "sheer ritualism" to confer immunity on an official record simply because facts of illegality do not appear on it. "That way lies tyranny."[278]

May an alien withdraw his plea of guilty to a felony entered on the erroneous assurance of his lawyer that no deportation proceedings could result from his plea? This issue was raised in *U.S. v. Parrino*.[279] When deportation proceedings nevertheless were started against him, Parrino sought to withdraw his plea of guilty.

Originally Parrino had been convicted of kidnapping after a jury trial and sentenced to a term of twenty-five years. The government then brought deportation proceedings against him. As an alien sentenced to a term of a year or more for a crime involving moral turpitude, he was deportable. However, on appeal to the Circuit Court of Appeals, the conviction was reversed and the case was remanded to the district court for a new trial. There was a sharp issue of law whether the statute of limitations had run against Parrino before he was arrested, and thus whether he could be prosecuted. That issue was referred back to the trial court.[280]

Upon the reversal of the conviction, the government had to abandon its deportation proceedings. Thereafter, Parrino pled guilty to a lesser charge of conspiracy to kidnap, and he was sentenced to a term of two years. At the time of his plea Parrino relied upon the categorical but erroneous assurance by his lawyer, a former Commissioner of Immigration, that no deportation order could be founded upon a plea of guilty, as distinguished from a conviction after trial. To Parrino's surprise, the abandoned deportation proceedings were reinstated. He then moved to set aside the plea of guilty. The question before the court was whether it would constitute "manifest injustice" within the meaning of Rule 32(d) of the federal Rules of Criminal Procedure to hold Parrino to his plea. The District Court denied his application.

Speaking for the majority of the court, affirming the lower court decision, Judge Hincks held that since the erroneous information had emanated from Parrino's lawyer, and not from an official source, Parrino had no recourse to this relief. Further, a failure to anticipate a "collateral consequence" of a plea of guilty is not a ground for the withdrawal of a plea of guilty.

In a spirited dissent, Judge Frank pointed to the practical import of the court's decision: two years in jail and the rest of Parrino's life in banishment or exile.[281] Deportation, though not considered a criminal punishment, may be far more drastic in effect than a prison sentence. Frank argued that Parrino's lawyer had had ample time in which to examine the statute and the clear Supreme Court decision in point before he made his "magnificent" mistake. Though he was a former Commissioner of Immigration, the lawyer was "hopelessly incompetent" and "egregiously derelict"[282] to the grave prejudice of Parrino. Of what utility, asked Frank, is the constitutional requirement that a defendant have counsel before entering a plea of guilty if his counsel is incompetent?

Frank would accord Parrino the chance of proving his innocense, if he could, at a retrial.[282a] Sometimes a judge regrettably must administer "injustice according to law" when a statute clearly is indifferent to justice. This should be regarded as exceptional and deplorable. The normal role of the judge is to administer justice.[283] "When, therefore, a Rule tells us in the plainest words to avoid manifest injustice, I believe we should eagerly embrace the opportunity, not extend earlier decisions to escape it."[284]

From Frank's judicial opinions in the area of civil liberties there emerges an image of a judge with an intense conscience. He was ever mindful that a democratic society in pursuing the self-protective aim of convicting the guilty should not in so doing sacrifice the equally important goal of not endangering the innocent. It is better that a culprit escape than that an innocent man be made to suffer. The guarantees of the Bill of Rights embodied for Frank a policy more important than that of crime detection and punishment. A civilized, democratic society must pursue its goals in a civilized fashion. He bade us reflect on the brutal consequences of the totalitarians' alleged efficiency in pursuing suspected criminals.

Judge Frank's fervor for the inviolability of the Fifth Amendment privilege against self-incrimination found eloquent expression in *U. S. v. Grunewald*.[148]

The foes of the privilege—beginning with Bentham—have mistakenly viewed it solely from a procedural angle; so considered, it seems to them an unjustifiable obstacle to judicial ascertainment of the truth. They ignore the fact that the privilege—like the constitutional barrier to unreasonable searches, or the client's privilege against disclosure of his confidential disclosures to his lawyer—has, *inter alia,* an important 'substantive' right of privacy, a right to a private enclave where he may lead a private life. That right is the hallmark of our democracy. The totalitarian regimes reject that right. They regard privacy as an offense against the state. Their goal is utter depersonalization. They seek to convert all that is private into the totally public, to wipe out all unique 'private worlds', leaving a 'public world' only, a la Orwell's terrifying book "1984". They boast of the resultant greater efficiency in obtaining all the evidence in criminal prosecutions. We should know by now that their vaunted efficiency too often yields unjust, cruel decisions, based upon unreliable evidence procured at the sacrifice of privacy. We should beware of moving in the direction of totalitarian methods, as we will do if we eviscerate any of the great constitutional privileges.[148a]

To Frank the administration of justice was the great aim of law—more important than that of maintaining order. The administration of justice should not be a mere ritual. His heart pulsated in harmony with the plight of all, regardless of their station in life. "The test of the moral quality of a civilization" lies in "its treatment of the weak and powerless."[285] It is true that at times Frank's zeal transported him away from the world of reality into an abstract realm of justice. But those moments were infrequent.

Frank urged a number of reforms. In his deeply ingrained vein of fact skepticism he called for the abolition of capital punishment to avoid the horrible and irreparable crime of executing an innocent man wrongly convicted. And though he advocated the abolition of the venerable jury system in civil cases, his respect for existing law is manifest in his strong statements that as long as the jury system prevailed, he would enforce punctiliously all rules and regulations governing it.

Jerome Frank was a man of compassion, of deep humane feelings. He would not permit an individual to be trampled upon by the juggernaut of society or by a false appraisal of the superior merits of societal order to individual liberty. The bedrock of Frank's judicial opinions in this area was his belief in the inherent dignity of all men, regardless of their station in life. A case before him was not just another case, to be dispatched with expedition, but a unique experience. As Justice Douglas remarked: "An insistence on fair procedure is the great truth by which Jerome Frank lived. Concern for it made him a truly great jurist of our time."[286] His colleague, Judge Charles E. Clark, who had often differed with him, said that Frank's greatest single contribution was "his passion for the defense of civil liberties."[287] He added that Frank was singular among judges in carefully considering and answering each communication, and there were many, from prison inmates sentenced in his court.[288]

Judge Frank had an instinctive feeling for the humanity in all men. From this followed his concern for the innocent wrongly convicted. This was his lifelong passion. His words bear the sincere stamp of a deeply etched empathy for those suffering injustice at the hands of the law.

131

# Chapter IV

## FREEDOM OF SPEECH AND PRESS

In an area critical to the lifeblood of a democracy—freedom of speech and of the press—Judge Frank wrote but three opinions: one involving the distribution on public streets of commercial handbills, and two on the issue of pornography, including the landmark case of *U.S. v. Roth*.[1]

### *Free Speech and the Distribution of Handbills*

The first case to engage Judge Frank's attention in this sphere involved the validity of a municipal prohibition against the distribution of commercial handbills on streets and other public places. *Chrestensen* v. *Valentine*[2] is tangential to the mainstream of cases involving the issue of the freedom to distribute on the public streets handbills of a religious, social or ideological content. An analysis of Frank's remarks in this case, representing a byway in the handbill cases, is revealing of his position on freedom of speech in the more crucial areas.

On a number of occasions the issue before the Supreme Court concerned the freedom to distribute on the public streets handbills directed to the communication of ideas. Whenever the issue raised by a handbill case was one of the communication of ideas, divorced from the "taint" of commercial advertising, the Supreme Court was quick to strike down as invalid under the First and the Fourteenth Amendments of the Constitution[3] any statute interfering with the untrammeled right of its distribution. Thus, in *Lovell* v. *Griffin*[4] the Court struck down as unconstitutional an ordinance requiring permission from the City Manager of Griffin, Georgia, to distribute pamphlets on the public streets. Jehovah's Witnesses had been arrested for distributing without permission pamphlets propagandizing their religion. The Court applied to these facts a previous opinion that freedom of speech and of the press which are protected by the First Amendment from Congressional infringement are among the fundamental liberties protected by the due process clause of the Fourteenth Amendment from state invasion.[5]

Likewise, in *Schneider* v. *State*[6] the Court invalidated a similar invasion of fundamental liberties. Involved were four simultaneous appeals from convictions in different states for the distribution on the public streets of handbills of the Friends of the Lincoln Brigade during the Spanish Civil War, labor picketing handbills, protest handbills on unemployment insurance, and Jehovah's Witnesses' handbills in house-to-house canvassing. Three of the ordinances involved sought to justify the prohibition imposed on the distribution of handbills by a need to keep the streets clean. In the *Jehovah's Witnesses* case the ordinance required the investigation, photographing and fingerprinting of all applicants for house-to-house canvassing in order to prevent fraudulent solicitations for money or an invasion of homes with criminal design. All four ordinances were held unconstitutional. The Court ruled that so important an interest as the dissemination of information could not be sacrificed because of the public interest in keeping the streets clean.[7] And conceding in the Jehovah's Witnesses' appeal that certain restrictions may be imposed in the public interest, such as reasonable hours for house canvassing, the Court prohibited prior licensing of the distributors as an invasion of constitutional liberty.[8]

Whether, however, there is a similar constitutional right to distribute on the public streets commercial handbills was the issue which confronted Judge Frank in *Chrestensen* v. *Valentine*.[9] The challenged section of the New York City Sanitary Code prohibiting such distribution, however, excluded from its ambit "the lawful distribution of anything other than commercial and business advertising matter."

The facts in the case, briefly, were these: In 1940 an application by Chrestensen, a Florida citizen and owner of a former U.S. Navy submarine, to dock it off Battery Park was refused by the New York City authorities. Subsequently, the New York State authorities granted him permission to dock the submarine at a state-owned pier in the East River. He then printed a draft of a handbill setting forth information about the submarine's location and its features, and fixing a popular admission price. The Police Commissioner denied his request for permission

133

to distribute this frankly commercial handbill on the streets, and advised him that a handbill could be legally distributed on the streets only if it contained non-commercial information or advertised a public protest. A revised handbill which Chrestensen then prepared had printing on both sides: on one side he advertised the submarine's location and solicited public patronage; on the reverse side appeared a vigorous protest against the "dictatorial" denial by the Police Department of his application to tie up at the city docks. The police authorities informed Chrestensen that distribution of a handbill bearing his protest would not be permissible unless the commercial advertising was removed from its text.

A district court granted Chrestensen's petition to enjoin the Police Commissioner from enforcing the municipal regulation against commercial advertising on the streets. In the Circuit Court of Appeals, the majority, speaking through Judge Clark, held it unconstitutional to prohibit a combined advertising and protest not shown to be a mere subterfuge—which it felt was the situation in this case.[10] Clark argued that no distinction could be drawn in law between group protest for religious or political principles and individual protest for business injuries. He added that an absolute prohibition even of exclusively commercial handbills from distribution on the streets was of doubtful constitutionality, but that a decision on that issue was not necessary on the facts of this case.

In his dissenting opinion, Frank argued that the protection of free speech under the First Amendment does not include a right to distribute commercial advertising on the public streets. He referred to Chrestensen's original draft which evinced an exclusively commercial motivation. There was a continuing presumption of this commercial purpose, and the second draft struck him as a subterfuge for circumventing the law after the Police Commissioner's rejection of the first draft. There was no inherent, organic relation between the two sides of the handbill to justify a claim of their inseparability.[11] "The two circulars are not Siamese twins."[12] A fission of the commercial and protest parts of the handbill could clearly be effectuated, since they were not inextricably interwoven one with the other. The fusion of the two parts, easily divisible without injury to either, was the "arbitrary choice" of Chrestensen.[13] It was clear to Frank that at least the dominant motivation for the handbill was a commercial one.

Clark had attacked as an incalculable calculus Frank's requirement for a motivation of at least a dominant protest in advertising in order to constitute protected free speech. He claimed that this called not only for an objective weighing of the relative quantum of advertising material and protest material, but also for a subjective assessment on the part of police officials of the non-commercial motives.[14] But Frank was not disturbed by the perennial and occasionally difficult question of where to draw the line—in this case, between a dominant and an auxiliary purpose. "Where to draw such lines 'is the question in pretty much everything worth arguing in the law,' Mr. Justice Holmes often noted."[15]

Rejecting the majority view that an absolute prohibition even of purely commercial expression in the marketplace was unconstitutional, Frank applied the thesis of the peaceful co-existence of legal principles in a world of compromise.[16] As Frank read the majority opinion, it had in effect advocated a victory for an absolute constitutional right of free expression in the public market, whether for the dissemination of ideas or the distribution of commercial advertising, in the battle between free expression and the police power which a city seeks to exercise for the group welfare. But in Frank's view, at times one principle yields, at other times the other. There are no absolutes. The role of a judge is to effect compromises, reconciliations of divergent principles.[17] And so in the instance of a clash between the city's inherent police power to prevent street cluttering and the constitutional principle against the abridgment of free speech, if the police power is sought to prohibit the distribution of "free speech" handbills, it must compromise and yield. In that case, though the city cannot prevent the distribution of "free speech" handbills, its police power, however, is not completely destroyed but is simply "chastened," since the city can still arrest and punish those who litter the streets. The police power in this instance is punitive and "after the fact" rather than preventive.[18] But the situation is different with respect to commercial handbills. Frank's thesis was that the historical background of free speech neither compels nor suggests its application to the distribution of commercial handbills.[19] The fight for free speech waged by Thomas Paine and John Milton did not include the right to "peddle" commercial advertising.[20] Businessmen can utilize means other than street distribution, such as newspaper advertising, to reach the public. It follows that there is no paramount constitutional principle in the case of commercial handbills before which the police power must yield. The police power need not be reduced in potency as in the case of "free speech" handbills "from prevention to punishment after the fact when pieces of paper, devised for business purposes, may litter its streets to the injury of public health or safety."[21]

Frank was on sound ground when he objected to the "thingifying" or reification of the words "free speech" and "free expression," which makes one forget the vital ideas behind these expressions—" 'the defense of liberty' and the functioning of 'the processes of popular rule' "[22] for which they stand. To "thingify"[23] them would mean to infuse them with a life of their own, independent of their historic past and historic delimitations.

## Judge Frank and Free Speech as a "Near Absolute"

In the course of his discussion in the *Chrestensen* case Frank set forth his stand on free speech. He deemed it

> . . . one of our fundamental liberties, singularly well protected; it therefore comes as *near* to creating *an absolute principle* as any fostered by our Constitution . . . For it is our challenge to dictatorship and its vaunted efficiency . . .
>
> But even the principle of free speech is not an absolute; it has its limitations. Thus one may commit a crime, or be guilty of an actionable wrong, if he wantonly shouts "fire" in a crowded theater; or utters certain kinds of untruths—or, in some circumstances, even truths.[24]

Frank's preceding reference to free speech as coming "near to creating an absolute principle as any fostered by our Constitution" was succinct, and no definitive gloss can be based on it

136

in an effort to ascertain his position on free speech. However, it is suggestive of the following analysis.

Three views can be discerned among the Supreme Court justices on the issue of the scope of freedom of speech under the First Amendment: (1) the "absolute"; (2) the "preferred status"; and (3) the "judicial restraint" views. Justices Black and Douglas have constituted the so-called absolute school of interpretation of the First Amendment. They have consistently maintained that the First Amendment is absolute and unequivocal on its face: "Congress shall make *no* law . . . abridging the freedom of speech, or of the press ..."[25] Thus, they have denied the validity of any abridgment of free speech, including seditious libel[26] even when maliciously uttered, and obscenity statutes,[27] unless the speech has become "brigaded"[28] with a action. But even Douglas excludes from the protection of the First Amendment the following two limitations listed by Frank as not protected by the First Amendment: (1) the wanton shouting of "fire" in a crowded theater,[29] on the theory that ti has transcended speech and become "brigaded" with action; (2) actions in libel and slander.[29a] Black goes even further than Douglas since he excludes the first of these limitations from the coverage of the First Amendment but includes the second in its coverage.[30] Though subsequently Frank showed his agreement with this school of thought in the area of obscenity,[31] he wrote no opinion or expressed any view in the area of seditious libel. It is therefore difficult to ascertain whether Frank fully aligned himself with this school.

The "preferred status" school does not go as far as the "absolute" school in interpreting the First Amendment. It excludes from First Amendment protection seditious libel maliciously uttered and obscenity. Frank cited in support of his "near" absolute position a famous footnote in *U.S.* v. *Carolene Products Co.*,[32] in which Chief Justice Stone had given expression to a preferred status doctrine for the Bill of Rights. This view was also championed by Justices Murphy and Rutledge.[33] The champions of the "absolute" school adopt the philosophy of this school, but, as indicated, go beyond it. That Frank at the very least adopted the philosophy of the preferred status school there can be no doubt. To understand fully the "preferred status" doctrine,

137

it is necessary to contrast it with the doctrine of "judicial self-restraint," of which the eloquent spokesman was Justice Frankfurter.

The justices in general[34] are today agreed that a statute enacted in the social or economic sphere dealing with problems such as housing, wages, hours of work, and regulation of public utilities enjoys a presumption of constitutionality unless it is shown that there is no reasonable or rational basis to believe that it could accomplish a valid legislative objective.[35] The Court will find no violation of "due process" under the Fifth or Fourteenth Amendments—applicable against the federal and state governments respectively—unless it can be shown that the legislature acted without reason, in a capricious manner. This it is difficult to do and so the invalidation of such legislation as unconstitutional is rare. "Due process of law" is a very vague standard and the absence of specifics in its phraseology gives the legislature, as representative of the popular will, broad latitude to enact experimental social and economic legislation. The Court will not interfere with the policy expressed by Congress or the state legislatures in their innovations, although it may disagree with them, so long as no constitutional principle is violated.

The parting of the ways between the proponents of the "preferred status" and of the "judicial self-restraint" doctrines does not arise in the above area, but with respect to the validity of statutes in the area of freedom of speech. The proponents of the judicial self-restraint doctrine argue that cases involving free speech are no exception to the rule that courts are not super-legislatures.[36] They contend that policy making in any area, including free speech, is not within the province of the courts.[37] The judiciary must, according to this school, balance against First Amendment rights the fact that Congress deems it necessary in times of stress to grant "government the power to do what it thinks necessary to protect itself, regardless of the rights of individuals."[38] There need be no proof of the imminence of any danger to the country.[39] Accordingly, these proponents indulge in the same presumption of validity of statutes in the area of free speech as in every other species of legislation, provided that there is a "rational basis" for it.

138

On the other hand, the proponents of the "preferred status" doctrine argue that legislation, federal or state, abridging the specific right of freedom of speech or of the press "cannot be sustained by any presumption of validity but is presumptively unconstitutional, throwing on its proponents the burden of justifying the abridgment, not doubtfully or remotely, but by demonstration of clear and present public danger involving the greatest abuses."[40] First Amendment freedoms may not be subordinated to the views of Congress that the dissemination of "dangerous" doctrines requires the exercise of the community's police power, without further proof to the satisfaction of the Court that an immediate danger threatens.[41] According to this position, the existence of a "rational basis" for adopting a restriction in the economic or social sphere of legislation will render it constitutional, whereas the mere existence of a "rational basis" for adopting a legislative restriction of free speech is insufficient to sustain the constitutionality of the statute under the specific and unqualified phraseology of the First Amendment or under the "due process" clause of the Fourteenth Amendment when it sheds its vagueness and is made specific in free speech cases through an incorporation of the First Amendment privileges into its concept of "liberty."[42] In the case of free speech, there must be much more than the existence of a "rational basis" for adopting a restriction—there must be proof of a grave and immediate danger.[43] It was the philosophy of this school that Frank at the very least adopted.

Shortly before his death, Frank wrote an article[44] in which he briefly discussed Learned Hand's opinion in the famous Communist conspiracy case, *Dennis* v. *United States*.[45] Hand had upheld the constitutionality of the Smith Act and sustained the defendants' convictions for wilfully conspiring to "teach and advocate the overthrow and destruction" of the government. Frank analyzed Hand's decision as resulting from a view that the First Amendment was intended as a mere "admonition of moderation" to Congress rather than enforceable constitutional law.[46] It was with some diffidence that Frank presented his own viewpoint, so profound was his respect for the wisdom and erudition of the man he deemed the wisest of America's judges. "So I warn you not to make up your minds without much reflection."[47] Frank proceeded to demonstrate Hand's subsequent contradictory approach in his volume, *The Spirit of Liberty*. Hand referred to the accepted fact that the Constitution would not have been ratified but for a promise of prompt amendment to include a Bill of Rights and had it not been believed that all the provisions of a Bill of Rights would be "mandates" against which " 'no statute will prevail.' "[48] Frank's query therefore is a most sequential one: "Why, then, one may ask, should not the courts respect that history[49] which discloses that the First Amendment was intended to be a legal "mandate," and not merely a "moral adjuration?"[50]

## Freedom of Speech and Obscenity

The common law of obscenity[51] prevailed down to Lord Campbell's Act of 1857, the first statute on obscenity in England.[52] In the United States the first statute on obscenity was passed by Congress in 1873.[53]

The leading case on the subject, followed both in England and the United States down to relatively recent times, was *Queen* v. *Hicklin*.[54] The Hicklin rule sanctioned a grossly restrictive test of obscenity for the normal adult population of the community by using as its yardstick the lewd influence a book or any portion of it may exert upon the moronic, the infantile and the adolescent.[55] Then in 1913, Judge Learned Hand, although feeling constrained to follow the Hicklin rule, criticized it roundly[56] in *U.S.* v. *Kennerley*.[57] But not until the 1930's did the American courts generally begin to reject this rule.[58] In 1933, in *U.S.* v. *One Book Called "Ulysses,"*[59] Judge Woolsey reversed a customs ban on James Joyce's famous stream-of-consciousness novel, and in a memorable opinion explicitly and forcefully repudiated the Hicklin rule. He stated that the law should be concerned only with the "person with average sex instincts" and the test of whether an author's intent is sensualistic or realistic in his portrayals is to be culled not by isolating obscene passages in the book but from a reading of the entire book.[60] In affirming the decision on appeal,[61] Judge Augustus N. Hand applied as the proper test that of the "dominant effect" of the book.[62]

These decisions did not, however, deal with the question whether obscenity, no matter how defined, is utterance within the protection of the First Amendment. Dicta in various Supreme Court decisions held that it was not.[63] In 1949, in a very comprehensive opinion, which Frank was later to acknowledge for the influence it had exerted upon his thinking in this area,[64] Judge Bok in *Commonwealth* v. *Gordon*[65] squarely decided an obscene literature case in the light of the First Amendment. Repudiating the Hicklin rule, he applied the preferred status doctrine for free speech to include obscenity.[66] It is only the presence of "a clear and present danger" which removes literature from the protection of the First Amendment. Such danger is possible only in connection with literature which is "dirt for dirt's sake"[67] and which "can be traced to actual criminal behavior either actual or demonstrably imminent."[68]

The first case in which the Supreme Court decided the issue whether obscenity is utterance which is protected by the First Amendment was *Roth* v. *United States*.[69] Judge Frank had written an opinion in the lower court decision of this case. This was the second of the two obscenity opinions written by Frank, both of which focused on Samuel Roth, a book and magazine publisher.

May a Postmaster General issue an order following an administrative hearing[70] to exclude from the mails a book on the ground that it is obscene under the postal laws? In the first Roth case, *Roth* v. *Goldman*[71], Roth sought to enjoin the Postmaster General from executing such an order against his book, *Magic Tales from the Czechs*. The District Court had sustained the action of the Postmaster.

In a brief Per Curiam opinion the Circuit Court of Appeals affirmed the lower court decision. Judge Frank wrote a lengthy concurring opinion. This was his first obscenity case and he decided to yield to "the more experienced judgment" of his colleagues. "But I do so with puzzlement and with the hope that the Supreme Court will review our decision, thus dissipating the fogs which surround the subject."[72] Despite his nominal concurrence, he expressed strong and unequivocal disagreement with his colleagues.

Frank was opposed to bestowing such immense administra-

141

tive authority and virtual literary dictatorship on one fallible man. Literary censorship not only bans finished products; it also cramps the imagination of authors who must write with one eye upon the Postmaster. Such suppression is compatible only with the foreign ideologies of "Hitlers, Czars and Commissars."[73] Art must remain free and unregimented. A democracy must cherish in practice the maxim "de gustibus non est disputandum" in order to prevent the blight of insidiously expanding anti-democratic practices.

Congressional authorization to an official largely to suppress a book by banning it from the mails might, in Frank's view, run counter to the First Amendment. A different question might arise if this were an instance of criminal punishment after the publication of a book rather than an administrative restraint prior to publication.[74] From his reading of the Supreme Court decisions on the preferred status doctrine for the First Amendment, Frank was of the opinion that a justification for suppression could result only from proof of a "clear and present danger" that a book "would bring about grave 'substantive evils' adversely affecting the public interest."[75] No such proof was adduced upon the administrative hearing in this case.[76] No sane man will argue that it is socially dangerous to arouse normal sexual desires, and there never has been "convincing proof" that reading obscene publications produces undesirable and harmful sexual conduct.[77] In addition, a suppression statute in order to be constitutional should have a sufficiently precise standard of obscenity providing that a book will in all probability have socially harmful effects upon average readers before it can be banned.[78]

Frank conceded that because of the "primitive state of our psychological knowledge"[79] it is perhaps impossible to obtain "convincing proof" of anti-social effects of literature, and for that reason the lower courts may have instead adopted as their standard of judgment for obscenity the current mores, the general community attitude of what is socially right and wrong.[80] But, countered Frank, the Postmaster in this case made no express finding on the current public atitude towards books like Roth's. Furthermore, assuming that he had, how would he have gauged the average American opinion? If the matter were entrusted to a jury, it too might not represent the "average" community views. And how does a judge take judicial notice of the contemporary mores in passing upon the Postmaster General's "guess"? Judges know best the views of lawyers, who are known to tell at their gatherings such tales as appear in Roth's book. Have they become depraved as a result? Are lawyers less susceptible to depravity than the rest of the population, an elite group worthy of a guardian status in a Platonic state? "The truth of the matter is that we do not know with anything that approximates reliability, the 'average' American public opinion on the subject of obscenity. Perhaps we never will have such knowledge . . . ."[81] Frank placed no stock in securing enlightenment from the "social sciences" in the present state of knowledge of community opinion. The social sciences, useful as they may be for some purposes, are "further away from the 'scientific' than were alchemy or astrology."[82]

Frank failed to find any more obscenity in Roth's book than in Balzac's *Droll Stories,* freely accessible in any public library or bookstore.[83] And if the degree of artistry of a book were to become the criterion for obscenity, is the Postmaster General to become a literary critic? And are the reviewing judges to become "super-critics"?

> Jurisprudence would merge with aesthetics. Authors and publishers would consult the legal digests for legal-artistic precedents. We might some day have a legal restatement of the Canons of Literary Taste. I cannot believe Congress had anything so grotesque in mind.[84]

The subsequent constitutional history of postal censorship indicates that Frank's position may yet be vindicated.[85] It has been gaining strength[86] and may yet emerge victorious. If there has to be any censorship, it were better left to the courts than to the Post Office authorities.[87] In the light of Frank's sound strictures of the Court's opinion, it is difficult to see why he was so diffident as to concur with his colleagues rather than candidly file a dissenting opinion.

The case of *Roth* v. *Goldman* was but a prelude to an even more significant opinion by Judge Frank in the landmark case of *U.S.* v. *Roth.*[88] Is obscenity an utterance which is protected by the First Amendment? *U.S.* v. *Roth* was the first case reaching the Supreme Court to decide that issue. The statute involved in the two Roth cases was identical, but the action instituted by the authorities differed. While the former case was an appeal from postal administrative action, the latter case was an appeal from a conviction by a federal jury for mailing "obscene" books and magazines.

In his short opinion affirming the conviction, Judge Clark referred to the fact that although the Supreme Court had never explicitly decided the constitutional issue, it has nonetheless affirmed a number of convictions resulting from prosecutions under the federal obscenity statute.

In a lengthy opinion Judge Frank concurred with the Court's majority solely because the lower court's charge to the jury was correct under the existing law.[89] But his concurrence was with very considerable reservations and the expressed hope that the Supreme Court would reverse the decision. As a judge of an inferior court, Frank felt constrained to affirm Roth's conviction by dicta[90] in Supreme Court opinions that obscenity was not protected speech under the First Amendment[91] but he stated that none of those dicta had "carefully canvassed the problem in light of the Supreme Court's interpretation of the First Amendment, especially as expressed by the Court in recent years."[92] Listing case after case, Frank demonstrated that all the Supreme Court cases in which convictions had been obtained under the federal obscenity statute never dealt with the constitutional issue in the light of the First Amendment.[93]

It was the preferred status doctrine for the First Amendment that was the source of Frank's doubt about the validity of the obscenity statute. Under that doctrine there is no presumption of constitutionality for a statute which curbs free expression.[94] As Frank read the Supreme Court opinions "uttered within the past twenty-five years," in order for the statute to be valid the government must show that it comes within either one of two exceptions to the preferred status doctrine: (1) a statute striking at so-called "fighting words" which are likely to incite to a breach of the peace,[95] or (2) a statute striking at words which "with sufficient probability tend either to the overthrow of the government by illegal means or to some other overt anti-social

144

conduct."[96] The danger or evil at which the obscenity statute intended to strike must be "clear (i.e., identifiable) and substantial."[97] And since the obscenity statute struck only at words, it is unconstitutional, unless it can be proven that words "tend, with a fairly high degree of probability, to incite to overt conduct which is obviously harmful."[98]

Frank was fearful of the path which leads from mild governamental censorship to governmental regulation of political and religious reading.[99] Censorship of publications which may arouse sexual thoughts, regardless of any nexus with anti-social behavior, may lead to censorship of political and religious publications, regardless of any nexus with "probable dangerous deeds."[100] Logically extended, censorship could ultimately enmesh reports and photographs, appearing in the daily press, which stimulate sexual thoughts. Frank expressed opposition to any "paternalistic guardianship by government of the thoughts of grown-up citizens."[101] This enervates their spirit and leads to a servile adoption of the attitude, "Papa knows best."[102]

In his opinion Judge Clark had made reference to the "strongly held view" that obscenity contributes to juvenile delinquency.[103] Judge Frank was highly dubious that a nexus can at the present time be demonstrated between children reading obscene literature and anti-social behavior. However, he had no doubt that if such a nexus could be proven, a statute drawn to prohibit the distribution of obscene publications to young people specifically would be constitutional. But he added that this was not an issue in this case since the statute under attack is not restricted to children.[104]

Frank acknowledged that since writing his opinion in the first Roth case his views on the subject had matured. At first, he felt that a purely punitive obscenity statute was constitutional, though he doubted that prior administrative restraint of allegedly obscene literature was constitutional.[105] But after reading Judge Bok's opinion in *Commonwealth* v. *Gordon*,[106] he was goaded into further reflection, leading to the skeptical views embodied in this opinion.[107]

Frank asked whether the obscenity statute is valid because there was a common law of obscenity at the time the First Amendment was adopted. In reply to the contention raised that it is, he referred to the fact of "scant recognition"[108] of a crime of obscenity prior to the First Amendment. But what was of crucial importance to him was that the First Amendment was a deliberate departure by the framers of the Constitution from the English common law on freedom of speech and press.[109] Thus, Madison wrote that " 'the state of the press . . . under the common law, cannot . . . be the standard of its freedom in the United States.' "[110] Frank was in accord with Justice Black that " '[N]o purpose in ratifying the Bill of Rights was clearer than that of securing for the people of the United States much greater freedom of religion, expression, assembly and petition than the people of Great Britain had ever enjoyed . . .' "[111]

The main critique leveled at the obscenity statute by Frank was the fact that the courts define it to authorize punishment, not for overt action, but for inducing "mere thoughts, and feelings, or desires."[112] No thoroughgoing studies have been made on probable anti-social, harmful sexual conduct resultant from reading or seeing "obscene" publications.[113] The extant studies conclude that the causes of sexual depravity are so manifold and complex that one cannot assign to "obscenity" a "ponderable causal factor in sexually deviant adult behavior,"[114] with any degree of assurance. The indications are to the contrary.

Scientific studies were cited by Frank which demonstrate that juvenile delinquents, the group most frequently sought to be protected by those advocating the suppression of "obscene" literature, read much less than normal children. Delinquents seek adventure, not inactive entertainment.[115] The Harvard authorities on crime and juvenile delinquency, Professors Sheldon and Eleanor Glueck, published a ten-year study on the causes of juvenile delinquency. Ninety contributing factors were studied. Nowhere in the study is the sort of reading engaged in by delinquents considered, for the simple reason that, as their findings point out, delinquents read very little.[116] Similar results were arrived at in the surveys by Dr. Marie Jahoda and her associates.[117] And we are confronted with the same lack of proof regarding the evil effects of reading "obscene" literature upon the conduct of adults. The available data are wholly insufficient to justify a conclusion that the obscenity statute "is within the narrow exceptions to the scope of the First Amendment."[118]

Arguing that the currently accepted test of obscenity is irreconcilable with the immunity from prosecution enjoyed by the classics, Frank cited Aristophanes' *Lysistrata*, Chaucer's *Canterbury Tales*, Rabelais' *Gargantua and Pantagruel*, Shakespeare's *Venus and Adonis*, Fielding's *Tom Jones* and Balzac's *Droll Stories*.[119] The greater artistry of these "obscene" writings should produce a greater influence upon readers than writings lacking artistry. Classics are not excluded as an exception in the postal obscenity statute. The fact, however, that judges have felt the necessity to except classics from its purview has obviated an absurdity in its application, and points to its illogicality and to the fact that it is in violation of the First Amendment.

If the definition of the "obscene" were of a limited and rather clear scope, the fear of prosecution and punishment might act as a deterrent for "restricted sorts of publications only."[120] But by reason of the exceedingly vague judicial definition of the term, a prosecutor who threatens suit against a publisher if he mails almost any book treating sex in an unconventional manner, virtually exercises a prior restraint upon him, since he will fear involvement in a criminal action, its attendant publicity and possible punishment.[121] Such capricious, non-judicial threats strikingly flout the First Amendment.

And so the "exquisite vagueness of the word 'obscenity'"[122] was an additional ground for the doubts entertained by Frank about the constitutionality of the obscenity statute. Frank felt that the standard of the "average conscience of the time" which courts today generally accept is a strikingly vague guide to judges and jurors and to those engaged in the mailing of books.[123] A statistician would not base a conclusion on community attitudes regarding obscenity drawn from so unfair a sample as a jury of twelve persons selected at random.[124] A particular jury may be representative of the moral sentiments of another age.[125] Frank assured us, without proof however, that the "reasonable man" standard in criminal negligence prosecutions and tort suits does not in the remotest manner approach the looseness of the obscenity standard.[126] It is excessively vague to serve as a basis for an exception to the First Amendment, even if it could be considered definite were freedom of speech not involved.[127]

147

In a challenge to Plato's concept of censorious guardians, Frank attributed to adult citizens in a democracy the need to be "self-guardians" and to "act as their own fathers and thus become self-dependent."[128] This in general was the burden of his volume, *Law and the Modern Mind*. The First Amendment ensures that the minority view of today may become the majority view of tomorrow.[129] No fallible men, be they prosecutors, judges or jurors, should be converted into what John Stuart Mill called a "moral police" and become the despotic arbiters of our literature.[130]

The lengthy Appendix to this landmark case represents one of Judge Frank's most noteworthy contributions to legal decision writing. Thurman Arnold referred to it as "[T]he best example of Judge Frank's method of supporting his conclusions of law by research into relevant social, scientific, psychological and economic information . . ."[131] In a surpassing panegyric Arnold claimed that there were "no opinions like it in American case law."[132] He added: "If a real union between the law and social science is at all possible, the method of Judge Frank, illustrated by the Roth case, points the way. His success in making the fusion may be his most enduring monument."[133]

Justice Douglas was also lavish in his praise of the Appendix.

> Legal precedents, sociology, juvenile delinquency, history, arts and literature, the First Amendment, the Great Books—all are discussed in a fascinating analysis of an ancient and perplexing "problem" . . . One can search the reports and not find a more interesting and profound canvass of an important legal problem than this one in obscenity . . . It will, I think, remain a classic.[134]

The constitutional development in obscenity for a number of years after the *Roth* case had taken a direction which vindicated Frank's position—in fact, though not in theory, since the Supreme Court in *Roth* held that obscenity is not protected speech under the First Amendment.[135] However, this development has not been uniform and two very recent 5-4 and 5-3 decisions by the Supreme Court making a determination that the literature involved was obscene point to a slight tightening of the reins.[136] The decisions are too recent to be able to predict any long-range position of the Court. Even if these latest decisions indicate a new trend, as well they may, the ramparts of censorship have already been too widely breached by the Court for it ever to become to any appreciable degree the Board of Supercensors feared by Judge Frank and Justice Black. The new trend, if such it be, is in a restricted portion of the broad spectrum of censorship, namely, commercial exploitation and pandering.[136]

In the area of free speech, Frank's expression of views was forthright and virile. Whether or not one is in accord with him, his was a voice calling for further social study and enlightenment on the effects of literature alleged to be obscene. He sought to break down the barriers of censorship. As such, he was in the vanguard of America's most liberal tradition. But Frank was no dogmatic libertarian, as is evidenced by his attempted exclusion of the distribution on the public streets of commercial handbills from the orbit of protection by the First Amendment.[137]

From our study this fact emerges: In the composite picture of the judicial voices which in the twentieth century have been raised in defense of the age-old battle for freedom of utterance and of the press, the voice of Judge Frank was not a "still small voice."

# Chapter V

# JUSTICE IS AS JUSTICE DOES

A New Deal functionary, a jurist on the bench of an outstanding appellate federal court, a legal philosopher and prolific author, Jerome Frank was one of the most colorful personalities of the New Deal era. He served as general counsel of the Agricultural Adjustment Administration and of the Federal Surplus Relief Corporation. While with the former agency he had evinced a deep concern for the underdog—the sharecropper—and this led to his cashiering. He then became special counsel to the Reconstruction Finance Corporation. Shortly thereafter he helped the Public Works Administration prepare and win its case against the Alabama Power Company. Before ascending the bench of the Circuit Court of Appeals he had served as Chairman of the Securities Exchange Commission. He wrote—and it may truly be said that his life was dedicated to the belief—that in America we can create "a unique civilization—an economic-political democracy every citizen of which will have a full life."[1]

Frank was an articulate spokesman for the constructive skeptical approach to man's all-encompassing problems—not only in the law, but in all the domains of thought. "We must put question marks alongside many of our inherited legal dogmas, since they are dangerously out of line with social facts . . ."[2] His skepticism entailed constant vigilance—an unceasing and unflagging interest in pitting legal formulations against their performance and their sufficiency. He opposed an investigation on all fronts at once.[3] But while some legal formulations are being investigated, others will temporarily be treated as fixed—those which he denominated as "temporary absolutes."[4]

The chief criticism levelled at Frank was that he ventured into the realm of psychoanalysis in which he was professionally inexpert and without the "necessary tools for an evaluation of the kind of legal 'behavior' he examines."[5] Frank was in the avant-garde of the psychological wing of American legal realism.[6]

There were different psychological approaches within this wing, such as Lasswell's use of the free-fantasy method, Frank's use of modern child psychology, and the use of behavioristic psychology by Oliphant, Schroeder and Malan.[7] Not all of these tools were scientific; some were tendentious. Granted that the shock Frank engendered in American jurisprudence was needed, his manner lacked the precision of a scientific approach. In fighting the myth of legal certainty, he created another myth—his notion of the law as a subconscious father-substitute, a replacement for the forfeited omnipotence of the father in the psyche of the child maturing out of infancy. Nevertheless, one should be able to distinguish the grain from the chaff, and disregarding Frank's unproven psychological theory, recognize the merits of his onslaught on legal fundamentalism. In essence, divorced of his unproven psychological theory, it was the skeptical approach that was Frank's answer to the "basic myth" of legal certainty.

Frank's efforts to arrive at a psychoanalysis of the law arose at a time when psychoanalysis was at the peak of its popularity in the United States.[8] What can be said of an interdisciplinary effort between psychoanalysis and the law and more generally, psychology and the law? Despite Frank's abortive effort in wedding psychoanalysis and the law insofar as an explanation for the myth of legal certainty is concerned—and we know of no reference to this effort in the professional psychoanalytic literature—, it is a non sequitur to deduce that this interdisciplinary labor has not borne fruit in other directions. Artificial boundary-lines between disciplines can often be transcended to their mutual profit. Thus, "[W]hen the Gluecks use psychological techniques in criminology, or courts call upon competent psychiatric experts in the treatment of certain types of criminal behavior, this is a far different and more expert use of psychological tools than is Jerome Frank's exposure of the myth of legal certainty . . ."[9] This interdisciplinary effort has also borne fruit in Frank's general psychological approach to the law, which, stripped of its mythological creation, has distinct merit. His analysis of the decisional process on a psychological basis was a necessary corrective to the false picture often painted of the law as a strictly logical process. And to touch upon one fragment of his suggestions, the writer's own observation of judicial behavior over the years leads him to agree with Frank upon the need for a psychoanalysis or its equivalent for judges—not as an elixir, but as a mollifying force for the dictatorial or erratic behavior of *some* members of the judiciary who are complex-ridden. The reach of this interdisciplinary effort may have greater extension and greater effect in the years ahead. Frank will be remembered as one of its pioneers.

Frank, however, may be charged with a degree of hyperbole in his views on the judicial process. He exaggerated in *Law and The Modern Mind* the extent of uncertainty in the legal rules. He seemed later to have realized this.[10] And while he performed a salutary service in dethroning logic from its supremacy in the legal process, he carried his militancy too far. His reformer's zeal to establish a more wholesome balance did not require that he utilize hyperbole to the extent he did. Later in *Courts on Trial* he exaggerated the extent of uncertainty in the facts. And while he rendered a beneficial service in pointing out the many elements of uncertainty which permeate fact determination, there too his zeal transported him beyond bounds. His skepticism seemed at times almost boundless. His reformer's zeal did not require the degree of magnification which he attributed to fact uncertainty.

While Frank rightly stressed the importance of the fact-finding process which has little to do with the formulation of legal principles, he was fully aware of the important role played by the ideal element—theoretical formulations of justice and legal principles—in the development of the law.[11] But he over-drew his early picture of the "completely adult judge" who "unfettered by paragraphs and precedents, finds justice through a clear and cool perception and valuation of the social issues at stake"[12]—a picture which has echoes of Plato's conception of the philosopher-king. Frank's original thesis in which he used psychology to demolish the myth of legal certainty at times gave the appearance of approximating the European school of *Freirechtslehre*,[13] which practically denied the existence of logic in the judicial process. On the other hand, to the credit of the realists in general and Frank in particular is their advocacy of the utilization of the social sciences in integration with the law. Realism has advocated and sought to have law avail itself of the use of statistics, economics, criminology, psychology, etc. in an effort to base law on scientific knowledge and experiment rather than on a fallacious logic.[14]

It is important to note that legal realism has made no claim that it is an exclusive jurisprudential school. Its validity rests on its supplementary role. In the everyday administration of justice, most legal matters—*quantitatively*—are of a routine nature, and analytical jurisprudence has its validity in this sphere.[15] But analytical methods prove unable to meet an impressive number of legal situations *qualitatively*.[16] It is there that legal realism has sought to rationalize the law and fill the gap by the use of scientific methods. The guidance for any legal system must stem from social ideals and the ideal element in the law. Legal realism has had its detractors who erroneously claimed that it was possessed of no ideal element.[17] It has also had its moderate defenders who asserted that in the course of time it came to admit that the search for justice was the paramount concern of the law.[18] Be that as it may, the record seems clear that regardless what may be the case with other realists, in the case of Frank a concern for justice was his paramount ideal and his guiding star at all times.[19]

It may truly be said that the legal realists involved the most creative minds in jurisprudence in a dynamic discussion of the quality of our laws and legal institutions, and of the need for reforms.[20] In a deserved tribute to a group of men who at times have been considerably maligned, Professor Patterson wrote that he had known nearly all of those in his list of legal realists, which includes Frank, and he could say

that he has not known any group of men who were more earnestly concerned than they were for the discovery of the true and the good and for the development of means of promoting ultimately the welfare of their fellowmen. The realists were (are) not cynical. The realists were seeking primarily to discover or invent the methods of a sociology of law. In these respects their aims and evaluations were not very different from those of Pound's sociological jurisprudence.[21]

In summation, what have the legal realists, of whom Jerome Frank was a leading proponent, and what has Jerome Frank in particular achieved? Frank has been referred to as "probably the foremost figure among the American legal realists and certainly one of the great legal thinkers of the present century."[22] Frank, and the other legal realists, were iconoclasts in revolt against the rigidities in our legal system resulting from the enshrinement of analytical positivism, a mechanical jurisprudence.[23] They represented the yeast in the sociological school of jurisprudence. Without the greater zeal and zest displayed by the legal realists in expanding the domains of sociological jurisprudence in dramatic form, the staid sociological jurisprudents probably would not have succeeded as rapidly and as effectively as they did.[24]

The defeat of the conservative, anti-New Deal majority on the Old Court under Roosevelt has been attributed to the legal realists.[25] Indeed, it has been said that this represented "the apogee of the legal realists' achievmnts."[26] This defeat, however, cannot be attributed directly to legal realism, except in the sense that legal realism was part and parcel of the intellectual turmoil of the period. The general economic and social turmoil brought about its defeat. Frank himself attributed the defeat to the ultimate influence of Holmes, Brandeis, Stone and Professor Thayer of Harvard Law School, and to the immediate influence of F.D.R.'s court fight.[27] He claimed that his attack on fatherly authority in *Law and The Modern Mind* came close to the view that the Supreme Court justices should not have a role as the infallible guardians of the social and economic values under which America should mould its destiny.[28] The moulding force should rather be the will of the people as expressed by its chosen representatives. Certainly, the views which began to prevail in the Supreme Court after Roosevelt's threat to pack it were in accord with the views of the legal realists and of sociological jurisprudents in general. The reconstituted Court sustained the New Deal legislation, refusing to read into the Constitution economic views of its own. It rejected the "positivist conception of the decision-making process,"[29] such as had been formulated by Justice Roberts in *U.S.* v. *Butler*: "[T]he judicial branch of the Government has only one duty—

lay the article of the Constitution which is invoked beside the statute which is challenged and to decide whether the latter squares with the former . . ."[30] This was an instance of the old "phonograph theory" of the law,[31] and was conceptualism at its worst. Legal realism had fought against such a restricted view of the judicial function. The repudiation of a spurious logic by the Supreme Court in effect represented a victory for legal realism.

Legal realism sought not only to expose a mechanical jurisprudence, but also to test pragmatically the functioning of the judicial machinery and seek means of ameliorating it. That has always been the function of legal reform. Despite extreme theoretical formulations on the part of some legal realists, essentially these realists were sociological jurisprudents, kinsmen in spirit of Pound and Cardozo.

Although the main exponents of legal realism, including Jerome Frank, have passed away, their influence has widely permeated many spheres of judicial thinking. They introduced a dynamic approach to law. The pendulum in the Supreme Court has swung to an ever-increasing degree in a constitutional direction favoring the civil liberties of the individual—revence for the individual, the leitmotif of Frank's approach to the law. Frank felt strongly that "we dare not overlook the microcosm, the more minute factors that loom large in the lives of individual men."[32] The legal realists, and particularly Frank, constituted one of the several constructive forces functioning simultaneously to widen the horizons of constitutional protection for the weak and humble. Frank polestar, his motive power, was an overwhelming concern with and passion for JUSTICE. "Thanks to avoidable court-room errors, innocent men are convicted of crimes; and every week, for similar reasons, someone loses his life's savings, his livelihood, his job. Most of such injustices stem not from lack of justice in the legal rules but from mistakes in fact-finding. And a high percentage of these mistakes derive from needless defects in the court-house methods of getting at the facts."[33] In addition, Frank championed the inclusion of social studies as an integral part of the law school curriculum. Yale Law School, as well as other law schools, has broadened its curriculum to embrace a host of technically non-legal subjects, including policy-making in the world community.[34] And Frank's advocacy of an interne plan for law schools still has current relevance.[35]

The continuance of the label legal realism is of no importance. What is of importance is that, so long as man remains fallible and his institutions fallible, legal realism in some form— whether by that name or by some other label or by no label at all—will from time to time perform its task of a sustained quest for greater justice. In so doing, it will accept sound insights from any of the jurisprudential schools or any of the social arts in solving problems as they arise. Its own contribution, in the main, will be the application of a constructive skepticism, with equal emphasis on the component elements of the phrase.[36]

The question of the efficiency of the law courts, of the judges and of the legal machinery in general will always be with us, and it will always be welcome for a "prophet" to arise and point to shortcomings as he sees them and to propose reforms. New York State, for example, has recently effected wholesale revision of its penal laws, and it has a enacted a law ablishing capital punishment, excepting in two instances.[37] As the leading exponent of fact-uncertainty Frank had advocated abolition of capital punishment.[38] The point is not whether Frank was correct on a particular issue, suggestion or proposed reform. It is rather that his reformer's zeal was a welcome antidote to the complacency which so often lays hold of so many of the leaders of legal thought. The desideratum is that a voice such as that of Frank's should not remain a "voice crying in the wilderness."

It has been pointed out that in "the past twenty years or so, the stress in the American literature about law has been on . . . the quest for standards and values in the progress of guiding the evolution of 'the law that is' into the law we think it ought to become."[39] Rostow singles out particularly as contributors to this development Felix Cohen,[40] F. S. C. Northrop, Messrs. Lasswell and McDougal, Henry Hart, Friedrich Kessler, Jerome Hall, Lon Fuller and Edmond Cahn[41]. And he concludes that "[T]heir work has helped to correct and offset the relative neglect of the problem of values which characterized the more positivistic outlook of the earlier legal realists."[42] Such quests for standards and values are, indeed, desirable and necessary. Men—including judges—need standards and criteria to guide them. But it is important to note that these quests for standards and values do not present us with absolutes as solutions to legal problems, nor could it be desirable that they do so and thereby foreclose future growth. Any insights which these thinkers manifest should be utilized by all workers in the vineyard of jurisprudence. That most legal realists did not concern themselves with normative theories and that some even looked askance at the pursuit[43] may be leveled as a long-range criticism of the realists. But their accomplishments far outweighed any justifiable impugning of the movement. And certainly with respect to Frank, stress was always placed by him upon the need for legal theory.[44]

The work of the so-called "rule skeptics" among the legal realists in their efforts to elaborate a science of prediction of legal decisions has been taken over by the judicial behavioralists in the past decade.[45] And in the last two decades normative jurisprudence has sprung into an ascendancy among legal thinkers.[46] The recrudescence of the latter arose after legal realism had performed its salutary function and the need for a systematic attack upon and pruning of the law was no longer among the felt necessities of the time.

Jerome Frank was a kaleidoscopic personality, but his greatest contribution, according to some admirers as well as critics, has been that of fact-skepticism as related to the fact-finding process, but even more so in its ecumenical proportions. Frank had stated in an article that fact-skepticism

> should, among other things, persuade us to make humane changes in the administration of criminal justice, such as abolition of the death sentence and increased stress on the "individualization" of punishment. Moreover, fact-skepticism transcends the legal realm. It raises, for instance, a serious question about the worth of much history-writing, with its cock-sureness as to the "facts" of history, whether of the distant or very recent past.[47]

It has been stated that the main value of *Courts On Trial* transcends its proposals for court reforms and it should be read as "a challenge to reconsider many established social policies in

157

the critical light of fact-skepticism."[48] It calls, for example, for a reconsideration of the death penalty, and if courts cannot be so sure of the facts of a case, should they continue to treat the slightest degree of contributory negligence in negligence cases as a complete defense to an action and dismiss, as the New York courts do, "a pedestrian's *entire* claim for injury in an automobile negligence case because it finds he was contributorily negligent, though in a much smaller degree than the driver? Fact-skepticism refutes the certitude behind harsh rules like this one."[49] It calls for a re-examination in the criminal law of the rationale of deterrence usually posited as a basic ground for punishment of criminals.[50] Though with some hyperbole, Professor Cahn felt the concept was epoch-making because of its universal and illuminating applicability in all spheres of thought —law, the social sciences, religion, philosophy and international relations.[51] And although a number of thinkers had recognized and utilized it, it was Cahn's contention that Frank alone had presented it systematically and in universal terms.[52]

It was in the juristic thought of Aristotle that fact-skepticism found close affinity.[53] Aristotle had urged the need for individualization of cases through equity because of their infinite divergences from patterns, and the constant need for adjustment of general mechanical rules to particular situations.[54] To Frank's delight, these chameleon-like particulars had been called by William James "wild facts," that is, facts which do not fit into any neat logical compartment, and "which furnish so much of the spirited element in our existence and which our logical propositions and scientific laws simply fail to net."[55]

Life to Frank was a challenging experience because it represented the challenge of the unknown, the possible, the changing, the chancy, the contingent. It was the challenge of an open and expanding world. In his search for meaning in life, Frank was beyond a peradventure of doubt a "liberal." It is true that he felt the term "liberal" was too vague and that a better word should be coined.[56] Lacking a better word, to him the main difference between a "liberal" and a "radical" was this: The liberal lives in a world of reality; the radical in an ivory tower. The liberal is pragmatically compromising and as a consequence achieves solutions; the radical is uncompromising and as a consequence lacks achievement. Compromise may be denounced by those on the extreme right and on the extreme left. But the word "compromise" is just another instance of an "anesthetizing ambiguous word."[57] "All compromises are not evil or foolish. Life is full of compromises . . Civilization is built on mutual yieldings and concessions. There are good and bad compromises. Some deserve applause and other condemnation."[58]

Frank's philosophy in the law, in politics and in economics was that of the Trimmer.[59] His philosophy was directed towards pragmatic reforms in the law and in the economic structure of America in the depression years of the 30s. He was opposed to any radicalism which would mean the attempted extirpation, root and branch, of the basic folkways of our American civilization.[60] Although the claim has been made that he started out as a radical in his philosophy of the law,[61] certainly the subsequent unfolding of his philosophy dispels such a notion, even if originally true.

Was Jerome Frank on the bench "the completely adult jurist," the laurels awarded by him to Holmes?[62] We believe that the answer must be in the affirmative.

> Judge Frank represented in a very articulate and at times eloquent sense the kind of adult jurist that he described in his own writings. His achievements as a judge of one of the greatest courts in the country gave concrete practical meaning to one of the most unusual and seminal careers in contemporary American law, and brought to fulfillment the ideas of the country's outstanding legal realist.[63]

On the bench it was particularly in the area of *stare decisis* that one would expect to find a radical transformation of the law if Frank were the radical he was charged to be. One would expect to see a judge freed from the bonds of tradition and of precedent-citing, deciding each case as it arose on the basis of his own notions of justice as hunch-directed. But from Frank's decisions in cases where the issue of *stare decisis* was directly involved, there emerges an image of Frank as a traditional judge with a liberal bent of mind. He abided by *stare decisis* as a fundamental tenet of our legal system, conducive to stability and certainty in the daily affairs and enterprises of men. He would not easily overrule long-established precedents despite his disagreement with their desirability. But he was no worshiper of tradition and precedent for the sake of certainty when, in his opinion, they interfered with a just disposition of a case or were out of line with changed circumstances. In criminal cases, where the liberty of the individual was at stake, he unhesitatingly dissented in a number of instances when he deemed the precedents erroneous or undesirable. The attainment of the goal of justice was more desirable than the attainment of certainty and uniformity in the law.[64]

It is true that in his early writings Frank exaggerated the extent of unique circumstances in cases which call for unique treatment. But by the time he ascended the bench his view on that score had changed. Although in his early period he laid less stress on rules than in the period of his service on the bench, at no time had he advocated the abandonment of *stare decisis*. By the time of his ascension to the bench, the gravamen of his writings had shifted from an emphasis upon rule uncertainty to fact uncertainty. By that time he had significantly changed his view with respect to the volume of cases which can be disposed of by routine application of rules from his original estimate of a limited number to his later view of a far greater number. In his early formulations, rules simply were one element of a compound entering into a judicial decision, and not too significant at that. In his later writings, rules were conceded to be a significant element in the compound. But even in his later formulations of the role of *stare decisis* he omitted mention of the significant role that *stare decisis* plays in bringing certainty and stability into the daily transactions and enterprises of people.[65] By the time he ascended the bench, his earlier expressed views on the extent of unique circumstances in cases had become obsolete. It is far easier to be revolutionary or radical in theoretical discussions than in the decision of actual cases. On the bench he was a little more ready than his brothers to overrule precedents of his court. This represented a difference of degree, but of a relatively minor degree. At no time, however, did he apply the principle of "free judicial decision." He was no starry-eyed iconoclast bent on demolishing rules in accordance with his subjective whims, but rather a staid interpreter of the laws of his government.

From Frank's judicial opinions in the area of civil liberties there emerges an image of a judge whose great concern was for even-handed justice—for the inconspicuous, the despised and the indigent as well as for the influential. For him "[T]he test of the moral quality of a civilization" was in its treatment of the weak and powerless.[66] In this area he dissented more often than his colleagues by reason of different views on social policy and constitutional interpretation. But this image must be somewhat qualified. At times the passion for justice with which he was imbued was so keen that his zeal carried him away and blinded him to facts which did not warrant its exercise in a particular instance.

Characteristically, Frank wrote: "But I, for one, cannot sleep well if I think that, due to any judicial decisions in which I join, innocent destitute men may be behind bars solely because it will cost the government something to have their appeals considered.[67] His concern was not only for the native indigent but for the friendless alien. He frequently dissented in cases involving aliens. His dialectical skill in interpreting Supreme Court cases to conform with his notions was but the outward garb for a heart pulsating in harmony with the plight of the despised alien. He would grant what he considered the full constitutional protection to safeguard procedural due process for all defendants, regardless of their station in life. To him the administration of justice was the great aim of law—more important than that of maintaining order. The administration of justice was not a mere ritual. Frank was in the mainstream of America's great liberal judges.

Frank was an iconoclast of the venerable jury system, except in criminal cases. His crusade for the abolition of the jury system in civil cases was not consistent with his justification for its retention in criminal cases. His respect for existing law, however, is apparent in his strong statements that as long as the jury system prevailed, he would enforce punctiliously all rules and regulations governing it. The private views of a judge become irrelevant on the bench.

The fundamental liberty of free speech was to Frank a "near

161

absolute." From his brief discussion on this aspect of free speech it is difficult to ascertain with any certainty whether or not he fully agreed with the champions of the so-called absolute school of interpretation of the First Amendment, Justices Black and Douglas.[68] That at the very least Frank adopted the preferred status doctrine of interpretation for the First Amendment, there can be no doubt.

In one of his outstanding opinions in a landmark case on obscenity,[69] Frank expressed strong opposition to a "moral police" in the guise of judges, jurors and prosecutors—all fallible men— becoming the despotic arbiters of our literature. In a democracy adult citizens should be self-guardians. To this opinion Frank attached a lengthy Appendix in which he brought to bear upon his analysis the fruits of the social studies, and it is a good example of the fusion which can be effected in the appropriate case between the two disciplines. His voice was one calling for further social study and enlightenment. He sought to break down the barriers of censorship. As such, he was in the vanguard of America's most liberal tradition.

The key to Jerome Frank's jurisprudential philosophy and to his career on the bench was the fact that he was not at ease in Zion. He knew the difficulties on the path and the arduous tasks confronting man in the uphill climb towards a saner world. But he was an inveterate optimist who believed in the perfectibility of man, though he will never attain perfection. He believed there was insufficiency merely in the intellectual formulation; the deed was more important to him than the abstraction. Although a firm believer in the scientific method and in the advancement of man's intellectual impulses, he was an equally firm believer in the paramount importance of the moral impulses. JUSTICE IS AS JUSTICE DOES.[70] Matthew Arnold spoke of the "alternations of Hebraism and Hellenism, of a man's intellectual and moral impulses,"[71] by which "the human spirit proceeds, and each of these two forces has its appointed hours of culmination and seasons of rule."[72] Of Frank it may be truly said that he synthesized in his philosophy and in his life the quintessence of Hebraism and Hellenism; a synthesis of the highest intellectual and moral impulses of man.

# BIBLIOGRAPHY

## I.

### a. OPINIONS OF JUDGE JEROME N. FRANK

*Aero Spark Plug Co.* v. *B. G. Corp.*, 130 F.2d 290 (1942), 69, 213 (con. op.)

*Archawski* v. *Hanioti*, 239 F.2d 806 (1956), 219. (con. op.)

*Biedler & Bookmyer* v. *Universal Ins. Co.*, 134 F.2d 828 (1943), 254.

*Broadcast Music* v. *Havana Madrid Restaurant Corp.*, 175 F.2d 77 (1949), 195.

*Ira S. Bushey & Sons* v. *W. E. Hadger Transportation Corporation*, 167 F.2d 9 (1948), 197. (dis. op.)

*Chrestensen* v. *Valentine*, 122 F.2d 511 (1941), 132. (dis. op.)

*Christensen* v. *United States*, 194 F.2d 978 (1952), 221. (dis. op.)

*Commissioner of Internal Revenue* v. *Beck's Estate*, 129 F.2d 243 (1942), 80.

*Commissioner of Internal Revenue* v. *Hall's Estate*, 153 F.2d 172 (1946), 213. (dis. op.)

*Dincher* v. *Marlin Firearms Co.*, 198 F.2d 821 (1952), 81. (dis. op.)

*Eastern Wine Corporation* v. *Winslow-Warren Ltd.*, 137 F.2d 955 (1943), 216.

*Fanelli* v. *Gypsum Co.*, 141 F.2d 216 (1944), 201.

*In Re Fried*, 161 F.2d 453 (1947), 84, 95.

*Guiseppi* v. *Walling*, 144 F.2d 608 (1944), 82.

*Hammon-Knowlton* v. *United States*, 121 F.2d 192 (1941), 69.

*Hentschel* v. *Baby Bathinette Corp.*, 215 F.2d 102 (1954), 72-73. (dis. op.)

*Hoffman* v. *Palmer*, 129 F.2d 976 (1942), 219, 238.

*Hume* v. *Moore-McCormack Lines, Inc.*, 121 F.2d 336 (1941), 71.

*Joseph* v. *Farnsworth Radio & Television Corp.* et al., 198 F.2d 803 (1952), 220 (dis. op.)

*Keller* v. *Brooklyn Bus Corp.*, 128 F.2d 510 (1942), 238. (dis. op.)

*Kleinman* v. *Kobler*, 230 F.2d 913 (1956), 202.

*La Touraine Coffee Co.* v. *Lorraine Coffee Co.*, 157 F.2d 115 (1946), 73. (dis. op.)

*In Re P. J. Linahan*, 138 F.2d 650 (1943), 200.

*In Re Marine Harbor Properties*, 125 F.2d 296 (1942), 68.

*McAllister* v. *Commissioner of Internal Revenue*, 157 F.2d 235 (1946), 221. (dis. op.)

*Michelsen* v. *Penny*, 135 F.2d 409 (1943), 81. (dis. op. in part)

*Morgan* v. *United States*, 229 F.2d 291 (1956), 221 (dis. op.)

*Morris* v. *Pennsylvania Ry. Co.*, 187 F.2d 837 (1951), 238. (con. op.)

*Old Colony Bondholders* v. *New York, New Haven & Hartford Ry. Co.*, 161 F.2d 413 (1947), 213. (dis. op. in part)

*Pabellon* v. *Grace Line*, 191 F.2d 169 (1951), 215.

*Perkin* v. *Endicott Johnson Corporation*, 128 F.2d 208 (1942), 203,- 220.

*Repouille* v. *United States*, 165 F.2d 152 (1947), 198. (dis. op.)

*Ricketts* v. *Pennsylvania Railway*, 153 F. 2d 757 (1946), 71-72. (con. op.)

*Rieser* v. *Baltimore & Ohio Ry. Co.*, 224 F.2d 198 (1955), 214. (con. op. in result)

*Roth* v. *Goldman*, 172 F.2d 788 (1949), 141. (con. op.)

*Schwartz* v. *Mills*, 192 F2d 727 (1961), 82. (dis. op.)

*Skidmore* v. *Baltimore & Ohio Ry. Co.*, 167 F.2d 54 (1948), 237.

*Slifka* v. *Johnson*, 161 F.2d 467 (1947), 79. (con. op.)

*Standard Brands* v. *Smidler*, 151 F.2d 34 (1945), 216. (con. op.)

*Triangle Publication* v. *Rohrlich*, 167 F.2d 969 (1948), 216. (dis. op.)

*U.S.* v. *Antonelli Fireworks Co., Inc.*, 155 F.2d 631 (1946), 115, 118. (dis. op.)

*U. S.* v. *Bennett et al.*, 152 F.2d 342 (1945), 71, 74. (dis. op.)

*U. S.* v. *Gonzalez Castro*, 228 F.2d 807 (1955), 214. (con. op.)

*U. S.* v. *Costello* 221 F.2d 668 (1955), 219, (con. op.)

*U. S.* v. *Courtney*, 236 F.2d 921 (1956), 234. (maj. op.)

*U. S.* v. *Delli Paoli*, 229 F2d 319 (1955), 217. (dis. op.)

*U. S.* v. *Denno*, 208 F.2d 605 (1953), 224. (dis. op.)

*U. S.* v. *Ebeling*, 146 F.2d 254 (1944), 240. (dis. op.)

*U. S.* v. *Farina*, 184 F.2d 18 (1950), 118. (dis. op.)

*U. S.* v. *Farley*, 238 F.2d 575 (1956), 241.

*U. S.* v *Field*, 193 F.2d 92 (1951), 235. (con. op. as to affirmance but dissenting as to one ruling)

*U. S.* v. *Forness*, 125 F.2d 928 (1942), 196.

*U. S.* v. *Gordon*, 236 F.2d 916 (1956), 233.

*U. S.* v. *Grunewald et al.*, 233 F.2d 556 (1956), 109. (dis. op as to defendant Halpern)

*U. S.* v. *Johnson*, 238 F.2d 565 (1956), 120, (dis. op.)

*U. S.* v. *Lennox Metal Mfg. Co.*, 225 F.2d 302 (1955), 221.

*U. S.* v. *Leviton*, 193 F.29 848 (1951), 93. (dis. op.)

*U. S.* v. *Masciale*, 236 F.2d 601 (1956), 98 (dis. op.)

*U. S. ex rel. Knauff* v. *McGrath*, 181 F.2d 839 (1950), 245.

*U. S.* v. *Mulcahy*, 169 F.2d 94 (1948), 214. (dis. op.)

*U. S.* v. *On Lee*, 193 F.2d 306 (1951), 74-76.

*U. S.* v. *On Lee*, 201 F.2d 722 (1953), 101, 103, 232. (dis. op.)

*U. S.* v. *Parrino*, 212 F.2d 919 (1954), 128, 243. (dis. op.)

*U. S.* v. *Pierre*, 161 F.2d 467 (1947), 78. (con. op.)

*U. S.* v. *Rosenberg*, 195 F.2d 583 (1952), 28-30.

*U. S.* v. *Roth*, 237 F.2d 796 (1956), 84, 143, 250. (con. op.)

*U. S.* v. *Sacher*, 182 F.2d 496 (1950), 196. (con. op.)

*U. S.* v. *Scully*, 225 F.2d 113 (1955), 76. (con. op. in result)

*U. S. ex rel. Accardi* v. *Shaughnessy*, 206 F.2d 897 (1953), 127. (dis. op.)

*U. S. ex rel. Fong Foo* v. *Shaughnessy*, 234 F.2d 715 (1955), 79.

*U. S.* v. *St. Pierre*, 132 F.2d 837 (1942), 107. (dis. op.)

*U. S.* v. *Ullmann*, 221 F.2d 760 (1955), 78, 218.

*U. S.* v. *Walker*, 190 F.2d 481 (1951), 239. (dis. op.)

*U. S. ex rel. Madeiros* v. *Watkins*, 166 F.2d 897 (1948), 125. (dis. op.)

*Usatorre* v. *The Victoria*, 172 F.2d 434 (1949), 220. (dis. op. in part)

*Wallace* v. *U. S.*, 142 F.2d 240 (1944), 214.

*M. Witmark & Sons* v. *Fred Fisher Music Co. et al.*, 125 F.2d 949 (1942), 80. (dis. op.)

*Zamore* v. *Goldblatt*, 201 F.2d 738 (1953), 71, 214. (con. op.)

*Zell* v. *American Seating Co.*, 138 F.2d 641 (1943), 219.

## b. BOOKS BY JUDGE FRANK

Frank, Jerome. *Courts on Trial: Myth and Reality in American Justice*. (Princeton: Princeton U. Press, 1949; Introduction of Edmond Cahn in paperback ed., New York: Atheneum, 1963).

——. *Fate and Freedom: A Philosophy for Free Americans* (New York: Simon & Schuster, 1945; rev. ed., Boston: Beacon Press, 1953).

——. *If Men Were Angels*. (New York: Harper & Brothers, 1942).

——. *Law and The Modern Mind* (New York: Brentano's, 1930; Preface to the Sixth Printing in paperback ed., Garden City, N.Y.: Doubleday & Co., Inc.—an Anchor Book, 1963).

——. *Save America First*. (New York: Harper & Brothers, 1938).

—— and Frank, Barbara. *Not guilty* (Garden City: Doubleday & Co., 1957).

——. *The Selected Writings of Jerome Frank: A Man's Reach* (ed. Barbara Frank Kristen, New York: Macmillan Co., London: Collier-Macmillan Co., 1965).

## c. ARTICLES BY JUDGE FRANK

Frank, Jerome. "Both Ends Against the Middle," *University of Pennsylvania Law Review*, C (1951), 20.

——. "Cardozo and the Upper-Court Myth," *Law and Contemporary Problems*, XIII (1948), 369. ............ ........ ........ ........ ........

——. "Civil Law Influences on the Common Law—Some Reflections on 'Comparative' and 'Contrastive' Law," *University of Pennsylvania Law Review*, CIV (1956), 887.

165

——. "A Conflict with Oblivion: Some Observations on the Founders of Legal Pragmatism," *Rutgers Law Review*, IX (1954), 355, 425.

——. "The Cult of the Robe," 28 *Saturday Review of Literature* (October 13, 1945), 12.

——. "Epithetical Jurisprudence and the Work of the Securities and Exchange Commission in the Administration of Chapter X of the Bankruptcy Act," *New York University Law Quarterly Review*, XVIII (1941), 317.

——. Introduction to Harold M. Hoffman and Joseph Bradley, "Jurors on Trial," *Missouri Law Review*, XVII (1952), 235.

——. "Are Judges Human?" *University of Pennsylvania Law Review*, LXXX (1931), 17, 233.

——. "Judicial Fact-Finding and Psychology," *Ohio State Law Journal*, XIV (1953), 183.

——. "A Lawyer Looks at Language," in S. I. Hayakawa, *Language in Action*. (New York: Harcourt, Brace, 1939).

——. "The Lawyer's Role in Modern Society: A Round Table," *Journal of Public Law*, IV (1955), 8.

——. "Memorable Victories in the Fight for Justice," *Life* (March 12, 1958) Vol. 30, p. 6.

——. "Modern and Ancient Legal Pragmatism—John Dewey & Co. vs. Aristotle," *Notre Dame Law Journal*, XXV (1950), 207, 460.

——. "Mr. Justice Holmes and Non-Euclidean Legal Thinking," *Cornell Law Quarterly*, XVII (1932), 568.

——. "The New Sin," *Saturday Review of Literature* (December 22, 1945) Vol. 28.

——. "Overhauling the Cabinet," *Fortune* (January, 1944) Vol. 29, p. 88.

——. "The Place of the Expert in a Democratic Society," *Philosophy of Science*, XVI (1949), 3.

——. "A Plea for Lawyer-Schools," *Yale Law Journal*, LVI (1947), 1303.

——. "Realism in Jurisprudence," *American Law School Review*, VII (1934), 1063; repr. sub. nom. "Experimental Jurisprudence and the New Deal," *U.S. Congressional Record*, 73rd Congress, 2d Session, Part 11, 12412.

——. "Red, White and Blue Herring," *Saturday Evening Post* (December 6, 1941) Vol. 214, p. 9.

——. Review, Franz R. Bienenfeld, *Rediscovery of Justice, California Law Review*, XXXVIII (1950), 351.

——. Review, Huntington Cairns, *Legal Philosophy from Plato to Hegel, Indiana Law Journal*, XXV (1949), 231.

——. Review, George M. Calhoun, *Introduction to Greek Legal Science, Harvard Law Review*, LVII (1944), 1120.

——. Review, Wolfgang Friedmann, *Legal Theory, Harvard Law Review*, LIX (1946), 1004.

———. Review, Karl N. Llewellyn, *The Bramble Bush, Yale Law Journal,* XL (1931), 1120.

———. Review, Hans Morgenthau, *Scientific Man vs. Power Politics, University of Chicago Law Review,* XV (1948), 462.

———. Review, Maynard E. Pirsig, *Cases on Judicial Administration, Yale Law Journal,* LVI (1947), 589.

———. "Say It With Music," *Harvard Law Review,* LXI (1948), 921.

———. "The Scientific Spirit and Economic Dogmatism," in Jerome Nathanson (ed.), *Science for Democracy,* (New York: King's Crown Press, 1946), 11.

———. "Self-Guardianship and Democracy," *American Scholar,* XVI (1947), 265 (an editorial).

———. " 'Short of Sickness and Death': A Study of Moral Responsibility in Legal Criticism," *New York University Law Review,* XXVI (1951), 545.

———. "A Sketch of an Influence," In Paul Sayre (ed.), *Interpretations of Modern Legal Philosophies* (New York: Oxford U. Press, 1947).

———. "Some Realistic Reflections on Some Aspects Of Corporate Reorganizations," *Virginia Law Review,* XIX (1933), 541.

———. "Some Reflections on Judge Learned Hand," *University of Chicago Law Review,* XXIV (1957), 666.

———. "Some Tame Reflections on Some Wild Facts," in Sidney Ratner (ed.) *Vision and Action* (New Brunswick: Rutgers University Press, 1953), 56.

———. "Something's Wrong with Our Jury System," *Collier's* (December 9, 1950) Vol. 126, p. 28.

———. "The Speech of Judges: A Dissenting Opinion," (under pseudonym, Anon Y. Mous of Middletown), *Virginia Law Review,* XXIX (1943), 625.

———. "To-day's Problems in the Administration of Criminal Justice," 15 *Federal Rule Decisions* (F.R.D.), (1958), 93.

———. "War Crimes," *Collier's* (October 13, 1945), Vol. 116, p. 11.

———. "What Constitutes a Good Legal Education," *American Bar Association Journal,* XIX (1933), 723; repr. in *American Law School Review,* VII (1933), 894.

———. "What Courts Do in Fact," *Illinois Law Review,* XXVI (1932), 645, 761.

———. "White Collar Justice," *Saturday Evening Post* (July 17, 1943), Vol. 216, p. 22.

———. "Why Not a Clinical Lawyer-School?," *University of Pennsylvania Law Review,* LXXXI (1933), 907.

———. "Words and Music: Some Remarks on Statutory Interpretation," *Columbia Law Review,* XLVII (1947), 1259.

## d. UNPUBLISHED MATERIAL

Columbia University Oral History Project—a taped interview with Jerome Frank (typewritten copy in possession of Mrs. Jerome Frank, New Haven, Conn.)

Selected Documents from the Papers of President Franklin D. Roosevelt and Richard Rovere concerning Jerome Frank (Franklin D. Roosevelt Memorial Library, Hyde Park, N. Y.)

## I. GENERAL WORKS USED IN THIS STUDY

### a. BOOKS

Abraham, Henry J. *The Judicial Process* (2d ed., New York, London, Toronto: Oxford University Press, 1968.)

Allen, Carleton Kemp. *Law in the Making.* (Paperback ed., London: Oxford University Press, 1961.

Arnold, Matthew. *Hebraism and Hellenism,* in Portable Matthew Arnold. (New York: Viking Press, 1960).

Arnold, Thurman W. *The Symbols of Government.* (New Haven: Yale U. Press, 1935).

———. *The Folklore of Capitalism.* (New Haven: Yale U. Press, 1937).

Association of the Bar of the City of New York. *Equal Justice for the Accused* (New York: Doubleday & Co., 1959).

Barth, Alan. *The Price of Liberty.* (New York: Viking Press, 1961).

Benedict, Ruth. *Patterns of Culture.* (Paperback ed., New York: Penguin Books, Inc., 1946).

Bodenheimer, Edgar. *Jurisprudence.* (New York: McGraw-Hill, 1940).

———, *Jurisprudence—The Philosophy and Method of the Law.* (Cambridge: Harvard University Press, 1962).

Burns, Edward McNeill. *Ideas in Conflict—The Political Theories of the Contemporary World* (New York: W. W. Morton & Co., 1959).

Busch, Francis X. *Trial Procedure Materials.* (Indianapolis: Bobbs-Merrill, 1961).

Cahn, Edmond N. *The Sense of Injustice* (New York: New York University Press, 1949).

Cardozo, Benjamin N. *The Growth of the Law.* (New Haven: Yale U. Press, 1924).

———. *Nature of the Judicial Process.* (New Haven: Yale University Press, 1921).

———. *Paradoxes of Legal Science.* (New York: Columbia University Press, 1927).

———. *Selected Writings.* (ed. Margaret E. Hall, New York: Falcon Publications, 1947).

Chafee, Jr. Zechariah. *Free Speech in the United States.* (Cambridge:

Harvard University Press, 1941): (Cambridge: Harvard University Press, 1954).

Cohen, Felix S. *Ethical Systems and Legal Ideals: An Essay on the Foundations of Legal Criticism.* (New York: Falcon Press, 1933).

Cohen, Morris Raphael. *American Thought: A Critical Sketch.* (Glencoe, Ill.: Free Press, 1954).

——. *Law and the Social Order—Essays in Legal Philosophy.* (New York: Harcourt, Brace & Co., 1933).

——. *Faith of a Liberal.* (New York: Henry Holt, 1946).

Commager, Henry Steele. *The American Mind.* (New York: Yale University Press, 1950).

Cowan, Thomas A. (ed.) *The American Jurisprudence Reader.* (New York: Oceana Publications, 1956).

D'Entrèves, A. P., *Natural Law—An Historical Survey* (New York: Harper Torchbooks, 1965).

Dillard, Irving (ed.) *One Man's Stand for Freedom.* (New York: Alfred A. Knopf, 1963).

Douglas, William Orville. *A Living Bill of Rights.* (Garden City, N.Y.: Doubleday & Co., 1961).

——. *The Right of the People.* (New York: Doubleday & Co., 1958).

——. *Stare Decisis.* (Association of the Bar of the City of New York, 1949).

Drinker, Henry S. *Some Observations on the Freedoms of the First Amendment.* (Boston: Boston University Press, 1957).

Dunham, Barrows. *Heroes and Heretics.* (New York: Alfred A. Knopf, 1964).

Ernst, Morris L. and Schwartz, Alan G. *Censorship—the Search for the Obscene.* (New York: The Macmillan Co., 1964).

Fellman, David. *The Defendant's Rights.* (New York, Toronto: Rinehart & Co., 1958).

Friedmann, Wolfgang W. *Legal Theory.* (3d ed., London; Stevens & Sons, Ltd., 1953).

Fuller, Lon S. *The Law in Quest of Itself.* (Chicago: Foundation Press, 1950).

Galston, Clarence G. *Behind the Judicial Curtain.* (Barrington House, 1949).

Garlan, Edwin N. *Legal Realism and Justice.* (New York: Columbia University Press, 1941).

Gellhorn, Walter. *American Rights: The Constitution in Action.* (New York: The Macmillan Co., 1960).

——. *Individual Freedom and Governmental Restraints* (Baton Rouge: Louisiana State U. Press, 1956).

Goodhart, Arthur L. *Modern Theories.* (London: Oxford University Press, 1953).

Green, Leon. *Judge and Jury.* (Kansas City, Mo.: Vernon Law Books Co., 1930).

Griswold, Edwin N. *The 5th Amendment Today*. (Cambridge: Harvard University Press, 1955).

Gurwich, Georges. *Sociology of Law*. (New York: Philosophical Library & Alliance Book Corp., 1942).

Hirschfield, Robert S. *The Constitution and the Court*. (New York: Random House, 1964).

Holmes, Jr., Oliver Wendell. *The Common Law*. (Boston: Little Brown & Co., 1881).

Inbau, Fred E. and Reid, John E. *Lie Detection and Criminal Investigation*. 3d ed., Williams & Wilkins Co., 1953).

*Interpretations of Modern Legal Philosophies: Essays in Honor of Roscoe Pound*. ed., Paul Sayre (New York: Oxford University Press, 1947).

Jahnige, Thomas P. and Goldman, Sheldon. *The Federal Judicial System: Readings in Process and Behavior*. (New York, Chicago, San Francisco, Atlanta, Dallas, Montreal, Toronto. London: Holt, Rinehart and Winston Inc., 1968).

James, William. *Pragmatism: A New Name for Old Ways of Thinking*. (Longmans, Green, 1949).

Kalven, Harry J. and Zeisel, Hans. *The American Jury* (Boston: Little, Brown, 1966).

Kilpatrick, James Jackson. *The Smut Peddlers*. (New York: Doubleday & Co., 1960).

Köhler, Wolfgang. *Gestalt Psychology—An Introduction to New Concepts in Modern Psychology* (a Mentor book—New York and Toronto: The New American Library, and London: The New English Library Limited, 1947).

Konefsky, Samuel J. *The Legacy of Holmes and Brandeis*—A Study in *the Influence of Ideas* (New York: Collier Books, 1961).

Konvitz, Milton R. *The Alien and the Asiatic in American Law*. (Ithaca: Cornell University Press, 1946).

——. *Civil Rights in Immigration*. (Ithaca: Cornell University Press, 1953).

——. *Expanding Liberties—Freedom's Gains in Postwar America* New York: Viking Press, 1966).

——. *Fundamental Liberties of a Free People*. (Ithaca: Cornell University Press, 1957).

Lasswell, Harold D. *The Impact of Psychoanalutic Thinking in the Social Sciences*, in Hendrik M. Ruitenbeck (ed.), *Psychoanalysis and Social Science*. (New York: E. P. Dutton & Co., 1932).

Lewis, Anthony. *Gideon's Trumpet*. (New York: Random House, 1964).

Llewellyn Karl N. *The Bramble Bush* (New York: Oceana Publications, 1951 ed.)

——. *The Common Law Tradition*. (Boston: Little, Brown & Co., 1960).

170

——. *Jurisprudence—Realism in Theory and Practice.* (Chicago: University of Chicago Press, 1962).

Lockhart, William B.; Kamisar, Yale and Choper, Jesse H. *The American Constitution—Cases and Materials* (2d ed., St. Paul, Minn.: West Publishing Co., 1967).

Mayers, Lewis. *The American Legal System.* (Rev. ed., New York: Harper & Row, 1964).

*Modern Introduction to Philosophy,* ed. Paul Edwards and Arthur Pap (rev. ed., New York: Free Press; London: Collier-Macmillan Ltd., 1965).

Murphy, Walter F. and Pritchett, C. Herman. *Courts, Judges and Politics.* (New York: Random House, 1961).

Paton, George W. *A Text-Book of Jurisprudence.* (3d ed., New York: Oxford University Press, 1964).

Patterson, Edwin W. *Jurisprudence: Men and Ideas of Law.* (Brooklyn: The Foundation Press, Inc., 1953).

Paul, James C. and Schwartz, Murray L. *Federal Censorship: Obscenity in the Mail.* (Glencoe, Ill.: Free Press, 1961).

Paul, Julius. *The Legal Realism of Jerome N. Frank.* (The Hague: Martinue Nijhoff, 1959).

Perry, Ralph Barton. *The Life and Character of William James.* (New York: George Braziller, 1954).

*My Philosophy of Law. Credos of 16 American Scholars.* (Boston: Boston Law Book Co., 1941).

Plucknett, Theodore F. T. *A Concise History of the Common Law.* (5th ed., Boston: Little, Brown & Co., 1956).

Pound, Roscoe. *Interpretations of Legal History.* (Cambridge: Harvard University Press, 1923).

——. *An Introduction to the Philosophy of Law* (New Haven: Yale U. Press, 1922).

——. *Justice According to Law.* (New Haven: Yale U. Press, 1951).

——. *Law Finding Through Experience and Reason.* (Athens, Ga.: University of Georgia Press, 1960).

Pritchett, C. Herman. *American Constitutional Issues.* (New York, San Francisco, Toronto, London: McGraw Hill Book Co., 1962).

Reuschlein, Harold Gill. *Jurisprudence—Its American Prophets.* (Indianapolis: Bobbs-Merrill, Inc., 1951).

Richardson, William Payson. *The Law of Evidence.* (8th ed. Brooklyn, N.Y.: Copyright by Jerome Prince, 1955).

Robinson, Edward Stevens. *Law and the Lawyers* (New York: Macmillan Co., 1935).

Rogge, John. *The First and the Fifth.* (New York: Thomas Nelson & Sons, 1960).

Rostow, Eugene V. *The Sovereign Prerogative: The Supreme Court and the Quest for Law.* (New Haven and London: Yale University Press, 1962).

171

Rumble, Wilfrid E., Jr. *American Legal Realism.* (Ithaca: Cornell University Press, 1968).

Schlesinger, Jr., Arthur M. *The Coming of the New Deal.* Boston: Houghton Mifflin Co., 1959).

Schwartz, Bernard. *Administrative Law.* (2d ed., London: Sir Isaac Pitman & Sons, Ltd.; Dobbs Ferry, N.Y.: Oceana Publications, Inc. 1960).

————. *American Constitutional Law.* (Cambridge: Harvard University Press, 1955).

Stone, Julius. *The Province and Function of Law.* (Cambridge: Harvard University Press, 1950).

Swisher, Carl Brent. *American Constitutional Development.* (2d ed., Boston: Houghton Mifflin Co., 1954).

Weber, Alfred. *History of Philosophy.* (New York: Scribner's, 1902).

## b. ARTICLES AND MISCELLANEOUS MATERIALS

Adler, Mortimer J. "Law and the Modern Mind: A Symposium," *Columbia Law Review,* XXXI (1931), 82.

Allen, Francis A. Review, Frank, *Law and the Modern Mind, Illinois Law Review,* XLIV (1949), 554.

Arnold, Thurman W. Review, Frank, *Law and the Modern Mind, Saturday Review of Literature* (March 7, 1931), Vol. 7, p. 644.

————. Review, Frank, *Fate and Freedom, Saturday Review of Literature* (June 23, 1945), Vol. 28, p. 10.

————. "Judge Jerome Frank," *University of Chicago Law Review,* XXIV (1957), 633.

————. "Jerome N. Frank," *Journal of Legal Education,* X (1957), 1.

Barrett, Edward F. "Confession and Avoidance—Reflections on Re-reading Jerome Frank's Law and the Modern Mind," *Notre Dame Lawyer,* XXIV (1949), 447.

Bingham, Joseph W. "What Is Law?," *Michigan Law Review,* XI (1912).

Black, Forrest Revere, Review, Frank, *Law and the Modern Mind, Kentucky Law Journal,* XIX (1931), 349.

Bodenheimer, Edgar. "Law as Order and Justice," *Journal of Public Law,* VI (1957), 194.

————. "A Decade of Jurisprudence in the United States—1946-1956," *Natural Law Forum,* III (1958), 44.

————. "Analytical Positivism, Legal Realism and the Future of the Legal Method," *Virginia Law Review,* XLIV (1958), 365.

Bohlen, Francis H. Review, Frank, *Law and the Modern Mind, University of Pennsylvania Law Review,* LXXIX (1931), 822.

Brennan, William J. "The Role of the Court—The Challenge of the Future," *New York Law Journal* (April 20, 1965), 4.

172

Cahn, Edmond. "Fact Skepticism and Fundamental Law," *New York University Law Review*, XXXIII (1953), 1.

——. "Judge Frank's Skepticism and Our Future," *Yale Law Journal*, LVI (1957).

Cardozo, Benjamin N., "A Ministry of Justice," *Harvard Law Review*, XXXV (1921), 1136.

Cavers, David A. Review, *Law and the Modern Mind*, West. Va. Law *Review*, XXXVII (1931).

Clark, Charles E. "Jerome N. Frank," *Yale Law Journal*, LXVI (1957), 817.

Clines, Francis X. "Law Schools Get an Intern Plan," *New York Times* (August 3, 1964), p. 1 (2d Section).

Cohen, Felix. Review, Frank, *Law and the Modern Mind*, *American Bar Association Journal*, XVII (Feb. 1931), 111.

Cohen, Morris Raphael. "Justice Holmes and the Nature of Law," *Columbia Law Review*, XXXI (1931), 352.

Corbin, Arthur L. "The Law and the Judges," *Yale Law Review* (n.s.), III (1914), 234.

Cox, Oscar. Review, *Law and the Modern Mind*, *Yale Law Journal*, XL (1931), 670.

*Current Biography* (New York: H. W. Wilson Co., 1941), pp. 301-03 (Biography of Frank).

DeGrazia, Edward. "Obscenity and the Mail: A Study of Administrative Restraint." *Law and Contemporary Problems*, XX (1955), 608.

Dewy, John. "Logical Method and Law," *Cornell Law Quarterly*, X (1924), 17.

——. "My Philosophy of Law," in *My Philosophy of Law: Credos of 16 American Scholars* (Boston: Boston Law Book Co., 1941), 73.

Dickinson, John. "My Philosophy of Law," in *My Philosophy of Law: Credos of 16 American Scholars* (Boston: Boston Law Book Co., 1941), 97.

Diplock, Sir William Kenneth. "The Jury and Civil Actions in England," *New York State Bar Journal*, Vol. 36, No. 4 (Albany, N.Y.: New York State Bar Association, August, 1964).

Douglas, William Orville. "Jerome N. Frank," *Journal of Legal Education*, X (1957), 1.

Elder, Robert H. "Resolved that Jury Trials in Civil Cases Should Be Abolished," *Bar General Pamphlets*, Vol. 15 (New York County Lawyers Association, Radio Address, Dec. 11, 1930).

*Encyclopaedia Britannica*. Vol. XIII (1961), article on "Jury" p. 205.

*Jerome N. Frank Memorial Issue*, *Yale Law Journal*, LXVI (May, 1957), 817.

*Jerome N. Frank Memorial Issue*, *University of Chicago Law Review*, XXIV (Summer, 1957), 625, 769.

173

Frank, John P. "The Top Commercial Court," *Fortune* (January, 1951), 92.

Fuller, Lon L. "American Legal Realism," *University of Pennsylvania Law Review,* LXXXII (1934), 429.

Galston, Clarence G. "Civil Trials and Tribulations," *American Bar Association Journal,* XXIX (1945), 195.

Graham, Fred R. "Law: Focus on Aid to Defense," *New York Times* (August 29, 1965), News of the Week Section, p. 4E.

Hagan, James E. and Snee, Joseph M. "The McNabb-Mallory Rule: Its Rise, Rationale and Rescue," *Georgetown Law Journal,* XLVII (1958), 1.

Haines, Charles Grove. "General Observations on the Effect of Personal, Political and Economic Influences in the Decisions of Judges," *Illinois Law Review,* XVII (1922), 98.

Hamilton, Walton H. Review, Frank, *Law and the Modern Mind, The New Republic,* Vol. 65 (January 21, 1931), 111.

Hoffman, Malcolm A. Review, Frank, *Law and the Modern Mind,* "Old Wine," *Federal Bar Journal,* VII (1946), 233.

Holmes, Jr., Oliver Wendell. "The Path of the Law," *Harvard Law Review,* X (1897), 457.

Hutcheson, Jr., Joseph G. "The Judgment Intuitive: The Function of the 'Hunch' in Judicial Decisions," *Cornell Law Quarterly,* XIV (1929), 274.

Inbau, Fred E. "Law and Police Practice: Restrictions on the Law of Interrogation and Confessions," *Northwestern University Law Review,* LII (1957), 77.

"Intellectual on the Spot," *Time* (March 11, 1940), 71.

Kalven, Jr., Harry. "The Dignity of the Civil Jury," *Virginia Law Review,* L (1964), 1055; *New York Law Journal,* (December 15, 16, 17, 1964), 4.

Kantorowicz, Herman. "Some Rationalism about Realism," *Yale Law Journal,* XLIII (1934), 1240.

Kennedy, Walter B. "Realism, What Next?," *Fordham Law Review,* VIII, Part II (1939), 45.

Knox, John C. "A Just Justice," *Saturday Evening Post* (July 24, 1943), Vol. 217, p. 22.

Iandynski, Jacob W. "The Making of Constitutional Law," *Social Research* (Spring, 1964).

Levy, Leonard W. "The Right against Self-Incrimination: History and Judicial History," *Political Science Quarterly,* LXXXIV (March, 1969), 1.

Llewellyn, Karl N. "A Realistic Jurisprudence—the Next Step," *Columbia Law Review,* XXX (1930), 431.

——. "Some Realism about Realism—Responding to Dean Pound," Harvard Law Review, XLIV (1931), 1222.

Lockhart, William B. and McClure, Robert C. "Literature, the Law of Obscenity and the Constitution," *Minnesota Law Review,* XXXVIII (1954).

Loevinger, Lee. Review of Courts on Trial, Jerome M. Frank, *Etc.*: *A Review of General Samantics,* VIII (1950), 34.

Lucey, Francis E. "Natural Law and American Legal Realism: Their Respective Contributions to a Theory of Law in a Democratic Society," *Georgetown Law Journal,* XXX (1942), 493.

McCormack, Charles T. "Jury Verdicts upon Special Questions in Civil Cases," *Judicial Administration Monographs,* Series A, 72 (Special Committee on Improving the Administration of Justice of the American Bar Association, 1942).

McDougal, Myres S. "The Law School of the Future: From Legal Realism to Policy Science in the World Community," *Yale Law Journal,* LVI (1947), 1345.

McWhinney, Edward. "Judge Jerome Frank and Legal Realism: An Appraisal," *New York Law Forum,* III (1957), 113.

———. "The Great Debate: Activism and Self-Restraint and Current Dilemmas in Judicial Policy-Making." *New York University Law Review,* XXXIII (1958), 755.

Meagher, Jefferson F. "Trial by Jury Deserves a Fair Trial," *New York State Bar Journal,* Vol. 36, No. 4 (Albany, N. Y.: New York State Bar Association, August, 1964), 303.

Mechem, Philip. "The Jurisprudence of Despair," *Iowa Law Review,* XXI (1936), 669.

Moore, Underhill. "Rational Basis of Legal Institutions," *Columbia Law Review,* XXIII (1923).

Morgan, Edmund M. Review, Frank, *Courts on Trial, Journal of Legal Education,* III (1950), 385.

Niebuhr, Reinhold. Review, Frank, *Fate and Freedom, The Nation,* (July 14, 1945), 40.

Oliphant, Herman. "A Return to Store Decisis," American Bar Association Journal, XIV (1928), 71.

Pound, Roscoe. "Do We Need a Philosophy of Law?," *Columbia Law Review,* V, (1905), 339.

"The Call for a Realist Jurisprudence," *Howard Law Review,* XLIV (1931), 697.

———. "Fifty Years of Jurisprudence," *Harvard Law Review,* II (1938), 444.

———. "How Far Are We Attaining a New Measure of Values in Twentieth Century Juristic Thought?," *Virginia Law Review,* XLI (1936), 81.

———. "Liberty of Contract," *Yale Law Journal,* XVIII (1909), 454.

———. "The Need for a Sociological Jurisprudence," *Green Bag,* XIX (1907), 107.

175

——. "Scope and Purpose of Sociological Jurisprudence," *Harvard Law Review*, XXIV (1912), 591.

Radin, Max. "Legal Realism," *Columbia Law Review*, XXXI (1931), 824.

Robson, William A. Review, Frank, *Courts on Trial, The Political Quarterly*, XXI (1950), 417.

Schroeder, Theodore, "The Psychologic Study of Judicial Opinions," *California Law Review*, VI (1918), 69.

Schuett, John T. "A Study of the Legal Philosophy of Jerome N. Frank," *University of Detroit Law Journal*, XXXV (1957), 28.

Warren, Samuel D. and Brandeis, Louis D. "The Right to Privacy," *Harvard Law Review*, IV (1890), 193.

Yale Law Faculty, "In Remembrance," *Yale Law Report*, III (1957), 10.

## c. DECISIONS OF THE U.S. SUPREME

## COURT AND OF OTHER COURTS

*Abrams* v. *U.S.*, 250 U.S. 616 (1919), 248.

*Accardi* v. *Shauggnessy*, 347 U.S. 260 (1953), 243.

*Alabama Power Co.* v. *Ickes*, 302 U.S. 464 (1937), 180.

*American Bank & Trust Co.* v. *Reserve Bank of Atlanta*, 256 U.S. 350 (1921), 248.

*Ashcraft* v. *Tennessee*, 322 U.S. 143 (1944), 88.

*Battaglia* v. *State of N.Y.*, 10 N.Y. 2d 257 (1961), 214.

*Beauharnais* v. *Illinois*, 343 U.S. 250 (1952), 247, 249, 252.

*Benton* v. *Md.*, 395 U.S. 784 (1969), 223.

*Betts* v. *Brady*, 316 U.S. 455 (1942), 241.

*Bihn* v. *U.S.*, 322 U.S. 633 (1946), 217.

*Blackburn* v. *Alabama*, 361, U.S. 199 (1960), 225.

*A Book* v. *Attorney General*, 383 U.S. 413 (1966), 251, 254.

*Boyd* v. *U.S.*, 116 U.S. 616 (1886), 230.

*Breard* v. *Alexandria*, 341 U.S. 622 (1950), 247.

*Bridges* v. *State of California*, 314 U.S. 252 (1941), 254.

*Brown* v. *Allen*, 344 U.S. 443 (1952), 224, 226, 228.

*Brown* v. *Mississippi*, 397 U.S. 278 (1936), 87.

*Bruton* v. *United States*, 391 U.S. 123 (1968), 218.

*Burnett* v. *Coronado Oil & Gas Co.*, 285 U.S. 393 (1932), 218.

*Callen* v. *Pennsylvania Railway Co.*, 332 U.S. 625 (1947), 215.

*Casey* v. *U.S.*, 276 U.S. 413 (1927), 229.

*Chambers* v. *Florida*, 309 U.S. 227 (1944), 88.

*Chaplinski* v. *New Hampshire*, 315 U.S. 568 (1942), 248, 252, 253.

*Chapman* v. *California*, 386 U.S. 18 (1967), 236.

*Cicenia* v. *Lagey*, 357 U.S. 504 (1958), 227.

*Commonwealth* v. *Gordon*, 66 Pa. D. &. C. 101 (1949), 141, 145.

*Crooker* v. *California*, 357 U.S. 433 (1958), 227.

*Curcio* v. *U.S.,* 354 U.S. 118 (1956), 235.
*Delli Paoli* v. *U.S.,* 353 U.S. 232 (1956), 218.
*Dennis* v. *U.S.,* 183 F.2d 201 (1950), 139.
*Dennis* v. *U.S.,* 341 U.S. 494 (1951), 235, 249.
*Emspak* v. *U.S.,* 348 U.S. 190 (1954), 235.
*Escobeda* v. *U.S.,* 378 U.S. 478 (1964), 227.
*Fabris* v. *General Foods Corp.,* 152 F.2d 660 (1945), 237.
*Fred Fisher Music Co.* v. *Witmark & Sons,* 318 U.S. 643 (1943), 220
*Fong Yue Ting* v. *U.S.,* 149 U.S. 711 (1893), 123.
*Gallegos* v. *Nebraska,* 342 U.S. 55 (1951), 226.
*Gemsco, Inc. et al* v. *Walling,* 324 U.S. 244 (1945), 222.
*Gideon* v. *Wainwright,* 372 U.S. 335 (1963), 241.
*Ginsberg* v. *State of New York,* 390 U.S. 629 (1968), 253, 255.
*Ginzburg* v. *U.S.,* 383 U.S. 463 (1966), 255.
*Gitlow* v. *New York,* 268 U.S. 652 (1925), 246.
*Goldman* v. *U.S.,* 316 U.S. 129 (1942), 102, 240.
*Griffin* v. *Illinois,* 351 U.S. 12 (1955), 120.
*Griswold* v. *Connecticut,* 381 U.S. 479 (1965), 248.
*Grove Press, Inc.* v. *Christenberry,* 276 F.2d 433 (1960), 252.
*Grove Press, Inc.* v. *Gerstein,* 378 U.S. 577 (1964), 255.
*Grunewald* v. *U.S.,* 353 U.S. 391 (1957), 236.
*Haley* v. *Ohio,* 322 U.S. 596 (1948), 88.
*Harris* v. *So. Carolina,* 338 U.S. 68 (1948), 224.
*Haynes* v. *Washington,* 373 U.S. 503 (1963), 225.
*Jacobellis* v. *Ohio,* 378 U.S. 184 (1963), 255.
*Jencks* v. *U. S.,* 353 U.S. 657 (1956), 240.
*Johnson* v. *U.S.,* 352 U.S. 565 (1957), 240.
*Johnson* v. *verbst,* 304 U.S. 458 (1938), 241.
*Katz* v. *U.S.,* 389 U.S. 348 (1967), 231.
*Kessler* v. *Strecker,* 307 U.S. 22 (1938), 241.
*Kovacs* v. *Cooper,* 336 U.S. 77 (1948), 248, 249.
*Leyra* v. *Denno,* 347 U.S. 556 (1954), 224.
*Lisenba* v. *California,* 314 U.S. 219 (1941), 88.
*Lopez* v. *U.S.,* 373 U.S. 427 (1962), 232.
*Lovell* v. *Griffin,* 303 U.S. 444 (1938), 132.
*Low Wah Suey* v. *Backus,* 225 U.S. 460 (1912), 241.
*Mahler* v. *Eby,* 264 U.S. 32 (1924), 241.
*Malinski* v. *N.Y.,* 324 U.S. 401 (1944), 224.
*Mallory* v. *United States,* 354 U.S. 449 (1956), 226.
*Manuel Enterprises* v. *Day,* 370 U.S. 478 (1962), 252, 255.
*Masciale* v. *U.S.,* 356 .S. 386 (1958), 98.
*McDonald* v. *Fless,* 238 U.S. 364 (1914), 238.
*McNabb* v. *U.S.,* 318 U.S. 332 (1943), 90, 226.
*Miller* v. *U.S.,* 317 U.S. 192 (1942), 240.
*Minersville School District* v. *Gobitis,* 310 U.S. 586 (1943), 209.

177

# Footnotes—Introduction and Chapter I
## Legal Realism and Jerome Frank

1. See, e.g., Philip Mechem, "The Jurisprudence of Despair," *Iowa Law Rev.*, XXI (1936), 669; John Dickinson, "My Philosophy of Law," in *My Philosophy of Law: Credos of 16 American Scholars* (Boston: Boston Law Book Co., 1941) p. 98. For a discussion of legal realism, see pp. 34-47, *infra*.

2. William Orville Douglas, "Jerome N. Frank," *Journal of Legal Education*, X (1957), 1, 2.

3. Frank, *Fate and Freedom: A Philosophy for Free Americans* (New York: Simon & Schuster, 1945; rev. ed., Boston: Beacon Press, 1953).

4. Julius Paul, *The Legal Realism of Jerome N. Frank* (The Hague: Martinus Nijhoff, 1959), p. 150.

5. *Current Biography* (New York: H. W. Wilson Co., 1941), p. 301.

6. *Ibid.*

7. Excerpt of a letter, dated October 28, 1946, from Professor Merriam to Richard Rovere in *Selected Documents from the Papers of President Franklin D. Roosevelt and Richard Rovere concerning Jerome Frank* (Franklin D. Roosevelt Memorial Library, Hyde Park, N.Y.), cited hereafter as Selected Documents.

8. Current Biography, *supra*. See also, "Intellectual on the Spot," *Time*, (March 11, 1940), 71, for a profile of Frank, and which cites Benjamin Cohen of New Deal fame as the other of the two brightest students. *Op. cit.*

9. See letter of Frank to Felix Frankfurter, dated November 30, 1932, in Selected Documents, *supra*.

10. Current Biography, *supra*.

11. *Columbia University Oral History Project*—a taped interview with Frank.

12. *Ibid.*

13. See pp. 80-82, *infra*. In none of his books or articles did Frank make mention of his psychoanalytic treatment.

14. See pp. 34-37, *infra*.

15. Frank, *Law and The Modern Mind* (New York: Brentano's, 1930). See discussion on this book, Chap. I, passim, *infra*.

16. He served in that capacity for a year. In 1946, Frank resumed his association with Yale Law School as a visiting lecturer in "Fact Finding," a post he held until his death.

17. Frank, *Save America First: How to Make Our Democracy Work* (New York and London: Harper & Brothers, 1938), Preface, p. ix. Later Frank was appointed a visiting lecturer at the New School for the school year 1946-47.

18. Columbia University Oral History Project, *op. cit.*

19. *Ibid.*

20. Current Biography, op. cit., p. 302.

21. Farley thought that Frank's father-in-law was a political enemy of his in New York. Although Frank had no father-in-law, "it proved difficult to erase the misapprehension." Arthur M. Schlesinger, Jr., *The Coming of the New Deal* (Boston: Houghton Mifflin Co., 1959), p. 49.

22. *Ibid.*, 278. At Frank's suggestion, the FSRC was set up as an independent corporation to purchase surplus food products for distribution to the unemployed. It expanded to include surplus cotton, blankets and coal. Some businessmen opposed it, charging it "with the sin of competing with private enterprise"—a groundless charge—, and its activities were restricted. In 1935 it was transferred to AAA.

23. *Op. cit.*, pp. 49, 50.

24. *Ibid.*, 50.

25. Current Bioghaphy, *op. cit.*, p. 302.

26. For a delineation of Peek, see Schlesinger, *supra*, 58. See also *op. cit.*, pp. 54-55, 56.

27. *Ibid.*

28. *Ibid.*, 57.

29. *Ibid.*, 58.

30. Douglas, *op cit.*, p. 2.

31. Schlesinger, *supra*, 79. See also *op. cit.*, pp. 77-80.

32. *Ibid.*, 80.

33. *Ibid.*

34. See *Alabama Power Company* v. *Ickes*, 302 U.S. 464 (1937).

35. *Ibid.*, 473.

36. F.h. 34, *supra*.

37. Douglas, *op. cit.*, p. 3.

38. Current Biography, *op. cit.*, p. 302.

39. See p. xv at f.n. 40, *infra*. This estimate of Frank was confirmed to the writer by Frank's widow upon his visit to her in New Haven during January 1965.

40. Douglas, *op. cit.*, p. 3.

41. *Ibid.*

42. Letter from Douglas, dated November 14, 1946, to Richard Rovere in Selected Documents, *op cit.*, in which he refers to Frank as having the sharpest mind of anyone he had ever met. See also *op. cit.*, letter from Abe Fortas, dated October 25, 1946, who refers to Frank's "kaleidoscopic brilliance."

43. Frank, "Realism in Jurisprudence," *American Law School Review*, VII (1934), 1063; repr. sub. nom. "Experimental Jurisprudence and the New Deal," *U.S. Congressional Record*, 73rd Cong., 2d Sess., 1934, Part 11, 12412.

44. First portrayed by Frank in Law and The Modern Mind, *op. cit.*

45. See p. 188, f.n. 175, *infra*.

46. Frank, "Realism in Jurisprudence," *op. cit.*, p. 1064; in repr., p. 12412.

47. *Ibid.*, in repr., 12413.

48. *Ibid.*

49. *Ibid.*, 1064-65, 1067-68; in repr., pp. 12413-14. For discussions on several of the New Deal agencies, see Frank, Save America First, *op. cit.*, passim. "New institutional arrangements are required which, by their nature, will call for cooperation. For changes in group sentiments are, it would seem, more often the result than the cause of changes in customs." *Op. cit.*, p. 347.

50. Op. cit. p. 180 f.n. 17, *supra*.

51. Frank, *If Men Were Angels* (New York: Harper & Brothers, 1942), p. 332; Frank, "Red, White and Blue Herring," Saturday Evening Post,

181

(December 6, 1941) Vol. 214. pp. 9, 9-10; Frank "The New Sin," *Saturday Review of Literature,* (December 22, 1945) Vol. 281, pp. 3, 27, all to the effect that after the fall of France, Frank became convinced that the military might of the Nazis was a peril to America and that collective security was necessary.

For Frank's evolution from an advocacy of isolationism to an advocacy of world government in order to escape international anarchy, see Frank, Review of *Scientific Man vs. Power Politics,* by Hans Morgenthau, in *U. of Chicago Law Rev.,* XV (1948), 462; Frank, "War Crimes." Collier's (October 13, 1945).

52. Frank, Save America First, *op. cit.,* pp. 185-201. "All wise students of mankind agree that not only geography, economic relations and physical science, but also ideas, prejudices, superstitions, play their part in producing the social institutions of all human groups. Those forces are variables which interact . . . Each one of them is a 'possible condition and not an explanation.' . . . Their interactions are bafflingly complicated. The history of any society is the history of the result of these baffling interactions. The mistake of the Marxists lies in confusing "necessary" with "sufficient" (i.e. fully explanatory) conditions." *Op. cit.,* pp. 200-01.

53. *Ibid.,* 416.

54. *Ibid.,* 415.

55. *Ibid.,* 246. "Production will fall off—the national income will decline —if so large a proportion of the national income becomes concentrated in the hands of a few citizens that domestic purchasing power does not expand." *Op. cit.*

56. *Ibid.,* 294.

57. *Ibid.*

58. Edward McWhinney, "Judge Jerome Frank and Legal Realism: An Appraisal," *N.Y. Law Forum,* III (1957), 113. See also, John P. Frank, "The Top Commercial Court, *Fortune* (January, 1951), 92, who states that some of the most important business disputes come before the "ablest group of judges, those of the U.S. Court of Appeals for the Second Circuit." For his discussion of Frank, see *op. cit.,* p. 108.

58a. Parties to a lawsuit who, after exhausting state court remedies, appeal on federal constitutional issues to the federal courts are bound by the decisions of the lower federal courts—the district courts and the circuit courts of appeals—unless there is a reversal upon a further appeal to the Supreme Court. However, a state court, even though it will regard an opinion of a lower federal court, particularly a circuit court of appeals, as persuasive, is under no obligation to follow it in cases other than the one appealed from, but is bound only by the pronouncements of the Supreme Court on federal constitutional issues.

59. Unlike the Supreme Court, however, where all the justices, unless disqualified or absent, sit in every case—carefully screened by it for review —originating from the breadth and length of the United States, usually only 3 out of the 8 or 9 judges in each of the eleven Circuit Courts of Appeals sit on a particular case in view of the work load. The opportunity for a Supreme Court justice to participate in a greater number of important cases than a judge of a circuit court of appeals is accordingly increased.

60. Op. cit., f.n. 51, *supra.*

61. Op cit., f.n. 15, *supra.*

62. *Op. cit.,* f.n. 3, *supra.* See pp. 32-33, *infra.*

63. Frank, *Courts on Trial: Myth and Reality in American Justice* (Princeton: Princeton U. Press, 1949). See Chap. I, passim, *infra*.

64. Frank, *Not Guilty* (with Barbara Frank) (Garden City: Doubleday & Company, Inc., 1957). See pp. 27-28 *infra*.

65. Jerome Frank, *Fate and Freedom—A Philosophy for Free Americans*, *op. cit.*

66. *Ibid.*, Preface, vi.

67. Jerome Frank, *If Men Were Angels*, *op. cit.* p. 307. For a brief survey of the various jurisprudential schools, see pp. 1ff., *infra*.

68. Julius Paul, *The Legal Realism of Jerome N. Frank*, *op. cit.*, p. 150.

69. *Ibid.*, 26.

70. For an opinion that a more appropriate term is the "teleological school" since this school "emphasizes the fundamental quest—the purpose of law"—and since some "philosophy overlaps many schools of jurisprudence," see George W. Paton, *A Text-Book of Jurisprudence* (3d ed., New York: Oxford U. Press, 1964), pp. 35-36. See re "transcendential idealism," p. 189, f.n. 208, *infra*.

71. Roscoe Pound, "Fifty Years of Jurisprudence," *Harvard Law Rev.*, LI (1938), 444, 446.

72. Morris Raphael Cohen, *American Thought: A Critical Sketch* (Glencoe, Ill.: Free Press, 1954), p. 137.

73. *Ibid.*

74. Julius Stone, *The Providence and Function of Law* (Cambridge: Harvard U. Press, 1950), p. 220.

75. Edwin W. Patterson, *Jurisprudence: Men and Ideas of the Law* (Brooklyn: The Foundation Press, Inc., 1953), p. 410.

76. "This school tended to romanticize primitive legal institutions, . . . to hinder changes in law through legislation and to perpetuate outmoded traditions." *Ibid.*, 16.

77. Sir Carleton Kemp Allen, *Law in the Making* (paperback ed., London: Oxford U. Press, 1961), p. 16.

78. Edgar Bodenheimer, *Jurisprudence—The Philosophy and Method of The Law* (Cambridge: Harvard U. Press, 1962), p. 71.

79. Thomas A. Cowan (ed.), *The American Jurisprudence Reader* (New York: Oceana Publications, 1956), p. 9.

80. George W. Paton, *op. cit.*, p. 18. For a sound critique of the historical school, see *op. cit.*, pp. 19-21.

81. Patterson, *op. cit.*, p. 83.

82. Stone, *op. cit.*, p. 4.

83. *Ibid.*, 55. See, however, Lon S. Fuller, *The Law in Quest of Itself* (Chicago Foundation Press, 1940), p. 19., who states that the father of legal positivism was Thomas Hobbes (1588-1679). Fuller is correct up to a point. As Friedmann points out, Austin, like Hobbes, divorced the study of law from justice, "but it was left to Austin to follow up this conception into the ramifications of a modern legal system." Wolfgang W. Friedmann, *Legal Theory* (3d ed., London: Stevens & Sons, Ltd., 1953), p. 151. It should be noted that many of the discoveries of the analytical positivists can be found in the literature of the laws of all nations, especially the Romans. "With Austin, however, the subject becomes differentiated from moral and political speculation." *Stone, op. cit.*

84. *Ibid.*

85. Edgar Bodenheimer, "Analytical Positivism, Legal Realism and The

Future of the Legal Method," *Va. Law Rev.*, XLIV (1958), 365, 368.

86. Friedmann, *op. cit.*, p. 153, quoting from Austin, Lectures on Jurisprudence, Vol. I, p. 176.

87. For a penetrating critique of this theory of law, see Paton, *op. cit.*, pp. 70-78.

88. Austin was a disciple of Jeremy Bentham (1748-1832), but he developed only one aspect of Bentham's interests in both legal analysis and legal reform, namely, legal analysis. Bentham may be considered the father of analytical positivism only in a limited sense, since his main interest was in reform. At any rate, he stressed no cleavage, as did Austin, between analysis and reform. See Paton, *op. cit.*, p. 4; Stone, *op cit.*, p. 56. That Austin, however, was a utilitarian and a follower of Bentham at least in the sense that he believed in utilitarianism as the proper guide for legislation, see Paton, *op. cit.*, p. 5; Bodenheimer, Jurisprudence, *op. cit.*, pp. 98-99. "Austin took from Bentham the tool of analysis which both wielded so well; Austin also adopted the theory of utility, but he regarded it as falling outside the sphere of jurisprudence proper. Finally, the two sides of Bentham's work each created a separate school—the pure analyst interested in the law as such and the teleological writer intedested in the ends which law should pursue. It was a disaster for English jurisprudence that Bentham's work was not taken in its entirety. Analysis is barren without a keen view of social utility; a study of the objectives of law is useless unless founded on an analytical appreciation of the *law that is*. But in the nineteenth century, for all Bentham's influence in the world of practical affairs, there was a tendency to deny this in the theory of jurisprudence . . .

". . . Austin's followers were even more rigorous than their master in confining jurisprudence to an analysis of the rules in force." Paton, *op. cit.*, pp. 5, 6.

89. Stone, *op. cit.*, p. 71.

90. *Ibid.*, 56.

91. Frank, *Law and The Modern Mind*, *op.cit.*, p. 193; Stone, *op. cit.*, p. 193; Stone, *op. cit.*, p. 48; Patterson, *op. cit.*, p. 85.

92. Bodenheimer, "Analytical Positivism, Legal Realism and The Future of the Legal Method," *op. cit.* Austin's analysis of the basic legal terms—rights, obligations, injuries, rights in rem, rights in personam, the main concepts of contracts, of torts, etc.—is to a considerable extent "textbook law on a high level of generality." Patterson, *op. cit.*, p. 14.

93. Pound, "Fifty Years of Jurisprudence," *op. cit.*, pp. 444-45. Allen makes the cogent distinction between "two antithetic conceptions of the growth of law . . . In the one, the essence of law is that it is imposed upon society by a sovereign will. In the other, the essence of law is that it develops within society of its own vitality." Allen, *op. cit.*, p. 1.

94. Stone, *op. cit.*, pp. 3, 4; Allen, *op. cit.*, p. 7. Despite some distinguished dissenters, it still is the dominant jurisprudence in England, Canada, Australia and New Zealand. Patterson, *op. cit.*, p. 84.

95. Cohen, *op. cit.*, p. 151.

96. *Ibid.*, 154. See also *ibid.*, 152-53.

97. Oliver Wendell Holmes, Jr., *The Common Law* (Boston: Little, Brown & Co., 1881).

98. *Ibid.*, 1.

99. Oliver Wendell Holmes, Jr., "The Path of The Law," *Harvard Law*

*Rev.*, X (1897), 457, reprinted in Holmes, *Collected Legal Papers* (1920), p. 167.

100. *Ibid.,* 465.

101. *Ibid.*

102. *Ibid.*

103. *Ibid.*

104. See. p. 17 at f.ns. 262, 263, 265, 266, *infra.*

105. *Supra,* 459.

106. *Ibid.*

107. *Ibid.* See Frank's discussion of Holmes's "prediction theory" in Frank, "A Conflict with Oblivion: Some Observations on the Founders of Legal Pragmatism," *Rutgers Law Rev.*, IX (2 parts, 1954), 425, 448, 449. Holmes stated that the law was to be looked at from the standpoint of a "bad man," who was not interested in legal axioms, but in what the courts are likely to do in fact if he acted in a certain manner. *Op cit.* See p. 18 at fn. 274, *infra.*

108. But in one respect Holmes was in accord with a major tenet of analytical positivism: He advocated for purposes of legal study—the study of the law as is—that there be a divorce between law and ethics. But that Holmes was not indifferent to morals is apparent from his remarks that the history of the law "is the history of the moral development of the race . . . When I emphasize the difference between law and morals, I do so with reference to a single end, that of learning and understanding the law." *Ibid.*, 461. See Frank, If Men Were Angels, *op. cit.*, p. 56. Professors Cohen and Friedmann have pointed out that the quotations in the text from Holmes represented but one facet of his thinking, which the legal realists were to appropriate to themselves as their basic philosophy in disregard of their context within a larger framework. Cohen pointed out that side by side with Holmes's characterization as a fallacy the notion that logic was "the only force at work in the development of the law," (*Ibid.*, 465) there appears in his article—and in his volume, The Common Law—a paean to logic, because without it the development of rational thought about the universe is impossible. Cohen further indicated that Holmes's work was full of a penetrating logical analysis of legal doctrines. Morris Raphael Cohen, "Justice Holmes and The Nature of Law," *Columbia Law Rev.*, XXXI (1931), 352; Friedmann, *op. cit.*, p. 198. See also A. L. Goodhart, *Modern Theories* (London: Oxford U. Press, 1953), p. 10, who states that Holmes was not attempting a philosophical analysis of the word "law," but was furnishing a definition for the restricted purpose of distinguishing it from ethics; Benjamin N. Cardozo, *The Nature of the Judicial Process* (New Haven: Yale U. Press, 1921), p. 33: "But Holmes did not tell us that logic is to be ignored when experience is silent."

109. Eugene V. Rostow, *The Sovereign Prerogative: The Supreme Court and The Quest for Law* (New Haven and London: Yale U. Press, 1962), p. 12.

110. *Ibid.*

111. *Ibid.*

112. Frank, "A Conflict with Oblivion: Some Observations on the Founders of Legal Pragmatism," *op. cit.*, p. 427.

113. There is not meant any connection with analytic positivism. Positivism is any philosophical system concerned with positive phenomena, ex-

cluding speculation about ultimate causes.

114. William James, *Pragmatism: A New Name for Some Old Ways of Thinking* (Longmans, Green, 1949), p. 55.

115. That is part of the book's title. James singled out Socrates, Aristotle, Locke, Berkeley and Hume as philosophers who had made fragmentary use of pragmatism in their philosophies. He stated that it was not until his time that pragmatism became conscious of a universal mission and destiny. *Ibid.,* 50.

116. *Ibid.,* 44.

117. *Ibid.,* 54.

118. *Ibid.,* 53.

119. That Dewey's pragmatism was more consistent than James's, see Ralph Barton Perry, *The Life and Character of William James* (New York: George Braziller, 1954), p. 305.

120. James, *op. cit.,* pp. 57-58. See also p. 197.

121. *Ibid.,* 58.

122. Patterson, *op. cit.,* p. 486.

123. John Dewey, "Logical Method and Law," *Cornell Law Quarterly,* X (1924), 17, 19.

124. *Ibid.,* 26.

125. *Ibid.*

126. John Dewey, "My Philosophy of Law," in *My Philosophy of Law: Credos of 16 American Scholars, op. cit.,* pp. 73, 76. pp. 73, 76.

127. *Ibid.,* 84.

128. Dewey, "Logical Method and Law," *op. cit.,* p. 27.

129. Friedmann, *op. cit.,* p. 199. For Frank's views on Dewey, see p. 26, *infra.*

130. Paton, *op. cit.,* p. 21.

131. Stone, *op. cit.,* p. 381. To similar effect, see Patterson, *op. cit.,* p. 509. For Pound's discussion of sociological jurisprudence, see Pound, *op. cit.,* Part IV, 777, 801-10.

132. *Ibid.*

133. Pound, *op. cit.,* p. 444, who claimed that all the nineteenth century jurisprudential schools were subject to the common criticism of dissociating law from "other phenomena of social control or of civilization."

134. Harold Gill Reuschlein, *Jurisprudence—Its American Prophets* (Bobbs-Merrill Co., Inc., 1951), p. 128.

135. Roscoe Pound, "Do We Need a Philosophy of Law?," *Columbia Law Rev.,* V (1905), 339. For other important early articles by Pound, see: "Liberty of Contract," *Yale Law Jour.,* XVIII (1909), 454; "Law in Books and Law in Action," *American Law Rev.,* XLIV (1910), 12; "Scope and Purpose of Sociological Jurisprudence," *Harvard Law Rev.,* XXIV (1912), 591.

136. The leading representatives of the Continental movement were Rudolph von Jhering, Rudolf Stammler, Joseph Kohler and Eugen Ehrlich. Pound also claimed Montesquieu as the "forerunner of sociological jurisprudence." See Reuschlein, *op. cit.,* p. 104. See also p. 109.

137. Lester F. Ward and A. W. Small. Reuschlein, *op. cit.,* p. 127 and Stone, *op. cit.,* p. 403, also list the French sociologist, Gabriel Tarde, as a progenitor of sociological jurisprudence.

138. See f.n. 136, *supra.* Jhering called the law of interests or purposes

"Zweckgesetz." See Reuschlein, *op. cit.*, p. 109; Friedmann, *op. cit.*, p. 224; Stone, *op. cit.*, p. 357. Pound adopted and developed Jhering's classification of interests. Friedmann, *op. cit.*

139. Allen, *op. cit.*, p. 36.

140. Professor Cohen pointed out the musty conservatism prevalent in American legal thought before Pound and its lack of contact with the "vigorous thinking and writing" on the Continent, and the vast influence exerted by Pound upon himself and on legal philosophy in general. Cohen *op. cit.*, p. 158, 158, f.n.

141. Friedmann, *op. cit.*, p. 238.

142. *Ibid.*

143. *Ibid.*, 238-39.

144. Stone, *op. cit.*, p. 406.

145. *Ibid.*, 407.

146. *Ibid.*, 406.

147. *Ibid.*, 411.

148. *Ibid.*, 408.

149. *Ibid.*, 410.

150. *Ibid.*, 412. This idea was later advocated by Cardozo in an article, "A Ministry of Justice," *Harvard Law Rev.*, XXXV (1921), 1136.

151. Prof. Gray wrote *Nature and Sources of Law* in 1909.
*Law* in 1909.

152. Friedmann, *op. cit.*, p. 197.

153. Frank, Law and The Modern Mind, *op. cit.*, p. 121.

154. Friedmann, *op. cit.*, p. 156.

155. *Ibid.*, 157; Frank, *supra*, 123.

156. *Ibid.; Ibid.*, 122. For a trenchant critique of Gray's views, see Benjamin N. Cardozo, *Nature of the Judicial Process* (New Haven: Yale U. Press, 1921), pp. 126-29. See also the criticism by Allen, *op. cit.*, pp. 66-67, of Austin's view that "custom cannot be conceived as command." "This conclusion certainly follows when it has once been assumed that all law must be an explicit command; but it is precisely the binding force of custom which challenges the initial assumption itself." *Op. cit.*, p. 67.

157. *Ibid.*, 197.

158. Frank, Law and The Modern Man, *op. cit.*, pp. 123-25. For a critique of the type of view expressed by Frank, see Morris Raphael Cohen, American Thought, *op. cit.*, p. 157.

159. Friedmann, *supra.*

160. *Ibid.*, 157.

161. His first article was "What Is Law?," *Michigan Law Rev.*, XI (1912), 1,109. See Stone, *op. cit.*, p. 415, f.n. 131. For a somewhat different view on the role of Bingham, see I. L. Fuller, "American Legal Realism," *U. of Pa. Law Rev.*, LXXXII (1934), 429, 429 f.n.

162. Frank, Law and The Modern Mind, *op. cit.*, pp. 275-79.

163. *Ibid.*, 275, f.n.

164. *Ibid.*

165. Cohen, American Thought, *op. cit.*, p. 319, f.n. 19.

166. See p. 17 at f.n. 265, *infra.*

167. See p. 185, f.n. 108, *supra.*

168. Bingham, *op. cit.*, p. 9.

169. *Ibid.*, 23.

170. *Ibid.*, 13, f.n. 31.

171. *Ibid.*, 15.

172. *Ibid.*, 17, 20.

173. *Ibid.*, 22, f.n. 24. For a penetrating critique of Bingham's position and of nominalism generally, see Morris Raphael Cohen, "Justice Holmes and The Nature of Law," *op. cit.*, pp. 360, 363.

Another early exegete of the realist position was Professor Arthur L. Corbin. See his article, "The Law and The Judges," *Yale Law Rev.* (*n.s.*), III (1941), 234. See p. 189 f.n. 207, *infra.*

174. See pp. 22-24, *infra.*

175. Note should be taken of the absence of kinship between legal realism and the venerable school of philosophic realism reaching back to Plato in the Athens of fourth century B.C. To Plato universals alone were real. The approach of legal realism to the philosophy of law, on the other hand, was a nominalistic one, regarding Ideas as mere concepts, mere names (nomina) lacking reality; particular, concrete things alone are real. See Alfred Weber, *History of Philosophy* (New York: Scribner's 1902), p. 83; Frank, Law and The Modern Mind, *op. cit.*, pp. 58-59, 64.

In still another philosophic context, realism posits the existence of a real world whether or not there is a mind to know it, and conversely idealism posits that reality lies in thought and ideas, and the external world has no independent existence absent a knowing mind. See *Modern Introduction to Philosophy*, ed. Paul Edwards and Arthur Pap (rev. ed., New York: Free Press; London: Collier-Macmillan Ltd., 1965), pp. 504ff.

The label "legal realism" was brought into currency in 1930 jointly by Professor Karl N. Llewellyn and Frank. Frank, If Men Were Angels, *op. cit.*, p. 54; Karl N. Llewellyn, "A Realistic Jurisprudence—The Next Step," *Columbia Law Rev.*, XXX (1930), 431. Frank, however, was soon of the opinion that the terminology was "unfortunate." Frank, *op. cit.*, pp. 54, 271; Frank, *Law and The Modern Mind* (paperback, Garden City, N. Y.: Doubleday & Co., Inc.—Anchor Books, 1963), Preface to the Sixth Printing, p. ix. In 1931 and 1933 he suggested substitute labels (never adopted). Frank, Law and the Modern Mind, *op cit.* He was motivated by the ambiguity resultant from the several historic connotations the term "realism" had assumed in philosophic discourse. Frank, If Men Were Angels, *op. cit.*, Appendix V, p. 276, f.n.; Frank, "Are Judges Human?," *University of Pa. Law Rev.*, LXXX (1931), Part II, 233, 258, f.n. 70, Frank, Law and the Modern Mind, *op. cit.*

176. Cohen, *op. cit.*, p. 159.

177. *Ibid.*, 160. See also Karl N. Llewellyn, *Jurisprudence: Realism in Theory and Practice* (Chicago: University of Chicago Press, 1962), pp. 7, f.n. 3; 8; Wilfrid E. Rumble, Jr., *American Legal Realism* (Ithaca: Cornell University Press, 1968), pp. 15-20, for the difficulties, inherent and other, encountered in converting sociological jurisprudence from an aspiration into a full-blown fact. Rumble states that Pound and Cardozo had distrust of the classical view of judicial decision-making before the legal realists emerged. But the latter "prosecuted this war more vigorously, more radically, and on a wider front." *Op. cit.*, pp. 38-39.

178. *Ibid.*, 161. Cf. Reuschlein, *op. cit.*, p. 162. Reuschlein credits the beginning of serious procedural legal reform in this country to Pound's St. Paul speech of 1906. *Op. cit.*
speech of 1906. *Op. cit.*

179. Paton, *op. cit.*, p. 23.

180. Bodenheimer, Jurisprudence—The Philosophy and Method of The Law, *op. cit.*, p. 116.

181. Frank, "Are Judges Human?," *op. cit.*, p. 18.

182. Bodenheimer, *supra*, 118, quoting Pound, "How Far Are We Attaining a New Measure of Values in Twentieth Century Juristic Thought," *Va. Law Rev.*, XL (1936), 81, 89.

183. Frank, Law and The Modern Mind, *op. cit.*, p. 207. Unless specific reference is made to the 1963 edition, all references to *Law and the Modern Mind* are to the 1930 dition.

184. Frank, "Are Judges Human?," *op. cit.*, p. 18.

185. *Ibid.*, 19. Emphasis supplied.

186. Paton, *op. cit.*, p. 27.

187. *Ibid.*, 28.

188. P. 10 at f.n. 185, *supra*.

189. *Supra*, 27.

190. *Ibid.*, 22.

191. Friedmann, *op. cit.*, p. 227.

192. *Ibid.*, 4.

193. *Ibid.*, 227.

194. Patterson, *op. cit.*, p. 196.

195. Friedmann, *op. cit.*, p. 196.

196 see e.g., p. 185, f.n. 108 and p. 188, f.n. 173, *supra*.

197. Frank, Law and The Modern Mind, *op. cit.*, p. 33.

198. Frank, "A Sketch of an Influence," in *Interpretations of Modern Legal Philosophies* (presented to Roscoe Pound), ed. Paul Sayre (New York: Oxford University Press, 1947), 222, 232. See also Frank, Law and The Modern Mind, *op. cit.*, p. 32.

199. Henry Steele Commager, *The American Mind* (New Haven: Yale U. Press, 1950), p. 375. See also his trenchant critique of the natural law and historical law schools, *op. cit.*, pp. 374-75.

200. Eugene V. Rostow, *The Sovereign Prerogative: The Supreme Court and The Quest for Law*, *op. cit.*, p. 8.

201. Stone, *op. cit.*, p. 72.

202. Friedmann, *op. cit.*, p. 150.

203. *Ibid.* See also William James, *op. cit.*, pp. 6, 9. James called it a "clash of human temperaments."

204. *Ibid.*

205. *Ibid.*, 171.

206. Patterson, *op. cit.*, p. 15. Patterson pointed out that a scientific study of law in a social milieu, akin to Comte's scientific sociology, would be vastly different from the approach of analytical positivism. The latter conducts an internal study of law—its structure, principles and corpus—which divorces itself from and lacks "society" in its orbit. *Op. cit.* See discussion in text, p. 12, *infra*.

207. *Ibid.*; Bodenheimer, "Analytical Positivism, Legal Realism and The Future of the Legal Method," *op. cit.*, p. 365. For mention of an analytical positivist of the 20th century who was also "warmly devoted to improving the law," Professor Arthur L. Corbin, see Patterson, *op. cit.* The two are not necessarily inconsistent. See p. 188, f.n. 173, p. 184, f.n. 88, *supra*.

208. Friedmann, *op. cit.*, p. 150. Friedmann added: "The antagonism

between such movements as analytical positivism and realism, is as strong as their common opposition to idealistic theories." *Op. cit.*, p. 151. The latter reference is to schools of thought known as "transcendental idealism," which sought to "deduce their legal philosophy from certain fundamental principles, which they discover through an inquiry into the human mind." *Op. cit.*, p. 77.

209. Frank, If Men Were Angels, *op. cit.*, p. 277; Karl N. Llewellyn, "Some Realism About Realism—Responding to Dean Pound," *Harvard Law Rev.*, XLIV (1931), 1222, 1233.

210. Frank, Courts on Trial, *op. cit.*, p. 73; Patterson, *op. cit.*, p. 538.

211. Frank, If Men Were Angels, *op. cit.*, p. 277, 278.

212. Rostow, *op. cit.*, p. 13. See also Reuschlein, *op. cit.*, p. 183. Rostow includes the realists and their antagonists in this description.

213. For one of the briefest but best presentations of legal realism, see Max Radin, "Legal Realism," *Columbia Law Rev.*, XXXI (1931), 824.

214. Llewellyn listed twenty legal realists and said there doubtless were twenty more. "Some Realism About Realism—Responding to Dean Pound," *op. cit.*, p. 1226, f.n. 18. See the enumeration in Patterson, *op. cit.*, p. 538; in Frank, If Men Were Angels, *op. cit.*, p. 54, f.n.

215. Frank, Courts on Trial, *op. cit.*, p. 75.

216. Llewellyn, *supra*, 1222.

217. Friedmann, *op. cit.*, p. 207. See Thurman W. Arnold, *The Symbols of Government* (New Haven: Yale U. Press, 1935)., *The Folklore of Capitalism* (New Haven: Yale U. Press, 1937). That Arnold, however, diverged somewhat from the general severe realist attack on conceptualism and was somewhat of an anomalous "mystic" realist, see Thurman Arnold, "Judge Jerome Frank," U. Chicago Law Rev., XXIV (1957), 634. In the course of his warm eulogy of Frank, he claimed that Frank did not "give adequate consideration to the importance of authoritarian law based on human reasoning and respected with mystical faith . . . This ideal is the cement which holds a free society together. The ideal of a judiciary which discovers its principles through the enlightened application of established precedents dramatizes that most important conception that there is a rule of law above men." He felt that realistic jurisprudence was "a good medicine for a sick and troubled society," such as the early '30s, but was "not a sustaining force for a stable civilization." *Op. cit.*

218. Friedmann, *ibid.* For various contemporary twentieth century theories which exerted an influence on the thinking of different realists, see Patterson, *op. cit.*, p. 538.

219. Patterson, *op. cit.*, pp. 546-48.

220. Friedmann, *op. cit.*, p. 200.

221. Allen, *op. cit.*, p. 41.

222. *Ibid.*, 43.

223. Frank, If Men Were Angels, *op. cit.*, p. 304.

224. Allen, *op. cit.*, p. 44.

225. *Ibid.*, 46.

226. Llewellyn, "Some Realism About Realism—Responding to Dean Pound," *op. cit.*, pp. 1236-37. He enumerated nine characteristics: (1) "The conception of law in flux . . ." (2) "The conception of law as a means to social ends and not as end in itself . . ." (3) "The conception of society in flux . . ." (4) "The *temporary* divorce of Is and Ought for purposes of study. By this I mean that whereas value judgments must

always be appealed to in order to set objectives for inquiry, yet during the inquiry itself into what Is, the observation, the description, and the establishment of relations between the things described are to remain as *largely as possible* uncontaminated by the desires of the observer or by what he wishes might be or thinks ought (ethically) to be . . . On the Ought side this means an insistence on informed evaluations instead of armchair speculations." (5) "Distrust of traditional legal rules insofar as they purport to *describe* what either courts and people are actually doing . . ." (6) ". . . the tentative adoption of the theory of rationalization for the study of opinions . . ." (7) The establishment of narrower categories in grouping of cases. "This is connected with the distrust of verbally simple rules—which so often cover dissimilar and non-simple fact situations." (8) An evaluation of law in terms of its effects. (9) "Insistence on *sustained and programmatic attack* on the problems of law along any of these lines . . ." Llewellyn stated that items 1, 2, 3 and 5, "while common to the workers of the newer movement, are not peculiar to them," but items 4, 6, 7, 8 and 9 "are to me the characteristic marks of the movement. . ."

227. Frank, Law and The Modern Mind, Preface to the Sixth Printing, *op. cit.*, pp. x-xi; Frank, Courts on Trial, *op. cit.*, pp. 73-74.

228. *Ibid.*, x; Frank, Courts on Trial, *op. cit.*, pp. 316, 321, 148, f.n. 3.

229. *Ibid.*, x; Frank, Courts on Trial, *op. cit.*, p. 73.

230. The theories of the "rule skeptics" Fred Rodell, Karl N. Llewellyn, Felix Cohen, Herman Oliphant and Underhill Moore are briefly summarized in Rumble, *op. cit.*, pp. 142-75. The success attained by them in their efforts to create a science of law is very questionable. The judicial behavior-alists, who unlike most legal realists are not lawyers but social scientists, have taken over in the last decade where the rule skeptics left off in their endeavor to develop a "science" of prediction of judicial decisions. See, e.g., Thomas P. Jahnige and Sheldon Goldman (eds.), *The Federal Judicial System:Readings in Process and Behavior* (New York, Chicago, San Francisco, Atlanta, Dallas, Montreal, Toronto, London: Holt, Rinehart and Winston, Inc., 1968). According to Rumble, they "seem to have advanced the cause of scientific progress beyond the point reached by the realists." *Op. cit.*, p. 177. See Rumble's discussion on the rule skeptics and the judicial behavioralists, *op. cit.*, pp. 167-82.

231. Frank, *supra,* xi; Frank, Courts on Trial, *op. cit.*, p. 74.

232. *Ibid.; Ibid.*

233. *Ibid.* See Patterson, *op. cit.*, p. 544; "Judge Jerome Frank has picked a different weak spot in the use of formal logic by hammering away for twenty years and more at the minor premise of the legal system . . ."

234. For Prof. Morgan's repudiation of this classification of himself, see his review of Courts on Trial in *Journal of Legal Education*, II (1949), 385, 386. It is of interest to note that a number of legal realists besides Frank were members of Franklin Roosevelt's New Deal. Thus, Douglas, Arnold, Oliphant and Felix Cohen were New Deal functionaries.

235. Frank, *supra,* xii.

236. *Ibid.*, xi. For Frank's rather sharp critique of Llewellyn as "perhaps the most brilliant of the rule skeptics," who, as a rule skeptic, is still addicted to "magic," a "semi-skeptical" believer in magic, see his Courts on Trial, *op. cit.*, pp. 74-77. And see Courts on Trial, *op. cit.*, pp. 148-49, for a similar critique of the rule skeptic Felix Cohen, "a brilliant younger member of this school," who looks for the motivating forces molding legal

decisions in "'the political, economic and professional backgrounds of our various judges.'" In Frank's view, the "'new psychology,' Freudian or otherwise, properly emphasizes" the "uniquely, highly individual" and "peculiarly individual factors." Frank, Courts on Trial, *op. cit.*, p. 151.

237. Patterson, *op. cit.*, p. 549.

238. *Op. cit.*

239. *Ibid.*, 12.

240. *Ibid.*, 326, f.n. 1. See David Elkind, "Giant in the Nursery—Jean Piaget," *New York Times*, Magazine Section (May 26, 1968), p. 25.

241. *Ibid.*, 15.

242. *Ibid.*, 18.

243. *Ibid.*, 16. See *ibid.*, 19 f.n., where Frank said that the law more than "most other departments of life" resembles "the child's conception of the Father-as-Judge," and thus the law "is looked to for an absurdly disproportionate degree of certainty." For Frank's discussion on religion, law and the father-substitute, see *ibid.*, 202, 203.

244. *Ibid.*, 19, 21.

245. *Ibid.*, 11, 11 f.n. "If it be true that greater legal certainty is sought than is practically required or attainable, then the demand for excessive legal stability does not arise from practical needs. It must have its roots not in reality but in a yearning for something unreal." *Op. cit.*, p. 11.

246. *Ibid.*, 13; 21 f.n. Frank listed fourteen other "suggested or possible explanations" in an Appendix, p. 263. See Patterson, *op. cit.*, p. 550, f.n. 58: "Most of these seem better than the Freudian one . . ."

247. *Ibid.*, 21 f.n.

248. *Ibid.* To same effect, see Frank, The Scientific Spirit and Economic Dogmatism, in *Science for Democracy*, ed. Jerome Nathanson (New York: Crown Press, 1946), pp. 11, 21.

249. *Ibid.*, 69 et seq.

250. See Frank, Review of *Rediscovery of Justice*, by F. R. Bienenfeld, *California Law Rev.*, XXXVIII (1950), 351.

251. See, e.g., Felix Cohen, *American Bar Ass'n. Journal*, XVII, (Feb. 1931), 111; Walton H. Hamilton, *The New Republic*, (Jan. 21, 1931) Vol. 65. p. 111; Malcolm A. Hoffman, "Old Wine," *Fed. Bar Jour.*, VII (1946), 223; Forrest Revere Black, *Ky. Law Jour.*, XVIV (1931), 349; Francis H. Bohlen, *U. of Pa. Law Rev.*, LXXIX (1931), 822; Francis A. Allen, *Ill. Law Rec.*, XLIV (1949), 554, a review of the 6th ed.; Oscar Cox, *Yale Law Jour.*, XL (1931), 670; William A. Robson, *The Political Quarterly*, XXI (1950), 417, a review of the 1st English ed.; David A. Cavers, *W. Va. Law Quar.*, XXXVII (1931); Mortimer J. Adler, "Law and The Modern Mind: A Symposium," *Columbia Law Rev.*, XXXI (1931), 82 (Llewellyn and Walter Wheeler Cook contributed to this symposium); Edward F. Barrett, "Confession and Avoidance—Reflections on Rereading Jerome Frank's Law and The Modern Mind (6th Printing), *Notre Dame Lawyer*, XXIV, 447; Thurman W. Arnold, *Saturday Review of Literature*, (March 7, 1931), Vol. 7, p. 644.

252. Karl N. Llewellyn, *Jurisprudence—Realism in Theory and Practice op. cit.*, p. 105. See pp. 101-15. These comments appeared originally as part of "Law and The Modern Mind: A Symposium," *ibid.*, 104.

253. Morris Raphael Cohen, *Law and The Social Order—Essays in Legal Philosophy* (New York: Harcourt, Brace & Co., 1933), p. 360. See Frank's

attempted explanation in Law and The Modern Mind, *op. cit.*, pp. 196-203; 19 f.n. See p. 192 f.n. 243, *supra.*

254. Allen, *op. cit.*, p. 47.

255. Frank, Law and The Modern Mind, *op. cit.*, p. 252.

256. *Ibid.*, 247.

257. *Ibid.*, 245.

258. See pp. 150-52, *infra,* for extended remarks on psychology and the law.

259. See p.3 at f.n. 95, *supra.*

260. *Supra,* 55. See Stone, *op. cit.*, p. 207.

261. *Ibid.*, 48.

262. *Ibid.*, 46. For Frank's later objection to the use of the word "law" in order to avoid formalistic polemics, see his If Men Were Angels, *op. cit.*, pp. 279-84; Courts on Trial, *op. cit.*, pp. 66-67.

263. *Ibid.*, 126.

264. *Ibid.*; Frank, "Mr. Justice Holmes and Non-Euclidean Legal Thinking," *Cornell Law Quar.*, XVII (1932), 568, 571; Frank, "Are Judges Human?," *op. cit.*, p. 17.

265. *Ibid.*, 128. In a footnote Frank added: "And predictions as to future decisions."

266. *Ibid.*, 46.

267. *Ibid.*, 51, quoting Holmes's famous "derisive phrase" in *Pacific Co. v.Jensen,* 244 U.S. 205, 255 (1917).

268. *Ibid.*, 62.

269. *Ibid.*, 167.

270. *Ibid.*, 276. See pp. 23-24, *infra.*

271. *Ibid.*, 167.

272. *Ibid.*, 125.

273. *Ibid.*, 127.

274. See p. 185, f.n. 107, *supra.*

275. *Supra,* 125.

276. *Ibid.*, 274.

277. Frank, *Law and The Modern Mind* (Garden City, N.Y.: Doubleday & Co., Inc., Anchor edition, 1963), p. xxvii. This is the paperback 6th edition, which was originally published in 1949. See p. 63 *infra.*

278. For a discussion of the other stimuli, see pp. 23-24, *infra.*

279. Frank, Law and The Modern Mind (1930 ed.), p. 128. The emphasis appears, however, only in the paperback edition of 1963, on p. 138. See f.n. 277, *supra.* Cf. this with Gray's view, p. 8, *supra.*

280. *Ibid.*, 58. See Frank, "A Lawyer Looks at Language," in S. I. Hayakawa, *Language in Action* (New York: Harcourt & Brace, 1939), p. 323 et seq.

281. *Ibid.*, 60. See also *ibid.*, 57.

282. *Ibid.*, 58.

283. *Ibid.*, 64.

284. *Ibid.*, 63.

285. Stone, *op. cit.*, p. 207.

286. *Supra,* 63.

287. Citing Piaget's studies, Frank felt that words cast a similar spell over children. *Ibid.*, Chapter VIII and IX.

288. *Ibid.*, 84, citing Ogden and Richards, The Meaning of Meaning (2d ed., 1927) and other books. For the considerable influence of Ogden

and Richards' book on American legal realism, see Patterson, *op. cit.*, pp. 287, f.n. 27; 546.

289. *Ibid.*, 91.

290. *Ibid.*, 84. See p. 5 at f.n. 118, *supra,* relative to William James and "magic words." See also Frank's discussion in *Chrestensen* v. *Valentine,* p. 136 at f.ns. 20, 22, 23, *infra.*

Frank's sound observations in this area are unnecessarily linked by him with his mythical theory of law as the father-substitute. He felt that this primitive and childish word-magic persisted in the law because of its function as the father-substitute. *Op. cit.*, p. 91. In If Men Were Angels, *op. cit.*, p. 312, Frank returned to this subject without any linkage to his father-substitute notion.

291. *Ibid.*, 65.

292. *Ibid.*, 67. For the influence of Schiller on William James, see p. 5 at f.n. 120, *supra.*

293. *Ibid.*

294. *Ibid.*, 68. See Frank, "What Courts Do in Fact," *Illinois Law Rev.,* XXVI (1932), 645, 777 f.n. 84: "Formal logic is misused in the effort to make it appear that formal law ensures certainty in decisions. But the result is rather to ensure mystery and uncertainty as to how decisions come into being."

295. For a discussion of John Dewey's "instrumental logic," and its influence on legal realism, see pp. 5-6 *supra.*

296. *Supra,* 67.

297. *Ibid.*, 68, f.n.; 66.

298. *Ibid.*, 131.

299. *Ibid.*

300. *Ibid.*, 98, 166.

301. *Ibid.*, 95.

302. *Ibid.*, 98.

303. *Ibid.*, 253.

304. *Ibid.* Emphasis supplied.

305. Frank, "Are Judges Human?," *op. cit.*, p. 44. The pejorative reference had been made by Professor Cohen. See also Frank, Review of *Legal Philosophy from Plato to Hegel,* by Huntington Cairns, *Indiana Law Rev.,* XXV (1949),231, 243; Patterson, *op. cit.*, p. 99. Patterson wrote that Frank in "writing able opinions expounding legal generalizations" has given evidence that he does not accept the so-called "do-law" theory that "law consists of what officials do, *independently of any generalization as to what they ought to do.* In this exclusive form, probably no person with any professional legal experience has ever adopted it."—For charges similar to Cohen's, see Mortimer Adler, "Symposium on Law and The Modern Mind," *op. cit.*, p. 98; Walter B. Kennedy, "Realism, What Next?," *Fordham Law Rev.,* VIII, Part II (1939), 73.

306. Frank, If Men Were Angels, *op. cit.*, pp. 303-04.

307. Frank, Law and The Modern Mind, *op. cit.*, p. 341. Frank was referring to two articles by Cohen.

308. Frank, "Mr. Justice Holmes and Non-Euclidean Legal Thinking," *op. cit.*, p. 571.

309. Frank, If Men Were Angels, *op. cit.*, p. 54.

310. See p. 18 at f.ns. 276-78, *supra;* p. 257, f.n. 10, *infra.*

311. See p. 196, f.n. 342, *infra;* p. 64, *infra.*

312. Frank, Law and The Modern Mind, *op. cit.*, p. 101.

313. Frank, Courts on Trial, *op. cit.*, p. 168.

314. Frank, Law and The Modern Mind, *supra*, 135. Cf. Frank, Courts on Trial, *ibid.*, 198; Frank, "Say It With Music," *Harvard Law Rev.*, LXI (1948), 921, 927.

315. Joseph G. Hutcheson, Jr., "The Judgment Intuitive: The Function of the "Hunch" in Judicial Decisions," *Cornell Law Quar.*, XIV (1929), 274. Hutcheson was a district judge of the Southern District Court of Texas.

316. Frank, *supra*, 103, quoting from Hutcheson, *ibid.*, 274. See Frank, "Both Ends Against the Middle," *U. of Pa. Law Rev.*, C. (1951), 20, 41-42.

317. Frank, Courts on Trial, *op. cit.*, p. 171. See Frank, "Both Ends Against the Middle," *op. cit.*, p. 41; Frank, "Short of Sickness and Death," *N.Y.U. Law Rev.*, XXVI (1951), 545-600.

318. *Ibid.*, 170.

319. Hutcheson, *op. cit.*, p. 287.

320. Frank, Courts on Trial, *supra*, 170. Frank cited the Gestaltists' favorite illustration of a melody which does not result from the summation of its parts, but is rather a basic unit determining the functions of its parts. The parts do not determine the melody. *Op. cit.*, pp. 170-71. For a leading book on Gestalt Psychology, see Wolfgang Köhler, *Gestalt Psychology: An Introduction to New Concepts in Modern Psychology* (a Mentor book— New York and Toronto: The New American Library & London: The New English Library, Limited, 1947).

321. *Ibid.*, 171.

322. *Ibid.*, 173. See Frank, "Say It With Music," *op. cit.*, p. 931.

323. *Ibid.*

324. *Ibid.*, 175.

325. For a critique that this approach is not universally true, see the views of a Yale Law School psychologist who was close to legal realism, Edward Stevens Robinson, *Law and the Lawyers* (New York: Macmillan Co., 1935), p. 174: "Whether, in his explicit statement of his reasons for concluding thus and so, a man gives a largely accurate or a largely fictitious account of himself is another one of those matters of fact. They are not always easy to settle, but certainly they can never be settled by the loose, lazy, and frequently cynical use of such terms as unconscious complexes and rationalization."

326. Frank, Law and The Modern Mind, *op. cit.*, p. 104.

327. *Ibid.*, 104-05.

328. *Ibid.*, 105.

329. Frank, Courts on Trial, *op. cit.*, p. 178.

330. Frank, Law and The Modern Mind, *supra*, 106.

331. *Ibid.*, 134. See *ibid.*, 105 f.n.

332. Frank, Courts on Trial, *op. cit.*, pp. 178, 150, 152.

333. *Ibid.*, 179, 180.

334. Frank, Law and The Modern Mind, *op. cit.*, p. 109.

335. Frank, Courts on Trial, *supra*, 17. 18. See Frank, *Not Guilty op. cit.*, p. 215: ". . . There is frequently an illusion of communication, an erroneous assumption that we invariably know what others mean. Frequently we talk past one another."

336. Frank, Not Guilty, *op. cit.*, p. 203.

337. Frank, Courts on Trial, *supra*, 18.

338. *Ibid.*, 20.

339. *Ibid.*, 22.

340. *Ibid.*, 23. See Frank's opinion in *Broadcast* v. *Havana Madrid Restaurant Corp.*, 175 F. 2d 77, 80 (1949): "For the demeanor of an orally-testifying witness is 'always assumed to be evidence.' It is 'wordless langauge.' The liar's story may seem uncontradicted to one who merely reads it, yet it may be 'contradicted' in the trial court by his manner, his intonations, his grimaces, his gestures, and the like—all matters which 'cold print does not preserve' and which constitute 'lost evidence' so far as the upper court is concerned . . ."

341. Frank, Law and The Modern Mind, *op. cit.*, p. 111. See also *ibid.*, 133.

342. In his Preface to the Sixth Printing of Law and The Modern Mind, Frank sought to dissipate a misunderstanding by "some legal pundits" to the effect that the burden of Law and The Modern Mind was that most uncertainty stems from rule-uncertainty. A careful reading of that book shows that Frank was referring to both rule-uncertainty and fact-uncertainty, though his emphasis was on the former in his attack on the "basic legal myth." See on fact-uncertainty, Chapter XII, "The Judging Process and the Judge's Personality," in Law and the Modern Mind. Frank admitted that perhaps he was "at fault in not so stating with greater emphasis." At any rate, the shift in emphasis is marked in Courts on Trial, where Frank dealt primarily with fact-uncertainty, as well as in the chapter devoted to that issue in If Men Were Angels. In Courts on Trial there is but one passing reference to Frank's basic notion in Law and The Modern Mind of the law as a father-substitute. It would appear that in the intervening years between the two books the hold of this psychological theory on him had become markedly attenuated. See Frank, Law and The Modern Mind, Preface to the Sixth Printing, *op cit.*, p. xvii; Frank, If Men Were Angels, *op. cit.*, Chap. VIII., Frank. Courts on Trial, *op. cit.*, p. 384.

For early articles by Frank, written in 1931 and 1932 respectively, in which he laid more stress on fact-uncertainty than on rule-uncertainty, see Frank, "Are Judges Human?," *op cit.*, and "What Courts Do in Fact," *op. cit.*

343. Frank, Law and The Modern Mind, Preface to the Sixth Printing, *op. cit.*, p. xv.

344. *Ibid.*, xvi.

345. Frank, Courts on Trial, *op. cit.*, p. 4; Frank, If Men Were Angels, *op. cit.*, pp. 68-80; 106-18, 284-93. In the latter volume, in an analysis of the hankering after certainty on the part of his critics, Frank does not mention the "psychoanalytic" theory of his *Law and The Modern Mind*. There is no indication he had given it up. It simply was not necessary for his purpose. He could make and develop his point without it.

346. Frank, Courts on Trial, *ibid.*, 14.

347. *Ibid.*, 15.

348. *Ibid.*

349. *Ibid.*

350. *Ibid.*, 24.

351. *Ibid.*, 33.

352. Frank, "Say It with Music," *op. cit.*, p. 956.

353. Frank, *supra*, 33. See p. 63 at f.n. 109 *infra*.

354. *Ibid.*

355. Frank, "Modern and Ancient Legal Pragmatism—John Dewey & Co. vs. Aristotle," *Notre Dame Lawyer*, XXV (1950), Part I, 207, Part II, 460.

356. *Ibid.*, 466.

357. *Ibid.*, 483.

358. *Ibid.*, 485.

359. *Ibid.*, 502.

360. Frank, Courts on Trial, *op. cit.*, p. 183. See Frank's opinion in *U.S.* v. *Forness*, 125 F.2d 928, 942 (1942): "It is sometimes said that the requirement that the trial judge file findings of fact is for the convenience of the upper courts. While it does serve that end, it has a far more important purpose—that of evoking care on the part of the trial judge in ascertaining the facts. For, as every judge knows, to set down in precise words the facts as he finds them is the best way to avoid carelessness in the discharge of that duty. Often a strong impression that, on the basis of the evidence, the facts are thus-and-so gives way when it comes to expressing that impression on paper. The trial court is the most important agency of the judicial branch of the government precisely because on it rests the responsibility of ascertaining the facts." (f.n. 43—"and because, too, the majority of decisions are not appealed.")

361. *Ibid.* "Even physicists and mathematicians frequently use logically-tested hunches." *Ibid.*

362. *Ibid.*

363. *Ibid.*, 185.

364. See Lee Loevinger, Review of Courts on Trial, in *Etc.: A Review of General Semantics*, VIII (1950), 42. See p. 152, *infra*.

365. See p. 119, *infra*.

366. Rumble, *op. cit.*, p. 135. See our discussion on fact-skepticism, pp. 157-58, *infra*.

367. Frank, *Not Guilty, op. cit.*

368. *Ibid.*, 248.

369. *Ibid.*, 38. It is different, of course, when a man should be in prison, without entering into a discussion of the pressing need for prison reform and a rational approach to rehabilitation of prisoners. For a brief comment by Frank on punishment, see his concurring opinion in *U.S.* v. *Sacher*, 182 F.2d 416, 458 (1950): "Criminologists disagree concerning the extent to which punishing one man deters other men. But there is general agreement that, in some instances at least, punishment acts both directly, as a preventive example to others, and indirectly, as a means of creating or strengthening social habits of conduct. There can be little doubt that summary punishment of contempt, in a case like this, will have both effects." Harry Sacher, the defendant in this case, was one of the obstructionist lawyers in the Communist conspiracy trial, *Dennis* v. *United States* (see p. 139, *infra*) who, after repeated warnings by the trial judge, Judge Harold Medina, was convicted, after the *Dennis* trial, of summary criminal contempt and sentenced to serve a term of six months. Medina filed thirty-nine specifications of flagrant obstruction by him. The other lawyers were also convicted of criminal contempt; the minimum sentence meted out was thirty days and the maximum six months. Sacher's conviction was sustained by a majority in the Circuit Court of Appeals and the Supreme Court denied certiorari in 341 U.S. 952 (1950). Judge Clark, who dissented in the Circuit Court of Appeals, based his

dissent solely on the pocedural ground of disapproving a summary conviction as distinguished from a conviction for contempt after a trial.

Frank's criticism of Sacher's conduct follows: "We affirm the orders punishing the lawyers not because they courageously defended their clients, or because those clients were Communists, but only because of the lawyers' outrageous conduct—conduct of a kind which no lawyer owes his client, which cannot ever be justified, and which was never employed by those advocates, for minorities or for the unpopular, whose courage has made lawyerdom proud. The acts of the lawyers for the defendants in this trial can make no sensible person proud.

"What they did was like assaulting the pilot of an aeroplane in flight, or turning out the lights during a surgical operation. To use homelier words, they tried to throw a wrench in the machinery of justice . . . The summary punishment here will tend to deter imitation of that behavior in other trials. If it is not deterred, the administration of justice in our courts is highly likely to break down.

". . . But we cannot agree that fearless discharge of that duty requires or permits a lawyer to turn a trial into a bar-room squabble." (A reading of the lengthy exchanges between the lawyers and the trial judge is convincing proof that Frank's charactrization of the trial as a "bar-room squabble" was close to the mark.)

370. Frank, If Men Were Angels, *op. cit.*, p. 316.

371. *Supra*, 326. See Frank's opinion in *Ira S. Bushey & Sons* v.W. E. *Hedger Transportation Corporation*, 167 F.2d 9, 36 (1948) (dis. op.): "I recall a 'small' businessman caught in the toils of the depression, who, in 1933, after listening to an eloquent address on liberty, sagely remarked: 'Yes, but you can't make a sandwich out of liberty.' To be sure, the purely 'economic man' is a bestial concept. Things of the spirit (such as civil liberties and what they make possible) are, or should be, more precious than material things. Yet for most mortals the former can have little value in the complete absense of the latter."

372. *Ibid.*

373. *Ibid.*, 327.

374. *Ibid.*, 327, 183. Paul wrote of Frank's volume, *Not Guilty:* "In its own modest way, *Not Guilty*, takes its place alongside the work of Beccaria, Bentham, and others in previous centuries who sought ways of making the judicial system a more compassionate and humane instrument of the ends of justice." Julius Paul, *The Legal Realism of Jerome N. Frank, op. cit.*, p. 103.

374a. 195 F.2d 583 (1952). A severance of trial was granted to Greenglass, who pleaded guilty, and to Yakolev. Sobell, who also appealed, had received a sentence of thirty years.

374b. See pp. 114-15, 118-19, *infra*.

374c. *Supra*, 604, 605, 607.

374d. *Ibid.*, 605.

374e. *Ibid.*, 607. The issue is at present before the Supreme Court again. Eleven of the fifty states have thus far abolished capital punishment, and three (including New York) have abolished it with reservations. There has been no excution in the U.S. since 1967. About 500 prisoners in the U.S. are waiting for the Supreme Court ruling on the Eighth Amendment. See *New York Times*, Dec. 26, 1969, p. 28.

374f. The reference is to the trial judge's opinion that the crime did incalculable damage to the security and vital interests of the United States.

374g. *Ibid.*, 608, 609. Certiorari was denied by the Supreme Court in 344 U.S. 838 (1952). Justice Black was of the opinion that the petition should have been granted. Subsequently, Justice Douglas granted a stay of execution while the Court was on vacation on an issue raised for the first time as to whether the District Court's power to impose the death sentence, conferred by the Espionage Act of 1917, under which the defendants were charged, had not been taken away from that court by the Atomic Energy Act of 1946, which authorized the death sentence only on a recommendation of the jury and where the proof was that the offense was committed with intent to injure the United States. However, the stay was later vacated by the Court and it affirmed the death sentence in 346 U.S. 273 (1953) in an opinion by Chief Justice Vinson. Justices Black, Douglas and Frankfurter dissented. Douglas felt that the power to impose the death sentence had been taken away from the trial judge. Black and Frankfurter felt that the court was acting in too much haste without adequate briefing by the parties and study by the court of the new issue raised.

On the question of a community standard discussed by Frank in his opinion, see pp. 142-43 *infra*. See also Frank's dissenting opinion in *Repouille* v. *United States*, 165 F.2d 152 (1947), in which he asserted that the moral sense of the community in the situation before him was to be sought in the views of the "ethical leaders of the community." For other views, see Julius Cohen, Reginald A. H. Robson and Alan Bates, "Ascertaining the Moral Sense of the Community: A Preliminary Report on an Experiment in Interdisciplinary Research," *Journal of Legal Education*, VIII (1955), 137-42, repr. in Thomas A. Cowan (ed.), The American Jurisprudence Reader, *op. ct.*, pp. 204-08. Involved in the Repouille case was the quest for citizenship by an alien whose "good moral character" over the preceding five years was questioned because he had practiced euthanasia—i.e., a mercy killing of his son who was a hopeless idiot. In a majority opinion, Judge Learned Hand felt that although the community standard of "good moral character was highly uncertain," yet he concluded that he was "reasonably secure in holding that only a minority of virtuous persons would deem the practice morally justifiable, while it remains in private hands, even when the provocation is as overwhelming as it was in this instance." *Op. cit.*, p. 153. The petitioner, however, did not lose much by this decision since he could file a new petition in a few days when the time lapse between the euthanasia and the new petition would be beyond the five year period. In his dissent on principle—since cases might be involved where the petitioner could lose much valuable time as a result of a decision—Judge Frank wrote: "I incline to think that the correct statutory test (the test Congress intended) is the attitude of our ethical leaders." *Op. cit.*, p. 154. Frank would have remanded the case to the district court to gather whatever information it could from both sides to be placed on the record as to the moral sense of the community leaders.

375. See pp. 1-2, *supra*.

376. See p. 1 at f.n. 67, *supra*.

377. Frank, Law and The Modern Mind, Preface to the Sixth Printing, *op. cit.*, p. xx. For a historical-philosophical survey of natural law, see A.P. D'Entrèves, *Natural Law—An Historical Survey* (New York: Harper Torchbooks, 1965).

378. Frank, Courts on Trial, *op. cit.*, p. 365. Whether labeled justice or natural law, agreement between them is only regarding the *broad* fundamental rights of life, liberty and the pursuit of happiness, or life, liberty and property (if the Lockean trinity is adopted), which must be regarded as imprescriptible rights.

379. *Ibid.* See: Edmond N. Cahn, *The Sense of Injustice* (New York: New York University Press, 1949), p. 12: "Why do we speak of the 'sense of injustice' rather than the 'sense of justice'? "Because 'justice' has been so beclouded by natural-law writings that it almost inevitably brings to mind some ideal relation or static condition or set of preceptual standards, while we are concerned, on the contrary, with what is active, vital, and experiential in the reactions of human beings." See p. 47, f.n. 509, *infra.*

380. *Ibid.*, 366.

381. *Ibid.*, 371. See Frank, "Memorable Victories in the Fight for Justice," *Life*, (March 12, 1951), Vol. 14, p. 86.

382. William J. Brennan, Jr., "The Role of the Court—The Challenge of the Future," *New York Law Journal* (April 20, 1965), 4. Justice Brennan states in this article that reverence for the individual is the distinct contribution both of legal realism and revived natural law to modern jurisprudence. He discusses the shift in emphasis from abstract rules to justice.

383. Frank, "Memorable Victories in the Fight for Justice," *op. cit.*, p. 104.

384. Frank, Fate and Freedom, *op. cit.*, "Polemic against Fatalism" is the title of Reinhold Niebuhr's review of Fate and Freedom in, *The Nation*, (July 14, 1945). Vol. 40.

385. *Ibid.*, 145.

386. *Ibid.*, Chapter I, passim.

387. *Ibid.*, 87. See also p. 182.

388. *Ibid.*, 17.

389. Thurman W. Arnold, Review of *Fate and Freedom*, *Saturday Review of Literature*, (June 23, 1945), Vol. 28, p. 10.

390. Frank, *supra*, 169.

391. *Ibid.*, 191, 193, 194.

392. *Ibid.*, 201.

393. *Ibid.*, 195.

394. *Ibid.*, 343. Frank wrote Fate and Freedom in the midst of World War II.

395. *Ibid.*

396. Frank, If Men Were Angels, *op. cit.*, p. 264. For a critique of Frank's discussion of determinism and voluntarism on the ground that the issue between them "is not so clear-cut as Judge Frank assumes," see Reinhold Niebuhr, *op. cit.* That there is no one version of free will or of determinism, see Barrows Dunham, *Heroes and Heretics* (New York: Alfred A. Knopf, 1964), p. 135, f.n. 4. For a good presentation of three broad views of and source material on free will and determinism, see Modern

Introduction of Philosophy, (ed. Paul Edwards and Arthur Pop), *op. cit.*, p. 2ff.

397. Frank, Courts on Trial, *op. cit.*, p. 239. See also Frank, "A Plea for Lawyer-Schools," *op. cit.*, p. 1326; If Men Were Angels, *op. cit.*, p. 13.

398. Frank, "A Plea for Lawyer-Schools," *op. cit.*, p. 1323. This was the view expressed by Professors Laswell and McDougal. See Paul, The Legal Realism of Jerome N. Frank, *op. cit.*, p. 109, who cites articles by two professors, pro and con, regarding the question of "preaching" by teachers.

399. Frank, Courts on Trial, *supra*, 239. See also, Frank, "A Plea for Lawyer-Schools, *ibid.*, 1325.

400. Frank, "A Plea for Lawyer-Schools," *ibid.*, 1325. See also Frank, Courts on Trial, *ibid.*, 240, 241, where Frank stated that "fortunately most of the judiciary is honest . . ." *Op. cit.*, p. 241.

401. Frank, Courts on Trial, *ibid.*, 240.

402. Frank, "Why Not a Clinical Lawyer-School?," *op. cit.*, p. 922.

403. Frank, Courts on Trial, *supra*, 2.

404. Frank, Law and The Modern Mind, *op. cit.*, p. 113.

405. *Ibid.* The reference is to Theodore Schroeder, "The Psychologic Study of Judicial Opinions," *California Law Rev.*, VI (1918), 69. Schroeder contended that from a judge's arguments, phrases, conclusions, and precedent-citing in his opinion, one could ferret out his dominant unconscious personal motives.

406. Frank, Courts on Trial, *op. cit.*, pp. 247, 250. Frank did not specifically refer to psychoanalysis in *Law and The Modern Mind.* His reference to treatment by a "psychologist" beyond a "searching self-analysis" is casual in the latter volume. See p. 34 at f.n. 409, *infra.*

407. Frank, Law and The Modern Mind, *supra*, 114. The reference is to Charles Grove Haines, "General Observations on the Effect of Personal, Political and Economic Influences in the Decisions of Judges", *Illinois Law Rev.*, XVII (1922), 98.

408. *Ibid.*, quoting from Haines. One of Frank's decisional gems, in which he distinguished social preconceptions or social value judgments from uniquely personal prejudices, will be found in *In re P. J. Linahan*, 138 F.2d 650 (1943). The case involved a "frivolous" charge of bias brought against a special master in Chapter X involuntary proceedings to reorganize a corporate debtor. It deserves quotation at length. "Democracy must, indeed, fail, unless our courts try cases fairly, and there can be no fair trial before a judge lacking in impartiality and disinterestedness. If, however, "bias" and "partiality" be defined to mean the total absence of preconceptions in the mind of the judge, then no one has ever had a fair trial and no one ever will. The human mind, even at infancy, is no blank piece of paper. We are born with predispositions; and the process of education, formal and informal, creates attitudes in all men which affect them in judging situations, attitudes which precede reasoning in particular instances and which, therefore, by definition, are pre-judices. Without acquired "slants," preconceptions, life could not go on. Every habit constitutes a pre-judgment; were those pre-judgments which we call habits absent in any person, were we obliged to treat every event as an unprecedented crisis presenting a wholly new problem he would go mad. Interests, points of view, preferences, are the essence of living. Only death yields complete dispassionateness, for such dispassionateness

signifies utter indifference . . An "open mind," in the sense of a mind containing no preconceptions whatever, would be a mind incapable of learning anything, would be that of an utterly emotionless human being, corresponding roughly to the psychiatrist's descriptions of the feeble-minded. More directly to the point, every human society has a multitude of established attitudes, unquestioned postulates. Cosmically, they may seem parochial prejudices, but many of them represent the community's most cherished values and ideals. Such social pre-conceptions, the "value judgments" which members of any given society take for granted, and use as the unspoken axioms of thinking, find their way into that society's legal system, become what has been termed "the valuation system of the law." The judge in our society owes a duty to act in accordance with those basic predilections inhering in our legal system (although, of course, he has the right, at times, to urge that some of them be modified or abandoned.) The standard of dispassionateness obviously does not require the judge to rid himself of the unconscious influence of such social attitudes.

"In addition to those acquired social value judgments, every judge, however, unavoidably has many idiosyncratic "learnings of the mind," uniquely personal prejudices, which may interfere with his fairness at trial. He may be stimulated by unconscious sympathies for, or antipathies to, some of the witnesses, lawyers or parties in the case before him . . . Frankly to recognize the existence of such prejudices is the part of wisdom. The conscientious judge will, as far as possible, make himself aware of his biases of this character, nullify their effect. Much harm is done by the myth that, merely by putting on a black robe and taking the oath of office as a judge, a man ceases to be human and strips himself of all pre-dilections, becomes a passionless thinking machine. The concealment of the human element in the judicial procss allows that element to operate in an exaggerated manner; the sunlight of awareness has an antiseptic effect on prejudices. Freely avowing that he is a human being, the judge can and should, through self-scrutiny, prevent the operation of this class of biases . . .

". . . Impartiality is not gullibility. Disinterestedness does not mean child-like innocence. If the judge did not form judgments of the actors in those court-house dramas called trials, he could never render decisions." *Op. cit.*, pp. 651-53, 654.

Although not germane to the text, we quote from another opinion by Frank as illustrative of his penchant, at the drop of a hat, to poetize the most humdrum situation. The issue involved in *Fanelli* v. *United States Gypsum Co.*, 141 F.2d 216 (1944) was a prosaic one: May an employee, in a suit for salary alleged to be due him for overtime work, refresh his recollection from a memorandum made by him, not simultaneously with his discharge but one month later, wherein he set down the details of his overtime work? Frank's reply follows: "Common experience, the work of Proust and other keenly observant literary men, and recondite psychological research, all teach us that memory of things long past can be accurately restored in all sorts of ways. The creaking of a hinge, the whistling of a tune, the smell of seaweed, the sight of an old photograph, the taste of nutmeg, the touch of a piece of canvas, may bring readily to the foreground of consciousness the recollection of events that happened years ago and which would otherwise have been forgotten. If a recollection thus reawakened be then set down on paper, why should not that paper properly serve in the courtroom, as it does in everyday life, to prod the memory at still a later date? . . . Since the workings of the human memory still remain a major mystery after centuries of study, courts should hesitate before they glibly contrive dogmatic rules concerning the reliability of the ways of provoking it . . ." *Op cit.*, p. 217.

At times Frank displayed in his opinions a sense of humor. See, e.g., *Kleinman* v. *Kobler*, 230 F.2d 913 (1956), involving an alleged infringement of a patent for a double-headed electric shaver. Writing the Court's opinion, Frank found the patent invalid in view of the prior art; it did not constitute an invention of such originality as to warrant the granting of a patent. Frank wrote: "Perhaps plaintiff's device yielded a size and shape of bulge preferable to what the prior art yielded, but the production of such a result is not invention. So plaintiff, we think, must lose the battle of the bulge . . .

". . . For merely to use two Acron shaver-heads on a razor would clearly not constitute invention. The Acron razor was capable of side-cutting and anticipated plaintiff's patent. Plaintiff's approach to invention is not even a close shave." *Op. cit.*, p. 914.

409. *Ibid.*, See f.n. 406, *supra*.

410. Frank, Courts on Trial, *op. cit.*, p. 250. Frank explained his use of the word "something" as resulting from the constant revisions of the theory and techniques of psychoanalysis "and some adequate, less prolonged and complicated, substitute may soon appear." *Op. cit.* See also, Frank, "Some Reflections on Judge Learned Hand," *Chicago Law Rev.*, XXIV (1957), 666, 678; Frank, "Judicial Fact-Finding and Psychology," *Ohio St. Law Jour.*, XIV (1953), 183, 188; Frank, Fate and Freedom, *op. cit.*, pp. 209-10; Frank, Courts on Trial, *op. cit.*, p. 404.

411. *Ibid.*, 249. See Frank, If Men Were Angels, *op. cit.*, pp. 111, 112.

412. *Ibid.*, 251.

413. *See* p. 24 at f.n. 341, *supra*.

414. Frank, Law and The Modern Mind, *op. cit.*, p. 133.

415. *Ibid.*, 133, 134.

416. *Ibid.*, 134.

417. *Ibid.*, 139-40. "Epieikia" is the Greek word for equity.

418. Frank, Courts on Trial, *op. cit.*, p. 99.

419. *Ibid.*, 80.

420. *Ibid.*, 81.

421. *Ibid.*, 85.

422. *Ibid.*

423. Frank, "Fact-Finding and Psychology," *op. cit.*, p. 186.

424. Frank, Courts on Trial, *supra*, 93.

425. *Ibid.* For an extended discussion on "disclosure," see Frank, Not Guilty, *op. cit.*, pp. 242-48. Frank claimed that this procedure was followed in every civilized land but the United States. See also, Frank, "Civil Law Influences on the Common Law—Some Reflections on 'Comparative' and 'Constrastive' Law," *U. of Pa. Law Rev.*, CIV (1956). 887. For the pros and cons of this procedure and the fact that it is still a very live issue today, see Fred P. Graham, "Law: Focus on Aid to Defense," *New York Times* (August 29, 1965), News of The Week section, p. 4E. Texas is the

most recent state to enact legislation mandating discovery in criminal proceedings, effective January 1, 1966. ". . . the Justice Department has approved a proposed rule that would allow a defendant's lawyer to see any confession, scientific report or grand jury testimony by his client—but not a list of the prosecution's witnesses.

"The Supreme Court is expected to submit such a rule to Congress next year. This should encourage more states to adopt liberal criminal discovery rules." Graham, *op cit.*

426. *Ibid.*

427. *Ibid.,* 96. See the discussion of Frank's dissenting opinion in U.S. v. Johnson, pp. 120-21, *infra.* The government has sought to overcome some of the "legal laissez-faire" (*ibid.,* 92) condemned by Frank through the passage of the Federal Criminal Justice Act of 1964, which mandates the assignment of counsel to indigent defendants in *all* criminal cases—misdemeanor as well as felony—in all federal and state jurisdictions, from the moment of arraignment. It provides a schedule of fees for lawyers, including fees for hiring investigators. The estimated cost nationwide for this task is $7,500,000 annually.

428. *Ibid.,* 94. See Frank., Review of *Cases on Judicial Administration,* by Maynard E. Pirsig, *Yale Law Jour.,* LVI (1947), 589, 594. For a comprehensive book on the Legal Aid Societies, Public Defenders, etc., see Association of the Bar of the City of New York, *Equal Justice for the Accused* (New York: Doubleday & Co., 1959). Since June 1, 1966, in New York, State, a.g., pursuant to Article 18B of the County Law, Legal Aid societies, Public Defenders, and any other kind of legal organization representing indigent defendants (whichever plan for representation among four types of plans listed is approved by each county or the city in which a county is wholly contained) are provided with funds for "investigative, expert and other services necessary for an adequate defense" in criminal cases.

429. *Ibid.,* 95.

430. *Ibid.*

431. *Ibid.*

432. *Ibid.,* 96.

433. *Ibid.,* 98.

434. *Ibid.,* 99.

435. *Ibid.,* 97. Under the Chandler Act of 1938, involving corporate reorganization cases, the expert staff of the SEC obtains evidence which is usually beyond the financial reach of private parties. For Frank's laudatory remarks of the administrative agencies, and particularly of the SEC, see his volume, If Men Were Angels, *op. cit.,* pp. 122-47. In *Perkins v. Endicott Johnson Corporation,* 128 F. 2d 208, 221 (1942), Frank wrote: "For the value of the specialist is that, in dealing with a selected area of experience, he is able to make inferences quickly—because in part intuitively —and with more likelihood of accuracy than his fellow men, since many of the criteria of judgment have, with him, become semi-automatic, having been transferred, so to speak, from the conscious processes to the spinal column (or, to use highbrow terms, from the cerebral cortex to the cerebellum.) He acquires unusual 'insight' and 'discernment' which are the 'funded outcome of long familiarity with like operations in the past' . . . " (The quotation is from John Dewey, How We Think, 104-05.)

See also, Frank "White Collar Justice," *Saturday Evening Post* (July 17, 1943), Vol. 216, pp. 22, 56, and the reply to this article by Senior Judge John C. Knox, "A Just Justice," *Saturday Evening Post*, (July 24, 1943). Vol. 216, p. 22. Commenting on Frank's call for a "public prosecutor for civil actions," Knox expressed his opposition to a "gumshoe army." *Op. cit.*, p. 75. See further, Frank, Courts on Trial, *op. cit.*: "In our own Domestic Relations Courts, government officers procure and present most of the evidence. Lawyers for any of the parties may cross-examine any witness, may offer additional evidence, and may argue about the applicable legal rules. The advantages of the adversary method are fully preserved, but the fighting spirit is much diminished."

436. *Ibid.*, 100. See Frank, Not Guilty, *op. cit.*, pp. 236, 241-42.

437. Frank, Not Guilty, *op. cit.*, p. 242.

438. Frank, Courts on Trial, *supra*. See Frank, "The Lawyers' Role in Modern Society," *Jour. Public Law*, IV (1955), 1, 22-23.

439. *Ibid.* See Frank, "Judicial Fact-Finding and Psychology," *op. cit.*, p. 185. "To a limited extent, such testimony has been employed in respect of complaining witnesses in prosecutions for sex offenses." *Op. cit.*

440. Frank, "Judicial Fact-Finding and Psychology," *op. cit.*, p. 185.

441. Frank, Courts on Trial, *supra*.

442. *Ibid.*, 225.

443. *Ibid.*, 225-28; Frank, "Why Not a Clinical Lawyer School?," *op. cit.*, pp. 907-08; Frank, "A Plea for Lawyer-Schools," *op. cit.*, p. 1320; Frank, "Both Ends Against the Middle," *op. cit.*, p. 21.

444. *Ibid.*, 226.

445. *Ibid.*, 230.

446. Frank, "What Constitutes a Good Legal Education," *American Law School Review*, VII (1933), 894, 895.

447. Frank, Courts on Trial, *supra*.

448. *Ibid.*, Frank, "Why Not a Clinical Lawyer-School?," *op. cit.*, p. 909.

449. Frank, Courts on Trial, *supra*, 231.

450. *Ibid.* Frank excepted the "brilliantly intuitive" teacher from this requirement.

451. *Ibid.*, 233, 227.

452. *Ibid.*, 233.

453. *Ibid.*, 234; Frank, "Both Ends Against the Middle," *op. cit.*, pp. 29-30.

454. *Ibid.*, 235.

455. Frank, "Why Not a Clinical Lawyer-School?", *op. cit.* p. 913.

456. *Ibid.*

457. Francis X. Clines, "Law Schools Get an Interne Plan," *New York Times* (August 3, 1964), p. 1 (Second Section): "The head of the largest organization of trial lawyers in this country announced yesterday a plan to rectify what he called 'one of the great failures of the nation's law schools' —the omission of practical courtroom experience in the training of law students.

"Under the plan, in which 20 law schools have expressed interest, students will take 'field trips' to courtrooms and work on cases under trial lawyers in an 'apprenticeship' program . . ."

458. Frank, Courts on Trial, *op. cit.*, p. 239; Frank, "Both Ends Against the Middle," *op. cit.*, p. 33. Julius Paul states that "as early as 1913, Wil-

liam Draper Lewis was urging the incorporation of the social sciences in legal education." Paul, *op cit.*, pp. 111, 112, f.n. 1. Cf. p. 143, at f.n. 82, *infra*.

459. *Ibid.*, Frank, "The Lawyers' Role in Modern Society," *op. cit.*, pp. 23-24.

460. *Ibid.*, 239, 161. For Frank's opposition to behaviorism, see p. 256 f.n. 7, *infra*. For his views on determinism, see pp. 32-33, *supra*.

461. Frank, "Why Not a Clinical Lawyer-School?," *op. cit.*, p. 922.

462. Frank, Courts on Trial, *supra*, 239. For Frank's reply to a critique by Professor Northrop regarding an alleged lack of theory among realists, see Frank, "A Plea for Lawyer-Schools," *op. cit.*, p. 1322 ff.

463. Frank, "A Plea for Lawyer-Schools," *op. cit.*, p. 1321.

464. Patterson, *op. cit.*, p. 554. See Patterson's qualification of this influence of legal realism on legal education: "To claim for legal realism all of the innovations in legal education after 1930 would be an exaggeration; to restrict the influence of legal realism to those who became its avowed followers would be no less misleading. A good many law teachers who rejected the extreme positions of legal realism were moved to incorporate more moderate versions of its ideas in their own work." *Op. cit.*

465. That Frank objected to such terminology and believed a "legal science" impossible because of fact uncertainty and the multiple and rapid changes which take place in society—in its mores and folk-ways—, see Frank, Courts on Trial, *supra*, 196-200, 214, 216-17; Frank, "A Plea for Lawyer-Schools," *op. cit.*, p. 1330, 1333; Frank, "The Scientific Spirit and Economic Dogmatism," in *Science for Democracy—Papers from the Conferences on the Scientific Spirit and Democratic Faith*, ed. Jerome Nathanson (King's Press, 1946), p. 11; Frank, "Short of Sickness and Death; A Study of Moral Responsibility in Legal Criticism," *op. cit.*, p. 623. See p. 256, fn. 7, *infra*.

466.. Roscoe Pound, "The Call for a Realist Jurisprudence," *Harvard Law Rev.*, XLIV (1931), 697, 697, 706.

467. *Ibid.*, 707, 699.

468. *Ibid.*, 703.

469. *Ibid.*, 706. See Pound, "Fifty Years of Jurisprudence," *op. cit.*, in which Pound's shafts seem directed mainly at the realists who had adopted behavioristic psychology. Frank, though not immune from some of his intended barbs, would seemingly not merit the brunt of them. For Frank's opposition to behaviorism, see p. 257, f.n. 7.

470. Frank, Law and The Modern Mind, *op. cit.*, p. 168.

471. Frank, If Men Were Angels, *op. cit.*, p. 298. Frank cited particularly his article, "Mr. Justice Holmes and Non-Euclidean Thinking," *op. cit.*

472. *Ibid.* Frank was replying to Professor Fuller. For a devastating and somewhat immoderate attack on the legal realists for allegedly seeking to eliminate value judgments and upon Frank in particular for allegedly seeking to substitute a psychoanalysis of lawyers for jurisprudence, see Georges Gurvich, *Sociology of Law* (New York: Philosophical Library & Alliance Book Corp., 1942), pp. 172-75.

473. Frank, Courts on Trial, *op. cit.*, p. 218.

474. *Ibid.*, 219.

475. *Ibid.*

476. *Ibid.*, 220.

477. *Ibid.*, 221.

478. Karl N. Llewellyn, "Some Realism about Realism—Responding to Dean Pound," *op. cit.* See also Llewellyn, "A Realistic Jurisprudence—The Next Step," *op. cit.*, p. 449. See his later expression of admiration for Pound in stressing the importance of the Ought—"the basic truth about the heart of Jurisprudence"—in Llewellyn, "Jurisprudence—Realism in Theory and Practice," *op. cit.*, p. 153.

479. Stone, *op. cit.*, p. 385.

480. *Ibid.*, 383.

480a. *Ibid.* See p. 190, f.n. 226, *supra*, with reference to the characteristic listed under (4) therein.

481. *Ibid.*, 385, f.n. 22. Stone dates this turning to the period when realism reached its "majority," taking as its birthplace Bingham's article appearing in 1912. See p. 9,, *supra.* For a scathing denunciaton of legal realism for its alleged lack of conceptualism, see Philip Mechem, "The Jurisprudence of Despair," *Iowa Law Rev.*, XXI (1936), 669. For an attempt to minimize somewhat the difference between realists and "conceptualists," as constituting "not so much a matter of specific beliefs as it is of mental constitution," see I. L. Fuller, "American Legal Realism," *U. Pa. Law Rev.*, LVVVII (1934), 429, 461. He claimed that the conceptualist is not as disturbed as the realist about the discrepancy between the IS and the OUGHT. Frank would clearly opt for a disturbed realist than for an undisturbed conceptualist, as delineated by Fuller.

For one of the most frequently cited critiques of legal realism (and like most critiques, it is bipolar), see Herman Kantorowicz, "Some Rationalism about Realism," *Yale Law Jour.*, XLIII (1933), 1240. For a scintillating presentation of the question of justice in legal realism, see Edwin N. Garlan, *Legal Realism and Justice* (New York: Columbia U. Press, 1941). He is convinced "that Legal Realism is not as indifferent to the theory of justice as some would suppose." *Op. cit.*, Preface, xii, ". . . justice as a conception used in law derives in good part from its very fluidity and its motive power rather than from its intellectual definition." *Op. cit.*, p. 121.

482. Frank should certainly be included in the "others."

483. Frank, Courts on Trial, *op. cit.*, p. 102.

484. *Ibid.*

485. Francis E. Lucey, "Natural Law and American Legal Realism: Their Respective Contributions to a Theory of Law in a Democratic Society," *Georgetown Law Jour.*, XXX (1942), 493, 508.

486. *Ibid.*, 513.

487. *Ibid.*, 515, 521.

488. *Ibid.*, 520.

489. *Ibid.*, 521.

490. *Ibid.*, 523.

491. Paul, *op. cit.*, p. 92.

492. Edward McNeill Burns, *Ideas in Conflict—The Political Theories of the Contemporary World* (New York: W. W. Norton & Co., 1959), p. 127.

493. *Ibid.*

494. See Robert S. Hirschfield, *The Constitution and the Court* (New York: Random House, 1964), pp. 22-25.

495. Friedmann, *op. cit.*, p. 209.

496. *Ibid.*

497. *Shaughnessy* v. *United States,* 345 U.S. 206, 224 (1952).

498. Frank, "Some Reflections on Judge Learned Hand," *op. cit.* This article was published posthumously.

499. *Ibid.,* 704. For a trenchant reply by Frank to a similar charge of totalitarianism by Mortimer Adler, see Frank, Fate and Freedom, *op. cit.,* pp. 217, 218. For another similar charge, See John T. Schuett, "A Study of the Legal Philosophy of Jerome N. Frank," *University of Detroit Law Jour.,* XXXV (1957), 28, 47-49 (his M.A. thesis at Loyola University).

500. *Ibid.,* 705.

501. *Ibid.*

502. See, e.g., Frank, Save America First, *op.cit.,* pp. 227, 228, 416 and passim.

503. Frank, "Self-Guardianship and Democracy," *American Scholar,* XVI (1947), 265 (Editorial).

504. *Ibid.,* 267.

505. Edgar Bodenheimer, *Jurisprudence* (New York: McGraw-Hill, 1940), p. 314. Bodenheimer wrote that realist jurisprudence substituted for the Austinian legislator the American judge as "the sovereign creator of the law." *Op. cit.* He also feared that the skepticism of legal realism might, against the wishes of its representatives, lead to totalitarianism. For a similar view by Paul, see p. 45 at f.n. 491, *supra.* Paul thought that Frank's reply to Bodenheimer's argument about the enthronement of judges would have been: "If it is the judges who make the law, that is a fact, and not a 'wish-assumption.'" Paul, *op. cit.,* p. 142.

Bodenheimer in his second edition, Jurisprudence—The Philosophy and Method of The Law, (1962) *op. cit.,* omits the sharp references to legal realism to be found in the first edition, *op. cit.* See also, Bodenheimer, "A Decade of Jurisprudence in the United States of America—1946-1956," *op. cit.*

506. Bodenheimer, "A Decade of Jurisprudence in the United States—1946-1956," *op. cit.,* p. 46.

507. *Ibid.,* 59.

508. Frank, Fate and Freedom, *op. cit.,* Courts on Trial, *op. cit.,* and Frank, "Memorable Victories in the Fight for Justice," *op. cit.*

509. See Edmond N. Cahn, The Sense of Injustice, *op. cit.* "Where justice is thought of in the customary manner as an ideal mode or condition, the human response will be merely contemplative, and conceptualism bakes no loaves. But the response to a real or imagined instance of injustice is something quite different; it is alive with movement and warmth in the human organism. For this reason, the name 'sense of injustice' seems much to be preferred . . . 'Justice', as we shall use the term, means the *active process* of remedying or preventing what would arouse the sense of injustice." *Op. cit.,* p. 12. See p. 200, f.n. 379, *supra.*

# Footnotes—Chapter II
## Stare Decisis

1. See discussion, pp. 60ff, *infra.*
2. Jerome Frank, *Courts on Trial* (Princeton: Princeton U. Press, 1950), p. 266.
3. Qoted by Frank in *Hammon-Knowlton* v. *United States,* 121 F. 2d 192, 204 (2d Cir., 1941).
4. Benjamin N. Cardozo, *The Growth of the Law* (New Haven: Yale U. Press, 1924), p. 1. See pp. 62ff., *op. cit.,* for Cardozo's analysis of the forces at work in the growth of the law: logic (philosophy), history, custom and justice (mores).
5. *Ibid.,* 19.
6. *Ibid.*
7. *Ibid.,* 129.
8. Roscoe Pound, *Interpretations of Legal History* (Cambridge: Harvard U. Press, 1923), p. 1.
9. For Frank's critique of this dichotomy, see pp. 52-53, *infra.* For Pound's views, see Roscoe Pound, *An Introduction to the Philosophy of Law* (New Haven: Yale U. Press, 1922), pp. 137-41.
10. Roscoe Pound, *Law Finding Through Experience and Reason* (U. Ga. Press, 1960), pp. 37-39.
11. For an illustration, see *ibid.,* 37.
12. *Ibid.,* 43.
13. Carleton Kemp Allen, *Law in the Making* (paperback ed., London: Oxford U. Press, 1961).
14. *Ibid.,* 344.
15. *Ibid.*
16. *Ibid.,* 203.
17. *Ibid.,* 345. "In the time of Lord Mansfield, the duty of judicial 'loyalty' was fully recognized and repeatedly asserted . . ." op. cit.
18. *Ibid.,* 207.
19. *Ibid.,* 335.
20. *Ibid.,* 235ff. However, on July 26, 1966, Lord Chancellor Gardiner announced that the House of Lords proposes to modify its present practice, so that despite the "indispensable' need for *stare decisis,* "a too rigid adherence to precedent may lead to injustice in a particular case and also unduly restrict the development of the law." *New York Times* (July 27, 1966), pp. 1, 6. See also, *New York Times* (July 31, 1966), Comment, Section IV, p. 6:1. The effect of this modification remains to be seen. But that the conservative Houes of Lords will not be as free in overruling its previous decisions as the United States Supreme Court seems reasonably certain for the foreseeable future.
21. *Ibid.,* 342.
22. Anthony Lewis, *Gideon's Trumpet* (New York: Random House, 1964), p. 85.
23. William Orville Douglas, *Stare Decisis* (Association of the Bar of the City of New York, 1949), pp. 13, 17. For a discussion regarding overruling on constitutional grounds, see p. 77, *infra.*

24. *West Va. Board of Education* v. *Barnette*, 313 U.S. 624 (1943), overruling *Minersville School District* v. *Gobitis*, 310 U.S. 586 (1940).

25. 354 U.S. 1 (1957), overruling 351 U.S. 487 (1956).

26. *Smith* v. *Allwright*, 321 U.S. 649, 669 (1944) (dis. op.)

27. Frank, Courts on Trial, *op. cit.*, p. 74.

28. Douglas, *op. cit.*, pp. 3, 31.

29. *Ibid.*, 31.

30. *Ibid.*, 30.

31. Jerome Frank, *Law and The Modern Mind* (New York: Brentano's 1930), Chapter XIV.

32. *Ibid.*, 149. Frank also cited with approval the argument of Professor Herman Oliphant, another legal realist, "that the courts have been paying too much attention to the language of prior cases and that the proper use of the doctrine of following the precedents should lead the courts to pay more attention to what judges in earlier cases have decided as against what they have said in their opinions." *Ibid.*, 151. See Herman Oliphant, "A Return to Stare Decisis," *American Bar Association Journal*, XIV (1928), 71.

33. *Ibid.*, 151.

34. *Ibid.*, 152.

35. *Ibid.*, 153.

36. *Ibid*, 159.

37. *Ibid.*, 153. See pp. 69-70, *infra*.

38. *Ibid.*, 154.

39. *Ibid.*

40. *Ibid*, 209.

40a. *See* p. 49, *supra*.

41. *Ibid.*, 213.

42. Jerome Frank, "Are Judges Human?", *U. Pa. Law Rev.*, LXXX (1931), 17, 32.

43. See Forrest Revere Black, Review of *Law and The Modern Mind, Ky. Law Jour.* XIX, (1931), 349; Francis H. Bohlen, Review of *Law and The Modern Mind, U. Pa. Law Rev.*, LXXIX (1931), 822; Benjamin N. Cardozo, The Growth of the Law, *op. cit.*, pp. 81-82.

44. Frank, Law and The Modern Mind, *op. cit.*, p. 7.

45. Frank, Courts on Trial, *op. cit.*, p. 266.

46. *Ibid.*, 269. To same effect, see an earlier article by Cardozo, "Jurisprudence," in *Selected Writings of Benjamin N. Cardozo* (ed. Margaret E. Hall; New York: Falcon Publications, 1947), pp. 7, 34-36.

47. *Ibid.*, 269-70.

48. *Ibid.*, 270.

49. *Ibid.*, 267-68, 271.

50. Cf. Ruth Benedict, *Patterns of Culture*, (paperback ed., New York: Penguin Books, Inc., 1946), Chap. I, "The Science of Custom."

51. Frank, *supra*, 272, at f.ns. 13, 14.

52. *Ibid.*, 272.

53. *Ibid.*, 273.

54. *Ibid.*, 275.

55. *Ibid.*

56. *Ibid.*, 276.

57. Frank, "The Place of the Expert in a Democratic Society", *Philosophy of Science,* XVI (1949), 3, 13.

58. Frank, *supra,* 276, quoting from his opinion in *United Shipyards v. Hoey,* 131 F. 2d 525 (2d Cir., 1940).

59. *Ibid.,* 277.

60. *Ibid.,* 278.

61. *Ibid.*

62. "As depicted by Jessel and some other legal writers, this idea has a delightful vagueness which makes it most helpful in 'sterilizing' an awkward precedent." *Ibid.,* 279. See Walter F. Murphy and C. Herman Pritchett, *Courts, Judges and Politics* (New York: Random House, 1961), p. 365; C. K. Allen, *op. cit.,* pp. 212-13. That the interpretation of *ratio decidendi* has not been a uniform one, see George Whitecross Paton, *Jurisprudence* (3d ed., Oxford: Oxford U. Press, 1964), pp. 180ff.; Edgar Bodenheimer, *Jurisprudence—Philosophy and Method of Law* (Cambridge: Harvard U. Press, 1962), pp. 375-82.

63. Frank, *supra,* 280. See Frank, Law and The Modern Mind, *op. cit.,* pp. 148-49, f.n.

64. *Ibid.,* 284. Frank, Law and The Modern Mind, *op. cit.* pp. 6-7, 10.

65. *Ibid.,* 285.

66. *Ibid.,* 284, f.n. 37.

67. Frank, *If Men Were Angels* (New York: Harper & Brothers, 1942), p. 303. Frank stated there that the basic difference between the realists and their critics has not been with respect to "rules," but with respect to "facts"—the uncertainty of fact-finding.

68. Frank, *supra,* 285.

69. See p. 54 at f.n. 46, *supra.*

70. See Paton, *op. cit.,* p. 200; "Modern business would be difficult without fixed rules of law by which men could order their conduct. Popular confidence in the courts is shaken if law is regarded as the mere *ipse dixit* of a judge. Moreover, the law is wiser than the individual view of one man." That Frank, however, recognized this role for *stare decisis* in his opinion writing, see p. 68 at f.n. 135, *infra.*

71. Frank, "Place of the Expert in a Democratic Society," *op. cit.*

72. See pp. 55-56, *supra.*

73. Frank, Courts on Trial, *op. cit.,* p. 288; Frank "Place of the Expert in a Democratic Society," *op. cit.,* p. 24.

74. *Ibid.*

75. *Ibid.,* Chap. XXIX.

76. *Ibid.,* 392.

77. *Ibid.,* 396.

78. *Ibid.*

79. *Ibid.,* 263. See Rumble, Jr., *op. cit.,* p. 50: "A strong case can be made for the proposition that it was still the dominant view in the first two decades of this century . . ." Some of Frank's discussion on this subject in *Law and The Modern Mind,* Chap. IV, is linked with his discredited theory of the "basic legal myth." The subject can be more profitably analyzed by presenting Frank's views, without any intrusion of a fictitious theory, as they appear in *Courts on Trial.* For Frank's theory of the "basic legal myth," see pp. 15-17, *supra.* For a discussion a judicial legislation, see pp. 53-54, *supra.*

80. Justice Holmes had written: "The common law is not a brooding omnipresence in the sky." *Pacific Co.* v. *Jensen,* 244 U.S. 205, 255 (1917). See p. 18, at f.n. 197, *supra.*

81. Frank, *supra,* 265.

82. *Ibid.,* 293.

83. *Ibid.,* 294.

84. *Ibid.,* 303.

85. *Ibid.,* 295, f.n. 10. The priority claimed by Frank was a letter he had written to Krenek preceding the reading of a paper by Maurois and the appearance of an article by Cassio on this subject. See Frank, "Words and Music: Some Remarks on Statutory Interpretation," *Columbia Law Rev.,* XLVII (1947), 1259.

86. *Ibid.,* 297.

87. *Ibid.,* 299.

88. Frank, "Words and Music: Some Remarks on Statutory Interpretation," *op. cit.,* p. 1271.

89. Frank, *supra,* 299.

90. *Ibid.,* 301. For Opinions on Judicial Legislation, see pp. 79 ff., *infra.*

91. *Ibid.,* 328. See dicussion p. 65, *infra,* for a critique of this position.

92. Karl N. Llewellyn, *The Common Law Tradition* (Boston: Little Brown & Co., 1960), p. 91.

93. *Ibid.,* 220, f.n. 214. (Emphasis supplied). See Frank, Review of *The Bramble Bush* by Karl N. Llewellyn, *Yale Law Jour.,* XL (1931), 1120, in which Frank claimed an inconsistency between Llewellyn's general views and his specific views on *stare decisis.*

94. Edward McWhinney, "The Great Debate: Activism and Self-Restraint and Current Dilemmas in Judicial Policy-Making," *N. Y. U. Law Rev.,* XXXIII (1958), 755, 760-61.

95. *Ibid.,* 760. For a decussion of the European free law schools, see pp. 61-62, *infra.*

96. *Ibid.,* 761.

97. *Ibid.* For similar views, see Julius Stone, *The Province and Function of the Law* (Cambridge: Harvard U. Press, 1950), p. 745, f.n. 207; Edwin W. Patterson, *Jurisprudence: Men and Ideas of the Law* (Brooklyn: The Foundation Press, Inc., 1953), p. 545.

98. See discussion at p. 258, f.n. 13, *infra.*

99. Frank, Law and The Modern Mind, *op. cit.,* p. 158, f.n.

100. *Ibid.,* 280. Freirechtslehre is the German for Free Law Theories or Free Judicial Decision School.

101. *Ibid.,* 283.

102. *Ibid.,* 284.

103. *Ibid.,* 131.

104. *Ibid.*

105 See pp. 22-24, *supra.*

106. Frank, "Are Judges Human?", *op. cit.,* pp. 47-48.

107. See p. 56 at f.n. 67, *supra.*

108. Frank, *Law and The Modern Mind* (paperback ed., an Anchor Book, Garden City, N. Y.; Doubleday & Co., Inc., 1963), p. xxvii. The

original sixth edition of which this is a reprint was published in 1949, and the Preface is dated Nov. 21, 1948.

109. *Ibid.*

110. See p. 25, *supra.*

111. Frank, Courts on Trial, *op. cit.*, p. 286. This book was published about a half year after the Preface to the Sixth Edition of *Law and The Modern Mind* had been written.

112. *Ibid.*, 267.

113. See p. 56, *supra.*

114. See p. 56, *supra,* and p. 211, f.n. 70, *supra.*

115. See p. 61 at f.n. 97, *supra.*

116. See p. 62 at f.n. 103, *supra.*

117. Frank, "Short of Sickness and Death: A Study of Moral Responsibility in Legal Criticism," *N.Y.U. Law Rev.*, XXVI (1951), 545, 555.

118. Selected Writings of Benjamin N. Cardozo, *op. cit.*, p. 11. Cardozo was a commanding philosopher of the sociological wing of jurisprudence.

119. *Ibid.*, 14.

120. *Ibid.*, 15.

121. *Ibid.*, 14.

122. *Ibid.*, 15.

123. *Ibid.*, 19.

124. Frank, "Cardozo and The Upper-Court Myth," *Law and Contemporary Problems,* XIII (1948), 369. See also, Frank, If Men Were Angels, *op. cit.*, pp. 285-93.

125. Benjamin N. Cardozo, *The Nature of the Judicial Process* (New Haven: Yale U. Press, 1921), p. 163.

126. Frank, *supra,* 380.

127a. This is apparent from the following statistics. Frank wrote the Court's opinion in 483 unanimously decided cases, the majority opinion of the Court (involving one dissent) in 55 cases, and concurring opinions (concurring either with a unanimous or a majority opinion) in 56 cases. He was a member of the court panel in 861 cases in which he did not write the opinion but joined either in a unanimous or a majority opinion. He joined in 369 Per Curiam opinions (short opinions of the Court bearing the name of no judge). Finally, he dissented only in 126 cases. The writer made no tally of the number of cases in which each of his colleagues dissented by way of contrast with Frank. But it is quite apparent from the above figures that Frank was no great dissenter. He was in agreement with his colleagues much more often than in disagreement. (Note: The above statistics excluded a small number of Per Curiam opinions of one line or so in which a decision is affirmed on the basis of the opinion in the Court below.)

128. Frank, Courts on Trial, *op. cit.*, p. 144.

129. *Ibid.*, 270. See discussion, *infra,* pp. 79-80.

130. See p. 59 at f.n. 90, *supra.*

131. See p. 80, *infra.*

132. See p. 81, *infra.*

133. See pp. 81-82, *infra.*

134. 125 F.2d 296 (2d Cir., 1942). The issue involved was a jurisdictional one in a bankruptcy reorganization case, as to whether the federal court could assume jurisdiction even though there was a pending state case,

or the state Supreme Court should retain jurisdiction. A prior decision in that Circuit had held that the state court retained jurisdiction.

Frank was recognized as an expert in corporate reorganization. See Frank, "Reflections on Some Aspects of Corporate Reorganization," *Va. Law Rev.*, XIX (1935), 541, 698; Frank, "Epithetical Jurisprudence and the Work of the S.E.C. in the Administration of Chapter X of the Federal Bankruptcy Act," *N.Y.U. Law Rev.*, XVIII (1940-41), 317. As a sample of his many opinions in cases involving corporate reorganizations, see *Old Colony Bondholders* v. *New York, New Haven & Hartford Ry. Co.*, 161 F.2d 413 (2d Cir., 1947) (dis. in part), involving the reorganization of the New Haven & Hartford Railroad Co. In the course of this rather lengthy, prosaic opinion, packed with figures, Frank discussed his gestalt theory of the decisional process in connection with the opinion rendered below by the commissioners of the Interstate Commerce Commission. *Op. cit., p.* 499. Subsequently he expatiated on this theory in Courts on Trial, *op. cit.,* pp. 170-75. See discussion pp. 22-23, *supra.*

135. That Frank in his jurisdictional writings never referred to legal certainty as a by-product of *stare decision,* see discussion on p. 56, *supra.*

136. 125 F.2d at 302. In 317 U.S. 78 (1942), the Supreme Court unanimously affirmed the lower court decision. Of course, the issue of *stare decisis* was not before the Supreme Court, as it is not governed by prior decisions of a lower court.

137. *Commissioner of Internal Revenue* v. *Hall's Estate,* 153 F.2d 172 (2d Cir., 1946). Gray said: "If he delayed to make a contract or to do an act until he understood exactly all the consequences it involved, the contract would never be made or the act done." *Op. cit.,* p. 175. At issue in this case was whether one Supreme Court decision had in effect over-ruled a prior decision by that court involving the Revenue Act. In his dissenting opinion, Frank claimed it had, and he would have remanded the case to the Tax Court to ascertain whether the testator in drawing up an irrvocable trust agreement had relied on the earlier Supreme Court case. No appeal was taken.

In *Aero Spark Plug Co.* v. *B. G. Corp.,* 130 F.2d 290 (2d Cir., 1942), Frank commented that in drafting instruments, lawyers undoubtedly rely on the decisions. But he asserted that the "great majority of men seldom consult lawyers before acting." 130 F.2d at 297, f.n. 23. Frank offered no facts to substantiate this bald statement other than reliance upon utterances of John Chipman Gray and Professor Edwin Patterson. Later, he apparently contradicted himself when he stated: "We know virtually nothing of the extent to which men do, in fact, rely on past judicial utterances." Could it be that Frank's reference was to men relying on past judicial utterances without consulting lawyers? Do not most men have lawyers draft their agreements and other instruments?

138. 153 F.2d at 175.

139. 121 F.2d 192 (2d Cir., 1941). Plaintiff had originally sued the Collector of Internal Revenue, but the court ruled that on the facts of this case he should have sued the United States directly. By the time he did, the statute of limitations had run against him. Could it be said that the Collector and the U.S. were in reality the same party, regardless of the formal requirements of suit? If not, plaintiff's action would have been

214

barred. The difficulty confronting Frank was the fact that the United States is a sovereign body, which cannot be sued unless it specifically waives its immunity to suit in any area of the law. The government contended that it was legally a different party from the Collector, and that a waiver of sovereign immunity in this type of case was not to be extended under the relevant statute to the Collector.

140. In 314 U.S. 694 (1941) a writ of certiorari was denied and thus the Supreme Court turned a deaf ear to Frank's supplication.

See *Wallace* v. *U.S.*, 142 F.2d 240 (2d Cir., 1944), in which Frank reiterated the distaste he had expressed in the *Hammon-Knowlton* case for the doctrine of governmental immunity from suit without its permission.

141. Thurman Arnold, "Judge Jerome Frank," *U. Chicago Law Rev.*, XXIV (1957), 633.

142. *Ibid.*

143. See p. 52, *supra.*

144. 130 F.2d 290 (2d Cir., 1942). See p. 214, f.n. 137, *supra.* This was a patent infringement and patent validity case, a staple of a federal judge's provender.

145. *Ibid.*, 296.

146. *Ibid.*

147. Frank cited Green's analysis of five factors, but discussed only two.

148. Frank cited *Mitchell* v. *Rochester Ry. Co.*, 151 N.Y. 107 (1896), barring recovery for alleged mental anguish. After Frank's demise, *Battaglia* v. *State of N.Y.*, 10 N.Y. 2d 257 (1961) reversed the *Mitchell* case. Green's "administrative factor" was thus withdrawn from this type of case in New York State.

149. 152 F.2d 342 (2d Cir., 1945).

150. *Ibid.*, 359. To same effect, see *U.S.* v. *Gonzalez Castro*, 228 F.2d 807, 810 (1955): "For, since a criminal action involves a man's life or liberty, we ought not in such an action, accord much sanctity to *stare decisis* by adhering to a precedent favorable to the prosecutor, if we now consider it markedly unreasonable, undesirable, or unjust . . . For that reason, while in civil suits I feel obliged to follow recent decisions of this court with which I disagree, I feel free to dissent from any of our decisions based on established rules adverse to on accused of crime, when I think those rules unjust."

151. As he had done in *In Re Marine Harbor Properties*, p. 68, *supra.*

152. 201 F.2d 738 (2d Cir., 1953).

153. *Ibid.* This was a bankruptcy proceeding, in which an appeal was filed from a denial of a demand for a jury trial. In a Per Curiam opinion, citing prior decisions, the Court held that the proper procedure was to file a petition for mandamus, and it dismissed the appeal. Frank regretted that a mere label should determine the outcome of a proceeding. For another case of a somewhat analagous nature, but involving more than a question of *stare decisis*, in which Frank attacked "antiquated procedural technicalities, the exaltation of labels . . . rigid antiquarianism . . . irrational procedural formalism, judicial red-tape-ism yielding injustice," see *U.S.* v. *Mulcahy*, 169 F.2d 94, 102 (2d Cir., 1948) (dis. op.)

To the same effect as *Zamore* v. *Goldblatt, ibid.*, see *Rieser* v. *Baltimore & Ohio Ry. Co.*, 224 F.2d 198 (1955), involving the appealability of an intermediate order in a suit, without awaiting the final outcome of the case. Frank concurred with reluctance by reason of prior decisions of his circuit. He added that had he participated in those decisions, he would have dissented.

In a case involving the question of appealability of an intermediate order, ordinarily not appealable until the final outcome of the case which may possibly obviate the need for any appeal (though the case is not germane to the issue of *stare decisis* as was *Rieser* v. *Baltimore & Ohio Ry. Co., op. cit.*) Frank proposed "a statute (modelled somewhat on the Supreme Court certiorari statute) which will confer on each court of appeals the authority, in its discretion, to allow an appeal from any order that is not final, whenever delay resulting from denial of the appeal will work substantial injustice by way of markedly heavy expense (of a trial) or great waste of time and effort." *Pabellon* v. *Grace Line,* 191 F.2d 169, 180 (1951).

154. 153 F.2d 757 (2d Cir., 1946).

155. 121 F.2d 336 (2d Cir., 1941).

156. Frank disputed the theory set forth in several cases that the special solicitude for seamen was a result of their rashness and improvidence. He argued that they were no more rash and improvident than other employees. His thesis was that the solicitude stemmed from a feeling of the importance of the sea and seamen to the national defense.

157. Judge Learned Hand who wrote the Court's opinion arrived at the same verdict as Frank but on entirely different, ad hoc, grounds. Judge Swan dissented.

For Frank's erudite analysis of two theories of contracts: the "actual intent", "meeting of the minds" or "will" theory, and the so-called "objective" theory, see 153 F.2d at 760 ff.

158. 153 F.2d at 767, 768.

159. *Ricketts* was not appealed. However, in *Callen* v. *Pennsylvania Railway Co..* 332 U.S. 625 (1947), a general release case, Frank's thesis was set forth in an amicus curiae brief submitted to the court. Justice Jackson, speaking for the court in a 5-4 decision, retorted: "Considerable reliance is placed upon a concurring opinion in the Court of Appeals for the Second Circuit in *Ricketts* v. *Pa. Ry. Co.*, 153 F.2d 757, 760. However persuasive the arguments there stated may be that inequality of bargaining power might well justify a change in the law, they are also a frank recognition that the Congress has made no such change. An amendment of this character is for the Congress to consider rather than for the courts to introduce. But until the Congress changes the statutory plan, the releases of railway employees stand on the same basis as the releases of others." *Op. cit.,* p. 630.

160. 215 F.2d 102 (2d Cir., 1954). The action originated in the federal court because of the diversity in citizenship of the parties. Plaintiffs resided in Michigan where the incident occurred; defendants were New York corporations.

161. *Ibid.,* 105.

162. *Ibid.,* 106.

163. *Ibid.,* 106, f.n. 7.

164. *Ibid.,* covering two pages of the opinion and in which Frank quoted at length from the article, "Proximate and Remote Cause," written in

216

1870 by Nicholas St. John Green, a law professor and one of the founders of American pragmatism.

165. In 349 U.S. 923 (1955) the Supreme Court denied a writ of certiorari.

166. As distinguished from patents, which are constitutionally buttressed (Art. I, sec. 8), the law relative to trade-names has been judge-made and statutory.

167. *Eastern Wine Corporation* v. *Winslow-Warren Ltd.*, 137 F.2d 955, 958 (2d Cir., 1943). Cf. Frank's analysis in *Chrestensen* v. *Valentine*, pp. 135-36, *infra*.

168. *Ibid.*, 959.

169. *Ibid.*, 958.

170. A person using another's trade name might sell to the public at a lower price than the other.

171. *Supra*, 959.

172. 157 F.2d 115 (1946).

173. As distinguished from patents, trade names require a user in order to become effective.

174. 157 F.2d at 125, f.n. 26.

175. *Ibid.* In 329 U.S. 771 (1946), the Supreme Court denied a writ of certiorari. For other cases involving a similar analysis by Frank, see *Eastern Wine Corporation* v. *Winslow-Warren Ltd.*, 137 F.2d 955 (2d Cir., 1943) in which Frank wrote the majority opinion of the Court, (cert. den. 320 U.S. 758 (1943); *Standard Brands* v. *Smidler*, 151 F.2d 34 (2d Cir., 1945), involving "V-8" juices and "V-8" vitamin tablets, in which Frank concurred with reluctance, saying he would not be sorry if the Supreme Court reversed (the case was not appealed); *Triangle Publication* v. *Rohrlich*, 167 F.2d 969 (2d Cir., 1948) (dis. op.), involving the teen-age magazine "Seventeen" published by plaintiff under a registered trade-mark and girdles traded as "Miss Seventeen." manufactured by defendant. In each case the issue was whether there had been an infringement of plaintiff's trade name monopoly of a registered trade mark. Dissenting from the majority opinion in the latter case, which granted an injunction to plaintiff on the ground of unfair competition, Frank wrote: "In the instant case, there is not even potential competition. For the defendants, as sellers of girdles, do not compete with plaintiff, which makes and sells nothing but a magazine, and which does not as much as intimate that it contemplates ever making or selling anything else . . .

"The question has been raised as to whether the trade-name doctrine, by its creation of 'perpetual monopolies,' has not injured consumers, a question of peculiarly serious import in these days when living cost are notoriously oppressive. Since, however, the Supreme Court has approved the doctrine, an intermediate court (such as ours) must enforce it. But. in the absence of legislation so requiring, we should not expand it . . .

"A few years ago there was much talk adverse to legal "conceptualism." Some of the talkers seemingly went so far as to deny all concepts. Others, more sagely, objected to the logical application of the wording of a legal concept unless adequate attention is given to the policy the words are designed to express. Long before (in 1891) Holmes, J. had said that legal doctrines have often been "generalized into fiction," and that "the whole outline of the law is the resultant of a conflict at every point be-

217

tween logic and good sense—the one striving to work fiction out to consistent results, the other restraining and at least overcoming that effort when the results become too manifestly unjust. In the light of subsequent criticism of such employment of the term "logic" it is perhaps well to rephrase Holmes' remark thus: Judges should peer behind the mere verbal articulation of a legal rule or concept to observe the policy it embodies, whenever a logical application of that rule or concept, as previously articulated, will yield socially disvaluable results. Such caution becomes especially important when an "analogical extension" of earlier elliptical judicial statements is proposed." No appeal was taken to the Supreme Court in this case.

176. See p. 71, *supra*.

177. P. 71, f.n. 149, *supra*.

178. At issue was the judge's charge to the jury, which Frank deemed prejudicial. Involved was a conspiracy to steal gasoline coupons. In his charge the judge had remarked with reference to one of the defendants: ". . . Did she steal them? *Who did if she didn't?* You are to decide that." (Emphasis supplied.) Frank argued the jury might have inferred from these remarks that the burden of proving her innocence was upon defendant and that she need establish the identity of another person as the thief in order to be exonerated. The majority of the court felt from reading the entire record that defendant was guilty and deemed the error cited a "harmless error," particularly since, in its belief, it had been neutralized by many correct, explicit instructions on the point elsewhere in the judge's charge. Frank, on the other hand, argued that the function of finding a defendant guilty belongs to a jury and not to an appellate court reading a cold record. Frank argued that a finding of "harmless error" should be arrived at independently of any opinion by the appellate court of the defendant's guilt and should be based exclusively on the likely importance of the error upon the jury at the trial.

In *Bihn* v. *U.S.*, 322 U.S. 633 (1946) (on appeal by Bihn, the co-defendant, Bennett did not appeal), the Supreme Court reversed the lower court, sustaining Frank's dissent.

179. 201 F.2d 722 (2d Cir., 1953). For a fuller discussion of this case, see pp. 103ff., *infra*.

180. *Ibid.*, 724.

181. *Ibid.*, 725.

182. 190 F.2d 687 (2d Cir., 1951).

183. *Rex.* v. *Taylor*, 2 K.B. 368 (1950), overruling *Rex* v. *Treanor*, 1 All. E.R. 330 (1939).

184. See discussion of U.S. v. Bennett, p. 71, *supra*.

185. 201 F.2d at 726. In 345 U.S. 936 (1953), the Supreme Court denied an application for a writ of certiorari. There was no issue of *stare decisis* before the Supreme Court, since none of its own prior decisions was involved.

For an issue of frequent occurrence in conspiracy trials, when one defendant has confessed and the other has not, and the confession admitted into evidence as an exhibit implicates the non-confessing defendant, see *U.S.* v. *Delli Paoli*, 229 F.2d 319 (2d Cir., 1955). Frank dissented and stated that he would discard as unjust the precedents of his circuit relied upon by the majority of the court. In a 5-4 decision, the Supreme Court in

*Delli Paoli* v. *U.S.*, 353 U.S. 232 (1956), affirmed the Circuit Court of Appeals. It is interesting to note that in *Bruton* v. *United States.* 391 U.S. 123 (1968), the Supreme Court overruled its decision in *Delli Paoli* v. *U.S.*, and thus Frank's dissent was ultimately vindicated by the Supreme Court.

186. See *discussion of Hammon-Knowlton v. United States, p. 69, supra.*

187. 225 F.2d 113 (2d Cir., 1955).

188. *Ibid.*, 116.

189. *Ibid.*, 120.

190. *Ibid.*, 119.

191. See Jacob W. Landynski, "The Making of Constitutional Law," *Social Research* (Spring, 1964).

192. *Burnett* v. *Coronado Oil & Gas Co.*, 285 U.S. 393, 406 (1932). In 350 U.S. 891 (1955), the Supreme Court denied a writ of certiorari in the Scully case, thus not acting on Frank's suggestion to it.

193. *U.S.* v. *Ullmann*, 221 F.2d 760, 762 (2d Cir., 1955).

194. *Ibid.* Ullmann had been linked by Elizabeth Bentley with an espionage ring allegedly headed by Nathan Gregory Silvermaster and of which Harry Dexter White was claimed to be a member. See O. John Rogge, *The First and the Fifth* (New York: Thomas Nelson & Sons, 1960), p. 271. At issue in this case was the Immunity Act of 1954, under which Ullmann, a former Treasury Department official, had been granted full immunity in return for his testimony about his knowledge of espionage and of membership in the Communist Party. See p. 219, f.n. 197, *infra.*

195. 132 F.2d 837 (2d Cir., 1942). For a fuller discussion of this case, see pp. 107-09, *infra.*

196. By virtue of his office—*ex officio*—and without any formal charge, a judge in the ecclesiastical courts of the Stuart period, on mere suspicion that an individual harbored "dangerous" thoughts, could compel him to submit to a so-called *ex officio* oath. It was a religious age and oaths were taken seriously. See David Fellman, *The Defendant's Rights* (New York, Toronto: Rinehart & Co., 1958), p. 155.

197. That the Fifth Amendment was intended as a shield against self-incrimination only, and not against the disclosure of "disgraceful" acts or acts which could lead to the economic or social detriment of the individual, see *Ullmann* v. *United States.* 350 U.S. 422 (1956). (See f.n. 193, *supra,* citing the lower court opinion in Ullmann). The issue in *Pierre,* however, was whether the disclosure went beyond that of a mere disgraceful act.

198. 234 F.2d 715 (2d Cir., 1955).

199. 218 F.2d 316 (2d Cir., 1954).

200. 234 F.2d at 718, 719. The Attorney General in the prior case (f.n. 199, *supra*) had found that Moon would not be subject to physical persecution if deported to Communist China despite the evidence of his anti-Communism.

201a. 161 F.2d 467 (2d Cir., 1947).

202. "Hearsay may be roughly (and somewhat inaccurately) described as the report in court by a witness of a statement made by another person, out of court, who is not subject to cross-examination at the trial, when the report of that statement is offered in evidence to prove the truth of a fact asserted in that statement. It is, so to speak, second-hand evi-

dence. Now doubtless hearsay should often be accepted with caution. But 90% of the evidence on which men act out of court, most of the data on which business and industry daily rely, consists of the equivalent of hearsay. Yet, because of distrust of juries—a belief that jurors lack the competence to make allowance for the second-hand character of hearsay—such evidence, although accepted by administrative agencies, juvenile courts and legislative committees, is (subject, to be sure, to numerous exceptions) barred in jury trials. As a consequence, frequently the jury cannot learn of matters which would lead an intelligent person to a more correct knowledge of the facts." Frank, Courts on Trial, *op. cit.*, p. 123.

203. 161 F.2d at 470. To same effect, see Frank's opinions in *Hoffman* v. *Palmer*, 128 F.2d 976, 987 (2d Cir., 1942); *U.S.* v. *Costello*, 221 F.2d 668, 679 (2d Cir., 1955); *Archawski* v. *Hanioti*, 239 F.2d 806 (2d Cir., 1956). In *Zell* v. *American Seating Co.*, 138 F.2d 641 (1943), Frank discussed in similar vein the judge-made parol evidence rule, namely, the rule that negotiations preceding a written contract are superseded by and merged in the executed written insrument. He wrote: "Although seldom mentioned in modern decisions, the most important motive for perpetuation of the rule is distrust of juries, fear that they cannot adequately cope with, or will be unfairly prejudiced by, conflicting 'parol' testimony. If the rule were frankly recognized as primarily a device to control juries, its shortcomings would become obvious, since it is not true that the execution by the parties of an unambiguous writing, 'facially complete', bars extrinsic proof. "*Op. cit.*, pp. 644-45. Frank then cited numerous exceptions which have been grafted onto the parol evidence rule. He suggested rather than extending the scope of the rule judicially, "it might be well by legislation to restrict it," and he proposed that if "the basic motive in perpetuating is fear of juries, the legislatures might dal with it somewhat as the proposed A.L.I. Code of Evidence deals with certain phases of the hearsay rule," (*op. cit.*, p. 650, f.n. 35), namely, the proposal in our text following immediately after this footnote.

204. To same effect, see *U.S.* v. *Delli Paoli*, 229 F.2d 319, 323 (2d Cir., 1955). See p. 218, f.n. 185, *supra*. See discussion on the hearsay rule at p. 67, *supra*.

205. 129 F.2d 243 (2d Cir., 1942).

206. *Ibid.*, 246.

207. *Ibid.*, 245.

208. *Ibid.*

209. 125 F.2d 949 (2d Cir., 1942).

210. *Ibid.*, 967, 968.

211. *Ibid.*, 967. The litigation arose over the popular song "When Irish Eyes Are Smiling," and other songs. At issue was whether the composer could sell his royalties and assign his renewal rights in the copyrights during the period of the first twenty-eight years of the copyrights before his renewal rights matured at the termination of the twenty-eight year period. Because of financial need, when the song had not yet attained the height of its fame, the composer sold his royalties and assigned his renewal rights "for a song." Despite this assignment of his renewal rights, at the termination of the twenty-eight year period the composer again assigned a renewal of the copyright to someone else. This litigation arose between the two assignees. In his dissent, Frank felt that the congressional

purpose evinced in the passage of the copyright legislation of protecting the old age of an author or composer cannot be reconciled with the right to make the original assigment in consequence of the interpretation of the Copyright Acts by the majority of the Court. Frank was of the opinion that his colleagues interpreted the Copyright Acts as if laissez-faire was still in fullest bloom when Congress passed the Copyright Acts.—The Supreme Court in *Fred Fisher Music Co.* v. *Witmark & Sons,* 318 U.S. 643 (1943) affirmed the decision.

For Frank's analysis of his conception of a faulty interpretation of legislation based upon a supposed spirit of institutions—the so-called *Zeitgeist,* see *op. cit.,* pp. 963-64; *Perkins* v. *Endicott Johnson Corporation,* 128 F.2d 208, 217, f.n. 25 (2d Cir. 1942).

212. 135 F.2d 409 (2d Cir., 1943).

213. Under the National Bank Act, directors of banks are required to be bona fide stockholders of the banks. Defendant, chairman of the board of directors, arranged to have as fellow-directors "de facto" stockholders who did not fulfill the "statutory provisions prescribing qualifications for that office." The directors apparently were prudent and responsible businessmen. Some loans which they had arranged and on which losses were sustained could just as well have been arranged by any prudent persons. Were they to be held as insurers of their acts because of their technical failure to comply with the statute? Judge Clark could see no connection between the violation of the statute and the loss. Judge Frank read the National Bank Act as a mandatory injunction, not a mere suggestion. He stated that one need not be a disciple of Hobbes or Austin to believe that a legislature intends to have its laws respected.

214. 198 F.2d 821 (2d Cir., 1952).

215. This was a diversity suit brought by a Pennsylvanian against a Connecticut corporation in the Connecticut Federal District Court (part of the Second Circuit Court of Appeals), and the Connecticut law was held applicable.

216. 198 F.2d at 827.

217. *Ibid.,* 823. "The policy behind a limitations statute is that of penalizing one who 'sleep(s) upon his rights.' The time to be considered is when the 'legal damage occurred, until then . . there was no actionable injury." *Op. cit.*

218. *Ibid.,* 825.

219. No appeal was filed. But see the later case of *Riccuiti* v. *Voltaic Tubes, Inc.,* 277 F.2d 809 (2d Cir., 1960), which seems to vindicate Frank's position.

For another case of equitable interpretation of a statute by Frank, see his dis. op. in *Joseph* v. *Farnsworth Radio & Television Corp.,* 198 F.2d 883 (2d Cir., 1952).

In *Usatorre* v. *The Victoria,* 172 F.2d 434, 439, 441 (1949), an admiralty case involving the application of Argentinian law, Judge Frank wrote: "The export witness's adherence to the literal words of the (Argentinian) code may have caused the trial judge to question his conclusions. For, we are told, the civilians. influenced by an interpretative theory which derives from Aristotle (citing in a footnote Aristotle's Nicomachean Ethics, Bk. V, ch. 10, 1137b) (and which has effected Anglo-American practice as well) are accustomed to interpret their statutory enactments 'equitably,' i.e., to fill in gaps, arising necessarily from the generalized terms of many statutes, by asking how the legislature would have dealt with the 'unprovided case.' . . . "This attitude finds expression in Art. I of the Swiss Civil Code (of 1907) which directs the judge to decide as if he were a legislator, when he finds himself faced with a definite gap in the statute.'" (quoting from Friedmann, Legal Theory (1944), 294).

220. 192 F.2d 727 (2d Cir., 1951).

221. *Ibid.*, 735.

222. *Ibid.*, 733. *To same effect, see Frank's opinions in McAllister* v. *Comm'r. Internal Revenue*, 157 F.2d 235, 240 f.n. 6 (1946) (dis. op.); *Christensen* v. *U.S.*, 194 F.2d 978, 983 (1952), in which Frank in his dissenting opinion expressed his opposition to the "lexiscographic logic of the literal languague litany," when to interpret a statute literally would, in his opinion, result in an inequity; *Morgan* v. *U.S.*, 229 F.2d 291, 294 (1956): "I had thought that our court, long taught by Judge Learned Hand, would never be the slave of literal language, would always recognize that it is 'one of the surest indexes of a mature and developed jurisprudence not to make a fortress of the dictionary.' (Cabell v. Markham, 2 Cir., 148 F.2d 737, 739). That is ancient learning. (Indeed an early seventeenth century English commentator suggested the removal of a judge, for violation of his oath of office, if he 'held himself in his judgments precisely or rather austerely to the letter of the law' without regard to its spirit. Hake, Epieikia, Yale Law Library Publications (1953), 29. Of course, I think that suggestion inapplicable here) . . ."

Likewise, in interpreting contracts Frank repudiated the plain language construction of considering only the text in utter disregard of its context. Thus, in *U.S.* v. *Lennox Metal Mf'g. Co.*, 225 F.2d 302, 311 (1955), Frank wrote: "Accordingly, it is regarded by many authorities as a fallacy that, in interpreting contractual language, a court may not consider the surrounding circumstances unless the language is patently ambiguous. Any such rule, like all rules of interpretation, must be taken as a guide, not a dictator. The text should always be read in its context. Indeed, text and context necessarily merge to some extent, just as an individual's 'inner environment' includes the air in his lungs." In a footnote, Frank quoted from Sullivan, The Aspects of Science (2d series. (1926), 15-17: "Prof. Rougier in his "Paralogismes du Rationalisme," instances the different significations so elementary and unambiguous a concept as a triangle has for different minds. He takes Euclid, Schopenhauer, Duns Scotus, Spinoza and Goethe . . ." In the balance of a long quotation, the different significations are set forth.

223. See Bernard Schwartz, *American Administrative Law* (2d ed., London: Sir Isaac Pitman & Sons Ltd.; Dobbs Ferry, N.Y.: Oceana Publications, Inc., 1962), p. 17.

224. 144 F.2d 608 (2d Cir., 1944).

225. *Ibid.*, 620. "In the case of the courts, we call it 'interpretation' or 'filling in the gaps'; in the case of administration we call it 'delegation' of authority to 'supply the details' . . . In both instances, the task is unavoidable.

"Indeed, those who today criticize the transfer of 'subsidiary legislation' to administrative officers forget that, inspired by somewhat similar motives, there has been and still is much criticism of the power exercised by judges in construing statutes, that Bentham, Livingston, and their disciples (some even in our time) have insisted that all 'law' must emanate solely from the legislature, and have tried, through codification, to destroy all 'judicial legislation.' . . ." Op. cit., pp. 620, 621.

226. See *Gemsco, Inc. et. al.* v. *Walling,* 324 U.S. 244 (1945), affirming Frank's majority opinion, which involved many issues.

# Footnotes—Chapter III
## Civil Liberties

1. Due process is guaranteed in the Fifth and Fourtheenth Amendments against the federal and state governments respectively. The right against unreasonable searches and seizures, against self-incrimination, the right to assistance of counsel in defense of criminal prosecutions and trial by jury in criminal prosecutions guaranteed against the federal government by the Fourth, Fifth and Sixth Amendments respectively, have been incorporated by Supreme Court decisions into the due process clause of the Fourteenth Amendment, and thus binding today against the states as well. Recently, in *Benton* v. *Md.*, 395 U.S. 784 (1969), the right against double jeopardy has also been incorporated. This case overruled *Palho* v. *Conn.*, 302 U.S. 319 (1937). Most of the Bill of Rights—the first eight amendments—have been gradually incorporated into the due process clause of the Fourteenth Amendment.

2. See pp. 111-19, *infra.*

3. See pp. 95-97, *infra.*

4. See pp. 143ff, *infra.*

5. See pp. 120-22, *infra.*

6. Roscoe Pound, *Justice According to Law* (New Haven: Yale U. Press, 1951), p. 37.

7. See p. 49, *supra.*

8. William Orville Douglas, "Jerome N. Frank," *Journal of Legal Education*, X (1957), 1, 7.

9. 222 F. 2d 698 (2d Cir., 1955).

10. Walter Gellhorn, *American Rights: The Constitution in Action* (New York: The Macmillan Co., 1960), p. 25.

11. *Ibid.*, 26.

12. *Ibid.*

13. *Ibid.*, 204, f.n. 8.

14. *Ibid.*, 25. The fact finders are the judge or jury. However, as to the admissibility of forced confessions in federal courts, see Alan Barth, *The Price of Liberty* (New York: Viking Press, 1961), p. 52: "From the beginning of the American Republic, forced confessions have been inadmissible in *federal courts.*" (Emphasis supplied).

15. 297 U.S. 278 (1936).

16. *Ibid.*, 285.

17. 309 U.S. 227 (1940).

18. Since a sharp conflict in the record relative to the infliction of physical violence was a question of fact, the Supreme Court relied on the jury finding in that respect, which by its verdict of guilty had resolved that issue against the defendant. The appeal revolved exclusively about the undisputed facts concerning the issue of mental coercion.

19. The administration of the criminal law rests in the main with the states. But the federal courts may review convictions in state courts on the basis of the due process clause of the Fourteenth Amendment, which

is applicable to and enforceable against the states. See *Watts* v. *Indiana*, 338 U.S. 49, 50, f.n. 1, 51 (1949).

20. 314 U.S. 219 (1941).

21. Defendant was convicted of the murder of his wife. But he had been arrested first on an unrelated charge of incest. He was questioned about the murder on a number of occasions during a two day period. There was a question whether he fell asleep or fainted as a result of the questioning. Remanded to jail after a hearing on the incest charge, he was questioned all day until midnight about the murder. See re this case, Fred E. Inbau and John E. Reid, *Lie Detection and Criminal Investigation* (3d ed., Williams & Wilkins Co., 1953), p. 214.

22. 322 U.S. 143 (1944), Justice Jackson wrote a brilliant dissenting opinion. See p. 226, f.n. 30, *infra*.

23. 322 U.S. 596 (1948).

24. 338 U.S. 49 (1949).

25. *Ibid.*, 53.

26. *Ibid.*, 52.

27. *Ibid.*, 57. See p. 92 at f.n. 59, *infra*. As to the meaning of "unlawful detention," see p. 89 at f.n.s. 34, 35, *infra*

28. See *White* v. *Texas*, 310 U.S. 330 (1940); *Ward* v. *Texas*, 316 U.S. 547 (1942); *Malinski* v. *New York*, 324 U.S. 401 (1944); *Turner* v. *Pa.*, 338 U.S. 62 (1948); *Harris* v. *So. Car.*, 338 U.S. 68 (1948); *Brown* v. *Allen*, 344 U.S. 443 (1952); and *Leyra* v. *Denno*, 347 U. S. 556 (1954). It should be noted that in the latter case, the Supreme Court sustained, though on different grounds, Frank's dissent in *U.S.* v. *Denno*, 208 F.2d 605 (2d Cir., 1953). This case is a variant of the run-of-the-mill mental coercion cases. Leyra was convicted of the hammer murder of his elderly parents and was sentenced to death. After intermittent questioning for two days and a night by the police and after complaints that his sinus was bothering him, Leyra was introduced to a psychiatrist summoned by the District Attorney (a fact unknown to Leyra), who talked to him in a wired room for one and a half hours. The District Attorney and the police were listening in an adjoining room. The doctor inquired about his sinus condition and the treatment he had received for it, and in the course of the interview remarked: "I'm your doctor." He told the doctor that he was very tired after only two hours of sleep the previous night. Reassuring him—"I am here to help you"—the psychiatrist placed his hand on Leyra's forehead to help him recollect the incidents of the murder. Seeking to minimize the homicide by suggesting it had been committed in a fit of temper, the physician stated: "Morally you are not to be condemned, right? . . . We're with you 100% . . . We'll play ball with you." The questioning was "persistent and unceasing." The New York Court of Appeals, reversing the conviction, was of the opinion that there had been created a "pseudoconfidential atmosphere of physician and patient," effecting a "subtle intrusion upon the rights of defendant and was tantamount to a form of mental coercion." The court held that Leyra's confession to the psychiatrist was invalid by reason of the mental coercion and also because of promises of leniency made to Leyra by the psychiatrist. *People* v. *Leyra*, 302 N.Y. 353, 358, 360. 362 (1951). On a retrial, the court in unmistakable language told the jury of the involuntariness and worthlessness of the confession to the psychiatrist and allowed it to be used only

225

to determine whether its effect carried over so as to permeate, taint and invalidate subsequent confessions made by Leyra within five hours to a police captain, a business associate and two assistant district attorneys. A second conviction was affirmed by a majority of the N.Y. Court of Appeals in *People* v. *Leyra*, 304 N.Y. 468 (1952). The New York court held that the question of a carry-over effect of the first confession upon subsequent confessions was a valid issue for determination by a jury. Upon appeal to the federal courts, raising a constitutional issue, a majority of the Circuit Court of Appeals agreed with the New York court. Frank dissented on the ground—disputed by the majority of the court—that the state had introduced no expert testimony to support a finding that the effect of the promise of leniency—as distinguished from the effect of the mental coercion—had worn off when Leyra made his last confession to the district attorneys. The majority was of the opinion that there was conflicting evidence by the experts on this issue and that it was a proper question for jury submission and determination. Morever, it found nowhere a "specific and definite promise of a lesser charge as the reward for a confession." If there had been a promise of a lesser charge, and its effect carried over to subsequent confessions, Leyra could not be prosecuted for first degree murder. The unspecific character of the threats and promises—Frank thought them specific enough—is to be found in the following language used by the psychiatrist when talking to Leyra: "These people are going to throw the book at you unless you can show that in a fit of temper, you got so angry that you did it. Otherwise, they toss premeditation in and it's premeditation. See?" 208 F.2d at 610. In a 5-3 decision, the Supreme Court held that the coercive character of the first confession to the psychiatrist controlled the character of all subsequent confessions; that they were part of "one continuous process." The court did not find it necessary to single out and discuss the issue of a promise of leniency raised in the lower courts. As a result, Leyra went free.

29. 346 U.S. 156 (1953).

30. Justice Jackson, who had written the minority opinion in *Ashcraft* v. *Tennessee* (f.n. 22. *supra*), and had joined in the dissenting opinion in *Haley* v. *Ohio* (f.n. 23, *supra*) now commanded a majority of the Court. See discussion following in the text.

31. Inbau and Reid, *op. cit.*, p. 207. For the Lisenba test, see p. 88, *supra*.

32. This is known as the "totality of circumstances" test. For subsequent decisions and developments in this area after the Caminito case, see *Spano* v. *New York*, 360 U.S. 315 (1959), *Blackburn* v. *Alabama*, 361 U.S. 199 (1960), *Rogers* v. *Richmond*, 365 U.S. 534 (1961) and *Haynes* v. *Washington*, 373 U.S. 503 (1963). The rationale of untrustworthiness for barring confessions was not the exclusive test in these cases, but was used in conjunction with a second rationale, namely, that due process bars evidence secured as a result of improper police procedure. As Chief Justice Warren said in the *Spano* case: "The abhorrence of society to the use of involuntary confessions does not turn alone on their inherent untrustworthiness. It also turns on the deep-rooted feeling that the police must obey the law while enforcing the law; that in the end life and liberty can be as much endangered from illegal methods used to convict those thought to be criminals as from the actual criminals themselves." 360 U.S. at 320. Checked with external evidence in the cases, the confessions could

sometimes be inherently believable, and yet at times have been barred as a violation of due process. See, e.g., opinions in *Watts* v. *Indiana*, 338 U.S. 49 (1949) and *Rogers* v. *Richmond, op. cit.* These cases thus represent a veering away from the exclusive test of untrustworthiness set forth in the Stein case.

33. The recent decision of *Miranda* v. *Arizona*, 384 U.S. 436 (1966) adds a new dimension with which we are not concerned in our analysis of Frank. This case bars a confession from evidence in a state court on constitutional grounds—namely, as in violation of the Fifth and Fourteenth Amendments—if the police fail to advise a defendant of his right to counsel, his right to remain silent and the fact that anything he says may be used against him, before any interrogation may start. Under this new constitutional interpretaion, Caminito may have chosen silence and the case might never have gone to trial. See p. 228, f.n. 50, *infra.*

34. Inbau and Reid, *supra; McNabb* v. *United States*, 318 U.S. 332, 342, f.n. 7 (1943).

35. Thus, e.g., under New York law "the fact that a confession was given during a period of illegal detention is one factor to be considered in determining whether or not it was voluntary; but it does not make the confession inadmissible per se." *Stein* v. *New York*, 346 U.S. 156, 187 f.n. (1953). See also, William Payson Richardson, *The Law of Evidence* (8th ed., Brooklyn, 1955), p. 305.

36. 318 U.S. 332 (1943).

37. Two of the McNabb brothers were subjected to two days of unremitting questioning; the third, arrested later, to five or six hours.

38. In the view he took of the case, Justice Frankfurter found it unnecessary to decide whether the confessions had been coerced in violation of the Fifth Amendment or were voluntary, as he would have had to do if this had been an appeal from a state court conviction, involving the Fourteenth Amendment. See 318 U.S. at 340.

39. 318 U.S. at 341.

40. *Ibid.*, 344.

41. See *Gallegos* v. *Nebraska*, 342 U.S. 55, 64 (1951); *Brown* v. *Allen*, 344 U.S. 443, 476 (1952).

42. See p. 227, f.n. 35, *supra.*

43. 335 U.S. 410 (1948). Upshaw was not questioned continually over many hours and by numerous officers as in *McNabb.* For the whittling away process of the *McNabb* doctrine in the lower federal courts by restricting it to facts as aggravating as those in the *McNabb* case, prior to its clarification in *Upshaw* and in *Mallory* v. *United States*, 354 U.S. 449 (1956) (decided after Frank's death), see James E. Hagan and Joseph M. Snee, The *McNabb-Mallory* Rule: Its Rise, Rationale and Rescue," *Georgetown L. Journal*, XLVII (1958), 1, 4, 5, 6. See also David Fellman, *The Defendant's Rights* (New York: Rinehart, 1958), p. 177. For the revolt which broke out against the *McNabb-Mallory* doctrine, see Hagan and Snee, *op. cit.*, pp. 34-36. The revolt has proven unsuccessful. The Judicial Conference of the U.S. has informed Congress of its opposition to any legislation setting aside this doctrine. See *N.Y. Law Journal* (Feb. 24, 1964) 1. In 1966 President Johnson vetoed a bill which would have modified the *McNabb-Mallory* doctrine for the area of Washington, D.C. For views pro and con this doctrine, see Hagan and Snee, *op. cit.*,

pp. 24, 25; Fred E. Inbau "Law and Police Practice; Restrictions in the Law of Interrogation and Confessions," *Northwestern U. L. Rev.*, LII (1957), 77, 79.

44. 335 U.S. at 413.

45. p. 224, f.n. 9, *supra*.

46. The record on appeal may be found in New York City in the library of the Supreme Court, Kings County and in the New York County Lawyers' Association, New York City.

47. See, e.g., Frank, *Courts on Trial: Myth and Reality in American Justice* (Princeton: Princeton Univ. Press, 1949), p. 182 and passim; Frank, *If Men Were Angels* (New York: Harper & Brothers, 1942), p. 109; Frank, "Cardozo and the Upper-Court Myth," *Law and Contemporary Problems*, XIII (1948), 369.

48. 161 F.2d 453 (2d Cir. 1947). See pp. 95-97, *infra*.

49. The District Attorney in his brief on appeal, attached to the record, contended that the cell was identical with all other detention cells.

50. At the time of this decision this was no violation of due process. See *Crooker* v. *California*, 357 U.S. 433 (1958) and *Cicenia* v. *Lagey*, 357 U.S. 504 (1958). Today, however, Frank's bald statement that this was an unconstitutional act is the law, as set forth in *Escobeda* v. *United States*, 378 U.S. 478 (1964). The 1966 decision of *Miranda* v. *Arizona* (see p. 227, f.n. 33, *supra*) will result in bringing the state cases on confessions in closer alignment with the federal cases. Regardless of the voluntariness of the confession, it will be held inadmissible in a state court as well if obtained without a warning to a defendant of his right to counsel, etc. However, a defendant may intelligently waive his right to counsel. But if a defendant in a state arrest chooses to talk after an intelligent waiver of his rights and this eventually leads to a confession, the question of a deferred arraignment on the issue of the voluntariness of the confession will still be decided by state—not by federal—law. For a host of questions which may arise as a result of the *Miranda* decision, see: William B. Lockhart, Yale Kamisar and Jesse H. Choper, *The American Constitution —Cases and Materials* (2d ed., St. Paul, Minn.: West Publishing Co., 1967) pp. 478-81.

51. These are Frank's statistics.—Frank related Caminito's version of a conference with his two co-defendants at 10:30 P.M. on the night he confessed. But at 9 P.M. Caminito had given his signed confession to a police stenographer, and so a conference as alleged by Caminito at 10:30 P.M. with his co-defendants as to whether they should all confess under duress and later seek their remedies, makes no sense. Frank, however, did not furnish the police version of defendant's conference alleged by them to have occurred at 2 P.M.

52. Caminito's account of a sleepless night, of course, is beyond the realm of proof. If true, could it have been caused by his predicament rather than by the sleeping accommodations?

53. 222 F.2d at 701, 703.

54. *Ibid.*, 706.

55. *Ibid.*, 700. See p. 89, *supra*.

56. In *Stein*, there were 12 hours of intermittent questioning; in this case Frank read into the record, mistakenly as we have sought to show, 27 hours of continuous questioning. See p. 91, *supra*. There was also

228

no element of so-called "kidnapping" in the *Stein* case. But see p. 91, f.n. 50, *supra*.

57. See p. 89, *supra*. It is possible Frank meant that questioning a man of Caminito's "type" for an alleged 27 hours was an unconstitutional act, an interpretation which would not be contradictory to the *Stein* principle.

58. See pp. 22 ff., *supra*.

59. See his concurring opinions in *Watts* v. *Indiana* p. 183 at f.n. 27, *supra* and *Reck* v. *Pete* 367 U.S. 435 (1961), and his dissenting opinion in *Stroble* v. *California*, 343 U.S. 181, 203-04 (1952). In the last case Justice Black joined in the dissent.

60. "An opinion by a judge in deciding a case, upon a matter not essential to the decision, and therefore not binding." American College Dictionary.

61. 222 F.2d at 702. In his concurring opinion, Chief Judge Clark referred to the delicacy of the problem created by the exercise of habeas corpus jurisdiction over the state courts by the lower federal courts—district and circuit courts of appeals—in cases involving state police activities, thereby raising an issue of comity and orderly federal-state relations. He made mention of the fact that in *Caminito* both the Appellate Division and the Court of Appeals of New York, the two highest courts of that state, had affirmed the conviction. Clark noted pending "wise" legislation drafted by a committee of the Judicial Conference of the United States and supported by the Conference of the State Chief Justices to permit only the United States Supreme Court to exercise jurisdiction by means of a writ of certiorari in cases involving state police activities; the appeal would be taken directly from the state's highest court to the Supreme Court. Such legislation, however, has not been enacted.

In 350 U.S. 896 (1955), the Suprme Court denied a writ of certiorari, and thus the *Caminito* decision stood. That a denial of certiorari may be for varied reasons, not necessarily related to the merits, and resulting from the fact that four members of the Supreme Court did not agree to hear the case, see *Brown* v. *Allen*, 344 U.S. 443, 491 (1952).

For an interesting analysis of the issues presented by detention of defendants prior to arraignment, see *U.S. ex rel. Williams* v. *Fay*, 323 F.2d 65, 73 (2d Cir., 1963).

62. 193 F.2d 848 (2d Cir., 1951).

63. This was a statement of the existing law. The standard "without unnecessary delay" was held in *Upshaw* v. *United States* (p. 90 at f.n. 43, *supra*) to imply no relaxation of the *McNabb* doctrine. Federal statutes have from time to time varied in their terminology with respect to the period when an arrestee must be presented to a committing officer. Thus, the Act of March 1, 1879, with reference to illicit distillery arrests, used the word "forthwith"; the Act of June 8, 1934, with reference to the F.B.I., used the word "immediately."

64. Leviton did not take the stand. 193 F.2d at 855.

65. *Ibid.*, 855, f.n. 1.

66. The officers admitted that Leviton was not free to come and go from 1:45 on.

67. *Supra*, 858. Rule 5(b) supplied the rationale for Rule 5(a) (see p. 93 at f.n. 63, *supra*), namely, its requirement that a judicial officer

inform a defendant of his rights, such as the right to counsel, to a preliminary examination of the People's case, and the provision that he shall admit a defendant to bail as provided in the rules.

68. 322 U.S. 65 (1944). In this case the Supreme Court held that a confession voluntarily made within a few minutes after the defendant's arrest was admissible in evidence in a federal court.

69. 193 F.2d at 861.

70. P. 227, f.n. 43, *supra*.

71. 193 F.2d at 860.

72. Edmond Cahn, "Judge Frank's Skepticism and our Future," *Yale Law Jour*. LVI (1957), 8, 29.

73. A writ of certiorari was denied by the Supreme Court in 343 U.S. 946 (1952), and Leviton's conviction was sustained. However, Justices Black and Douglas were of the opinion that the writ should have been granted.

74. p. 228, f.n. 48, *supra*.

75. *Ibid.*, 458.

76. *Ibid.*, 459.

77. A confession physically or psychologically coerced would constitute a violation of due process under the Fifth Amendment.

78. Such as a confession obtained during illegal detention, even without proof of any coercion.

79. The Fourth Amendment deals with illegal search and seizure.

80. Since this view of Frank about statutory violations did not muster the support of any other member of the bench, it was a minority opinion in that aspect of the case, and was a partial dissent by him. In any event, it was an *obiter dictum*.

81. 161 F.2d at 461.

82. See p. 90 at f.ns. 38-40, *supra*.

82a. *Ibid.*, 462.

83. See 161 F.2d at 465, f.n. 35: "One wonders whether statutes should not provide governmental compensation for persons wrongfully indicted."

84. *Ibid.*, 465. See Frank, "To-day's Problems in the Administration of Criminal Justice," 15 *Federal Rule Decisions* (FRD) (1958).

Judge Augustus N. Hand dissented on formalistic grounds: the absence of a governing statute. Both parties appealed. Certiorari was granted the government in 331 U.S. 804 (1947), but denied to Fried et al. in 331 U.S. 858 (1947). Subsequently, the Government moved to dismiss its own writ. 332 U.S. 807 (1947). No reason was assigned for the Government's action.

85. Dis. op in *Casey* v. *U.S.*, 276 U.S. 413, 423 (1927). "But it may not provoke or create a crime and then punish the criminal, its creature."

86. 287 U.S. 435 (1932).

87. *Ibid.*, 451.

88. *Ibid.*, 457.

89. 236 F.2d 601 (2d Cir., 1956).

90. 236 F.2d at 603, quoting from *U.S.* v. *Sherman*, 200 F.2d 880, 882 (2d Cir., 1952).

91. *Ibid.*, 604.

92. *Ibid.*

93. *Ibid.*

94. *Ibid.*, 605, quoting from *U.S. v. Sherman, op. cit.* The majority referred to *U.S. v. Sherman*, but Frank felt it did not support its view. The *Sherman* case interpreted the *Sorrells* case. The *Sherman* case held that the proof of predisposition and criminal design of a defendant may be shown "by evidence of his past offense, of his preparation, *even of his 'ready complaisance.'* Obviously, it is not necessary that the past offenses proved shall be precisely the same as that charged, provided they are near enough in kind to support an inference that his purpose included offenses of the sort charged." (Emphasis supplied) 200 F.2d at 882. The different interpretations of the Sherman case by Judges Hincks and Frank will be found in *U.S. v. Musciale*, 236 F.2d at 603, f.ns. 1 and 604, respectively.

95. *Ibid.*

96. 287 U.S. at 441.

97. 200 F.2d at 882. See f.n. 94, *supra.*

98. *Masciale* v. *U.S.*, 356 U.S. 386 (1958).

99. 356 U.S. 369 (1958), handed down during the same term as *Masciale* v. *U.S., ibid.*

100. 356 U.S. at 389. The Supreme Court affirmed the conviction by a divided court (5-4). The dissent by Justice Frankfurter (Justices Douglas, Harlan and Brennan joining) was based on his view that the issue of entrapment should have been decided by a judge, not by a jury. It was thus a dissent on a procedural issue.

101. 193 F.2d 306 (2d Cir., 1951).

102. Alan Barth, *op. cit.*, p. 145. See p. 105 at f.n. 125, *infra.*

103. *Ibid.*, 112.

104. Quoted *ibid.*, 129. "General warrants" could be served on any one. They contained no information as to any specific person to be arrested or specific papers to be seized. They authorized fishing expeditions. See Fellman, *op. cit.*, pp. 129-33.

105. 277 U.S. 438 (1928).

106. *Ibid.*, 457. The wires were inserted in the basement of an office building nearby, and in the streets near some private residences.

107. *Ibid.*, 464.

108. *Ibid.*, 463. The defense claimed that the Government had also violated the Fifth Amendment against self-incrimination. The Chief Justice replied: "There is no room in the present case for applying the Fifth Amendment unless the Fourth Amendment was first involved. There was no evidence of compulsion to induce the defendants to talk over their many telephones." 277 U.S. at 462.

109. *Ibid.*, 470. Taft wrote that the Washington statute did not declare the evidence obtained by interception inadmisible. *Op. cit.*, p. 469.

110. *Ibid.*, 478. See Samuel D. Warren and Louis D. Brandeis, "The Right to Privacy," *Harvard Law Rev.*, IV (1890), 193. In the *Olmstead* case Brandeis quoted in support of his position memorable words from *Boyd* v. *U.S.*, 116 U.S. 616, 630 (1886), as follows: " 'It is not the breaking of his doors, and the rummaging of his drawers, that constitutes the essence of the offense, but it is the invasion of his indefeasible right of personal security, personal liberty and private property, where that right has never been forfeited by the conviction of some public offense—it is the invasion of this sacred right which underlies and constitutes the es-

231

sence of Lord Camden's judgment. Breaking into a house and opening boxes and drawers are circumstances of aggravation, but any forcible and compulsory extortion of a man's own testimony or of his private papers to be used as evidence of a crime or to forfeit his goods, is within the condemnation of that judgment. In this regard the Fourth and Fifth Amendments run almost into each other." The *Boyd* case was a civil suit and the issue involved was whether a man's compulsory production of his private papers "to be used in evidence against him in a proceeding to forfeit his property for alleged fraud against the revenue laws" constituted an unreasonable search and seizure. The reference to Lord Camden's judgment is to his decision in *Entick* v. *Carrington,* 19 Howell's State Trials 1030.

111. See Barth, *op. cit.,* p. 132; O. John Rogge, The First and the Fifth (New York: Thomas Nelson & Sons, 1960), p. 228; Fellman, *op. cit.,* pp. 114-46. However, under the Omnibus Crime Conrol and Safe Streets Act of 1968. Title III, the federal government is authorized to use electronic eavesdropping and wiretapping in investigations of specified types of serious crimes. Judges may authorize their use up to 30 days.

112. 316 U.S. 129 (1942).

113. *Ibid.,* 133.

114. *Ibid.,* A dictum in the *Goldman* case is to the effect that conversation can be the subject of illegal seizure as well as tangible objects. This is contrary to the Olmstead case. See p. 102 at f.n. 108, *supra.*

115. P. 231, f.n. 101, *supra.*

116. P. 232, f.n. 112, *supra.*

117. 193 F.2d at 308.

118. *Ibid.* The Fourth Amendment refers to "persons or things to be seized."

119. *Ibid.,* 315. Justice Murphy dissented in the *Goldman* case.

120. *Ibid.*

121. *Ibid.,* 315, f.n. 18.

122. *Ibid.,* 311, citing a case.

123. See p. 102 at f.n. 105, *supra.*

124. *Supra,* 313. For opinions in accord with Frank's view, see: (a) dis. op. in *On Lee* v. *U.S.,* 343 U.S. 747 (1951); (b) the later decision of *Silverman* v. *U.S.,* 365 U.S. 505 (1960). The majority in the *On Lee* case in the Supreme Court did not have to rule on this point, since it found that no trespass had been committed.

125. *Ibid.,* 315. See reference to this passage by Justice Stewart in *Silverman* v. *U.S.,* 365 U.S. 505, 512, f.n.: "The late Judge Jerome Frank made the point in more contemporary language" than William Pitt.

126. *Ibid.,* 317. For a somewhat similar picture, see Justice Brandeis' concurring opinion in *Olmstead* v. *U.S.,* 277 U.S. 438 (1928).

127. *On Lee* v. *U.S.,* 343 U.S. 747, 752 (1951).

128. 193 F.2d at 314.

129. See dis. op. by Justice Douglas in *Silverman* v. *U.S.,* 365 U.S. at 512-13. Justive Douglas held that it made no difference. See *Katz* v. *U.S.,* 389 U.S. 348 (1967), wherein the court finally adopted the position that it makes no difference. Involved was the transmission of wagering information by telephone across state lines. The F.B.I. attached electronic listening and recording devices to the outside of a telephone booth from which the calls were made. The court said: "For the Fourth Amendment

protects people, not places. What a person knowingly exposes to the public, even in his own home or office, is not a subject of Fourth Amendment protection . . .

"We conclude that the underpinnings of *Olmstead* and *Goldman* have been so eroded by our subsequent decisions that the "trespass" doctrine there enunciated can no longer be regarded as controlling. The Government's activities in electronically listening to and rcording the petitioner's words violated the privacy upon which he justifiably relied while using the telephone booth and this constituted a search and seizure within the meaning of the Fourth Amendment. The fact that the electronic device employed to achieve that end did not happen to penetrate the wall of the booth can have no constitutional significance." 339 U.S. at 351, 353. The court concluded that a search warrant was required as a "constitutional precondition of such electronic surveillance." 339 U.S. at 347 (Headnote).

*On Lee,* unlike the *Katz* case, does not involve the attachment of an electronic device to any part of the defendant's premises. That *On Lee* remains undisturbed by the *Katz* decision, see the concurring opinion in *Katz* by Justice White, at p. 363, f.n.: "In previous cases, which are undisturbed by today's decision, the Court has upheld, as reasonable under the Fourth Amendment, admission at trial of evidence obtained (1) by an undercover agent to whom a defendant speaks without knowledge that he is in the employ of the police, *Hoffa* v. *U.S.,* 385 U.S. 293 (1966); (2) by a recording device hidden on the person of such an informant, *Lopez* v. *U.S.,* 373 U.S. 427 (1963); and (3) by a policeman listening to the secret micro-wave transmissions of an agent conversing with the defendant in another location, *On Lee* v. *U.S.,* 343 U.S. 747 (1952). When one man speaks to another he takes all the risks ordinarily inherent in so doing, including the risk that the man to whom he speaks will make public what he has heard. The Fourth Amendment does not protect against unreliable (or law-abiding) associates. *Hoffa* v. *U.S., supra. It is but a logical and reasonable extension of this principle that a man takes the risk that his hearer, free to memorize what he hears for later verbatim repetitions, is instead recording it or transmitting it to another.* The present case deals with an entirely different situation, for as the Court emphasizes the petitioner 'sought to exclude . . . the uninvited ear,' and spoke under circumstances in which a reasonable person would assume that uninvited ears were not listening." (Emphasis supplied)

130. See p. 84, *supra.*

131. 193 F.2d at 311.

132. For the denounement of the case, see *U.S.* v. *On Lee,* 201 F. 2d 722 (2d Cir., 1953), discussed on pp. 74-76 *supra.* It may be of interest to note that Chin Poy was not called as a witness because he had been convicted fifteen times of narcotics. See *U.S.* v. *On Lee,* 201 F.2d 722, 724. That the government probably never intended to call him, see op. by Chief Justice Warren in *Lopez* v. *U.S.,* 373 U.S. 427 (1962). Though the government, any more than a private person, is under no obligation to call all witnesses, it is submitted that it is morally wrong for the government to conceal a witness from a jury, which should be in a position to judge the facts by the testimony of all important available witnsses, disreputable as well as reputable. Further, the conversation with On Lee oc-

curred after his arraignment, and as Warren stated in the *Lopez* case, *op. cit.*, this alone should have been sufficient for a reversal. The issue, however, was not raised. As not infrequently happens, a judge arrives at the right decision for the wrong reasons. This was the case with Frank's decision in the *On Lee* case.

133. Edwin N. Griswold, *the Fifth Amendment today* (Cambridge: Harvard U. Press, 1955), p. 7.

134. *Ibid.*

135. Fellman, *op. cit.*, p. 154.

136. *Ibid.*

137. See page 219, f.n. 196, *supra.*

138. *Supra.* Lilburne refused to submit to an ex-officio oath in the Court of Star Chambers after an accusation of importing subversive books from Holland, and later of treason. Severely beaten in jail, he eventually won a montary vindication from Parliament. See Griswold, *op. cit.*, p. 3.

139. *Ibid.*, 154, 156.

140. 132 F.2d 837 (2d Cir., 1942).

141. *Ibid.*, 841.

142. See, e.g., pp. 24-27 and passim, *supra.*

143. 132 F.2d at 848.

144. *Ibid.*, 847. See Frank's opinion in *U.S.* v. *Gordon*, 236 F. 2d 916, 919, 920 (1956), in which the secretary-treasurer of a local of the International Brotherhood of Teamsters refused to answer questions about his local on the ground the answers might incriminate him under the Anti-Racketeering Law and as a result was held in contempt. Reversing the conviction, Frank wrote regarding the Fifth Amendment: "That provision unquestionably does sometimes impede enforcement of the criminal laws. But that was on of the clear purposes of the constitutional privilege, i.e., to prevent a court from compelling a witness—who migh or might not be a criminal—to give testimony which might incriminate him. All privileges not to testify have the same impeding effect. This fact was emphasized by Bentham, the first doughty foe of the anti-self-incrimination privilege. He depicted it as an absurd interference with the expeditious punishment of criminals. But, on the same grounds, he argued for the abandonment of the client-lawyer privilege. Yet few today want that privilege abandoned, although it enjoys no explicit constitutional protection . . . The framers of the Constitutional Amendments thought those guarantees embodied an even more important policy than that of detecting and punishing crime. Considered solely in terms of procedure, those constitutional safeguards seem logically indefensible. Considered, however, as conferring substantive rights, they assume a different significance: They express the high value our democracy puts on the individual's right of privacy . . .

"At any such right of privacy, be it noted, the despotic rulers of the totalitarian regimes sneer . . . Their position, which logically renders asinine any privilege not to testify, occasionally justifies them logically in subjecting their subjects to consant spying and snooping, for such despotic surveillance plainly aids in the detection of those who violate the laws. . . Before we accept their criticism and sacrifice all our other values to effective law enforcement, we should reflect on the brutal consquences of the totalitarians' alleged efficiency in pursuing suspected criminals . . . Such reflections should teach us this: An overzealous prosecutor's heaven may be everyone else's hell."

145. *Ibid.*, 850.

146. See pp. 111 ff., *infra*.

147 *Supra*, 848. In 318 U.S. 751 (1952), the Supreme Court granted certiorari. Thereafter because St. Pierre's five month term had expired when the case reached the Supreme Court, it ruled in a Per Curiam opinion in *St. Pierre v. U.S.*, 319 U.S. 842 (1943), that the issue was moot. See discussion of this case, pp. 78-79, *supra*.

The contempt cases, where the issue of a waiver of the Fifth Amendment privilege has usually arisen, have involved investigations of the Communist Party. See, e.g., *Rogers v. United States*, 340 U.S. 367 (1950), a 5-3 decision, in which the witness admitted before a grand jury, investigating the Communist Party of Denver, her membership in the Communist Party, but refused to disclose to whom she, as the admitted former Treasurer of the Denver Communist Party, had turned over the mmbership lists and dues books. Her conviction for contempt was sustained. By waiving her privilege against self-incrimination regarding her membership in the Communist Party, she was held bound to answer a mere "detail" in connection with the admission she already had voluntarily made and which did not entail any further crimination. "As to each question to which a claim of privilege is directed, the court must determine whether the answer to that particular question would subject the witenss to a 'real danger' of further crimination. After petitioner's admission that she held the office of Treasurer of the Communist Party of Denver, disclosure of acquaintance with her successor presents no more than a 'mere imaginary possibility' of increasing the danger of prosecution." 340 U.S. at 374. In a footnote (no. 19) to this passage, the Court made the following reference to the *St. Pierre* case: "U.S. v. *St. Pierre*, 132 F. 2d 837 . . . presented a closer question since the "detail" which St. Pierre was required to divulge would identify a person without whose testimony St. Pierre could not have been convicted of a crime. We, of course, do not here pass upon the precise factual question there decided by the Court of Appeals."

Cf. with the *Pierre* case *U.S. v. Courtney*, 236 F. 2d 92 (1956), involving a somewhat similar situation, but in which Judge Frank mustered a majority of the Court in favor of his opinion. The case was not appealed. Courtney was engaged in the trucking business and admitted to an investigative grand jury paying gratuities to certain businesses but he refused to state to whom and in what amounts. Frank held that answers to further questions would have supplied leads to evidence on the basis of which Courtney could possibly be convicted under the Internal Revenue Code, that he was within his constitutional rights in refusing further answers and was not guilty of contempt. It was Frank's contention that in *Rogers* v. *U.S., op. cit.*, the defendant had already implicated herself by admitting membership in the Communist Party in violation of the Smith Act and that in *U.S.* v. *St. Pierre, op. cit.*, assuming it still had vitality, the defendant had admitted committing a crime. But in the *Courtney* case, the defendant had not yet admitted to the commission of any crime since it was necessary to pass $600. or more to any one person within any one year before one could become guilty under the relevant Internal

Revenue Code section. Frank also read into a couple of Supreme Court cases decided since the *Rogers* case—*Emspak* v. *U.S.*, 348 U.S. 190 (1954) and *Trock* v. *U.S.*, 351 U.S. 976 (1956)—a more generous interpretation of the Fifth Amendment privilege.

For another contempt of court action involving the Fifth Amendment, in which Frank wrote an opinion concurring as to affirmance but dissenting in one ruling, see *U.S.* v. *Field*, 193 F. 2d 92 (2d Cir., 1951). The defendants in this case were the bail bondsmen for the defendants who failed to surrender themselves but went into hiding after the affirmance of their convictions in the famous Smith Act conspiracy trial reported in *Dennis v. U.S.*, 341 U.S. 494 (1950). (See p. 254, f.n. 98, *infra*) Frank agreed with the majority of the Court that the records of the Bail Fund of the Civil Rights Congress had to be produced in court and that the defendants, trustees of the Bail Fund, were required to testify regarding matters "auxiliary to the production" of the record. Such records are kept in a representative rather than in a personal capacity and are not protected by the personal privilege against self-incrimination. But the defendants were asked to answer other questions not pertaining to the records, as when they last had seen or about their acquaintance with the "Dennis-case refugees." 132 F.2d at 102. It was in this connection that Frank disagreed with his colleagues, contending that defendants' constitutional rights under the Fifth Amendment were being infringed. Frank denied that upon becoming bail, each defendant thereby entered into a contract with the government validly surrendering his constitutional privilege "long before there arises a judicial inquiry in which he is asked to give self-incriminating oral testimony under oath." 132 F. 2d at 107. He analogized to one contracting away his right to trial by jury in all future criminal proceedings. Such a waiver of a constitutional right can be effected only after indictment. "Advance abandonment is forbidden to prevent the right being thoughtlessly foregone. And, for like reasons, the same rule governs the advance abandonment of the privilege against oral testimony which tends to incriminate." 132 F.2d 108. In the course of his remarks, Frank wrote: "So that if, at times, this privilege protects the guilty, yet often it serves as a shield to the innocent." 193 F.2d at 109. Dean Griswold championed this defense of the Fifth Amendment as a shield to the innocent in his discussion of the Fifth Amendment, and he furnished concrete supporting examples. See Edwin N. Griswold, *op. cit.*, Chap. I and passim. For a vindication of Frank's dissenting position in the *Field* case, see *Curcio* v. *U.S.*, 254 U.S. 118 (1956). The *Field* case was not appealed.

148. 233 F.2d 556 (2d Cir., 1956).

149. Only the People's witnesses testify before a regular grand jury, unless the defendant, where permitted by statute, asks permission to testify.

150. 233 F.2d at 568.

151. 271 U.S. 494 (1924). This case involved two trials, not a grand jury situation. Reference was permitted to be made at the second trial to defendant's failure to testify at the first trial.

152. 233 F.2d at 572.

153. 318 U.S. 189 (1942). This case involved one trial, during which the prosecutor made a reference to the defendant's refusal to answer a question on the ground it might incriminate him of an aspect of the case he was

not charged with on this trial. The judge in his charge limited defendant's failure to answer to the issue of credibility. On appeal, the remarks of the prosecutor and the judge were held to constitute error.

154. 233 F. 2d at 575. See comment thereon in Edmond Cahn, "Fact Skepticism and Fundamental Law," *N.Y.U. Law Rev.*, XXXIII (1953), 1, 16. That an error involving a constitutional right may be classified as "harmless" was decided by the Supreme Court recently in *Chapman* v. *California*, 386 U.S. 18, 22 (1967). "We conclude that there may be some constitutional errors which in the setting of a particular case are so unimportant and insignificant that they may, consistent with the federal constitution, be deemed harmless, and not resulting in the automatic reversal of the conviction."

155. There are two grades of crime: misdemeanors and felonies. Felonies are the more aggravated of the two.

156. 233 F.2d at 578.

157. Now 18 U.S.C., sec. 3481.

158. 233 F.2d at 579.

159. *Ibid.*, 580.

159a. No witness hears the testimony of any other witness in a grand jury room.

160. *Grunewald* v. *U.S.*, 353 U.S. 391,423 (1957), in which the Supreme Court unanimously reversed the Circuit Court of Appeals and granted Halperin a new trial, thus sustaining Frank's dissent. It did not find it necessary to determine if the Raffel case had been stripped of vitality by the Johnson case. See p. 110 at f.n. S. 151, 153, *supra.*

Attached to the Grunewald case is an Appendix in which Frank furnished a bird's-eye view of the practice in several European countries regarding the privilege against self-incrimination and excerpts from articles and books on the validity and effects of a statute authorizing an accused to testify.

161. "Jury," Encyclopaedia Britannica, 1961 ed., Vol. XIII, p. 205. See p. 111, *infra*, for a definition of compurgation.

162. See Lewis Mayers, *The American Legal System* (rev. ed., New York: Harper & Row, 1964), p. 113; Francis X. Busch, *Trial Procedure Materials* (Indianapolis: Bobbs-Merrill, 1961), p. 92; Morris Raphael Cohen, *The Faith of a Liberal* (New York: Henry Holt, 1946), p. 92. The oft-quoted clause 39 of Magna Carta did not guarantee jury trials. It guaranteed only that "peers of the realm" would be tried by judges who were themselves peers and similarly clerics would be tried in their own courts by clerics. See Cohen, *op. cit.*

163. Encyclopaedia Britannica, *supra.* See also Busch, *op. cit.*, p. 1; Mayers, *op. cit.*, p. 111; Frank, Courts on Trial, *op. cit.*, p. 108.

164. Encyclopaedia Britannica, *ibid.*; Theodore F. T. Plucknett, *A Concise History of the Common Law* (5th ed., Boston: Little Brown & Co., 1956), p. 116.

165 *Ibid.*; Plucknett, *ibid.*, 111, 118.

166. *Ibid.*

167. Mayers, *op. cit.*, p. 113.

168. Frank, Courts on Trial, *op. cit.*, p. 109.

169. Encyclopaedia Britannica, *supra.* Many areas of the law—such as admiralty, bankruptcy, and almost all "equity" suits—in which there were

no jury trials at common law, accordingly have no jury trials guaranteed under the Seventh Amendment.

170. In *Law and The Modern Mind*, Frank made use of his theory of the "basic myth" (see p. 15, *supra*) in his analysis of the jury system. But since his theory, as we have seen, was itself a myth and is unnecessary to his critique of the jury system, we omit its discussion. See Frank, *Law and The Modern Mind* (New York: Brentano's, 1930), p. 177.

171. Frank, *Law and The Modern Mind, op. cit.*, p. 184.

172. *Ibid.*, 182. Frank rendered the Hebrew word as "Schemhamphora." It should be rendered as two words: Schem hamphorash (the Tetragrammaton).

173. *Ibid.*, 174.

174. Frank, Courts on Trial, *op. cit.*, p. 132.

175. *Ibid.*, 127, quoting Dean Pound, Wigmore and an English judge, Chalmers.

176. *Ibid.* See also Frank's opinion in *Skidmore* v. *Baltimore & O. Ry. Co.*, 167 F. 2d 54, 58 (2d Cir., 1948); Frank, "Words and Music: Some Remarks on Statutory Interpretation," *Columbia Law Rev.*, XLVII (1947), 1259, 1274-76; Frank, If Men Were Angels, *op. cit.*, pp. 87, 88.

177. *Ibid.*, 130.

178. *Ibid.*, 132. Frank referred to the fact that judges decide thousands of cases annually without juries, where a state constitution or a statute permits a waiver of trial by jury, and their decisions are often made with flexibility and individualization. However, he claimed that the judges "purport to be governed largely by rules and principles, standards and such, and thus perpetuate the public apprehension of the cold formalism of their decisions." Frank, Law and the Modern Mind, *op. cit.*, p. 176.

179. *Ibid.*, 130.

180. *Ibid.*, 132.

181. *Ibid.*

182. Frank, *Law and The Modern Mind, op. cit.*, p. 181. See also, *Skidmore* v. *Baltimore & O. Ry Co.*, 167 F. 2d at 64, 65.

183. Frank, Courts on Trial, *op. cit.*, p. 117. To same effect, see Leon Green, *Judge and Jury* (Kansas City, Mo.: Vernon Law Books Co., 1930), p. 351.

184. Frank, *Law and The Modern Mind, supra*, 181.

185. Frank, *Courts on Trial, supra*, p. 135.

186. *Ibid.* See p. 237, f.n. 169, *supra*.

187. *Ibid.*, 124, 125.

188. *Ibid.*, 137.

189. *Ibid.*, 139.

190. *Ibid.*, 109.

191. *Ibid.*

192. *Ibid.*, 136.

193. 155 F. 2d 631 (2d Cir., 1946).

194. *Ibid.*, 663, f.n. 68.

195. See p. 115, *supra*.

196. Frank, *Courts on Trial, op. cit.*, p. 132.

197. *Ibid.*, 122, derived from Osborn, *The Mind of the Juror* (1937), p. 92.

198. *Ibid.*, 114-15. See also Per Curiam opinion in *Fabris* v. *General Foods Corporation*, 152 F. 2d 660 (2d Cir., 1945), a case in which Frank

was a member of the court. An affidavit submitted by eight jurors alleged that their verdict was the result of an agreement to abide by a majority vote. Yet, on the authority of *McDonald* v. *Fless,* 238 U.S. 264 (1914), the Circuit Court of Appeals affirmed the judgment for defendant. "If evidence thus secured could be thus used, the result would be to make what was intended to be a private deliberation, the constant subject of public investigation—to the destruction of all frankness and freedom of discussion and conference." 238 U.S. at 267.

199. *Ibid.,* 141-42.

200. *Ibid.* Frank stated that the jury is less able to know whether its findings will favor one or the other side in those jurisdictions where the judge need not and thus should not give any charge on the substantive legal rules beyond what is necessary for the jury to answer the questions submitted to it.

201. *Ibid.,* 142.

202. *Ibid.* See Frank's opinion in *Skidmore* v. *Baltimore & O. Ry. Co.,* 167 F. 2d at 67, in which Frank mentioned his preference for the Texas procedure, which makes a special verdict mandatory when a party demands it, over the federal procedure giving the judge absolute discretion to use the "old-flashioned general verdict" despite the request of a party. See also Frank's praise for special verdicts in his dis. op. in *Keller* v. *Brooklyn Bus Corp.,* 128 F. 2d 510 (2d Cir., 1942), and in his concurring opinion in *Morris* v. *Pennsylvania Ry. Co.,* 187 F. 2d 837 (1951). In the latter case, Judge Clark wrote that special verdicts were valuable in some situations and of doubtful value in others. Frank expressed his disagreement with this partial critcism.

For adverse comments on the special verdict, see Green, *op. cit.,* pp. 411, 412, 416, 354-55, and Douglas, "Jerome N. Frank," *op. cit.,* p. 2. For a favorable comment, see Charles T. McCormick, "Jury Verdicts upon Special Questions in Civil Cases," *"Judicial Administrative Monographs,* Series A, 72-78 (Special Committee on Improving the Administration of Justice of the American Bar Association, 1942).

203. *Ibid.* The jury will know "whether its findings will favor one side or the other." *Op. cit.*

204. Frank, Law and The Modern Mind, *op. cit.,* pp. 180-81.

205. Frank, Courts on Trial, *supra,* 252. See Robert H. Elder, "Resolved that Jury Trials in Civil Cases Should Be Abolished," *Bar General Pamphlets,* Vol. 15, (New York County Lawyers' Association, Radio Address, Dec. 11, 1930.)

206. *Ibid.,* 123.

207. *Ibid.* See Frank's opinion in *Hoffman* v. *Palmer,* 128 F. 2d 976, 987, f.n. 20 (2d Cir., 1942), in which Frank referred to "a dispute as to whether the hearsay rule and its corollaries derive solely from the jury system and a mistrust of the capacity of juries to deal with so-called 'second-hand' evidence."

208. Is the figure 90% hyperbole?

209. *Supra,* 144. Cf. with discussion on hearsay evidence, pp. 79-80, *supra.*

210. 132 F. 2d 837 (2d Cir., 1942). See discussion of this case, pp. 78, 107-08, *supra.*

211. *Supra,* citing Clarence G. Galston, "Civil Trials and Tribulations,"

*Am. Bar. Ass'n. Jour.*, XXIX (1945), 195. See also, Clarence G. Galston, *Behind the Judicial Curtain* ,Barrington House, 1959), pp. 34, 46.

212. *Ibid.*, 145.

213. *Skidmore* v. *Baltimore & O. Ry. Co.*, 167 F. 2d at 67, f.n. 31.

214. *Supra.*

215. *Ibid.*

216. *Ibid.*, 109.

217. 184 F. 2d 18 (2d Cir., 1950).

218. In 340 U.S. 875 (1952), the Supreme Court denied certiorari in the *Farina* case.

219. 155 F. 2d 631 (2nd Cir., 1946).

220. In 239 U.S. 742 (1946), the Supreme Court denied certiorari in the *Antonelli* case. For an analogous case in which Frank again dissented, see *U.S.* v. *Walker*, 190 F 2d 481 (2d Cir., 1951), and in which the Supreme Court again denied certiorari, in 342 U.S. 868 (1951).

221. In 1964 a subcommittee of the Judiciary Committee of the New York State Senate conducted hearings regarding a proposal by Chief Judge Desmond of the N.Y. State Court of Appeals to abolish jury trials in civil actions. The abolitionists have in mind a proposed amendment to the State Constitution.

222. Sir William Kenneth Diplock, "The Jury and Civil Actions in England," *New York State Bar Journal*, Vol. 36, No. 4 (Albany, N.Y.: New York State Bar Association, August, 1964), 297, 300.

223. Jefferson F. Meagher, "Trial by Jury Deserves a Fair Trial," New York State Bar Journal, *ibid.*, 303, 306.

224. William Orville Douglas, "Jerome N. Frank," *Journal of Legal Education*, X (1957), 2.

225. See Harry Kalven, Jr., and Hans Zeisel, *The American Jury* (Boston: Little, Brown, 1966), p. 11, in which the authors refer to their study of the operation of the jury system in the United States as "a contribution to what has often been called realist jurisprudence; it is an effort to find out how the law in operation, as contrasted to the law on the books, is working."

226. Harold M. Hoffman and Joseph Bradley, "Jurors on Trial," *Missouri Law Rev.*, XVII (1952), 235.

227. *Ibid.*

228. Harry Kalven, Jr., "The Dignity of the Civil Jury, *Virginia Law Review*, L. (1964), 1055. This article also appeared in the *New York Law Journal*, (December 15, 16 and 17, 1964), 4.

229. *Ibid.*, N.Y. Law Journal, (Dec. 16, 1964), 4.

230. *Ibid.* Another statistic furnished by Kalven, resulting from a canvass of 1,060 trial judges throughout the U.S., concerned their degree of satisfaction with jury trials. For criminal cases, 75% were thoroughly satisfied, 20% "satisfactory if certain changes were made," and 3% "unsatisfactory." Regarding civil cases, 64% were thoroughly satisfied, 27% expressed satisfaction if certain changes were made, and 9% declared they were unsatisfactory.

231. For additional source material on the jury system, see the footnotes to the discussion on "The Merits of Trial by Jury," in David Fellman, *op. cit.*, pp. 109-11. For a critical view of the jury system, somewhat

similar to Frank's, see Abraham, Henry J., *The Judicial Process* (2d ed., New York, London, Toronto: Oxford University Press, 1968), pp. 128-33.

232. 238 F. 2d 565 (2d Cir., 1956).

233. A Latin phrase meaning "in the manner of a pauper."

234. 351 U.S. 12 (1955).

235. Another "distinguishing" feature was stated by the Court: "In Griffin v. People of the State of Illinois, 351 U.S. 12 . . ., the majority opinion proceeded on the assumption that in that case 'errors were committed in the trial which would merit reversal'; it was not addressed to the problems involved in frivolous appeals. . " 238 F. 2d at 566.

236. Since the Fifth Amendment, unlike the Fourteenth Amendment, does not contain an Equal Protection clause, Judge Hincks' statement that the statute also does not violate the Equal Protection clause of the Fifth Amendment is in error. See 238 F. 2d at 567.

237. *Ibid.*, 572.

238. *Ibid.*, 571, 572. See discussion by Frank as to what the "less opulent Scandinavian countries" do to insure equal justice under the law, *op. cit.*, 573, 573, f.n. 14c.

See *U.S.* v. *Ebeling*, 146 F. 2d 254 (2d Cir., 1944), for Frank's dis. op., in which he wrote in a vein similar to *U.S.* v. *Johnson*: "I, for one could not sleep well if I thought that, out of a desire for unnecessary expedition, I had helped to affirm the conviction of a man who may be innocent." *Op. cit.*, p. 258. During the trial of a spy conspiracy charge, defense counsel asked to see a statement which had been furnished to the Government by the People's main witness. The statement was handed up to the court, which refused to show it to the defense, stating that it had the earmarks of a confidential communication. Frank thought this procedure was wrong; that the defense was entitled to see the statement. This case was not appealed, but Frank's minority view ultimately became the procedure sanctioned by a majority of the Supreme Court in *Jencks* v. *United States,* 353 U.S. 657 (1956), which virtually overruled its previous decision in *Goldman* v. *U.S.* 316 U.S. 129 (1942).

239. 238 F. 2d at 571. Frank referred to the manner of statement provided in *Miller* v. *U.S.*, 317 U.S. 192 (1942), in which the District Court (although not involving a statute like the one in the *Johnson* case) had permitted the appeal *in forma pauperis.*

240. ". . . the judge may and should interrogate the witnesses, the counsel who represented the government and the defendant at the trial, and any other persons having reliable information. Outstanding among such other persons is the official reporter who took stenographic notes during the trial. The judge may request the reporter to read to the judge from those notes. However, in order to avoid so laborious a task, the judge may avail himself of 28 U.S.C.A., sec. 753(b) by directing the official reporter to transcribe the notes and, free of charge, deliver a transcript to the judge." 238 F. 2d at 570.

In *Johnson* v. *U.S.*, 352 U.S. 565 (1957), in a Per Curiam opinion, the Supreme Court vacated the majority judgment and sustained Frank's dissent. See Douglas, "Jerome N. Frank," *op. cit.*, p. 7: "His dissent in *U.S.* v. *Johnson* called for a liberal construction of the *in forma pauperis* statute so that an indigent defendant with a meritorious case would not

241

suffer a penalty 'because he is guilty of being poor'—a plea that did not go unnoticed. . ."

For a similar decision by Judge Frank at the same term, see *U.S.* v. *Farley,* 238 F. 2d 575 (2d Cir., 1956).

Since Frank's demise there has been considerable progress in aiding indigents charged with any felony in state courts. The state is required to supply them with free counsel. See *Gideon* v. *Wainwright,* 372 U.S. 335 (1963), overruling *Betts* v. *Brady,* 316 U.S. 455 (1942). This rule had already been made applicable in federal court trials in a 5-4 decision in *Johnson* v. *Zerbst,* 304 U.S. 458 (1938). Prior to the *Gideon* case, indigent defendants only in capital cases or in cases where denial of counsel would result in fundamental unfairness—such as, where the defendant is young, or ignorant, or is a mental case, or the case is a highly technical one—were entitled to free trial counsel in the states. See Anthony Lewis, *Gideon's Trumpet* (New York: Random House, 1964).

241. See p. 37, *supra.*

242. 238 F.2d at 573. See his f.n. 14b: "Frank, White Collar Justice, Sat. Ev. Post, July 17, 1943. See also, Frank, Courts on Trial (1949) 94-99; Frank, Administration of Criminal Justice, 15 F.R.D. (1953), 95, 100-101."

243. Bernard Schwartz, *American Constitutional Law* (Cambridge: Harvard University Press, 1965), p. 276.

244. Milton R. Konvitz, *The Alien and the Asiatic in American Law* (Ithaca: Cornell U. Press, 1946), pp. 1-2. The first immigration statute was enacted in 1875 barring prostitutes and convicts.

245. Milton R. Konvitz, *Civil Rights in Immigration* (Ithaca: Cornell U. Press, 1953), p. 4.

246. Fellmann, *op. cit.,* p. 249.

247. Zechariah Chafee, Jr., *Free Speech in the United States* (Cambridge: Harvard U. Press, 1954), pp. 196-97; Konvitz, The Alien and the Asiatic, *op. cit.,* p. 14. The leading case on this is *Chae Chan Ping,* 130 U.S. 581 (1889).

248. Thus, the Chinese Exclusion Acts barred Chinese laborers only, not "students, teachers, merchants and travelers for curiosity." Konvitz, *ibid.,* 9. A Chinese alien at our gates, claiming to be a student and not a laborer, could be barred by an administrative determination, without the right to court review. Similarly, with respect to aliens barred for holding opinions proscribed by Congress.

249. *U.S. ex rel. Knauff* v. *Shaughnessy,* 338 U.S. 537, 544 (1950).

250. *Ibid.* See also *Shaughnessy* v. *U.S. ex rel. Mezei,* 345 U.S. 206 (1953).

251. 149 U.S. 698 (1893).

252. See *Low Wah Suey* v. *Backus,* 225 U.S. 460 (1912); *Zakonaite* v. *Wolf,* 226 U.S. 272 (1912); *Wong Yong Sung* v. *McGrath,* 339 U.S. 33 (1950).

253. See *Kessler* v. *Strecker,* 307 U.S. 22, 34 (1938); Konvitz, Civil Rights in Immigration, *op. cit.,* p. 107.

254. See *Mahler* v. *Eby,* 264 U.S. 32 (1924), in which a resident alien was held deportable for a crime—violation of the Selective Service Act—for which he was not deportable at the time of its commission.

255. Schwartz, *op. cit.,* p. 277.

256. 198 U.S. 253 (1904).

257. 273 U.S. 352 (1927).
258. P. 124, f.n. 256, *supra.*
259. 259 U.S. 276 (1921).
260. P. 124, f.n. 257, *supra.*
260a. "To deport one who so claims to be a citizen obviously deprives him of liberty . . . It may result in loss of both property and life; or of all that makes life worth living. Against the danger of such deprivation without the sanction afforded by judicial proceedings, the Fifth Amendment affords protection in its guarantee of due process of law. The difference in security of judicial over administrative action has been adverted to by this court . . ." 259 U.S. at 284.
261. 166 F. 2d 897 (2d Cir., 1948).
262. *Ibid.,* 899.
263. *Ibid.,* 900-01.
264. *Ibid.,* 901. This case is a very confusing one on the facts. When Madeiros was arrested in New York City, in connection with one of his two convictions referred to in the text, his fingerprint record shows that he gave his name as Harry Brown and his birthplace as Bermuda. He escaped from prison and upon recapture gave his name as Henry C. Brown. In his other arrest in Virginia, he was questioned by Immigration officers in the penitentiary, and he then claimed to have been born in Portugal. His father, Jose Madeiros, was Portuguese. After his release, it was "discovered" that he had not been born in Portugal. A consular investigation in Bermuda convinced the authorities that he had been born in Bermuda. He was ordered deported to Bermuda. However, the British authorities conducted their own investigation of his citizenship and refused to issue to him travel documents for Bermuda. At this point the American government induced him to sign an agreement to depart voluntarily in lieu of deportation—a fact, as indicated by Frank, which cannot affect his rights, if he is an American citizen. It was then that he departed as a crew member on a British ship.

The Board of Immigration order of exclusion in this case "apparently rested on the theory that Madeiros was in fact one Henry Brown, born in Bermuda, who had deserted from the British navy and came to the United States in 1920 or 1921." 166 F. 2d at 903. Madeiros claimed that Henry Brown, whom he had known, died in Boston in 1927. The order of the Board of Immigration Appeals admitted that it was "extremely difficult to ascertain the true facts as to this man's identity," and conceded that no one had checked to ascertain whether a Henry Brown had died in Boston in 1927. Madeiros' attorney, after the decision by the Board of Immigration Appeals, found a death certificate, dated in 1927, of one Henry Brown, who answered to Madeiros' description of him. Frank felt that the district court, with this new evidence, might arrive at a different decision. If deported, Frank remarked, Madeiros would become a man without a country, since Bermuda would not accept him.
265. P. 124, f.n. 256, *supra.*
266. P. 124, f.n. 259, *supra.*
267. 166 F. 2d at 901.
268. P. 124, f.n. 257, *supra.*
269. 273 U.S. at 356. Emphasis supplied.
270. 166 F. 2d at 902.

243

271. See pp. 22 ff, *supra*.

272. 166 F. 2d at 902. Madeiros did not appeal the case.

273. 206 F. 2d 897 (2d Cir., 1953).

274. *Ibid.*, 902.

275. *Ibid.*, 900.

276. *Ibid.*, 901.

277. *Ibid.*, 902.

278. *Ibid.*, 903. In *Accardi* v. *Shaughnessy*, 347 U.S. 260 (1953), the Supreme Court in a 5-4 devision, reversed the lower court and sustained Frank's dissent. The case was remanded for trial on the issue raised. See Frank's opinion—this time a majority opinion—on an appeal from the trial, in 219 F. 2d 77 (2d Cir., 1954). The trial court had sustained the government's position. Frank reversed. He would not accept the Board members' testimony that they had not been influenced by the Attorney General's list, and had interpreted the list as a call to expedite the hearings— purely an administrative technique. Frank was sure that there must have been an unconscious influence upon the Board members. "Yet the rejection of the finding does not imply any challenge of the intelligence or integrity of the Board members. One need not turn to the works of Freud and his disciples to learn that the unconscious influences importantly affect the memory of honest men. Such teachings will be found in the writings of Plato, Aristotle, Euripides, Dante, Montaigne, Shakespeare, Molière, Pascal, Pope, Byron, Dr. Oliver Wendell Holmes and his sagacious son, to say nothing of the novels since Fielding to the present. Indeed, the courts have long recognized that, stimulated by interest, pride or other motives, thoroughly honest and intelligent witnesses may tell unrealiable stories . . ." Accardi was not accorded the opportunity to testify at the above trial. "Although the Board has already found that he has a good moral character, he should have the opportunity at the new hearing to offer evidence that he is not and never has been a racketeer. For it may be that in so characterizing Accardi, the Attorney General has confused him with someone else of the same name." 219 F.2d at 83. Frank accordingly ordered a new hearing.

A majority of the Supreme Court reversed Frank's decision in *Shaughnessy* v. *Accardi*, 349 U.S. 280 (1955). It held that there was nothing in the evidence to indicate that the Board had acted under subconscious psychological pressure. A minority of the Supreme Court would have accorded Accardi an opportunity to testify in line with Frank's opinion.

279. 212 F. 2d 919 (2d Cir., 1954).

280. *U.S.* v. *Parrino*, 180 F. 2d 613 (2d Cir., 1950). After his indictment in 1934, Parrino went into hiding until 1940. In 1937 the government nol prossed the case. Upon his return in 1940, Parrino lived an "innocent life in Brooklyn." He obtained a Social Security card; registered as an alien with the Department of Justice; opened a savings bank account; registered under the Selective Training and Service Act; registered his commercial truck and passenger car and renewed his driving licenses; started a grocery buiness and insured it; procured a marriage license and was married in a church; took out ration books; filed income tax returns and employer's information returns and filed a petition for naturalization, supported by a certificate of good conduct from the police. Despite his open living, the Federal Bureau of Investigation did not discover him

until 1948, when he was arrested. There is a three-year statute of limitations unless the person kidnapped was returned harmed, in which case there is no statute of limitations (and on this issue the proof at the trial was apparently contradictory). The question therefore was whether the original flight tolled the three-year statute of limitations (i.e. made it null) or whether a fugitive from justice who openly returns and resumes his accustomed activities and so continues for the full period of limitation fixed for the crime, does not thereby gain the immunity from prosecution which it is the purpose of these statutes to confer.

281. 212 F. 2d at 924.

282. *Ibid.*, 925.

282a. "He has already served his two-year jail sentence. Yet he is willing to take the chance of a new trial, as a result of which, unless the jury acquits him, he will not be sent again to jail but to death chair, so that the sentence he has served will count for nothing." 212 F. 2d at 926. We believe that the sentence should read: *may* be sent to the death chair, rather than *will* be sent to the death chair.

283. For the thesis that order and justice are both essential if a legal system is properly to fulfill its function, see Edgar Bodenheimer, "Law as Order and Justice," *Journal of Public Law*, VI (1957), 194, 204.

284. *Supra*, 926. In 348 U.S. 840 (1954), the Supreme Court denied a writ of certiorari.

It should be noted that by his silence Judge Frank missed a grand opportunity of delivering a dissenting opinion in a case fully deserving of it—*U.S. ex rel. Knauff* v. *McGrath*, 173 F. 2d 599 (2d Cir., 1949). Mrs. Knauff, of excellent background and with many contributions to the allied war effort, was married to a naturalized American citizen, a civilian employee of the U.S. Army in Frankfurt. She sought admission to the U.S. in order to be naturalized. Detained at Ellis Island, the Attorney General ordered her excluded on the alleged ground that her admission would be prejudicial to the U.S. The Attorney General's regulations sanctioned the denial of a hearing to an alien on the ground of confidential information, "the disclosure of which would be prejudicial to the public interest." In a unanimous opinion—to which Judge Frank, by not filing a dissent, agreed—Judge Chase affirmed the Attorney General's action. He referred to the plenary power of Congress to deny admission to aliens. The Attorney General in issuing his regulations had relied on an act of Congress of 1941. Judge Chase further held that the War Brides Act of 1945 which relieved alien spouses of American citizens who had served in World War II (Mr. Knauff had so served) of the immigration quota provisions, was subject to the prior act of Congress (of 1941). There was not one word of commiseration with the plight of Mrs. Knauff; not one word of criticism of the procedure inducing her plight. Although a majority of the Supreme Court affirmed the decision in 338 U.S. 537 (1949), two vigorous dissents were filed by three dissenting justices. The dissenters contended that Mrs. Knauff was entitled to a hearing under the War Brides Act and her entry was not to be governed by the Act of 1941. We would have expected to hear from Judge Frank something akin to the aroused indignation of Justice Frankfurter, who referred to the mere say-so of an official as sufficient to sever secretly the deepest tie an American soldier could form. Perhaps five minutes of cross-examination could enable Mr.

Knauff (the petitioner) to dissipate any erroneous information about his wife. The outcome of the case vindicated the minority opinions. After her plight had stirred up indignation in both houses of Congress, the Attorney General recommended her admission. She had been detained three years at Ellis Island. It should, however, be noted that after the Supreme Court decision adverse to Mrs. Knauff and before the Attorney General reversed himself, a private bill had been introduced in the Senate by Senator William C. Langer of North Dakota to admit her to the United States. Pending action by the Senate, a habeas corpus proceeding was instituted in Mrs. Knauff's behalf to enjoin the Commissioner of Immigration from deporting her. To Judge Frank's credit, he wrote an opinion in *U.S. ex rel. Knauff* v. *McGrath*, 181 F.2d 839 (1950), sustaining the writ on the ground alleged by petitioner that an invariable practice existed for the Attorney General to stop all deportation proceedings when a congressional bill is introduced to save a person from deportation. The Attorney General, however, was granted the right to controvert this contention. Judge Learned Hand's concurring opinion was on narrower grounds than Frank's. Hand concurred since the Attorney General had neither denied the general practice nor had given an excuse that the alien's continued presence in the United States would be prejudicial to its interests, even though she was not at large but was detained at Ellis Island. But were the Attorney General to plead that excuse, no court, in Hand's opinion, could inquire whether it was supported by facts. This certainly could be very prejudicial to the alien, and Frank specifically disagreed on this point. Judge Swan dissented on the ground that the court has no power to inquire into the reasons upon which an administrative official acts, should he decide to deport an alien. The case was remanded to the district court. A hearing on the petitioner's contention about the invariable practice was held and the District Court judge wrote an unpublished opinion. The Circuit Court of Appeals—Judges Swan, Augustus N. Hand and Chase—in 182 F.2d 1020 (1950) affirmed without opinion. Nothing in this opinion discloses what determination had been made by the district court judge, but it appears from the action of the Supreme Court that Mrs. Knauff's petition for a writ of habeas corpus had been denied and she was ordered deported. The Supreme Court granted certiorari in 340 U.S. 940 (1950), the judgment of the circuit court of appeals was vacated and the case was remanded to the district court to vacate its order and dismiss the proceedings as moot—since the Attorney General had acted in the meantime to admit Mrs. Knauff into the United States.

285. P. 86 at f.n. 8, *supra.*
286. Foreword, Not Guilty, *op. cit.,* p. 12.
287. Charles E. Clark, "Jerome N. Frank," *Yale Law Journal,* LXVI
288. *Ibid.*

# Footnotes—Chapter IV
# Freedom of Speech and Press

1. 237 F. 2d 796 (2d Cir., 1956).
2. 122 F. 2d 511 (2d Cir., 1941).
3. See p. 133, f.n. 5, *infra.*
4. 303 U.S. 444 (1938).
5. *Ibid.,* 450, citing its opinion in *Gitlow* v. *New York,* 268 U.S. 652,666 (1925), as well as subsequent Supreme Court decision for the principle of incorporation of a provision of the Bill of Rights, which is is binding only on the federal government, into the "liberty" guarantee of the due process clause in the Fourteenth Amendment, which is binding only on the states. "Freedom of speech and freedom of the press, which are protected by the First Amendment from infringement by Congress, are among the fundamental personal rights and liberties which are protected by the Fourteenth Amendment from invasion by State action." 268 U.S. at 666. The *Gitlow* case involved the New York Criminal Anarchy Act of 1902. In that case the court merely assumed "for present" purposes this principle of incorporation. It has since become established doctrine not only for the First Amendment but for most of the other provisions in the Bill of Rights. Between *Gitlow* and *Lovell* v. *Griffin,* the Supreme Court in a number of cases mentioned in the *Lovell* case, involving different aspects of freedom of speech and assembly, definitively incorporated the First Amendment into the Fourteenth Amendment. On the principle of "incorporation," see p. 224, f.n. 1, *supra;* p. 248, f.n. 30 and p. 249, f.n. 42, *infra.*

For facts about the Jehovah's Witnesses, see Milton R. Konvitz, *Fundamental Liberties of a Free People* (Ithaca: Cornell U. Press, 1957), p. 110, citing the World Almanac (1933); Walter Gellhorn, *American Rights— The Constitution in Action* (New York: Macmillan Co., 1960), p. 47.
6. 308 U.S. 147 (1939).
7. *Ibid.,* 162. See Gellhorn, *op. cit.,* p. 52.
8. *Ibid.,* 165. See Zechariah Chafee, Jr., *Free Speech in the United States* (Cambridge: Harvard U. Press, 1954), p. 406. Chafee is critical of the Court's striking down the ordinance in the *Jehovah's Witnesses* case.
9. P. 247, f.n. 2, *supra.*
10. *Ibid.,* 516.
11. *Ibid.,* 517.
12. *Ibid.*
13. *Ibid.,* 515. In the *Friends of Lincoln Brigade* case, one of the four cases constituting *Schneider* v. *State,* f.n. 6, *supra,* there was an invitation to a political meeting and an admission price was fixed. Both the majority and minority opinions in the *Chrestensen* case drew inferences from that case favorable to its own position.
14. *Ibid.*
15. *Ibid.,* 520.
16. See p. 135 at f.n. 17, *infra.*

17. *Supra*, 522. Frank quoted from Demogue, "Analysis of Fundamental Notions of Modern French Legal Philosophy," *Modern Philosophy Series* (1921), 570, 413, 394. See Benjamin N. Cardozo, *The Paradoxes of Legal Science* (New York: Columbia U. Press, 1927) p. 5: "The goal of judicial effort, says Demogue, is not logical synthesis, but compromise. . ."

18. *Ibid.*, 524.

19. *Ibid.*

20. *Ibid.*

21. *Ibid.*

22. *Ibid.*, 525.

23. *Ibid.*

24. *Ibid.*, 523. (Emphasis supplied.) In *Valentine* v. *Chrestensen*, 316 U.S. 52 (1942), the Supreme Court unanimously reversed *Chrestensen* v. *Valentine*, sustaining Frank's dissent. This was the first ruling by the Supreme Court on this issue. For a subsequent decision on somewhat variant facts, see *Breard* v. *Alexandria*, 341 U.S. 622 (1950).

25. Emphasis supplied. See, e.g., *Beauharnais* v. *Illinois*, 343 U.S. 250 (1952) (dis. op. by Justices Douglas and Black); William O. Douglas, *The Right of the People* (New York: Doubleday & Co., 1958), p. 21; Irving Dilliard (ed.), *One Man's Stand for Freedom* (New York: Alfred A. Knopf, 1963), II, IV.

26. Seditious libel is public libel brought because of criticism of public officials. See *N.Y. Times* v. *Sullivan*, 376 U.S. 254 (1964) (con. ops. by Justices Black and Goldberg, Justice Douglas joining); Dilliard (ed.) *op. cit.*, p. 476.

27. See *Roth* v. *U.S.*, 354 U.S. 476 (1957) (dis. op. by Justice Douglas, Justice Black concurring). See discussion of this case in the Circuit Court of Appeals, pp. 143 ff.

28. A favorite word of Douglas in many of his decisions and books. See, e.g., *U.S.* v. *Roth*, 354 U.S. 476, 514 (1957).

29. Citing Holmes's classic example in *Schenck* v. *U.S.*, 249 U.S. 47 (1919).

29a. That the First Amendment does not bar civil libel or slander actions, see William O. Douglas, *A Living Bill of Rights* (Garden City: Doubleday & Co., 1961), p. 26; William O. Douglas, *Right of the People* (Garden City: Doubleday & Co., 1958), p. 36: "The First Amendment gives no license to defame the citizen." They were actionable in the states long before the Union was established and were not intended to be barred by the First Amendment and so are not to be incorporated into the Fourteenth Amendment concept of "liberty" in the due process clause. (On the principle of "incorporation," see p. 224, f.n. 1, *supra*, and p. 249, f.n. 42, *infra*.) Black disagrees with Douglas on the issue of libel and slander actions. He wrote that the First Amendment bars all libel and slander actions, in the federal courts, and that by the incorporation of the First Amendment into the Fourteenth, libel and slander actions in the state courts should be held in violation of the Constitution. Oddly, he added: "I realize that sometimes you have a libel suit that accomplishes some good." "Justice Black and First Amendment Absolutes: A Public Interview," in Dilliard (ed.), *op cit.*, pp. 557-58.

30. Judge Frank added "or, in some circumstances, even truths." That the reference is to the very rare instance of a malevolent action taken by

one without a word of falsehood, is evidenced by Frank's citation in his footnote of *American Bank & Trust Co.* v. *Reserve Bank of Atlanta*, 256 U.S. 350, 358 (1921): "Banks as we know them, could not exist if they could not rely upon averages, and lend a large part of the money that they receive from their depositors on the assumption that not more than a certain fraction of it will be demanded on any one day. If, without a word of falsehood, but acting from what we have called disinterested malevolence, a man by persuasion should organize and carry into effect a run upon a bank, and ruin it, we cannot doubt that an action would lie." This is not a matter within the orbit of protection of the First Amendment, but is a question of tort law. The cause of action in the case cited was a bill in equity for an injunction.

31. *U.S.* v. *Roth*, p. 247, f.n. 1, *supra*.

32. 304 U.S. 144, 152, f.n. (1948): "There may be a narrower scope for operation of the presumption of constitutionality when legislation appears on its face to be within a specific prohibition of the Constitution such as those of the first ten amendments." *Carolene* was a commercial case.

33. See Justice Murphy's dictum in *Chaplinsky* v. *New Hampshire*, 315 U.S. 568, 571-72 (1942), in which he excluded from First Amendment protection "the lewd and obscene, the profane, the libelous." See dis. op. by Justice Rutledge in *Kovacs* v. *Cooper*, 336 U.S. 77 (1948). See Zechariah Chafee, Jr., *Free Speech in the United States* (Cambridge: Harvard U. Press, 1941), p. 150.

34. For an exception to this view, see Justice Black's opinions in *Rochin* v. *California*, 342 U.S. 165, 174 (1952) (con. op.) and in *Griswold* v. *Connecticut*, 381 U.S. 479 (1965) (dis. op.). Black does not feel that the Court should strike down any type of statute on the basis of its notions of reasonableness or the lack of it.

35. That this view has not always prevailed, see Jerome Frank, "Some Reflections on Judge Learned Hand," *University of Chicago L. Rev.*, XXIV (1955), 666, 689.

36. See concurring op. by Justice Frankfurter in *Dennis* v. *U.S.*, 341 U.S. 494 (1951). See Anthony Lewis, *Gideon's Trumpet* (New York: Random House, 1964), pp. 82-84.

37. See 341 U.S. at 552.

38. Dilliard, (ed.), *op. cit.*, p. 45, from the James Madison Lecture on The Bill of Rights delivered by Justice Black at N.Y.U. Law School.

39. See *ibid.*: "And laws adopted in times of dire need are often very hasty and oppressive laws, especially when, as often happens, they are carried over and accepted as normal."

40. Henry S. Drinker, *Some Observations on the Four Freedoms of the First Amendment* (Boston: Boston U. Press, 1957), p. 27.

41. See Konvitz, *op. cit.*, p. 278; dis. op. by Holmes in *Abrams* v. *U.S.*, 250 U.S. 616, 630 (1919); *Whitney* v. *California*, 274 U.S. 357 (1927), for a famous opinion by Brandeis. In *Abrams* v. *U.S.*, *Holmes* wrote: "Only the emergency that makes it immediately dangerous to leave the correction of evil counsels to time, warrants making any exception to the sweeping command, 'Congress shall make no law abridging the freedom of speech.'" *Op. cit.*

42. See Carl Brent Swisher, *American Constitutional Development* (2d ed., Boston: Houghton Mifflin Co., 1954), pp. 1032-33, who states that

the incorporation of the First Amendment into the Fourteenth Amendment and the inclusion of freedom of speech in the concept of "liberty" guaranteed by the states in the due process clause of the Fourteenth Amendment was not dictated by the Constitution but was evolved by the Supreme Court. See *West Va. Board of Education* v. *Barnette*, 319 U.S. 624, 639 (1943).

43. The doctrine of "clear and present danger" was first stated by Holmes in *Schenck* v. *U.S.*, 249 U.S. 47 (1919. See Douglas, the Right of the People, *op. cit.*, pp. 53-54. Holmes and Brandeis did not use the nomenclature "preferred status" for the First Amendment, but their opinions, mainly dissents, in which they pressed for a strict interpretation of the clear and present danger doctrine by the judiciary, unshackled by what Congress may deem a clear and present danger, project them into the role of progenitors of the preferred status doctrine. See their opinions cited in f.n. 41, *supra*. It was at one time contended by Justice Frankfurter, and disputed by Justice Rutledge, that the preferred status doctrine "had never commended itself to a majority of the Court." *Kovacs* v. *Cooper*, 336 U.S. 77, 90 (1948). See Rutledge's dis. op. at p. 106. Frankfurter referred to "preferred status" as a "mischievous phrase" which had "uncritically crept into recent opinions." *Op. cit*, p. 90. See *W. Va. State Board of Education* v. *Barnette*, 319 U.S. 624 (1943), which adopted the preferred status doctrine. Justice Jackson's majority opinion in that case is a clear exposition of the doctrine, as is the dis. op. by Justice Douglas in *Beauharnais* v. *Illinois*, 343 U.S. 250 (1952). See also Frankfurter's later statement in *Dennis* v. *U.S.*, 341 U.S. 494, 526 (1951), in which he admitted that the preferred status doctrine at times had commanded a majority of the court.

Justice Douglas' clear exposition of the preferred status doctrine in his dis. op. in *Beauharnais, op. cit.*, follows: "The First Amendment is couched in absolute terms—freedom of speech shall not be abridged. Speech has therefore a preferred position as contrasted to some other civil rights. For example, privacy, equally sacred to some, is protected by the Fourth Amendment only against unreasonable searches and seizures. There is room for regulation of the ways and means of invading privacy. No such leeway is granted the invasion of free speech guaranteed by the First Amendment. Until recent yars that had been the course and direction of constitutional law. Yet recently the Court in this and other cases has engrafted the right of regulation onto the First Amendment by placing in the hands of the legislative branch the right to regulate "within reasonable limits" the right of free speech. This is to me an ominous and alarming trend. The free trade in ideas which the Framers of the Constitution visualized disappears. In its place is substituted a new orthodoxy— an orthodoxy that changs with the whims of the age or the day, an orthodoxy which the majority by solemn judgment proclaims to be essential to the safety, welfare, security, morality, or health of society . . . Limits are drawn—limits dictated by expediency, political opinion, prejudices or other desideratum of legislative action . . . Freedom of speech, freedom of press, free exercise of religion are placed separate and apart; they are above and beyond the police power; they are not subject to regulation in the manner of factories, slums, apartment houses, production of oil, and the like." 343 U.S. at 285-86. It should be noted that both

250

the advocates of the "absolute" position and those of the so-called "preferred status" position grant to the First Amendment a "preferred status"—the "absolutists" only the more so.

44. Frank, "Some Reflections on Judge Learned Hand," op. cit.

45. 183 F. 2d 201 (1950). This case was in effect an onslaught on the preferred status doctrine. Judge Learned Hand read "clear and present danger" to mean in effect clear and probable danger, and the prevailing opinion in the Supreme Court, renederd by Chief Justice Vinson, adopted Hand's modification of the doctrine. Dennis v. U.S., 341 U.S. 494 (1951). (Vinson's opinion was joined in by Justices Reed, Burton and Minton; Justices Frankfurter and Jackson filed separate concurring opinions, and Justices Black and Douglas dissented in separate opinions.) Hand had written in his opinion that "(I)n each case (courts) must ask whether the gravity of the 'evil', discounted by its improbability, justifies such invasion of free speech as is necessary to avoid the danger." 183 F. 2d at 212. Vinson accepted this formulation: "We adopt this statement of the rule." For a softening of the Supreme Court's position and a partial retreat, see Yates v. U.S., 354 U.S. 298 (1957).

Frank's article reinforces the writer's argument that at the least Frank adopted the position of the advocates of a preferred status for the First Amendment. See p. 139, supra. For a good account and analysis of the Dennis case, see Samuel J. Konefsky, The Legacy of Holmes and Brandeis— A Study in the Influence of Ideas (New York: Collier Books, 1961), pp. 221-35, and Konvitz, op. cit., pp. 307-41. For an analysis of the Yates case, see: Milton R. Konvitz, Expanding Liberties—Freedom's Gains in Postwar America (New York: Viikng Press, 1966), pp. 124-26; C. Herman Pritchett, American Constitutional Issues (New York, San Francisco, Toronto and London: McGraw Hill Book Co., 1962), pp. 309-11.

46. See James C. N. Paul and Murray L. Schwartz, Federal Censorship: Obscenity in the Mail (Free Press of Glencoe, Inc., 1961), p. 6.

47. Frank, supra, 698.

48. Ibid., quoting from Hand. According to Frank, Hand loathed the Smith Act, the legislation upon which the Dennis conviction was based. But he attributed Hand's position on the First Amendment to a theory of constitutional law first announced by Professor James Bradley Thayer of the Harvard Law School that the Supreme Court should not be a superlegislature in passing upon Congressional acts. For this reason the First Amendment becomes merely an "admonition of moderation" to Congress. See Frank, op. cit., p. 697.—It would appear from this article that Frank would have aligned himself in the Dennis case with the dissenting opinions of Justices Douglas and Black.

49. For historic facts adduced by Frank, see ibid. and Frank's opinion in U.S. v. Roth, 237 F. 2d 796, 808 (2d Cir., 1956), particularly in the latter reference, his quotation from Madison's speech in Congress urging the adoption of a Bill of Rights which would be enforceable in the courts against the Legislature and the Executive. For a criticism of Hand identical with Frank's, see Douglas, The Right of the People, op. cit., p. 45.

50. Ibid. For a marshalling of different views as to the contemporary understanding of the First Amendment, see Paul and Schwartz, op. cit., pp. 5-6. The issue is left far from clear. The authors apparently are not prepared to accept the "absolutist" position on historical grounds. And even if the First Amendment is a legal mandate and not an "admonition of

moderation," the question of interpretation of the scope of that legal mandate—whether absolute or preferred—still remains, and Frank did not address himself to that.

On the question whether the justices' reading of constitutional history is not infrequently a rationalization for their "judgment resting on other grounds," see Leonard W. Levy,"The Right against Self-Incrimination: History and Judicial History," *Political Science Quarterly*, LXXXIV (March, 1969), 1. "The justices stand censured for abusing historical evidence in a way that reflects adversely on their intellectual rectitude as well as their historical competence." Op. cit., p. 1. Although making no claim to be a historian, it would appear to the writer that this criticism might apply to the "absolutist" school of interpretation of the First Amendment but not to the "preferred status" school.

51. See Walter Gellhorn, *Individual Freedom and Governmental Restraint* (Baton Rouge: Louisiana State U. Press, 1956), p. 99: "The heart of the common law approach, it seems to me, is this: No person should be deemed free to obtrude upon another an unwilling exposure to offensiveness—or, if you will, to obscenity." There was no definition of the term "obscenity" at common law. "The extent to which the publication of 'obscenity' was a crime at common law is unclear." *A Book* v. *Att'y. Gen.*, 383 U.S. 413 (1966) (op. by J. Douglas). See p. 146 at f.n. 108, *infra*.

52. Lord Campbell told the House of Lords that his bill was intended to apply to works "calculated to shock the feelings of decency in any *well-regulated* mind." (Emphasis supplied). See Konvitz, *op. cit.*, p. 163. Cf. f.n. 55, *infra*.

53. Gellhorn, *supra*, p. 99. A patron saint in this country in the battle against obscenity, was a psychopathic grocery clerk, Anthony Comstock. See Morris L. Ernst and Alan U. Schwartz, *Censorship—The Search for the Obscene* (New York: Macmillan, 1964), p. 29.

54. L.R. 3Q.B. 360 (1868). This case involved Henry Scott who had sold "Confessional Unmasked," an attack upon the Roman Catholic confessional, containing "obscene" passages.

55. This case misrepresented Lord Campbell's Act. See *Commonwealth* v. *Gordon*, 66 Pa. D. & C. 101 (1949). See f.n. 52, *supra*.

56. Hand's criticism was in a dictum (plural-dicta) which is an ellipsis for "obiter dictum," defined by the American College Dictionary as "an opinion by a judge in deciding a case, upon a matter not essential to the decision, and therefore not binding." See lengthier definition to same effect in Black's Law Dictionary (4th ed., St. Paul: West Pub. Co., 1951).

57. 209 Fed. 119 (D.C. N.Y., 1913). Hand was then a district court judge.

58. William B. Lockhart and Robert C. McClure, "Literature, The Law of Obscenity and the Constitution," *Minnesota L. Rev.*, XXXVIII (1954), 295, 327.

59. 5 F. Supp. 182 (1933). Woolsey was a district court judge.

60. Woolsey found Joyce's intent to be realism, not "dirt for dirt's sake."

61. 72 F. 2d 705 (2d Cir., 1934).

62. *Ibid.*, 708. The decision was not appealed to the Supreme Court.

63. See: *Chaplinsky* v. *N.H.*, 315 U.S. 568 (1942); *Near* v. *Minnesota*, 283 U.S. 697 (1931); *Beauharnais* v. *Illinois*, 343 U.S. 250 (1952). Obscenity was not involved in any of these cases. The first case squarely to raise the issue of the constitutional protection for literature assailed as

obscene was *People* v. *Doubleday & Co.*, 335 U.S. 848 (1948). However, the issue was left unresolved since the Supreme Court divided equally— 4-4—and as is customary in an equal division, no opinions were written. The conviction in the case was thus automatically affirmed.

64. See p. 145 at f.ns. 105, 106-07, *infra.*

65. 66 Penn. D. & C. 101 (1949). This was a lower Pennsylvania court.

66. *Ibid.*, 139. This would extend the "preferred status" doctrine to include obscenity. Cf. with p. 137 *supra.*

67. *Ibid.*, 128, 136, 151. Yet it was not clear to Bok "nor would I venture to state, would it be clear to the Supreme Court, if faced directly by an appropriate case of literary obscenity, what words inflict injury by their very utterance or how much injury is inflicted." *Op. cit.*, p. 167.

68. *Ibid.*, 104.

69. 354 U.S. 476 (1957).

70. The duty of a hearing in this type of case was imposed upon the Post Office in *Walker* v. *Popenoe*, 149 F. 2d 511 (2d Cir., 1945).

71. 172 F. 2d 788 (2d Cir., 1949).

72. *Ibid.*, 790.

73. *Ibid.*, 795.

74. See p. 145 at f.ns. 105-07, *infra*, for a change of view by Frank

75. *Supra*, 792.

76. *Ibid.*, 795.

77. *Ibid.*, 792.

78. *Ibid.*, 794.

79. *Ibid.*, 795.

80. *Ibid.*

81. *Ibid.*, 796.

82. *Ibid.* Cf. with Frank's views on the social sciences expressed in *Courts on Trial*, p. 40 at f.n. 458 supra.

83. Balzac's books had been banned by the U.S. Customs in 1930, but the ban was later lifted.

84. *Supra*, 797. On appeal to the Supreme Court, certiorari was denied in 337 U.S. 938 (1948). There was no dissent. One ventures to ask: Were Justices Douglas and Black nodding?—For an interesting discussion and analysis of a distinction between the operation of the Customs Bureau and the Post Office Department in the area of obscenity, see Gellhorn, Individual Freedom and Governmental Restraint, *op. cit.*, pp. 94-95. The identical book banned by one agency has been passed by the other.

85. See *Grove Press, Inc.* v. *Christenberry*, 276 F. 2d 433 (2d Cir., 1960), and esp. *Manual Enterprises* v. *Day*, 370 U.S. 478 (1962). In the Manual case the Supreme Court for the first time gave plenary review in connection with a Post Office ban on the ground of obscenity. Three of the five justices constituting the majority held that the Post Office had never been given authorization in section 461 of the U.S. Code, under which it operates in banning books, to ban any book without a prior criminal conviction, aside from the more basic question whether Congress could "constitutionally authorize any process other than a fully judicial one." 370 U.S. at 510. The two other justices in a concurring opinion bypassed this issue in their decision of the case on a substantive basis (finding the magazines involved not obscene) rather than on a procedural basis. The issues raised by the above three justices have not been

finally resolved by a full bench of the Supreme Court. See Paul and Schwartz, *op. cit.*, p. 29: "It is far from clear that Congress had intended to authorize the Post Office to stop suspect obscene materials in transit except as an incident to the arrest or indictment of the man who mailed them . . ."

86. Ernst and Schwartz, *op. cit.*, p. 229.

87. De Grazia states that "probably 95% of what is obscene to the postal censors is not obscene to the U.S. Attorneys or to the judges and juries . . ." Edward De Grazia, "Obscenity and the Mail: A Study of Administrative Restraint," *Law and Contemporary Problems*, XX (1955), 608, 615.

88. P. 247, f.n. 1, *supra*.

89. Namely, that the standard of obscenity is that of the normal adult, and that the material as a whole is to be weighed, not extracts from it.

90. See p. 252, f.n. 63, *supra*.

91. See p. 252 at f.n. 63 and f.n. 63, *supra*.

92. 237 F. 2d at 803.

93. Thus, e.g., in *U.S.* v. *Rosen*, 161 U.S. 29 (1895), the issue was whether an indictment under the obscenity statute contained sufficient information to apprise the defendant of the specific charge against him which he was called upon to defend, and "not the validity of that legislation, and the Court did not discuss its validity." 237 F. 2d at 803.

94. *Supra*, 803: "As I read the Supreme Court's opinions, the government, in defending the constitutionality of a statute which curbs free expression, may not rely on the usual 'presumption of validity.'"

95. See *Chaplinski* v. *New Hampshire*, 315 U.S. 568 (1942).

96. 237 F. 2d at 802.

97. *Ibid.*

98. *Ibid.* Frank referred to *Dennis* v. *U.S.*, 341 U.S. 494 (1951), as watering down somewhat the "clear and present danger" doctrine. "The test now involves probability . . ." *op. cit.* That Frank was critical of this case, see pp. 139-40, *supra*.

99. *Ibid.*, 805.

100. *Ibid.*

101. *Ibid.*

102. *Ibid.*

103. *Ibid.*, 799.

104. *Ibid*, 804. See *Ginsberg* v. *State of New York*, 390 U.S. 629 (1968), wherein a majority of the Supreme Court upheld a New York penal statute prohibiting the sale to minors under 17 of obscene materials "harmful to them." See p. 256, f.n. 136, *infra*.

105. See p. 142 at f.n. 74, *supra*.

106. See p. 253, f.n. 65, *supra*.

107. 237 F. 2d at 806.

108. *Ibid.*, 809. See p. 252, f.n. 51, *supra*

109. *Ibid.*

110. *Ibid.*, 809, f.n. 24a.

111. *Ibid.*, quoting from Black's majority op. in *Bridges* v. *State of California*, 314 U.S. 252, 265 (1941).

112. *Ibid.*, 811.

113. *Ibid.*, 811, 812. That there are "medical experts who believe that such stimulation (from reading erotica) frequently manifests itself in

254

criminal sexual behavior or other anti-social conduct," see *A Book* v. *Att'y. General*, 383 U.S. 413 (1966) (dis. op. by Justice Clark).

114. *Ibid.*, 812.

115. *Ibid.*, 813.

116. *Ibid.*

117. *Ibid.*, 814. Frank pointed out that youngsters get a vast amount of "education" in sexual smut from their companions. *Op. cit.*, p. 816.

118. *Ibid.*, 818.

119. *Ibid.*, 820.

120. *Ibid.*, 821.

121. *Ibid.*, 820-21.

122. *Ibid.*, 826.

123. *Ibid.*

124. *Ibid.*, 822.

125. *Ibid.*

126. *Ibid.*, 826. See *Biedler & Bookmyer* v. *Universal Ins. Co.*, 134 F. 2d 828, 830, f.n. (1943), wherein Frank said: "The 'reasonable man,' as Pollock observed, was the common law way of taking over the 'natural law' concepts of the Roman law and of Scholastic jurisprudence. Like the principles of 'natural law,' the applications of the 'reasonable man' standard vary with time, place and circumstance . . ." Frank spoke of the "numerous conflicting meanings" given to natural law. See discussion on Natural Law, pp. 1-2, 31-32, *supra*. See Walter Murphy and C. Herman Pritchett, *Courts, Judges and Politics* (New York: Random House, 1961), p. 4: "Natural-law thinking permeated every Western legal system, including that of the common law."

127. *Ibid.*, 827.

128. *Ibid.*, 823.

129. *Ibid.*, 824.

130. *Ibid.*, 825.

131. Thurman W. Arnold, "Judge Jerome Frank", *U. Chicago L. Rev.*, XXIV (1957), 633, 639.

132. *Ibid.*, 641.

133. *Ibid.*, 642.

134. William O. Douglas, "Jerome N. Frank," *Journal of Legal Education*, X (1957), 1, 5.—On appeal, the Supreme Court in *Roth*, v. *U.S.*, 354 U.S. 476 (1957), by a majority (three justices dissenting) affirmed the conviction and held that "obscenity is not within the area of constitutionally protected speech." 354 U.S. at 485. Since it is not protected speech, the issue of "clear and present danger" is inapplicable to it. *Op. cit.*, p. 486. For an illuminating discussion of this case, see Lockhart & McClure, *op. cit.*, pp. 20, f.n. 99, 25-26, 60 at f.n. 149 and 150.

It should be noted that on appeal, Roth advanced a very perfunctory argument on the issue of the obscenity of his specific publications. The court, as a result, did not pass on the specific publications, but ruled on a constitutional question practically in a vacuum—whether the federal obscenity statute violated the First Amendment. See Lockhart & McClure, *op. cit.*, p. 20, f.n. 99.—For a pragmatic justification of a modicum of censorship on the ground that though there may not be immediate effects of reading obscene literature, its reading will cause a "slow rotting of the social fabric," see James Jackson Kilpatrick, *The Smut Peddlers* (New

York: Doubleday, 1960), p. 289. See also *op. cit.*, pp. 234-41, 293, and Paul Schwartz, *op. cit.*, p. 215.

135. See: *One Inc.* v. *Olsen*, 355 U.S. 371 (1958); *Sunshine Book* v. *Summerfield*, 355 U. S. 372 (1958); *Times Films Corp.* v. *Chicago*, 355 U.S. 35 (1957). Citing the *Roth* case, these three Per Curiam opinions struck down postal restrictions on homosexual and nudist magazines and a French motion picture treating of the illicit sex acts of a seventeen-year-old boy as not violative of the Roth standard.

Recent Supreme Court decisions indicate that the Court has been circumscribing the *Roth* decision to "hard-core" pornography, which seems to mean that the book, etc. must have no redeeming features whatever, must be utterly devoid of social significance, before the Court will divest it of constitutional protection. The libertarian approach of Douglas, Black, Bok and Frank seems substantially to have been adopted in these cases—in fact, though not in theory. See: *Manual Enterprises* v. *Day*, 370 U.S. 478 (1962); *Jacobellis* v. *Ohio*, 378 U.S. 184 (1963), involving "Les Amants", a French film; and *Grove Press, Inc.* v. *Gerstein*, 378 U.S. 577 (1963), which in a 5-4 decision reversed a Florida conviction of Henry Miller's novel, *Tropic of Cancer*, abounding in four-letter words, etc.

136. See *Ginzburg* v. *United States*, 383 U.S. 463 (1966); *Mishkin* v. *New York*, 383 U.S. 502 (1966). These cases added to the *Roth* obscenity test—"whether to the average person, applying contemporary standards, the dominant theme of the material taken as a whole appeals to prurient interest" (353 U.S. at 489)—another dimension, namely, the test of commercial exploitation and pandering which in close cases, such as the Ginzburg case, may result in a determination that the material is obscene "even though in other contexts the material would escape such condemnation." 383 U.S. 463. See also *Ginsberg* v. *State of New York*, 390 U.S. 629 (1968), involving the New York Penal Law, section 4846, prohibiting the sale of obscene materials to minors under 17. The New York statute was held constitutional; the Court in a 6-3 decision adopted the theory of "variable concepts of obscenity." "It is not constitutionally impermissible for New York, under this statute, to accord minors under 17 years of age a more restricted right than that assured to adults to judge and determine for themselves what sex material they may read and see." (Headnote, p. 629.) In other words, even though the same material may not be prohibited to adults it may be to children, so long as the Court cannot say that the state prohibition is irrational. See p. 254, f.n. 104, *supra*.

Cf. *A Book* v. *Attorney General*, 383 U.S. 413 (1966).

137. P. 132, f.n. 2, *supra*.

# Footnotes—Chapter V
## Justice Is as Justice Does

1. See p. XVII. at f.n. 53, *supra.*
2. Frank, *Law and The Modern Mind* (New York: Brentano's, 1930), p. 245.
3. *Ibid.,* 251.
4. *Ibid.,* 252. "Some of them will be accepted because repeated checkings show them still to be working well; others because the attention, at the moment, will be too occupied." *Op. cit.*
5. Julius Paul, *The Legal Realism of Jerome N. Frank* (The Hague: Martinus Nijhoff, 1959), p. 61.
6. *Ibid.,* 59.
7. *Ibid.,* 62. Frank disclaimed any kinship between himself and behaviorism, a questionable and much-criticized school of modern psychology. He criticized at length those "rule-skeptics," like Professor Herman Oliphant, who had turned dogmatically to Watsonian behaviorism as "a new road to legal predictatbility and legal certainty." Frank, *Courts on Trial: Myth and Reality in American Justice* (Princeton: Princeton U. Press, 1949), p. 159. See also Frank, *If Men Were Angels* (New York: Harper & Brothers, 1942), p. 78. That Frank believed a "legal science" impossible of attainment, see p. 206, f.n. 465, *supra.* In the writings of some of the legal realists, however, as Llewellyn, Oliphant, Moore, Cook and Bingham, "the model of a natural science of law can be found." Rumble, Jr., *American Legal Realism* (Ithaca, N. Y.: Cornell U. Press, 1968), p. 32. ". . . some of the legal realists advocated a sociology of law, modeled along the lines of a natural science. The subject matter of such a science would be the behavior of officials rather than antecedent norms; its objective would be the description, explanation, and prediction of such behavior; and its students would not be concerned with the evaluation of law. For this precise reason, indeed, Pound reacted strongly against the model of legal science propounded by some realists. For him. . . '(W)hat ought-to-be has no place in physical science. It has first place in the social sciences.'
". . . Today this interest finds expression in the work of the judicial behavioralists. They are the step-children of the legal realists in the development of a sociology of law." Rumble, *op. cit.,* pp. 31-32.
8. Harold D. Lasswell, "The Impact of Psychoanalytic Thinking on The Social Sciences," in *Psychoanalysis and Social Science,* ed. Hendrik M. Ruitenbeek (New York: E. P. Dutton & Co., 1932), p. 6. Among social scientists in this country influenced by psychoanalytic thinking were Alfred L. Kroeber, Bronislaw Malinowski and Edward Sapir, anthropologists; William F. Ogburn, sociologist, and Charles E. Merriam, political scientist and Frank's teacher at the University of Chicago. For a reference to Merriam, see p. XII at f.n. 6, *supra.*
9. Paul, *op. cit.,* p. 61.
10. Cf., e.g., Frank, "Are Judges Human?," *U. of Pa. Law Rev.,* LXXX (1931), 17, 47-48, with Frank, "'Short of Sickness and Death': A Study

of Moral Responsibility in Legal Criticism," *N.Y.U. Law Rev.*, XXVI (1951), 545, 555. In the former article he wrote: "...(1) Many of the legal rules are unsettled or vague. (2) Some legal rules are clear and precise ..." In the latter article he wrote: "Most of those rules are well settled and precise."

11. Wolfgang W. Friedmann, *Legal Theory* (3rd ed., London: Stevens & Sons, Ltd., 1953), p. 206. Cf. the brief analysis by the Yale Law Faculty of Frank's views on the judicial process upon his demise: "He always maintained that he had insisted, in his works, on the personal and irrational elements in the judicial process in order to redress a balance, because so many other earlier thinkers had overemphasized the role of concepts and precedents. Those who read him with care know that he never underrated either the importance or the value of legal traditions." Yale Law Faculty, "In Remembrance," *Yale Law Report*, III (1957), 10.

12. *Ibid.*, 209.

13. *Ibid.* See p. 61 at f.n. 100, *supra*. At the close of the nineteenth century, at about the time Holmes was writing, this school arose independently on the Continent, especially in Germany. It never attained the influence of the American school of legal realism, and was more radical and theoretical in its approach. See *op. cit.*, pp. 244-45.

14. *Ibid.*

15. *Ibid.*, 208. Some writers have criticized Frank for ignoring the function of law in preventing disputes or in leading to settlements without litigation, based on the belief in the certainty of legal rules. See Francis H. Bohlen, Review of *Law and The Modern Mind*, *U. of Pa. Law Rev.*, LXXIX (1931), 822, 823; Morris Raphael Cohen, *Law and The Social Order—Essays in Legal Philosophy* (New York: Harcourt, Brace & Co., 1933), p. 225; Herman Kantorowicz, "Some Rationalism about Realism," *Yale L. Jour.*, XLIII (1934), 1240, 1247; E. M. Morgan, Review of *Courts on Trial, Journal of Legal Education*, II (1949), 355. Frank replied that his treatment of the law was restricted to court decisions. See Frank, If Men Were Angels, *op. cit.*, pp. 282-83; 103 f.n.

16. *Ibid.*

17. See pp. 41ff, *supra*.

18. Such as Professor Friedmann. See Friedmann, *supra*, p. 208.

19. See Frank, Review of *Legal Theory*, by Wolfgang W. Friedmann (1st ed.), *Harvard Law Rev.*, LIX (1946), 1004. Frank cited some of his writings, published in 1931-33, by way of refutation of Friedmann's assertion that only belatedly had the realists begun to recognize the importance of the ideal element in the law.

20. Paul, *op. cit.*, pp. 139-40.

21. Edwin W. Patterson, *Jurisprudence: Men and Ideas of the Law* (Brooklyn: The Foundation Press, Inc., 1953), p. 552.

22. Edward McWhinney, "Judge Jerome Frank and Legal Realism: An Appraisal," *N.Y. Law Forum*, III (1957), 113.

23. *Ibid.*

24. McWhinney wrote that this mechanical jurisprudence was comparable to the Pandectists of nineteenth century Germany. See p. 3 at f.n. 90, *supra*.

25. *Supra*, 116.

26. *Ibid.*

27. Frank, Courts on Trial, *op. cit.*, p. 312; Frank, "Some Reflections on Judge Learned Hand," *U. of Chicago Law Rev.*, XXIV (1957), 666, 691.

28. Frank, "Some Reflections on Judge Learned Hand," *op. cit.*, p. 687.

29. Edward McWhinney, "The Great Debate: Activism and Self-Restraint and Current Dilemmas in Judicial Policy-Making," *N.Y.U. Law Rev.*, XXXIII (1958), 775, 780.

30. 297 U.S. 1, 62-63 (1936).

31. See p. 11 at f.n. 197, *supra*.

32. Frank, Courts on Trial, *op. cit.*, p. 428.

33. *Ibid.*, 35.

34. For criticisms of legal realism from the standpoint of its alleged lack of relevance to the solution of policy conflicts of the Cold War and post-Cold War eras, see McWhinney, "Judge Jerome Frank and Legal Realism: An Appraisal," *op. cit.*, pp. 117, 119; Myres McDougal, "The Law School of the Future; From Legal Realism to Policy Science in the World Community," *Yale Law Jour.*, LVI (1947), 1345, 1355. See Frank's reply to McDougal's article, "A Plea for Lawyer-Schools," *Yale Law Jour.*, LVI (1947), 1303, 1340.

35. See p. 40, *supra*.

36. Frank would apply the same mode of thinking in helping solve, as they arise, new policy conflicts. See Frank, "A Plea for Lawyer-Schools," *op. cit.*, p. 1340.

37. The two exceptions are the murder of a police officer in the line of duty and the murder of any person—most likely a warden or another inmate—by a prisoner serving a life sentence.

38. See p. 27, *supra*.

39. Eugene V. Rostow, *The Sovereign Prerogative: The Supreme Court and the Quest for Law* (New Haven and London: Yale University Press, 1962), p. 20.

40. Felix Cohen was a legal realist who, unlike most legal realists, wrote on general principles and ethical values in the judicial process. See Felix Cohen, *Ethical Systems and Legal Ideals: An Essay on the Foundations of Legal Criticism* (New York: Falcon Press, 1933).

41. Rostow, *supra*, pp. 20-21.

42. *Ibid.*, 21.

43. See, e.g., Underhill Moore, "Rational Basis of Legal Institutions," *Columbia Law Rev.*, XXIII (1923), 612.

44. See pp. 31, 33, 34, 41, 43, 153, *supra*.

45. See p. 191, f.n. 39, *supra*.

46. See p. 156, at f.n. 39, *supra*.

47. Frank, "A Conflict with Oblivion: Some Observations on the Founders of Legal Pragmatism," *Rutgers Law Rev.*, IX (1954), Part II, 425, 451-52.

48. Edmond Cahn, Introduction to Frank, Courts on Trial, (paperback. New York: Atheneum, 1963), p. ix. See this thesis developed by Cahn in "Fact Skepticism and Fundamental Law," *N.Y.U. Law Rev.*, XXXIII (1958), 1.

49. *Ibid.*

50. Edmond Cahn, "Judge Frank's Skepticism and Our Future," *Yale Law Journ.*, LVI (1957), 829.

51. *Ibid.*, Cahn, Introduction to Frank, *Courts on Trial*, (paperback) *op. cit.*, p. ix.

52. Edmond Cahn, Introduction to Frank, *Courts on Trial*, (paperback) *op. cit.*, p. ix. The view that fact-skepticism was Frank's outstanding contribution to legal thought is shared by Bodenheimer and Paul. See Edgar Bodenheimer, "A Decade of Jurisprudence in the United States of America —1946-1956," *Natural Law Forum*, III (1958), 51, f.n. 34; Paul, *op. cit.*, p. 120. Paul regards Frank as the valiant champion of the struggle, not only in jurisprudence, but in all spheres of thought against dogmatic authoritarianism. See Julius Paul, "Jerome Frank's Attack on the 'Myth' of Legal Certainty," *Nebraska Law Rev.*, XXXVI (1957), 555. As such he has earned a well-earned niche "in the history of the liberal tradition." Julius Paul, The Legal Realism of Jerome Frank, *op. cit.*, p. 150. See also Rumble, Jr., *op. cit.*, p. 38: "Fact-skepticism is his (Frank's) particular creation."

53. Edmond Cahn, "Judge Frank's Fact-Skepticism and Our Future," *op. cit.*, p. 287. See Frank, Review of *Introduction to Greek Legal Science*, by George M. Calhoun, *Harvard Law Rev.*, LVII (1944), 1120.

54. *Ibid.*

55. *Ibid.* See Frank, "Some Tame Reflections on Some Wild Facts," in *Vision and Action: Essays in honor of Horace M. Kallen*, ed. Sidney Ratner (New Brunswick: Rutgers U. Press, 1953), 56.

56. Frank, *Save America First* (New York: Harper & Brothers, 1938), p. 417.

57. *Ibid.*

58. *Ibid.*

59. Frank, "Some Reflections on Judge Learned Hand," *op. cit.*, p. 670: "I was most pleased to learn soon after I joined him (Judge Hand) on the bench in 1941, that we shared an admiration for George Saville, Lord Halifax. In 1684, attacked as a political 'Trimmer,' Halifax replied in a tract that he delighted in that label. This innocent word 'T r i m m e r', he wrote, 'signifieth no more than this, that if men are together in a Boat, one part of the Company would weight it down on one side, another would make it lean as much to the contrary: It happeneth there is a third opinion, who conceive it would do as well if the Boat went even, without endangering the Passengers' (The Character of the Trimmer 3 (1689). Halifax's definition of a Trimmer satisfies, in large measure, Judge Hand's definition (and mine) of a true Liberal..."

60. Frank, Save America First, *op. cit.*, p. 223, and passim.

61. See pp. 60ff, *supra.*

62. Frank, Law and The Modern Mind, *op. cit.*, p. 253.

63. Paul, The Legal Realism of Jerome Frank, *op. cit.*, p. 154.

64. See pp. 53-54, *supra.*

65. See p. 56, *supra.*

66. See p. 92 at f.n. 54, *supra.*

67. See p. 121 at f.n. 238, *supra.*

68. See p. 137, *supra.*

69. U.S. v. Roth. SeSe pp. 143ff, *supra.*

70. See, e.g., p. 97, *supra.*

71. Matthew Arnold, *Hebraism and Hellenism*, Portable Matthew Arnold (New York: Viking Press, 1960), p. 568.

72. *Ibid.*

# ADDENDA

(1)*Aristotle and Natural Law* (*p.* 1)

That Aristotle in the brief references to natural law in his *Rhetoric* (*The Rhetoric and Poetics of Aristotle*. New York: The Modern Library, 1954, trans. W. Rhys Roberts, Book I, Ch. 15, pp. 1375a-1375b) and in his *Nicomachean Ethics* (*The Nicomachean Ethics of Aristotle*. Everyman's Library, London and Toronto: J. M. Dent & Sons Ltd., and New York: E. P. Dutton & Co., 1920, trans. D. P. Chase, Book V, ch. 7, p. 1134b) was most likely stating the position of the advocates of natural law rather than advancing his own views, see Francis D. Wormuth, "Aristotle on Law," in *Essays in Political Theory* (eds. Milton R. Konvitz and Arthur E. Murphy, Ithaca: Cornell U. Press, 1948), p. 59.

(2) *U.S.* v. *Rosenberg* (pp. 28-30).

While this book was in press, the writer spoke to Patricia (Mrs. Robert) Wald, Esq. of Washington, D.C., Judge Frank's law secretary at the time of the Rosenberg decision. Although she could recall no conversation by Frank regarding his views on capital punishment generally or on the special facts of the case before him, Frank did express the hope that the Supreme Court would reverse the decision and, by overruling its prior cases, grant authority to the Circuit Court of Appeals to modify sentences. This implies Frank's disapproval of capital punishment even on the special facts of the Rosenberg case. The possibility of the Supreme Court taking this action had been referred to by Frank in f.n. 41 of his opinion (195 F.2d at 609):" The Rosenbergs, of course, may ask the Supreme Court, considering 38 U.S.C., 2106, to over-rule the decisions precluding federal appellate modification of a sentence not exceeding the maximum fixed by a valid statute, and to direct us accordingly to consider whether or not these sentences are excessive; or the Rosenbergs, pursuant to Federal Rule of Criminal Procedure 35, may move the trial judge for a reduction of their sentences; or, if these alternatives fail, these defendants may seek relief from the President . . ." But Frank himself directed no supplication to the Supreme Court to overrule its decisions, a technique he employed in other cases. (See pp. 69 and 76, *supra*.)

261

The problem posed therefore still remains unanswered: Why did not Frank express his abhorrence of capital punishment despite the Supreme Court decisions tying his hands and even though he may have entertained a hope for a reversal by the Supreme Court? How sanguine could such a hope be?

The writer also had the benefit of a lengthy conversation with Sidney M. Davis, Esq. of the New York City, Judge Frank's law secretary from 1942 to 1944, and was informed that the second conjecture advanced in the text at page 29, namely, that Frank had not as yet formulated his views on capital punishment when the Rosenberg decision was written, is incorrect. In conversations as early as 1942, Frank had expressed to Davis his abhorrence of capital punishment. And on second thought, it does not appear plausible that Frank's lifetime had almost gone by without formulating his views on capital punishment.

Judge Thomas W. Swan, the only surviving member of the Learned Hand court, who sat on the Rosenberg case together with Frank and the late Judge Harrie Brigham Chase, replied in a letter that he cannot answer the question raised regarding Frank's failure to express his personal views on capital punishment in the opinion.

Finally, Judge Frank's inter-court confidential memoranda in a repository at the Yale Law School are not in the public domain. Some of Frank's memoranda contained among Judge Clark's inter-court confidential memoranda were made available for scholarly use as part of the Clark papers (see Marvin Schick, "Judicial Relations on the Second Circuit, 1941-1951," *New York University Law Review*, XLIV (1969), 939), but the Clark papers have since been removed from the public domain. At any rate, Clark was not a member of the Rosenberg panel and his file would throw no light on the case.

(3) Page 202, f.n. 412, *On Selection of Judges.*

For the various methods—appointive, elective and compromise —of selecting judges, see Henry J. Abraham, *The Judicial Process* (2d ed., New York, London, Torono: Oxford University Press, 1968), pp. 26-41. "In France, and in many other countries on the Continent, the trained judges are appointed to, rise in, and are promoted from a type of career service which is an adjunct of the general civil service . . . Political patronage plays scarcely a role in their selections. They have all been either schooled as judges for four years at the Center of Judicial Studies (established in 1959) or have had experience as such, and they enter the judicial service on the basis of passing competitive examinations." *Op cit.*, p. 33. In England, extolled for its superior judges, "judges are designated by the Crown with little or no surrender to politics . . . Since the group of barristers from whose ranks the Lord Chancellor chooses judges is small and select, he will certainly not hesitate to cross party lines to make appointments. If he does not personally know, or know of, a candidate, he will consult with the head of the division to which the judge is to be appointed and obtain his views—but *not* his prior approval . . . No letters of recommendation are accepted, and efforts to put political pressure on the Lord Chancellor are scouted strongly. R. M. Jackson, Reader in Public Law and Administration in the University of Cambridge, in his excellent study on the machinery of justice in England, contends that political considerations have hardly entered the process of judicial selection since 1907—although they died a slower death in the case of the office of Lord Chief Justice; and he insists that, as a consequence, there has been no apparent connection between the 'political antecedents' of the judges and their decisions in over a century." *Op. cit.*, pp. 31, 32. In the United States, federal judges are appointed by the President subject to confirmation by a simple majority vote of the Senate, more or less on a political basis. As a result of the Jacksonian revolution, the members of the state and municipal judiciary, for the most part, are elected by the people after selection by local political leaders. In the opinion of many, the appointive method has proven more effective generally than the elective method in elevating judges of superior ability on the trial court level. However, as a desideratum, judges should as far as possible, be removed from political selection. A judiciary in politics has always appeared to the writer objectionable. Cf. *op. cit.*, p. 40. For the commendable features in the Missouri Plan, a so-called "happy compromise" between the elective and appointive systems of selection of judges on the state level, see *op. cit.*, pp. 37-40.

(4) *U.S. ex rel. Caminito* v. *Murphy* (pp. 90-93).

Judge Frank's law secretary at the time of this case unfortunately died in an automobile accident, and the possibility of his throwing any light on the issue presented in the text has perished with him. Chief Judge William H. Hastie of the United States Court of Appeals for the Third Circuit, who sat on this case as a visiting judge and is the only surviving member of its panel, replied in a letter that he has no recollections regarding it and has preserved no notes which shed any light on the question raised.

In his opinion Judge Frank stated that Caminito confessed twenty-seven hours after arrest, and one page later we are told that Caminito was interrogated "almost continuously for 27 hours with only a brief interval for rest" during the night. This "brief interval" turns out to have been seven or eight nighttime hours spent alone in a cell. Even overlooking the question of the discontinuity of the interrogation, Frank's figures are on their face self-contradictory. "If "almost continuously for 27 hours" is a typographical error and some other numeral, such as seventeen, was intended, it would still not cure Frank's listing it among his facts designated as "not disputed." The People's evidence pointed to a much shorter period of interrogation and, more significantly, to a discontinuous one. Caminito's brief on appeal alleging that Caminito maintained his innocence for twenty-seven hours cannot be equated with a claim that he was interrogated for almost twenty-seven hours.

The People had no eyewitness to this crime. But a witness, looking out of a window when he heard screaming, saw a black automobile leave the scene, and on the trial he testified that Caminito's automobile resembled in a number of details the car which he had seen on the night of the killing. Before dying, the victim furnished the police with a description of the three perpetrators of the crime. Although there was a sufficient basis for Caminito's arrest, there was no proof of his identity as one of the perpetrators sufficient to warrant a conviction without his confession.

(5) *Miranda* v. *Arizona* (pp. 227, f.n. 33; 228, f.n. 50)

This landmark 5-4 decision has well-reasoned majority and minority opinions. The Omnibus Crime Control and Safe Streets Act of 1968 (Public Law 90-351; 82 Stat. 197) which modified *Miranda* will survive, of course, only if it meets the test of constitutionality. This legislation provides that in any criminal prosecution brought by the United States or by the District of Columbia, a confession "shall be admissible in evidence if it is voluntarily given." The trial judge must preliminarily in the absence of the jury determine its voluntariness. If he determines that it was voluntarily made, it is admitted in evidence. The jury then may hear relevant evidence on the issue of voluntariness and it is instructed to give such weight to the confession as it feels it deserves under all the circumstances. The judge in determining the issue of voluntariness is to take into consideration "whether or not such defendant was advised or knew that he was not required to make any statement and that any such statement may be used against him"; also, "whether or not such defendant had been advised prior to questioning of his right to the assistance of counsel . . ." Note should be taken that the act does not refer to criminal prosecutions brought by the states, since Congress has no jurisdiction over state courts. The state courts are still bound by the *Miranda* ruling unless and until the Supreme Court decides otherwise as a matter of constitutional interpretation. Under this act, in addition, a confession is not inadmissible solely because of delay, if it is made voluntarily and the confession was made within six hours following arrest or other detention. This latter provision modifies the McNabb-Mallory Rule. See p. 227, f.n. 43, *supra*.

(6) *U.S.* v. *Antonelli* (p. 115 *at f.n.* 193)

See page 218, f.n. 178, *supra*, with reference to the "harmless error" doctrine (which is based upon the "harmless error" statute). In the *Antonelli* case, this doctrine once again was at issue. Writing the majority opinion, Judge Clark disputed Judge Frank's claim that the Court was passing upon the guilt of the defendant based on its reading of the record, and if it was of the belief from reading the testimony that guilt had been established, it relied on the "harmless error" doctrine beyond its intended application. If the Court expressed its opinion that there was sufficient evidence for a finding of guilt from reading the entire record, that was not tantamount to abdicating the exercise of an independent judgment on the importance of the error committed in the light and in the context of the record. Despite its belief in the sufficiency of the evidence supporting the conviction, if the error committed, in the Court's opinion, was of sufficient gravity to affect the deliberations of the jury and the outcome of the case, it would reverse and order a new trial. Judge Clark wrote: "There are assertions (referring to Frank's claim) that this circuit has a unique rule of harmless error, unlike any other federal court. But the record does not bear out his contention. Not only has no such divergent rule ever been announced or assumed, but the members of this court have been scrupulous according to their lights in carrying out the announced principles of F.R. 61, 28 U.S.C.A. following section 723c, 28 U.S.C.A. section 391, 777, 18 U.S.C.A., section 556, and now of F.R.Cr. Proc., rule 52 (the "harmless error" statute). Errors there have been, of course; but they seem more like honest differences of opinion than blind intransigence.

There are certainly many cases in this circuit ordering reversals beyond what Wigmore would have thought permissible or desirable in an era less sensitive to the plaints of the accused, as stated in his famous criticism of presumption of error, 1 Wigmore on Evidence, 3 ed. 1940, section 21; and there are cases where members of this court remained in doubt . . ." 155 F.2d at 61, f.n. 4. Whereas in *U.S.* v. *Bennett et al.* (see p. 218, f.n. 178, *supra*) the Supreme Court on the facts of that case sustained Frank's dissent, in the *Antonelli* case Frank's dissent was not sustained. The issue of "harmless error" (though the doctrine itself is clear), like many other issues in the law, lends itself in the main to an ad hoc determination, i.e., case by case. However, that the quantum of evidence adduced against the defendant may at times have a bearing on the determination of the issue of "harmless error", see *Bihn* v. *U.S.*, 322 U.S. at 638, (see p. 218, f.n. 178, *supra*) wherein the Supreme Court said: "The 'harmless error' statute . . . means that a criminal appeal should not be turned into a quest for error. It does not mean that portions of the charge are to be read in isolation to the full charge and magnified out of all importance to their likely importance at the trial . . . We certainly cannot say from a review of the whole record that lack of prejudice affirmatively appears. While there was sufficient evidence for the jury, the case against petitioner was not open and shut. Since the scales are quite evenly balanced, we feel that the jury might have been influenced by the erroneous charge. Hence we cannot say it was not prejudicial and hence treat it as a minor aberration of trivial consequence. Nor is it enough for us to conclude that guilt may be deduced from the whole record . . ."

(7) *On Natural Law* (pp. 31-32)

Among many other examples of conflicting natural law claims, Frank listed the following: "In this country Natural Rights, an offspring of Natural Law, inspired the wording of the Declaration of Independence which speaks of the 'Laws of Nature and of Nature's God.' . . . But later, during the 19th century, some American judges, in the name of Natural Rights, made extreme extensions of laissez-faire doctrines to maintain the status quo; these judges succeeded in upsetting, as opposed to Natural Rights, much humane social legislation . . .

"Often Natural Law has been called upon to justify slavery; in modern times, slavery has been denounced in its name . . ." Frank, Courts on Trial, *op. cit.*, pp. 348, 349.

Some natural law advocates have argued that positive law

which, in their opinion, is contrary to natural law is a nullity and is not law; others have claimed that positive law of this quality should be changed to conform to natural law, but until changed, it is law. *Op. cit.*, p. 364.

"Some Natural Law adherents have maintained that from the Natural Law principles men can logically deduce a detailed code of legal rules valid forever and everywhere.

"The last notion is rejected in the Roman Catholic conception of Natural Law . . ." *Op. cit.*, pp. 362-63. Frank described the Thomistic version of natural law as positing but a few "basic, universal and eternal principles of justice, such as, 'Seek the common good,' which may be subdivided analytically into, 'Live in society, do good to others, avoid harming others, and render to each his own.' . . . From these basic principles, there can be deduced, logically, rationally, some secondary principles or precepts, such as, for instance, that one should not kill or steal." *Op. cit.*, p. 363. But the concrete application of these natural law principles requires man-made rules or positive law, which may vary with time, place and circumstance. The natural law principles, however, "assist in measuring the rules that exist by the standard of what they ought to be." *Op. cit.*

"As the enlightened Catholic acknowledges, a notable characteristic of Thomistic Natural Law is that it is not concrete. No one has ever been able to work out anything like a complete set of legal rules, deduced from Natural Law principles, acceptable to all honest and just lawyers, or non-lawyers, even in a given time and place." *Op. cit.*, p. 364.

That civilized man cannot find his precepts in nature is easily proven by the millions of Nazis who "recently desclosed what horror nature can be." "To say that is not to reject religion" nor invite cynicism. Man does not find his "oughts" "spelled out for him in nature; he puts them there. Religion means faith that man's ideals are achievable and will be achieved, his hope that the universe, of which he understands but a portion, will not prevent those ideals from being actualized and from, in some part, surviving." *Op. cit.*, pp. 355, 356.

(8) P. 45, at f.n. 494—*re U.S. Supreme Court.*

The constitutional powers of Congress and the President regarding the Supreme Court are the following: Congress may regulate the types of cases which the Supreme Court may hear under its appellate jurisdiction; Congress and the President control the size of the Supreme Court; Congress may introduce Constitutional amendments to overcome judicial decisions constitutionally bottomed, and it may impeach and convict justices. Hirschfield, *op. cit.*, pp. 22-23. The constitutional powers have been most infrequently resorted to in order to restrain the Supreme Court. The political powers, however, operating to restrain the Supreme Court have been more consistently applied. Thus, President Franklin Roosevelt's pressures on the Court by threatening to "pack" it in 1937 impelled "a change in the judiciary's attitude. Similarly, pressure generated by the contemporary conservative attacks on the Court have had an effect on several recent decisions dealing with civil liberties. There can be no doubt that the Justices, despite the aura of detachment and dispassion which surrounds them, are sensitive to public opinion and conscious of political realities." *Op. cit.*, p. 24. To the same effect, see Robert G. McCloskey, *The American Supreme Court* (Chicago and London: U. Chicago Press, 1960), pp. 224-25 and passim.

"Recognition of the constitutional and political power potentially available to check judicial authority has led the Supreme Court to impose restrictions on itself." Hirschfield, *op. cit.*, p. 24. The following constitute the catalogue of "rules of self-restraint" developed by the Supreme Court: The Court will not pass on the motives of legislators or the wisdom of legislation; it will presume a statute constitutional until the presumption is overcome by the challenging party; it will not render advisory opinions; it will avoid constitutional questions whenever possible to decide the case on some other ground; it will avoid many so-called "political questions" as defined by the Court. "Thus 'gerrymandering' of election districts for purely partisan purposes is a political question, according to the Court, but as a device for limiting Negro voting rights it is not. The doctrine of political questions has been applied most consistently in the field of international relations, leaving the problems in this area to be determined by the President and Congress, but it is an ill-defined rule and may be expanded or contracted in the Court's discretion"; and it will avoid decision on governmental operations in time of war. Hirschfield, *op. cit.*, pp. 24-25.

# INDEX

Abt, John: on Frank's AAA staff, xiv

Aenesidemus, 32

Agriculture Adjustment Administration: Frank general counsel to, xiv; 60

Alabama Power Company, P.W.A. versus, xv

Alfred the Great: trial by jury attributed to, 111

Allen, Carleton Kemp, 16; on *stare decisis*, 50-51

Analytical (also known as imperative or positivist) school of jurisprudence, 2-3, 11-12

Anderson, Sherwood, xiii

Aquinas, Thomas, 31

Aristophanes' *Lysistrata*, 146

Aristotle, 1, 26, 32, Nicomachean Ethics (on "equity"), 35; *Politics*, 82; 158

Arnold, Matthew: essay on "Hebraism and Hellenism", 162

Arnold, Thurman: on Frank's staff at AAA, xiv; legal realist and analyst of the economic order, 13; "fact skeptic," 14; 69, 148

Association of American Law Schools: Frank's address before, xvi

Austin, John: father of modern analytical jurisprudence, 2-3; 8

Balzac's *Droll Stories*, 143, 147

Barth, Alan, quoted, 101

Beale, Joseph H.: leading American Austinian, 3; 17

Bentham Jeremy: Utilitarian, 5; Austin's relationship to, 183.

Bill of Rights: privilege against self-incrimination not mentioned in, 107; right to trial by jury in criminal cases mentioned in, 112

Bingham, Joseph W., initiator of the realist exegesis, 9

Black, Hugo: on First Amendment, 137; 146, 149, 162.

Bok, Curtis, opinion in *Commonwealth v. Gordon*, 145

Borchard, Edwin M.: author "Convicting the Innocent," 115

Brandeis, Louis D.: on error by Supreme Court in constitutional interpretation, 77; 97; "right to be let alone", 102; claim of citizenship during deportation proceedings, 124; 154

Butler, Pierce: criticism of, 59

Cahn, Edmond: quest for standards and values, 156; on fact-skepticism, 158

Capital punishment, 27-30

Cardozo, Benjamin N., xii, on *stare decisis*, 48-49; on legal realism, 64-65; 155.

Charles I: persecution of Puritans under, 107

Chaucer's *Canterbury Tales*, 147

*Chicago Bar Association*: Frank's address before, 27.

Chinese Exclusion Acts, 122

Cicero: and natural law, 1

Civil liberties, 84-86; Coerced confessions, 86-95; advance suppression of coerced confession, 95-97; entrapment, 97-101; eavesdropping, 101-06; self-incrimination, 106-11; trial by jury, 111-19; poverty and equal justice, 120-22; aliens, 122-29; freedom of speech and the distribution of handbills, 132-36; Frank and free speech as a "near absolute", 135-40; freedom of speech and obscenity, 140-49.

Clark, Charles, E., xvii; legal decisions by: 93-94, 125, 131, 134, 144, 145

Clark, William (former judge): suggestion regarding juries, 117.

Cohen. Felix: "rule skeptic", 14; quest for standards and values, 156

Cohen, Morris Raphael, xiii, "phonograph theory", 11; on Frank's idea of the "basic legal myth", 16; 21

Coke, Sir Edward: on *stare decisis*, 50

Commager, Henry Steele: revolt against mechanistic jurisprudence, 11-12.

"The Common Law," by Holmes, Oliver Wendell, Jr., 4

Compurgation, 111

Comte, August: gospel of "scientific positivism" for study of society, 12

Cook, Walter Wheeler: legal realist, 13; 14

Corbin, Arthur L.: early exegete of realist position, 187

Coster: Frank's view on, 28

Court of Appeal (England), 50

Court of High Commission, 107

Court of Star Chamber, 107

"Courts on Trial," xviii, 53, 57, 63, 67, 112, 152, 157

Criminal prosecutors: suggestion on, 38

Darwin, Charles: influence upon Holmes, 5

Davis, Chester, xiv; clash with Frank at A.A.A., xv

Democracy: Frank's views on, 32-34

Democritus, 32

Determinism: Frank's views on, 32-33

Dewey, John: "instrumental logic", 5-6; Frank on, 26

Dickens, Charles: on antics to browbeat witnesses during cross-examination, 36

Diplock, Sir William: on trial by jury, 118

"Discovery" procedure, 36

Douglas, William O.: and Frank at S.E.C., xv, xvi; "fact skeptic", 14; on *stare decisis*, 51; eulogy of Frank, 86; 89; 92; on trial by jury, 119; on First Amendment, 137; 162

Eastman, Max, xiii

Ehrlich, Eugen: influence on Pound, 185

Fair Labor Standards Act, 82

Farley, James, xiv

"Fate and Freedom," xviii

Federal Communications Act, section 605, 102, 103

Federal Emergency Administration of Public Works: suit by Alagama Power Company against, xv

Fichte, Johann Gottlieb, 11

Fielding's *Tom Jones*, 147

Fortas, Abe: in Frank's AAA group, xiv; opinion of Frank, 180

Frank, Jerome, xii; biography, xii-xviii; psychological interpretation of law, 15-17; attack on conceptualism, 17-21; judging process and fact-skepticism, 22-27; on capital punishment, 27-30; on natural law, 31, 44; on free will, determinism and democracy, 32-33; program of reform, 34-41; controversy with Pound, 41-44; on *stare decisis*, 51ff; on civil liberties, 84ff; on freedom of speech and press, 132ff

Frankfurter, Felix: friendship with Frank, xiii, xiv; on "judicial self-restraint", 138

Freedom of speech, "absolute", "preferred status" and "judicial restraint" views, 137-39.

Free Will: Frank's views on, 32-33

*Freirechtslehre*, 61, 152

Freud, Sigmund, 32

Fuller, Lon: quest for standards and values, 156

Fuller, Lon: quest for standards and values, 156

Galston, Clarence G.: proposal on juries, 117

Gellhorn, Walter: revolt in American law against police brutality, 87

Gestalt psychology, 22-23

Glueck, Eleanor: juvenile delinquency, 146, 151

Glueck, Sheldon: juvenile delinquency, 146, 151

Gmelin: moderate in a continental *wing of Freirechtslehre*, 61

Gray, John Chipman: mental father of realist movement, 8; 68

Green, Leon: legal realist, 13; "fact skeptic", 14; 70

Green, Nicholas St. John: article cited, 216
Griswold, Erwin N.: on privilege against self-incrimination, 106
Haines, Charles Grove: blueprint of psychological study of Supreme Court justices, 34
Hall, Jerome: quest for standards' and values, 156
Hand, Augustus N., xvii; legal opinion, 140
Hand, Learned xvii, Frank's article on, 46, 139, 140; legal opinions, 96, 107
Hansen, Harry, xiii
Hart, Henry: quest for standards and values in the law, 156
Hearsay rule 67, 79-80, 116-17
Hegel, Georg Wilhelm Friedrich, 32
Henry II: and jury trials, 111-12
Henry III: and jury trials, 112
Hincks, Carroll C.: legal opinions, 120, 129
Hiss, Alger: member of Frank's AAA group, xiv; psychiatrist a witness at his trial to the testimonial capacity of Whittaker Chambers, 138.
Historical school of jurisprudence, 2
Hobbes, Thomas, 11; relationship to legal positivism, 182
Holmes, Oliver Wendell, Jr., xii, xvi; "The Common Law" and "The Path of The Law", 3-5; "bad man" theory of law, 18; Frank's conception of the "completely adult jurist", 20-21; 35, 44, wiretapping as a "dirty business", 102, 124, 135, 154, 159
House of Lords (as a court), 50
Hughes, Charles Evans, legal opinion, 98
Hume, David, 32
Hutcheson, Joseph G., Jr.: concept of the "judgment intuitive", 22; 35
Huxley, Thomas Henry: influence upon Holmes, 5
Ickes, Harold L.: asked Frank to prepare government power case, xv

"If Men Were Angels," xviii, 63
Ihering, Rudolf von: "interests" are the chief subject matter of law, 7, influence on Pound, 185
Imperative (also known as analytical or positivist) scool of jurisprudence, 2-3, 11-12
Insull, Samuel: opposition to Frank's trolley car plan for Chicago, xiii
Interstate Commerce Commission, 82
Investment Bankers' Association: bouts of Frank with, xvi
The "Is" and the "Ought," (Battle of), 42-44
Jackson, Robert H.: quoted, 45; legal opinion, 89
Jahoda, Marie: juvenile delinquency studies, 146
James, William: founder of Pragmatism, 5; 20, 32, 42
Jefferson, Thomas, 33
Joyce, James: Ulysses, 140
Judicial legislation, 57-58; Frank's opinions in, 79-83.
Judiciary: training for, 34-35
Jurisprudence: four schools, 1ff
Kalven, Jr., Harry: empiric jury studies, 119
Kant, Immanuel, 11
Kessler, Friedrich: quest for standards and values in the law, 156
Kipper, Florence (Mrs. Jerome Frank), xiii, quoted xiv.
Kohler, Joseph: influence on Pound, 185
Krenek: criticism of "musical purists" and inspiration to Frank, 59
Kroeber, Alfred L.: social scientist influenced by psychoanalysis, 256
Langdell, Christopher Columbus: American Austrian, 3; law library method of legal education and Frank's attack thereon, 39-40
Lasswell, Harold D.: quest for standards and values in the law, 156
"Law and The Modern Mind," xiv, 9, 15, 17, 47, 51, 52, 61, 62, 63, 66, 112, 148, 152, 154

Peirce, Charles: founder with William James of Pragmatism, 5; 32, 46

Petition of Right: privilege against self-incrimination not mentioned in, 107

Piaget, Jean: Frank's reliance on his psychological writings, 15

Pitt, William: on a man's home is his castle, 101

Plato: universalistic Ideas, 19; 32; Frank's chalenge to Plato's concept of censorious guardians, 148

Pope Innocent III: proscribed participation of priests in trials by ordeal, 112

Positivist (also known as analytical or imperative) school of jurisprudence, 2-3, 11-12

Pound, Cuthbert, 35

Pound, Roscoe: outstanding proponent of sciological jurisprudence in America, 7, legal realism an offshoot of sociological school and the contrast between the two, 9-11; controversy with legal realism, 41-44; on *stare decisis*, 49-50, 52; on training common to judges brought up in the common law tradition, 85; 155

Pragmatism, 5

Pressman, Lee: on Frank's staff at the AAA, xiv

Psychologists: recommended use as court experts regarding capacities of witnesses, 38-39

"Public prosecutor of civil actions": recommended use of, 37-38

Public Works Administration: Frank's preparation of its case against the Alabama Power Company, xv

Pythagoras, 32

Rabelais' *Gargantua and Pantagruel*, 147

Radin, Max: legal realist, 13; "fact skeptic", 14

Reconstruction Finance Corporation: Frank special counsel to, xv

Reeves, Judge: founder of first American law school, 39

Roberts, Owen J., 51, Legal opinions, 98, 103; "positivist conception of the decision-making process", 154

Rodell, Fred: "rule skeptic", 190

Roosevelt, Franklin D.: conflict in AAA between Feek and Frank's group, xiv, xv; "master experimentalist", xvi; defeat of anti-New Deal majority on Supreme Court, 154

Rostow Eugene V.: on the exponents of a mechanical jurisprudence, 12; on the quest for standards and values in the law, 156

Rousseau, Jean Jacques, 11

Rutledge, Wiley B.: champion of "preferred status' for First Amendment, 137

Sandburg, Carl, xiii

Sapir Edward: anthropologist influenced by psychoanalysis, 256

"Save America First," xvi

Schiler, F.C.S.: influence on William James, 5; on vices of "formal logic", 19

Schlesinger Jr., Arthur M.: profile of Frank, xiv

Scholastic philosophers, 11

Schroeder, Theodore: behavioristic psychologist, 151

Securities Exchange Commission: Douglas and Frank as chairmen of, xv; Frank's experience as chairman, 38; 60

Sextus Empiricus, 32

Shakespeare's *Venus and Adonis*, 147

Small, A. W.: American sociologist, a forerunner of sociological jurisprudence, 185

Social studies: Frank advocated inclusion in law school curriculum, 40

Sociological jurisprudence, 6-7

Special interrogatories, 116

Spinoza, Baruch, 11

"The Spirit of Liberty", by Learned Hand, 140

Stammler, Rudolf: influence on Pound, 185

273